Pour Roger Hollingsworth

Amicalement

MARKETING DEMOCRACY

MARKETING DEMOCRACY

Public Opinion and Media Formation in Democratic Societies

Romain Laufer
Catherine Paradeise

Transaction Publishers
New Brunswick (U.S.A.) and London (U.K.)

Copyright © 1990 by Transaction Publishers.
New Brunswick, New Jersey 08903

Library of Congress Catalog Number: 89-5196
ISBN: 0-88738-199-5
Printed in the United States of America

Library of Congress Cataloging-in-Publication Data

Laufer, Romain.
   [Prince bureaucrate. English]
   Marketing democracy : public opinion and media formation in
democratic societies / Romain Laufer, Catherine Paradeise.
     p. cm.
   Translation of: Le prince bureaucrate.
   Includes index.
   ISBN 0-88738-199-5
   1. Public relations and politics. 2. Public opinion.
I. Paradeise, Catherine. II. Title.
JF2112.P8L3813 1989
320.5′1—dc20

                                                   89-5196
                                                   CIP

Contents

Acknowledgments

We would like to express our gratitude to all those who have helped us write this book from its inception to its publication.

First, we are indebted to Véronique Aubert, political and administrative sciences specialist, to Francis Bailly, physicist and epistemologist, and to Pierre Triper, sociologist, who have generously shared with us their erudition and their advice.

We would like to express our gratitude to those who have supported us with their encouragement: the questions and criticisms of Jacqueline Laufer, Frédéric Langer, Emile Laufer and Charles Leben have without any doubt led us to clarify our arguments.

We are particularly endebted to Fernando Fajnzylber who encouraged us in our effort to have this book published in the United States.

It is difficult to express the debt we owe to the translator Noel Castelino as well as to Nora Scott who helped in the establishment of the final version of the manuscript. They should be thanked for the patience and the sympathy with which they devoted their knowledge and their skills to the heavy task they had undertaken.

The translation was funded by the French Ministry of Culture, the Centre HEC–ISA at Jouy–en–Josas and the Fondation Nationale pour l'Enseignement de la Gestion (F.N.E.G.E.). Our gratitude extends to all, people and organizations, who have helped us in these circumstances and without whom this book could not have been published.

We feel it is a great privilege to be able to offer this book to the American public, and an opportunity which has been made possible due to the decision of a publisher, Professor Irving Louis Horowitz. To him we are deeply grateful.

Communicating across an ocean does not make the work of producing a book easier. It requires even more patience and understanding than is required when people are able to meet face to face to discuss delicate points. For this reason we would like to express our gratitude to Scott Bramson who had the heavy responsibility of bringing the manuscript to a form in which it could finally be printed.

Introduction

The intensive development of communication techniques between individuals and organizations—and above all marketing—is undoubtedly one of the most significant facts of our time. No economic, political nor administrative activity has escaped it. This book aims to show that the emergence of marketing has been a major feature in the intellectual and social changes of the contemporary world. This statement may seem surprising in so far as the increasingly widespread use of the technique has been accompanied by protest and suspicion. On the one hand, consumers decry the manipulation of markets and opinion; on the other hand, many suspect that Machiavellian spirits are at work in these modern techniques of persuasion and seduction. These attitudes identify marketing as an instrument of power and pose the question of legitimacy. The question of marketing is a direct expression of the crisis of legitimacy democratic and free-market societies are undergoing.

The system of legitimacy which is the basis of modern society is rooted intellectually in the Enlightenment and socially in political democracy and laissez–faire capitalism born at the end of the 18th century. Despite the specificity of French and American intellectual traditions, the heart of legitimacy of power in each country with specific national intellectual tradition is to be the found in the representation of the social order as the natural result of interaction—via the ballot and the market—between reasoning individuals spurred by selfish interests. That is how the problem of the relationship between the community and individual is resolved: society can henceforth think of itself in terms of an ordered community without having to explain this order as the result of the regulating activity of the Prince or God.

The symbolic hierarchy which traditionally subordinated nature to culture is reversed. The social order is directly and completely rooted in the natural order. The cultural sphere of social organization—that is, an indivisible community and a nation bound by indivisible collective interests, find itself restricted to activities which ensure the orderly functioning of natural interactions between rational, free individuals with equal rights. The role of the state is reduced to a minimum. Its activities are carefully monitered by the political sphere and its intervention is subordinated to the natural expression of the will of individuals. Civil society is naturally constituted of and reproduced by the interaction between individuals all of whom have the power of absolute freedom to think and act, and as such, have no power over each other.

A considerable rearrangement of ideas occurred at the end of the 19th century. This was the price democratic legitimacy had to pay for the deep transformations, which, springing from the re-emergence of social processes within society, resulted in organizations developing beyond their legitimate boundaries both in the administrative and free-market spheres. This development led to the questioning of the effectiveness of subordinating the administrative to the political sphere and private enterprise to the rule of the market.

Post-modern society is the result of this further weakening of the sources of legitimacy available to private and public bureaucracies in contemporary society. Organizations cannot impose themselves by violence since it is incompatible with the liberty and autonomy of the individual in a democracy. They have to find justification and a mode of action which rekindle belief in the legitimacy of the social order whose *prima facie* nature is being questioned.

Playing with beliefs is playing a cultural game for the benefit of rebuilding belief by persuasion. The game conjures up in post-modern society the question of Machiavellianism which the Enlightenment philosophers thought they had routed by making each individual a king unto himself by eliminating "the will of the Prince." The modern Prince is a bureaucrat and his modus operandi is marketing. By playing the marketing game, post-modern society is rediscovering the relevance of Sophism, the theory and practice of persuasive speech, which flourished in Greece in the 4th century B.C. What we know of Sophism today has come down to us by the negative view philosophers have had of it through the ages. The philosopher, a rational man par excellence, views the Sophist as the enemy: the one who use fallacious reasoning and constantly threatens the rule of reason. In so far as power in contemporary society draws its legitimacy from reason, crisis of legitimacy corresponds to a crisis of reason and the emergence of Sophism. The comparison between marketing and Sophism as persuasive techniques and as manifestations of the crisis of reason leads us to argue that marketing is the modern—bureaucratic—form of Sophism. A legitimate system founded on the interrelations of rational individuals is thus transformed by the emergence of bureaucracies which establish new relations of interdependence within civil society. The scope of the founding ideas of the democratic order such as the individual, reason, majority, opinion, and will, are profoundly affected by this change.

As the founding father of the intellectual tradition of comparison between France and the United States, de Tocqueville showed that both societies occupy opposite ends on a spectrum which joins liberty and equality to the two concepts which comprise democracy. De Tocqueville ascribed the triumph of the democratic idea to the ineluctable spread of a penchant for equality in modern society. Placing major emphasis on the tension in democracy between equality and liberty, he was apprehensive that characteristics proper to France's cultural tradition and opposed to those of the U.S., might in his country sacrifice liberty to equality. Spurred by this concern, he invented, in the wake of Montesquieu, a new, pragmatic approach to the question of democracy which had stirred such passionate debate.

His historical, scientific and comparative method made him nevertheless fundamentally different from most of the doctrinaires around him who, at the time, saw no antagonism between liberty and equality, but rather considered them as mutually reinforcing concepts as expressed in the motto "liberty, equality, fraternity."

De Tocqueville's method allowed him to draw consequences from what doctrinaire thought hid: that "general will"—a central concept in the building of French democracy—could not be naturally deduced from the collection of the will of individuals. It required that equality between citizens be established and guaranteed. If administrative action was to establish equality it could only perform this task by infringing on individual liberties. There laid the contradiction—the implementation of the "general will"—which justified as a way of increasing the future exercise of liberty could also be considered dangerous as it forces civil society to give up certain aspects of its liberty. This danger was especially serious in France which had long-standing tradition of state intervention in civil society. The idea that liberty and equality could be mutually exclusive did not become determinant in political and administrative thought until later in the country. Then the extension of the role of the state became such that the contradiction resulted in practical disfunctions, thus shaking the until then unquestioned belief in the unity of the founding dogma.

In the United States the situation was very different due to the manner in which history viewed liberty. The taste for liberty there, unlike France, was not channelled through centralizing institutions inherited from the past. American democracy from the outset was founded above all on a suspicion of macroregulating state institutions and gave predominance to microregulation by individuals or small groups within civil society. The majority was simply viewed as the sum of individual opinions which were incapable of founding a superior reason like the "general will" as a unified expression of the nation. Although Condorcet had already firmly stated this point in his famous paradox, the United States did not build intellectual devices to globally legitimize the right of the state to intervene in various aspects of national life. The state, as necessary evil, could be called upon at any time to justify any of its actions which required the authorization of its citizens. The legitimacy of state intervention, as that of any of the social agents, had to be constantly confirmed in the courts of civil society at the request of civil society. As long as the State, the states and the organizations do not offend the law they can extend their sphere on intervention solely on the basis of the legitimizing power of the constitution.

It should nevertheless be pointed out that although our countries have such strongly divergent views on democracy, they converge with regard to the stumbling blocks present in post-modern society following the growing encroachment of the state on civil society and in organizations. In France and the United States the debate on the antagonism between liberty and equality is coming to the fore in the public realm in analogical or symmetrical terms. This is because both nations originate in the same history of Western reason and share a common social and intellectual history. In France, the dominant mode is critical reason based on the principle of the general will which makes equality the best way of attaining liberty. In the United States, pragmatic reason is the rule. It is based on the decentralized expression of individual will and interests in which liberty is the best possible path to equality. In the course of their respective developments, these opposite traditions necessarily confront one another by meeting the practical contradiction between equality and liberty required by democracy.

It goes without saying that by analyzing the configuration of the French crisis of legitimacy in post–modern society, emphasis is being placed on the solutions the French tradition has used to reduce the tension inherent to democracy between liberty and equality. Starting out from liberty, the opposite end of the democratic spectrum, America has invented its own formulas on different historical ground. Today both countries are confronted with converging problems of legitimation and can benefit from the mutual examination of their respective experiences. By cross–examining each other's past, each country can seek out the memory of failures and positive solutions which can shed light on the particularities of its own tradition by unveiling what it has hidden. The two countries can provide one another with other food for thought on the resources of legitimacy which today could help deal with problems arising from each country's history of democracy.

Chapter 1

Sophism and Marketing

Most people speak of ignorance without really knowing what it is all about.

Everybody agrees, if only to complain about it, that bureaucracy is a characteristic feature of the modern world. The mainstream of intellectual opinion has acknowledged the central importance of bureaucracy ever since Max Weber gave a rigorous definition of the concept.

This is not the case with marketing: hard as it is to ignore the fact of marketing in all its striking manifestations, it is harder still to appreciate the significance of this phenomenon. Only fifteen years ago, many sectors of the economy, banks, manufacturing companies, hotels and publishers were managing quite well without it; political marketing was then just winning its first laurels in France; the public sector, for its part, treated marketing with high disdain, deeming it incompatible with its own characteristic goals and mode of management. The word "marketing," was hardly ever seen in print, except in the classified advertisements of the big dailies. Now these very same dailies make frequent use of the word in their background articles. Yet this development is too recent for anyone to see more in it than a fashion or superficial phenomenon conditioned by what are assumed to be fundamental realities: the processes of production, finance and the advent of the age of communication.

As for Sophism, the term in its usual sense denotes a fallacious argument[1] of a kind condemned by the man of good faith. It is this conflict that philosophy teachers describe to their pupils when, in teaching Plato's *Dialogues*, they recount the clash between Socrates and that group of Greek rhetoricians who called themselves the Sophists. Socrates holding the Sophists to ridicule: such is the inevitable outcome of that engagement as it is told in our high schools.[2]

Today, however, there is growing interest in a more positive and more detailed study of Sophism while increasing attention is being paid to the discipline of rhetoric[3] which, not so long ago, was held in contempt (at least

1

in its modern forms). Yet its audience is still too narrow for the Sophists to be known otherwise than in a caricatural form.

We believe that the words Sophism and rhetoric designate notions that are sufficiently close to each other for us to advance the following proposition: *marketing is the bureaucratic form of Sophism.* We shall elucidate the proposition in this chapter. Only then shall we turn to the task of showing how the phenomenon of bureaucracy makes marketing different from Sophism: this will be the subject of the next four chapters.

With the contemporary victory of opinion over reason, as revealed by a host of symptoms ranging from a growing taste for efficiency to an emphasis on public opinion and a decline in the teaching of philosophy, we might ask if Plato's victory is not coming to its end as a pure fable, a pious lie which can no longer be sustained. The reason the philosophical tradition found it necessary to devote so much energy to denigrating the Sophists lies precisely in the great force of their arguments.

We shall first illustrate how Sophism and marketing do indeed correspond to the negative connotations of their use as invective. We shall then show how they also share a positive definition and we shall propose that this definition is essential to an understanding of marketing and, therefore, of contemporary society. Finally we shall ask how, through the centuries and in two profoundly different societies (albeit linked by ties of lineage) one and the same movement, known in one age as Sophism and in another as marketing, could have acquired such strength.

The Same Accusations

The indictment against Sophism and marketing contains the same accusations, point for point: their preference for appearances to the point of untruth, their technicist orientation which goes with an indifference to higher values, a mercantile attitude and the rejection of culture.

All is but appearance. The primary charge against marketing and Sophism is that they do not tell the truth. Marketing stands accused of manipulation: advertising spins out beautiful lies in order to sell; it attributes qualities they do not possess to the objects it promotes and wraps products up in flattering packages. Marketing feigns the better to beguile and dupe the consumer. Production engineers are very often at one with consumers in the contempt with which they regard the sales talk of those windbag merchants who call themselves marketing men. People who take up cudgels to warn the consumer against the carefully laid pitfalls of commercial propaganda find an echo in Plato's charge against Sophism when he said that "Sophistic is to legislation what beautification is to gymnastics and appearance to reality."[4]

This accusation is meaningless to those for whom it is intended since the reason men of marketing (like the Sophists) hold appearance (or the "plausible") "in more honor than the true"[5] is that, for them, there is nothing but appearance. It is the consumer's perception of the advantages and disadvantages of the product, the analysis of his motivations and the image of the product in the public mind that govern the preparation of marketing programs. Even the price of the product is an element of its presentation and is therefore fixed at levels that have no bearing on what would seem to be appropriate. Only the fascination of appearances can win the approval of potential customers.

There is nothing but appearance. Did Protagoras mean anything else by his famous assertion that "man is the measure of all things?"[6] If men have no common point of reference except perhaps the belief that they share the same feelings about things, no opinion can lay claim to a truth that does not exist. Man is limited to what his senses perceive of the world. His approval can be won only by influencing that perception. He can be enticed only by playing skillfully on his sensations and feelings. And the art of enticement requires a knowledge of how to conjure up appearances out of words and to present objects and people in a flattering light. Marketing men and Sophists claim to possess this technique.

The pragmaticians as technicians of enticement. Marketing men and Sophists regard themselves as technicians. They are doers or, better still, they know how to get things done. Only ask, and they perform. They are men of action. They know the art of playing with the sensations of men. Their role is limited to that of winning the public—the potential buyer or the member of the Greek city–state—over to the desire or the opinion towards which their client wishes it to be pulled. Since it is generally an effective weapon in their work of enticement, they generally behave as if they believed in it all. But this cannot be a condition of their action. For they are not concerned with the ends for which their services are bought. There is no dishonor in this for the value of every end is itself nothing but the effect of the conviction of the person who sets that end. Since there is no common measure between convictions, there is no yardstick by which to establish the superiority of any one end over the others.

Mercenaries. Thus the marketing men, like the Sophists, have no reason to take offense when certain people, fallen victim to other appearances, accuse them of being mercenaries. Their success, which brings them wealth and glory in this world, does not lie in the beauty of speculative thought that is devoid of efficiency; it is the success of those whom they charge for their services and who come back for more. People who accuse marketing of baseness for selling services very dearly echo, across the centuries, the philosophers at the end of the golden age of Greek philosophy, scandalized by the mercantile behavior of the Sophists who threw away their lessons for money.[7].

A pointless accusation for both marketing men and Sophists since, according to them, nothing, unless it be appearance, can confer any superiority whatsoever on disinterested acts. For the same reason, they do not question the purpose of those to whom they sell themselves. It is enough for them that their buyers have the money to purchase their services. The power they display in doing this is sufficient proof of their efficiency or their strength; and efficiency is the only conceivable sign of their value. Thus marketing is able to praise in turn the convenience of any brand of washing powder, or to show the most varied political programs in a favorable light using highly persuasive arguments. Thus it is that we can see praise being lavished on the attentiveness to the public of a policy that agrees with the results of an opinion poll and, in the same breath, on the courage of another action that disagrees with public opinion. "The art of persuading," says Gorgias, "far surpasses all others and is far and away the best, for it makes all things its slaves by willing submission, not by violence."[8] The means he proposes are better ones because they make it possible to keep power or to win it peacefully. In other words, Sophistical reflection is possible only in a society with an already democratic orientation in which discussion is a normal form of political relationship.

Just as commercial marketing is possible only in a society whose members have the real possibility of buying, that is to say both the means to procure products and the opportunity of choosing among them. Marketing adopts a program of enabling firms to maintain their position in the market or to win a position. Thus it presents itself as the means of defending the interests of both the producer and the consumer, that is of defending the conditions for maintaining the possiblities of choice. Neither the Sophist's technique nor that of marketing challenges the powers that be, any more than these techniques challenge anyone who, deeming himself the mightiest, might be tempted to appropriate power. When these techniques support an establishment in power—business or government—they set themselves the goal of ensuring the most efficient conditions for discussion and for winning consent, without any reference to some absolute virtuous power, by postulating the concomitantly legitimate and perfectible character of the power establishment.

Nor do they challenge the hegemonically inclined individual or group when placing themselves at the service of a conqueror—in the market or the agora—for they then postulate that it is preferable for the mightiest to win.[9] For the Sophists as well as for the marketing men, the instruments of power—the means to obtain or maintain it—take precedence over the ends. Because the ends are pointless, since there is no universal standard, all that is left is to act "in the most opportune manner."[10] As Thrasymachus says: "the purpose of government is to be efficient and to succeed. This is the criterion by which it should be judged."[11] The point to be justified is not why one governs or why one sells but how to govern or how to sell better. Like all techniques, Sophism and marketing are indifferent to power. They place no limit whatsoever on the exercise of power unless it be weakness, which carries its own sanction: elimination by the strongest. Only those who can afford to pay the Sophists and the marketing men can hope for the assistance of their services: those with power, in order to preserve it so that they may continue to protect the weak: those without power, in order to win it so that the strongest may triumph.

Technique versus culture. Technique requires apprenticeship. Technique also requires knowledge related to a practical purpose. If this knowledge serves as the basis for power, it no longer constitutes the innate quality of distinguished and disinterested minds but a collection of vulgar processes within the reach of anyone who wishes do take the trouble, time and money to learn them. This disrespect for culture is quite characteristic of marketing, which retains from traditional culture nothing but a motley collection of stereotypes that are effective for purposes of persuasion. Equally characteristic is the contempt in which marketing is held by the scholars in the fields surrounding it—economics, philosophy and sociology—which (considering themselves to be the bearers of "true values") have, until recently, denied it entry into those temples of cultural legitimacy, the universities. (Marketing was not introduced into the French university curriculum until after World War II.)

"Nowadays, the words 'success' or 'a successful man' suggest most immediately the world of business, and only secondarily that of politics. As an analogy, one might assign to rhetoric the place now occupied by advertising. . . . As we have our business schools and schools of advertising, so the Greeks had their teachers of politics and rhetoric: the Sophists." So Guthrie puts it.[12] Just as professors of marketing face opposition from the "noble" disciplines, so the Sophists faced it from the "philosophers of truth" because they declared themselves to be "technicians" and offered technical apprenticeship in their knowledge to all. A sacrilegious proposition this was, since it made talent not a moral and intellectual gift, reserved by the gods for a small elect, but a capacity that could be cultivated by anyone through a suitable apprenticeship organized by "teachers" with the help of text books. Sophistry was a democratic art that sapped the legitimacy of the power exercised by the elites in Athens by placing itself at the service of "the uncultured whose desire is not for wisdom but for scoring off an opponent."[13]

The Sophists were iconoclasts, all the more so as, possessing specialist

knowledge, they transmitted it not through the free and disinterested contact that the divinely elected philosopher might maintain with his disciples,
but through nothing less than the business relationship that linked the
master craftsman with his apprentice. Their minds perverted by money,
the Sophists sold technical instruction that was divorced from culture—
and were very successful at it. Here were minds whose distinction was
acknowledged by their most prestigious adversaries,[14] but they abandoned
the cult of virtue to place themselves at the service of efficiency in the
management of profane matters. Their aim was to train good talkers, capable of making points in a debate, not to arouse scientific interest in a
subject for its own sake.[15]

Foreigners. There is another criticism that Sophism and marketing share
across the centuries. The one like the other is accused of coming from
abroad. Indeed the Sophists came, in the main, from Asia Minor; marketing in France is perceived as coming from the United States. This is no
matter of chance. In order to change, a culture, a tradition must, by definition, take in that which is foreign to it. At the time Sophism appeared, the
Greek world was shaken by the upheavals of the Median wars which
brought temporal and spiritual troubles into the Greek body politic.[16] It is
not surprising that the answers came from outside, nor that the common
opinion, attached to tradition, resented them as foreign intrusions. The
same is true of marketing, a term for which the *Academie Française* has
not yet given up seeking a French equivalent because the original is too
strong a reminder of its North American origins. Marketing, after all, is a
symbol of a youthful America besieging an aging Europe. Taught, first of
all, on the other side of the Atlantic, where it earned its references, marketing has brought with it the notion, impious in the eyes of our old humanistic culture, that the problems of this world are above all problems of
management: that is, issues formulated as "problems" to be dealt with by a
universal method which brooks no cultural particularism.

For marketing then, as for Sophism, all questions are practical ones; all
answers relate to action on opinion, based on an operational knowledge of
the state of the market. These similarities between the characteristics of
Sophism and marketing are not purely rhetorical. They throw light on
fundamental resemblances between two techniques which hold identical
positions with respect to action, justify themselves in the same manner and
have appeared in structurally analogous historical conditions.

Marketing and Sophism, Techniques of Action

To act on the world, one needs a method by which to apprehend it, a
means of action and a goal. Hence three words suffice to characterize a

technique of action. Both marketing and Sophism choose empiricism as their method, rhetoric as their means and pragmatism as their goal.

The Method: Empiricism

The question that preoccupies marketing is not one of establishing the objective character of the need its products meet—goods, services, men or ideas. It accepts that its definition may be taken from another area (in the administrative or political spheres) and that the need lies in the irrational desire of the consumer (business); the problem is to tune in to the expressed need or to convince and, for this purpose, to explore the opinion of the consumer, the user, the citizen. The effectiveness of its work depends upon knowledge of "targets" and the fitting of persuasive techniques to subjectively felt needs, to the instincts of opinion. The opinion poll and the market study have become almost indispensable descriptive tools, and advertising the means of implementation.

The question that marketing asks is that of the Sophist: what empirical means can be used to find out the convictions of the governed so as to gear action to these convictions or transform them by the most efficient—that is the most skillful—processes? The Sophists did not question the foundations of opinion but took a purely phenomenological view of it, with efficiency as their goal. "Man is the measure of all things."

Rhetoric: The Art of the Commonplace

The technique of enticing is one of communication. Communication with the consumer, the user, the citizen—this is what marketing men propose. And they make images, words and sounds their favorite raw materials. Like Gorgias, they might say that words are all–powerful despots.[17] Their golden rule is to use the power of evocation, inherent in all languages that ensure communication between men, on behalf of what they want to sell. Advertising men are past masters in the art of selling a package holiday by a suggestion of palm trees waving in the breeze. Marketing men are experts in the use of the cultural stereotypes of the groups to which they address their images just as the Sophists were skilled in the art of "commonplaces,"[18] those all–purpose formulae and expressions they invented to hold the attention and win the approval of their audiences. For both, the key discipline is rhetoric, the technique of eloquence, which Gorgias named the queen of sciences who holds all the rest in her power[19] and which Aeschylus called "the charmer to whom nothing is denied."[20]

Any advertising man knows that a campaign for bathing costumes is ineffective in winter. Similarly, the Sophistical orator learned to take the floor at a time of his own choosing, to acquire a sense of timing, that is, the moment when his argument would have maximum efficiency, when, having allowed his adversary to speak, he could turn his own arguments against him according to the rules of the art of controversy (Eristics) and Sophistical prosody.[21]

To convince, it is not enough to choose the right arguments and use them at the right moment. They should also be well presented, that is, the message has to be organized in the way that is most propitious for its reception. For this purpose too, there are techniques. One well–known method for the temporal division of the message is based on what is called the hierarchical effect of advertising and has been christened AIDA in France because it seeks to awaken first the attention A of the target, then foster his interest I so as to uncover his desire D which makes it possible to take action A. A technique that irresistibly recalls the angler's art, but which is also similar, in all aspects, to the one Protagoras taught his pupils when he asked them to divide their speech into four basic modes: the request (or prayer), the question, the answer and the command.[22]

The art of the commonplace and the technique of effective discourse find applications everywhere. Marketing has given sufficient empirical proof of the universality of its method ever since it came out of private enterprise, where it was born, and went into the service of great national causes, politicians and even of God whose "popularity rating" was recently ascertained in a poll commissioned by the Bishop of Paris.[23] Protagoras too proclaimed that his teaching was useful in all matters and "proudly advertised his ability to teach a young man 'the proper care of his personal affairs, so that he may best manage his own household, and also of the State's affairs, so as to become a real power in the city, both as speaker and man of action'."[24]

And since he wished to make his knowledge serve many masters, the Sophist too had to learn the art of turning arguments inside out. Protagoras maintained that "there are two (opposite) arguments on every subject."[25] This is what he called antilogism. And one of his favorite methods of teaching was the exercise that consisted in developing arguments which prove one thing and then its contrary by turning the weakest argument into the strongest.[26]

The Goal: Pragmatism

Efficiency, the pragmatic criterion, is the only criterion possible, since no law of man or God can provide a transcendental criterion of judgment by which legitimate acts can be distinguished from illegitimate ones. The division of the market among companies can be regarded solely as the effect of a specific conjunction of buying desires which may be altered by various circumstances. Similarly, the Sophists were unable to see society as anything but the product of a consent arrived at by men under specific circumstances, subject to endless fluctuation at the whim of fresh circumstances. The laws of society are human artifacts, whether they constitute the "law of the mightiest," in Thrasymachus's opinion,[27] or the protection that society provides to the weakest, according to that of Protagoras.[28] To govern, therefore, can only mean to impose one's decision, either by the exercise of pure force—but it is well known that tyranny creates its own sanctions—or by proving one's actions are founded. As for the men in business marketing, they address their services to people who have no choice in the matter: incapable of applying constraint, firms are forced to resort to persuasion if they wish to get rid of their products. Unless marketing also claims to be an alternative to State coercion.[29]

The Sophists, like the men in political marketing, aim at increasing efficiency—in government or business—by giving leaders the instruments with which they can convince citizens or customers of the justice of their procedures, the legitimacy of their actions or the qualities of their products.[30]

The Justification of Marketing and Sophism

Every practice must justify its action before those who question its success. Sophism and marketing techniques of justification, are not exempt from this fate. Both have to answer questions on the underlying values of the knowledge they propose and the goals they pursue. They claim to be versatile and indifferent to the ends of the action that they bring about. How then are they to escape the accusation that they may be both the "best and the worst of things," depending on the cause to which they sell their services? How indeed if not by invoking the thesis that knowledge is relative, thereby asserting that if the technician does not take a stand it is not because he does not want to do so, but because he cannot do so? For all is relative. This is a theoretically strong argument, but a morally insufficient one, needing the supplement of a further proposition that assumes the social character of morality and thus provides assurance that the technician's lack of concern about the ends of his action does not indicate a lack of morality in the solutions that he proposes.

All is relative. There is no lack of proverbs available to marketing men: "What is truth in Athens is falsehood overseas" is how the members of the Greek city-state might have put it, as the Sophists suggested they do, when they heard of practices, which looked monstrous to their society, but which, they saw, were perfectly acceptable in other parts of the vast world then opening up before them.[31]

The variegated nature of the purchasing done by consumers is patent proof, say marketing men, that the relativity of demand must be respected if freedom is to be preserved in a society of plenty such as ours. Each person should be the sole master of the definition of his need. Need is a subjective matter. It is what one perceives to be such. There is nothing then, they add, to stop companies (on the contrary, everything encourages them) from anticipating their customers' desires by obtaining information about their tastes through market research and by seeking, through advertising, to emphasize the satisfactions they will obtain from the product on offer.

The same proposition is advanced by political marketing men: when they analyze the characteristics of a politician's electorate, suggest changes in tone or theme that should enable him to preserve or "win" new targets, the marketing men claim to be carrying out a job of information-gathering whose necessity derives from the fact that opinions vary, and which enables the candidate to take into account the citizens' aspirations. In the end, they say, they are working in the interest of the citizen.

By the manner in which he presents himself on the political scene, the candidate equipped with this knowledge can then inform the voters of his capacity to fulfill his role. The defenders of political marketing claim that it is essentially a means of improving communication in a democracy. The political debate is thus shifted from the idealistic search for the perfect society to the search for the best candidate, that is, the one who will be able to show that he is the most fit to meet the demands of the greatest number of voters.

Finally, the development of marketing in the public services can be seen as the means to establish communication—non–present but necessary all the same in view of the relativity of need—between users and the administration. Market research enables the administration to determine the nature of the public goods whose need is felt by the public and to take corresponding administrative action; the promotion of public goods and services by advertising enables every user to become aware of the possibilities that the State offers him. Once again, marketing presents itself as the means to ensure proper communication in a developed and pluralistic society, that is, as the means by which the subjects of administration can be made to benefit from the many opportunities offered them, while at the same time efficiently organizing the management of common resources.

Relativity and Morality

It is all very well to claim to be neutral about ends by arguing that they are relative. But what then of morality? To adopt efficiency as a goal, and to insist that this cannot be otherwise, does not suffice to disarm the defenders of morality, whose benediction is also a necessary condition of efficiency.

Neither marketing men nor Sophists are disturbed by this obstacle. It is true, they say, that the notions of the True, the Beautiful and the Good are relative. But this relativity is a cultural one. In any one society, the members share the same point of view on each of these notions. It is as if, in a given society, these values were absolute, but only so long as they do not change. ". . . what a city thinks just and fine is just and fine for so long as it is thought so. . . ."[32] These "cultural absolutes" therefore act as bounds beyond which it is useless for the man of action to try and act, for his arguments would then be held to be immoral and would therefore be ineffectual. Thus if marketing has considerably increased the number of products sold on the market, it has done so, say its promoters, only because it has met needs that had as yet had no opportunity to be expressed since the corresponding goods did not yet exist. Similarly, the effectiveness of the Sophistical discourse was conditioned by its capacity to relate to the commonplaces of those to whom it was addressed.

Thus argued Protagoras and Gorgias in an optimistic mode. The argument may also be put in the manner of Thrasymachus, for whom morality and the law that proceeds from it are not the product of a collective formulation but that which those in power define as being morality and law. For them nothing is unjust but an injustice that does not succeed, and "if treason never prospers, it is only because if it prospered no one would dare call it treason." This point of view does not challenge the role of the Sophist. It operates in a society whose order is based on the fact of domination as a substitute for physical violence. To the conception of society as a community, Thrasymachus opposes his vision of society as the place where "the mightiest lays down his law"[33] and where the weak are without protection.

Thrasymachus's view is basically that of marketing when it proposes itself as an alternative to coercion rather than the means to achieve communication based on the consensus of moral values. The argument of technical neutrality, a theoretically strong one, is socially tenable only when it concerns methods which can be placed at the service of all causes because they can be placed at the service of any cause. The position of technical efficiency is morally defendable only if it claims to be the means of persuading each citizen in the "agora," each user and each customer, not of the "truth" of a cause but of its "superiority." The foundation of the value of knowledge—efficiency—cannot do without a statement justifying the value of the goal that it serves to pursue.

Humanism. The goal, in both instances, is *man*: man who seeks fulfillment through a utilitarian conception of the politico–economic world according to marketing, and through political equality according to the Sophists. It is clearly to the individual man, as voter, user and consumer, that marketing is addressed. This man is a being with social and economic characteristics, endowed with irrational desires and instincts that shape his subjective perception of his needs. It is this human entity that marketing studies and not, as the classical economist did, that disembodied being, the liberal individual. It is the being in the humanness of his instincts, weaknesses and loves that marketing examines, not the cold, unfathomable and rational calculating being invented by the classical liberals. Its favorite science is psychology, or even psychoanalysis, but not economics. Statistics too, which enables marketing to think in big numbers, to address "most" of the people, those in the midst of the social system, all equal in their humanity but sovereign in their individuality.

For the Sophists, too, man was at the center. They were perhaps the first to propose the hypothesis of the equal humanity of all men, going so far as to campaign for the abolition of slavery in the name of the idea that freedom was incompatible with any form of submission other than that due to the law.[34] Thrasymachus himself, who saw inequality as the ineluctable order of society, and Callicles, who recommended it as the best possible social order, granted the status of human being to the weakest as well as the strongest, to the dominators as well as the dominated.[35] The same concern with the universality of human attributes and the perfectibility of all men can be noticed in the Sophists' view of education which led them to denounce, by their own practice, what classical philosophy would later as an "ideology of giftedness."

Marketing, Sophism and History

No matter how rigorous the demonstration that marketing and Sophism correspond across the ages, an explanation is still needed of why societies so distant from each other could have witnessed the emergence of such similar movements. As the narration of the succession of powers, history questions their legitimacy. An examination of this notion of legitimacy shows us that the legitimacy of the power of both Sophism and marketing spring from the crisis of legitimacy of other forms of power.

System of Legitimacy

"Experience shows that in no instance does domination voluntarily limit itself to the appeal to material or affectual or ideal motives as a basis for its continuance. In addition, every such system attempts to establish and to cultivate belief in its legitimacy. But according to the kind of legitimacy that is claimed, the type of obedience, the kind of administrative staff developed to guarantee it, and the mode of exercising authority will all differ fundamentally. Equally fundamental is the variation in effect. Hence it is useful to classify the types of domination according to the kind of claim to legitimacy typically made by each."[36] Can Sophism and marketing, these two techniques of power and domination, claim affinity with one of the types of legitimacy identified by Max Weber? Or, are they means for exercising power without legitimacy? If this is the case, what do they tell us about the societies in which they tend to become omnipresent techniques of domination?

The effectiveness of a principle of legitimacy relates to its capacity to define a stable referent of the social order, one located outside society and defined as an immutable court of truth. This referent justifies the nature of domination and the way in which it is exercised by defining the source of domination, the areas it controls and the form of the relationship between the orders of power and the obedience required of the objects of power.

Each type of legitimacy is distinguished from the others by the source of legitimacy it claims: charismatic legitimacy has its source in the Sacred, traditional legitimacy in History, and rational–legal legitimacy in Nature. The spheres over which domination is legitimately exercised derive from these sources: all aspects of existence in the first case, the sectors demarcated by Tradition in the second case, and those demarcated by Law in the third case. In the charismatic model, the relationship of domination is manifested and imposed by the communion of believers, in the traditional model by respect for customary law, and in the rational-legal model by the rational evidence of the rule revealed by the law.

Charisma has its source outside the world of mortals and imposes itself through the Prophet, God's Chosen One. God's Word flows through him and receives spontaneous adhesion. Adhesion is an act of faith, born of Revelation. He who does not adhere does not belong to the chosen people. The traditional model of legitimacy establishes, on the basis of History, the right of the leader to command and the duty of the members to obey. Mediation between the leader and the led is provided by respect for the historical institutions that represent Tradition. The rational model makes a leader of every individual who has the capacity for it: a leader of his own existence, a leader of society as a whole, through its representatives chosen to set up the anonymous laws of Nature and see to it that they are abided by.

Sophism, Marketing and Legitimacy

As compared to these models, the relativism of Sophism and marketing lies in the fact that they recognize no criterion of Truth, whether in heaven, history or nature. Belief makes no reference to Truth. If Sophism and marketing accord belief a central place, they do so only to the extent that belief is useful to action. The referent–less world of relativism is emptied of meaning. All that remains is an endless cloud of opinions. Power is therefore reduced to *de facto* power, and domination to a pragmatic problem: that of its preservation through the manipulation of opinion.

Although Sophism and marketing do not belong to any of the identified forms of legitimacy, they at least possess attributes of each of these forms. With charisma, they share the attribute of emotional adhesion. If "no prophet has ever regarded his status as being dependent on the opinion that the crowd has of him"[37] no product of marketing or Sophism has virtues independent of the opinions of the crowd. Whereas adhesion to the charismatic leader is spontaneous, adhesion to the product of marketing is constructed; whereas every word of the charismatic leader meets with immediate adhesion because it is his word, the Sophist and the marketing man seek to transfer the adhesion of the public, aroused by the evocation of words and ideas, to the person or the product that they wish to sell. Whereas faith is Revelation, adhesion to the product of marketing is the result of applying a technique of enticement.

As the rational–legal model, Sophism and marketing both refer to individual preferences. But where the former conceives these preferences as the effect of rational choice among natural needs ordered with respect to a norm, the latter conceives desires as the effect of impulses, attitudes, irrational opinions which cannot be ordered by a non-existent reason. It is this whole set of tendencies to act that the marketing man seeks to mobilize by seduction. The rational–legal model uses the evidence of the Truth (of the price, product or program) as the means to convince; marketing assesses its power of persuasion by the means of seduction it possesses for affecting the subjective perceptions of needs or products. The objectivity of the former, which unveils the truth of nature through science, contrasts with the impossible neutrality of the latter for which nothing is exempt from subjectivity.

It is from the traditional model that Sophism and marketing are undoubtedly the most distant. For the traditionalist, history is the resource that is perpetually recreated by the legitimate acts of the Prince; for the Sophist, the past is an eminently exhaustible resource. Sophism and marketing seem to be built on the destruction of tradition,[38] since their fragmented use of it weakens the identification of individuals with history as belief. Separated from the total system of interpretation that provides continuity and identity, tradition becomes folklore. It loses its value as a mark of the community of belonging; it is made over to chaos, to incoherence. Marketing and Sophism are consumers of tradition.

Marketing, Sophism and the Crisis of Legitimacy

While possessing some of their features, Sophism and marketing lie outside the systems of legitimacy defined by Max Weber. Moreover, all the criticisms made of these two techniques reveal that while they represent a threat to the other modes of legitimation, they are unable to supplant them. They threaten these modes of legitimation because they destroy their referents; but, since they do not rely on any alternative referent, they are by definition unfit to act as systems of legitimacy of their own.

Finally, marketing and Sophism, like all systems of legitimate domination, set out to substitute the gentle manner for violence. This proves that they aim to resolve, by the same recourse to appearances, the problem of all domination: to ensure obedience by the renewal of belief in legitimacy. Sophism and marketing propose themselves as substitutes for the methods of legitimation identified by Max Weber in periods of crises of referents or crises of legitimacy. The impossibility of identifying types of legitimation other than those described by Max Weber stems from the very logic of legitimation systems. For every system of legitimacy is organized around the division of the world into two elements, one of which is the source of the legitimate power, the other, the element through which this power is applied. Thus charisma subjects the profane to the sacred; traditionalism gives culture all the characteristics of the sacred, to which it subordinates natural life; finally, the rational–legal model identifies in eternal nature the immutable laws of the game by which culture must abide.

Hence a new system of legitimacy should be based on a new opposition between two terms, the immutability of one founding the legitimacy of the other. Neither marketing nor Sophism can provide the stable ground for such a system. For both deny the existence of a reality beyond appearances and treat the variety of beliefs—in God, tradition or reason—as phenomena. Using techniques, they seek to transfer the manifestations of belief to the products or opinions to be "sold." The art of the marketing man lies in his capacity to construct the perception of the ephemeral in terms of an absolute opposition between the eternal categories of the Beautiful and the Ugly. His victory comes when the new products of culture, including ideas, can no longer be identified in the traditional system of the categories of truth (divine, traditional or natural) unless mediated by labels that characterize their ephemeral modernity and their traditional eternalness, like the "new right," "new philosophy," "nouvelle cuisine" or "nouvelle histoire" which have cropped up in recent years. Yet, although nature and culture are not absolutely separate metaphysical categories but ambiguous notions, the fact remains that, because every belief is expressed in these terms, every pragmatic use of the resources of belief can be imagined only in these very same terms. Nature and culture—these are manners of speaking, but the moment one speaks, one must do so in the appropriate way, that is, from the viewpoint either of culture or nature. This is really what brings together, under the label of marketing, all those who draw arguments from the so-called "natural" or "cultural" need of the consumers in order to promote an article or service; this indeed is what brought together, under the banner of Sophism, all those, defenders of the *nomos* or the *physis*, who saw man as the sole common measure of all things.

Thus the whole task of marketing depends on the pragmatic consideration of need. In dealing with "something" that it calls "need" or "opinion," marketing justifies its role as a medium of communication between a product and a customer. However, the need itself still has to be justified by identifying the essential characters which require that it be satisfied. Only the two languages of nature and culture, of natural economy and cultural society, are then available. On the one hand there is a language of economy, namely the language of natural need or need as obligation that only the scarcity of economic goods prevents satisfying. Marketing comes forward then as a means of meeting the imperious requirement of vital need, of physiological need and of instinct by organizing an abundance of goods corresponding to needs. On the other hand, there is a language of sociology, namely the language of cultural need or need as aspiration, which appropriates marketing as soon as its thesis of need as obligation is belied by the observation of its great cultural variety. The satisfaction of need can appear as the legitimate task of marketing only if marketing cannot be accused of orchestrating these variations. It becomes necessary to assume both the founding value and the cultural relativity of tradition: needs are shaped by culture, not by the marketing man. Hence, to offer new products is still to meet a vital need of man. For, in every culture, it is the "need for distinction" that allows new objects to fulfill the need to signify that one is different. Man's nature is immersed in culture: this is the second type of position that marketing, following in footsteps of sociologists from Bataille to Bourdieu and Baudrillard,[39] has advanced in support of its activity. No other argument is possible. Similarly, when they did not set aside the problem of legitimacy, as Thrasymachus did in his pragmatic approach, [40] the Sophists had to seek a moral foundation in either nature or culture to support their standpoint on the best form of government. Protagoras and Gorgias and their disciples sought this foundation by asserting that "law exists for the benefit of human life,"[41] ensuring the supremacy of the *nomos* over the *physis*, of society over the king and the tyrant. But how then can the superiority of the law be explained if not by the intervention of some divine entity, the founder of morality, whose the Law is superior to all human laws;[42] if not by the virtue of those who make the law, that is, by an ultimate nature of man?

Callicles, on the contrary, seeks the basis of his argumentation in nature. For him, "force has priority over law"[43] because the best society is one governed by the strongest and not one in which the greatest number of the weak come together to make the law designed to protect them against the strongest. If natural power is said to be superior to conventional power, it is because the strongest is the one who can display the most courage and the most practical sense in dealing with the business of the polity to the advantage of all.

To tell the truth, the Sophists and marketing men seem to have a happier relationship with the exercise of power than do the philosophers of today or than did Plato. This is easily understood if their respective forms of discourse are compared to their real positions. Someone who holds power and someone deprived of it have opposite relationships with appearance. To the former, appearance brings confirmation of the evidence that suits him. To the latter, appearance recalls his deprivation. Hence Sophism, as a philosophy of power, should agree with appearance while Plato exposes appearance as illusion, as a veil that must be pulled aside to show the truth it conceals.

It remains for the Sophist and Plato each to achieve his desires in his respective relationships with the realities that he depicts for himself. For the Sophist, it will be the realm of power, by developing his pragmatic point of view, by bringing methods of persuasion to bear, by adopting efficiency as the sole criterion of action which is a purpose unto itself. For Plato and the philosopher, the achievement of desire, which cannot come through a relationship with power, must come through a relationship with knowledge: they will make their lack of power, a regrettable sign of the temporary triumph of appearances, the moral mark of the superiority of their ends. Their present lack of success will be answered for by their idealism.

What distinguishes Sophism and marketing from the other concrete approaches to power is that, as children of the crisis of legitimacy, they know the contradiction involved in removing the veil that is cast over reality. Thrasymachus alone refused to abandon pragmatic observation for morality. The others, from Protagoras to Callicles, were caught in the trap of their relativism. They failed in their attempts to put back a veil of morality on the reality of domination. The linguistic fate of the term "Sophist" is proof of this, for even the fact that the Sophists could have expressed a moral viewpoint on the world has been forgotten. Seeing legitimacy as nothing but the effect of a belief, hence not allowing themselves to adopt a superior principle which alone could have given meaning to domination, they did away with the question of "why" and had to restrict themselves to the question of "how," which is Machiavelli's question par excellence.

It is likely that, in its functioning, all power, however sacred, has knowledge of the Machiavelianism with which it is always associated; but not all power knows the fate that consists in revealing the technique of this power. It is in this sense that it might be said that Sophism and marketing are both naive techniques of non-naive power; and their naiveté lies in the fact that they call themselves techniques of power.

Notes

1. Sophism: (a) "Argument, reasoning that is false despite an appearance of truth (generally implies bad faith)—*Petit Robert* (b) "A specious but fallacious argument, either used deliberately in order to deceive or mislead, or employed as a means of displaying ingenuity in reasoning," *Shorter Oxford English Dictionary.*
2. This phenomenon is not unique to French schools (which, however, are now experiencing an opposite trend). W. K. C. Guthrie notes: "Until comparatively recently, the prevailing view, the view in which a scholar of my own generation was brought up, was that, in his quarrel with the Sophists, Plato was right. He was what he claimed to be, the real philosopher or lover of wisdom, and the Sophists were superficial, destructive, and at worst deliberate deceivers, purveyors of Sophistry in the modern sense of that term," in *The Sophists,* Cambridge University Press, 1971.
3. E. Dupréel, *Les Sophistes,* Neuchât el, Editions du Griffon, 1948; W. K. C. Guthrie, *The Sophists,* Charles Perelman & Olbrechts–Tyteca, *Traité de l'argumentation* Brussels, Editions universitaires, 1970; C. Perelman, *L'Empire rhétorique,* Vrin, 1977.
4. Plato in Guthrie, *op. cit.,* p. 176.
5. Plato, ibid., p. 189.
6. Cf. Plato, *Thaetetus,* 152, a.
7. This is one of the traits that most brought opprobium to the Sophists in the eyes of posterity.
8. Gorgias in Guthrie, *op cit.,* p. 192.
9. As Callicles did.
10. The *Kairos* or the "sense of timing, of the right moment," cf. Guthrie, *op. cit.,* p. 272.
11. Thrasymachus, *ibid.,* p. 298.
12. Guthrie, *op. cit.,* p. 50.
13. Plato, in Guthrie, *ibid.,* p. 187.
14. Cf. the famous debate between Socrates and Protagoras.
15. Cf. Guthrie, *op. cit.,* p. 54
16. Gomperz tells us: ". . . they relied absolutely on their own efforts, they resided more frequently abroad than at home, and thus handicapped, they were compelled to enter on a keen competition among themselves," *op. cit.,* p. 413; he calls them half professors and half journalists (p. 414). ". . . their business," he adds, was "to advertise themselves in difficult circumstances," p. 419. On this

last point, see H. I. Marrou, *Histoire de l'éducation dans l'Antiquite*, Paris, Seuil, UH series, re–edited 1965, p. 91.
17. Gorgias, in *The Sophists, op. cit.*
18. Gomperz, *op. cit.*, p. 474; H. L. Marrou, *op. cit.*, p. 98; *The Sophists, op. cit.*
19. Gorgias, *ibid.*, p. 271.
20. Aeschylus, in Guthrie, *op. cit.*, p. 50.
21. The art of language was of central concern to Sophists so much so that some of them worked on the theory of language and one tried to cure illnesses by language.
22. Guthrie, *op. cit.*
23. *Le Matin*, Paris.
24. Protagoras, in *The Sophists*, p. 20.
25. *Ibid.*, p. 24.
26. *Ibid.*
27. Thrasymachus, *ibid.*
28. Protagoras, *ibid.*
29. This is the approach taken by people like Kotler and Drücker for example. The argument runs as follows: to survive, companies must sell. To sell they must advertise. Innovation and the survival of the free society are bound up with the collective survival of companies. P. F. Drücker, *The Practice of Management*, London, Heinemann, 1955, and P. Kotler, *Le Marketing*, Paris, Editions d'organisation, 2 vols., 1974.
30. Guthrie, *op. cit.*
31. Which naturally overturned the notion of the divine origin of the law.
32. Guthrie, *op. cit.*, p. 180.
33. Thrasymachus, *ibid.*
34. Antiphon, in Guthrie, *op. cit.*
35. See for example Robin L., *La Pensée Grecque et les Origines de l'Esprit Scientifique*, Paris, Albin Michel, 1963.
36. M. Weber, *Economy and Society,* Berkeley, University of California Press, 1978, p. 213.
37. *Ibid.*
38. Cf. J. Habermas, *Raison et Légitimité*, Paris, Payot, 1980.
39. G. Bataille, *La Part Maudite*, Paris, Editions de Minuit, 1967; J. Baudrillard, *Le Systéme des Objets*, Paris, Gallimard, 1968 and *Pour une critique de l'économie politique du signe*, Gallimard, 1972; P. Bourdieu, *La Distinction*, Paris, Editions de Minuit, 1980.
40. As Taylors says, quoted by Guthrie, *op. cit.*, p. 96: "He (Thrasymachus) feels no need to justify the absolutism of the sovereign by appeal to the social contract by which he has been invested with his sovereign powers; since he does not regard right as having any meaning, he has not to show that the sovereign has any right to obedience; it is sufficient to observe that his power to enforce obedience is guaranteed by the simple fact that he is the sovereign." A more pragmatic solution, more elaborate in strategic terms, is provided by Antiphon, who, positing the absolute relativity of culture, suggests that "the conventional law should be respected" "in the presence of witnesses" "for reasons of appearance and reputation," but that it should be "violated whenever possible" for "reasons of reality," in Guthrie, *ibid.*
41. Democritus, *ibid.*
42. This is what Guthrie suggests about Protagoras when he says that man's nature,

his physical weakness would have led to his destruction without political organization. Consequently, laws are dictated by "nature." It is therefore, just to observe laws but they have neither the scope nor the effectiveness of divine or natural laws. Antiphon too says that the wise man will be guided not by the established laws, but by the laws of the *areté*. Guthrie on Protagoras, *op. cit., ibid.*

43. Calliclés, *ibid.,* p. 112.

Chapter 2

Laissez-Faire and the Crisis of Legitimacy

Some call a mask what others call a face.

The opposition between Plato and the Sophists was the opposition between the theory of power and its practice. Theory—in the etymological sense of *theoria*—means contemplation. To contemplate power, one must be at a distance from it. To practice power, one must be very close to it. Then, it is possible to forget that, to practice power, one must make it possible for those who are the objects of power to contemplate it. Every exercise of power calls for a representation of this power. To distinguish this representation of power from power itself, we shall call the former a system of legitimacy.

What distinguishes power from a system of legitimacy is the fact that the latter assumes the existence of a subjectivity contemplating the former. This may be as much the subjectivity of the one who acts, knowing that he acts, as that of the one who submits, knowing that he submits. In other words, once power ceases to be blind, it partakes of a system of legitimacy, regardless of the cruelty of its gaze.

Every representation of power assumes the presence of two subjects, one of whom asks the other a number of questions: Who exercises power? How does he exercise his power? In the name of what does he exercise his power? A system of legitimacy implies that any question can be asked about power, and that there is an answer to all questions.

The exercise of legitimate power assumes that the time needed to formulate the question of power and to reply to it is short enough to leave some time for action. This is what all parents understand in the end when, overwhelmed by incessant questioning from their children, they reply to everything with "Because." Thus sooner or later everyone rediscovers the essence of all legitimacy systems, namely that they should accept all questions and should provide an answer to each of them. History also shows that such a system of legitimacy wears out in the end, that the child is

21

increasingly dissatisfied with the answer even if it may be the best one that he will ever get. This system of legitimacy must yield to one more capable of coping with new demands: "So that curious children can ask questions," is the standard French reply. Thus do they move, in a matter of weeks, from the realm of truth to the rule of Sophism.

The legitimacy system of a society must meet a twofold requirement: it must be valid for both the multiplicity of beings who make up that society and for the multiplicity of circumstances in which an act must be legitimated. To be valid for a large population, the system must first of all be simple and rather brief. Although it may be developed in long treatises, it should be capable of being summarized by a single sign: this may be the flag, the anthem, the name by which a community recognizes itself. Thus the French Revolution was able to sum up its legitimacy system in three words: Liberty, Equality, Property, soon to be transformed into Liberty, Equality, Fraternity.

To be valid for an entire population, the system must be known to all. What would be the purpose of waving a colored cloth if it were not recognized as a flag? But if the symbolic value of this sign is acknowledged by all, its practical consequences will soon be seen to unfold in all their power. To be valid in all circumstances, the legitimacy system should constitute a system of logic. This enables it to frame an adequate response to each question. By itself, "because" contains the logic of the cause to which we owe the development of science and technology. Variants have been used: e.g. "because it is in the nature of things," "because things are what they are," "because this is how it always has been," "because such is our good pleasure," "because it is in the general interest."

Finally, if they are to constitute well-formed systems of legitimacy, these forms of logic should make reference to a representation of the world divided into two places, the first of which is the source of legitimate power (the sacred, nature) and the second, the site of this legitimate power (the profane, culture). It is thus that Weber distinguishes three types of legitimacy: charismatic, which makes reference to the distinction between the sacred and the profane; traditional, which makes reference to the distinction between culture (place of tradition, an institution whose sacred origins are lost in the mists of time) and nature (treated as it is laid down in tradition); and rational-legal, which refers to the distinction between nature (the place where laws emerge) and culture (the place where laws reign in conformity with the laws of nature).

The Ancien Regime in France was charismatic inasmuch as the king "by divine right" was consecrated at Rheims. But the Ancien Regime was above all traditional: power was handed down according to the principle of descent. The question of legitimacy in the Ancien Regime was therefore an explicit part of the legitimacy system: the king was the legitimate heir, consecrated at Rheims.The French Revolution saw the advent of a new legitimacy system of the rational–legal type. Henceforth, it was no longer individuals that ruled, but an impersonal norm, the law, a norm that proceeded from the most impersonal element in the cosmos, namely nature. And it must be an effect of the logic of legitimation that systems of "personal" legitimacy (charisma and tradition) allow the legitimacy of those who reign to be questioned explicitly whereas in impersonal systems the question of legitimacy disappears completely behind that of legality. The exclusion of the issue of legitimacy is thus part of the free-market system of legitimacy, so much so that the very idea of a crisis of legitimacy may be deemed self-contradictory so long as legal procedures still function. However there are numerous signs that such a crisis exists. Among them, for example, numerous protest movements against private enterprise (Consumer defense associations, the ecological movement, plans for business reform etc.) and administration (of late, the improvement of relations between the administration and the administered has become a theme of government while there is a growing trend, starting in the United States, towards cuts in public spending). Another indication is the outpouring of writings that speak explicitly of a crisis of legitimacy, in particular the works of Jurgen Habermas on the "problems of legitimation in late capitalism."[1] And then, in recent years, there has been the extraordinary interest shown in analyses in terms of power.

The crisis of the representation of power leads to its logical conclusion: the notion of power must henceforth assume responsibility for its own representation. So much so that approaches made in terms of legitimacy are often criticised for attaching more importance to the superficial aspect of things than to their substance, for giving more place to ideologies than to the real forces that these ideologies express. However, those who claim to get to the bottom of things forget that they cannot do so without contemplating their appearances, and that their understanding of the nature of power comes to them only from the variation of its representations. To analyze variations in systems of legitimacy is therefore to describe a phenomenon that each may then interpret according to his own cosmological framework, his own conception of the world.

The history of the free-market system of legitimacy goes from its founding, at the time of the French Revolution, to its present crisis. The argument can be summed up thus: every social actor (individual or organization) draws his or its legitimacy from a principle; when this principle happens to be contradicted too sharply by the way this actor functions in reality, he or it is then led to modify the initial principle in order to develop a new discourse that legitimizes his or its action.[2]

The Principle of the Free-Market System of Legitimacy

The free-market system of legitimacy results from the victory of the universal light of reason over superstition and the personal power of the king. Reason is born, first of all, with the science of nature, which establishes a distinction between nature and culture. Then comes the science of economics, which shows that society, too, can be governed by the laws of nature if it is freed of the traditional sovereign's tyranny. It is therefore necessary that, in place of the king's former power, should be enthroned reason, whose only role is to enable the laws of nature to exercise their benevolent domination over free and equal citizens. Nature is reason, it necessarily obeys the laws that constitute it. Culture becomes reason and should also become aware of the laws that are to govern it. Hence the free-market system of legitimacy assumes that society is divided into two sectors: the private, over which the laws of nature hold sway, and the public, entrusted with letting the laws of nature exercise unhampered legislation over the private sector. The public sector, successor to the traditional sovereign, is responsible for justice (ensuring compliance with contracts), the police (the prohibition of the use of violence), foreign affairs, national defense and transport (the safety and efficiency of exchange within the national market).

Each of these two sectors is the seat of a legitimacy of the rational–legal type, to use Max Weber's terms again: the *private sector* because, in it, the *laws of nature* express the rationality that political economy espouses; the public sector because a *system of laws* (the constitutional laws) organizes the reign of reason in government, the assemblies and courts of justice.

The history of the free-market crisis of legitimacy is the history of the crisis of the boundary between the public and private sectors. Every crisis of the private sector must necessarily have repercussions in the public sector that complements it. It is therefore not surprising that the major turning points in the history of the legitimacy of the private sector and that of the public sector should have come at the same time: 1880-1890 and 1945-1960.

The History of Legitimacy in the Private Sector

The Old System of Legitimacy

It was classical political economy that provided the brief and coherent discourse by which it was possible to legitimate the action of business firms. Four propositions sufficed here:

- Pure and perfect competition
- Profit maximization
- Entrepreneural risk
- The right to property

The theory of pure and perfect competition justified individual profit seeking. Economic laws ensured that, when each person pursued his maximum advantage, the invisible hand of the market, acting in the role of Providence, would bring about an optimum use of resources and ensure the remuneration of economic activities at their just price. It still had to be pointed out that this would lead to a sort of overall optimum for society. This is what Pareto's theory of the optimum established.[3]

The theory of the profit maximization implied that the entrepreneur had sufficient good taste not to be indifferent to the lure of profit. If not, it would no longer be certain that those who owned capital would strive for the utmost profit. The example of the latifundia–owners of Latin America, who keep huge tracts of land uncleared, gives an idea of the extent to which such an attitude can harm an economy.

The theory of entrepreneurial risk gave the finishing touches to the justification of the right to property. This was especially true because the entrepreneur could, without consultation, formulate the policy of his firm and appropriate its profits. According to this theory, the firm could function only because an investor was prepared to take the risk of losing his investment. If he took the risk, it was because he hoped to benefit from the profit that would result from good management. It was therefore the risk of failure that justified the authority of the owner and his right over the profits of his firm.[4]

It was, in fact, the right to property that, in the end, ensured the coherence of the system and translated it from the language of economics into that of law, for the free-market system of legitimacy had to find its complete expression in the language of legality.

The Turning Point of 1880-1890

If the legitimacy system of the firm in the free market had to be summed up in one sentence, it could be said that it was able to exercise freely all the power available to it since the power available to it was nil. For pure and perfect competition assumes that firms are infinitely small in relation to the market, and that none of them can by itself affect either the level of the quantities of products offered on the market or that of their prices.

The first turning point in the crisis of legitimacy of free enterprise was provided by the challenge to what was called the "atomicity" of firms.

Competition became less pure and less perfect. In the United States, the Vanderbilts, Rockefellers, Morgans and Du Pont de Nemours could no longer pass themselves off as small, meritorious entrepreneurs. They set up groups some of which dominated the market.

The free-market system of legitimacy was endangered if firms became "too big." To avoid this, it sufficed to add a sentence to the legitimacy system, a law to the system of legality: the anti-trust law. To see if a firm was "too big," it was brought before a judge. If it was acquitted, that meant it was "small enough." If it was condemned, it was broken up into entities that were "small enough" to be compatible with the free-market system.

The concentration of firms created a vacuum in the free-market system of responses; the anti-trust law made it possible to fill this vacuum by symbolically establishing a return to the previous situation. Thurman Arnold, who presided over the anti-trust legislation of the late thirties was able to point out that, rather than stopping it, the anti-trust laws went along with the concentration of firms, which continued apace in a spectacular manner. In *The Folklore of Capitalism*, he wrote as one disillusioned: ". . . the anti-trust laws enabled men to look at a highly organized and centralized industrial organization and still believe that it was composed of individuals engaged in buying and selling the free market."[5]

The Turning Point of 1945–1960

The effort made to preserve the old legitimacy system appears to have been crowned with success for more than half a century. However, during this period, all the other propositions of the free-market system of legitimacy found themselves in contradiction with actual practices.

The separation of managers from proprietors, which dealt a blow to the principle of profit maximization since, henceforth, those who decided sought "power" rather than profits, also affected the principle of entrepreneurial risk since the decision-maker was no longer the one who risked his capital, and finally touched on the relationship between the right to property and the power of management inasmuch as the control exercised by the share-holders was imperfect. In a study conducted in 1932 for the United States Research Council, Adolf Berle and Gardiner Means showed that the separation of managers from owners was transforming the very bases of the legitimacy of firms: "The institution considered here (the limited company) calls for analysis in terms of social organization: on the one hand, it implies a concentration of power in the economic realm, one comparable to the creation of religious power in the medieval Church or political power in the nation State; on the other hand, it engenders a wide variety of interrelationships among partners with many economic interests: those of the 'owners' who provide the capital, those of the workers who produce and sell, those of the consumers who assign value to the products of the firm and those of the managers who hold the levers of power."[6]

The principle of profit maximization was also to stumble over a second obstacle: the fact that a constantly increasing number of big companies no longer made profits. What this situation suddenly revealed was that bankruptcy was becoming ever more impossible, whether because the activities of a "pool of labour" had to be kept going or because national independence had to be maintained by continuing to produce, at a loss, certain goods deemed strategically essential or because it was necessary to avoid upsetting balances of payments that were already in the red. With the end of bankruptcy (for the "big firms"), the final element of the entrepreneur's risk disappeared. But the legitimacy of free enterprise lies entirely in the subjugation of the firm to the sanction of the market. It might have been believed that the economic crisis was going to reestablish the harsh law of the market. On the contrary, the concentration of firms was accelerated, with failure being replaced by takeover. For a takeover to bring salvation, the entity taking over must have sufficient legitimacy. It therefore became necessary for firms to have a new system of legitimacy.[7]

To avoid remaining silent in the face of the new questions about big firm power from law was once again called upon: the law on the social balance sheet which all big firms henceforth had to furnish, a balance sheet that stated what the firm provided not only to shareholders but also to employees, consumers and the environment. From the viewpoint of legitimacy, however, this law had a significance profoundly different from that of the anti-trust law. The latter restricted itself to controlling the size of firms in order to preserve free-market legitimacy; the former abandoned all controls over size and, in so doing, lost the very essence of free enterprise— so much so that it had to define new objectives for these big organizations and new ways of controlling them.

Henceforth, the big private organizations became institutions whose purpose ("social responsibility") and permanence made them similar to public organizations, all the more so since public organisations, for their part, had also undergone far–reaching transformations since the French Revolution.[8]

The History of the Legitimacy in the Public Sector

Although the story of the crisis of legitimacy has some universality, it is most often necessary to illustrate it with specific examples. We turned to the United States to trace the development of the private sector, which, with some variations, holds good for French firms.[9] It is in France that we shall follow the history of the legitimacy of the public sector, because it is particularly easy to trace here. France has two systems of jurisdiction, one for the public sector and one for the private. This raises the problem of drawing the line between the spheres of competence of the judiciary and the administrative courts respectively. A court, the Tribunal des Conflits,[10] has constantly to redefine the criteria by which a dispute can be assigned to one or the other of the jurisdictions. The "criterion of administrative law" thus defines the limits of public legitimacy and should therefore serve as a summary expression of its principle. The history of the criterion of administrative law can be divided into three periods: before 1880-1890, from 1880-1945, and after 1945.

First Period: The Old System of Legitimacy—The Criterion of Public Power

Administration subjected to government authority was the heir to traditional sovereignty governed by constitutional law alone. It did not render accounts to the private sector. Every agent of the State, defined by statute or by law, came solely under public jurisdiction, for he embodied "public power." This is what was known in France as the "Etat-Gendarme" (Garrison-State). With the criterion of public power, the foundation of legitimacy lay in the source of power.

Second Period: From 1880 to 1945—The Criterion of Public Service

Administration extended its activities to the social and economic spheres. With urban development especially, administration came to encroach with increasing frequency upon the right of the agents of the private sector to property. The visible arm of the State was increasingy substituted for the "invisible hand" of the market. The authority of public power could not extend to realms outside the classical notion of sovereignty without arousing fears of arbitrariness.

A new criterion of legitimacy was then sought. In the economic and social fields, the authority of the State could not rest upon the nature of its power but shifted to the end pursued: this point of view saw the triumph of jurists like Duguit and Jeze at the beginning of the century, when the criterion of public service was developed (a famous administrative court decision, the Blanco judgment of 1873 was the first step). Since it came as a solution to the crisis of legitimacy that public administration was experiencing, this notion was well received, as Jacques Chevalier explains: "The notion (of public service) then met with an extraordinary success, for it founded and limited the powers of governments on the philosophical duel while at the same time it constituted a juridical yardstick for the application of administrative law. Indeed, its conceptual clarity is remarkable: the right of the State is the right of the public services and, hence, not only does every administrative activity constitute, in principle, a public service but also only an administrative service can constitute a public service."[11]

It is by virtue of this principle that jurisprudence had to isolate the category of acts of private management which, although accomplished by the administration, had to be part of the legal system of the private sector. It was decided that the administration too could enter into private law contracts and the notion of public industrial and commercial service grew up, bringing certain public services under ordinary law.[12]

Conversely, "certain services are, by nature, of the very essence of the State or public administration."[13] Even if the service is managed by a private sector firm, it comes under public law if the end pursued is in the nature of a public service (for example, a ferry used to cross a river). The criterion of public service corresponds to a period that is called, in France, the Etat Providence (Welfare State), which, as we all know, is devoted to the welfare of the public. Henceforth, the foundation of the legitimacy of power lay in the end pursued.

Third Stage: After 1945—The Crisis of the Criterion

The crisis of the criterion is, by definition, the crisis of the boundary between the public and private sectors and, by the same token, it is the crisis of the legitimacy of free enterprise. Henceforth, it is not known where the State begins or ends.

To determine if an act is fish or fowl, private or public, the *Tribunal des Conflits* must conduct what is virtually a phenomenological examination of the various constituent elements and must decide, on the basis of the "sheaf of criteria" thus identified, whether the dispute is to be sent before the administrative jurisdiction or before the legal one. Mr. Bernard Chenot, when he was vice-president of the *Conseil d'Etat*, called this method "legal existentialism."

If this method enables the judge to continue to speak, it does not make for a satisfactory answer to the question of administrative legitimacy. Charles Debbasch, professor of public law, noted in an article called "The Administration Versus The Law":[14] "In the end, it is because the administrators are convinced that the rules of classical law are outmoded and that, in a certain way, they embody legitimacy that they feel permitted to stretch the very limits of laws or act against them." Administration can no longer legitimate its actions by either the source of its power (for it acts in spheres that exceed those of traditional sovereignty) or the ends of its power (it acts in far too many, and at times contradictory, circumstances to be able to sift out unambiguously the purpose of its action). Henceforth, it must seek its legitimacy in the sole resource that remains available: the methods of power.

Now what are the two essential grievances voiced against administration? Waste and inhumanity. Against waste, administration will resort to rational methods of management. Against inhumanity, administration will resort to the participation of the users: they cannot consider their own decisions to be inhuman. Against waste and inhumanity taken together, administration will use marketing, which combines the rationality of management with the humanity of those who take human needs into account.

The Case of Public-sector Firms

Looking at the history of public-sector firms in France, we can verify the consequences of the history of legitimacy that we have just traced. The crisis of legitimacy of private enterprise (after 1900) led to a movement of nationalization in France (in 1936): to legitimate a monopolistic firm, it became enough to bring it under the legitimate public authority since the latter (by definition) promised to place it at the service of the public.

After 1945, the public sector crisis of legitimacy led to public enterprise coming under challenge. The famous *Nora Report* (1968) notes: "The nationalized firms of the basic sectors have been used by the authorities at their discretion directly in the service of their general policies. . . ." But thereafter, to be legitimate, it no longer sufficed to be public; it was necessary to be well managed. The recommendations of the *Nora Report* were put into effect: management in general and marketing in particular made their entry into the big public-sector companies.

The crisis of legitimacy in the free market, is the crisis of the legitimacy of big organizations, public as well as private. For private firms, this crisis leads not so much to a change in method (management) as to a change of purpose: henceforth, the goal of profit is subordinated to a higher goal, which is none other than "organizational legitimacy." It is this legitimacy that must be won through marketing, the bureaucratic form of Sophism. For administrations, the crisis of legitimacy leads, less to a change of purpose than a change in methods of management. This change entails the introduction of management methods from the private sector and, in particular, the methods of marketing by which the legitimacy of the actions undertaken may actually be ascertained.[15]

This crisis of legitimacy thus leads to marketing just as another crisis of legitimacy once led to Sophism. Sophism was a technique of action that was pragmatic in its goals and empirical in its methods, using rhetoric as its essential resource. It remains to be seen how marketing is different from Sophism since it is deployed in a bureaucratic universe and not in the agora.

Notes

1. Jurgen Habermas, *Raison et Légitimité: problémes de légitimation dans le capitalisme avancé, op. cit.* See also Romain Laufer, "Crise de légitimité dans les grandes organisations," *Revue françáise de gestion*, 1977.
2. Cf. R. Laufer & A. Burlaud, *Management public, gestion et légitimité*, Paris, Dalloz, 1980, p. 9.
3. The "optimum" in Pareto's meaning of the word is defined by the fact that it is impossible to improve the condition of one person without another having his condition worsened.
4. Cf. Knight, *Risk, Uncertainty, Profit*, Chicago, Chicago University Press.
5. *The Folklore of Capitalism*, New Haven, Yale University Press, 1947.
6. A. A. Berle and G. C. Means, *The Modern Corporation and Private Property*, New York, Macmillan, 1933.
7. In Detroit, in the very heart of the world of classical capitalism, the firm of Chrysler was reduced to asking the U.S. Government for financial aid.
8. The history of the so–called crisis in legal language consists of the sequence anti–trust law/law on the social balance sheet. Since "laissez faire" is rational–legal in essence, it was normal that changes in legality should be matched by changes in the micro–economic language to account for "rationality." In this sense, Joan Robinson and Chamberlin's theory of monopolistic competition corresponds to the antitrust law. Robbins and Williamson's managerial theory of the firm corresponds to the law on the social balance sheet, etc.
9. For example, anti-trust laws were introduced into France belatedly, in particular with Common Market legislation on trust. It was by nationalization (rarely used in the U.S.) that France reacted to the private sector's crisis of legitimacy. This shows the importance of the public sector in France and its legitimating force while, in the United States, the legitimation of the system is essentially a matter of the private sector.
10. The "tribunal des conflits" arbitrates in cases of conflict of jurisdiction between the administrative and judiciary courts. Half of its members belong to the Conseil d'Etat (France's highest administrative jurisdiction and advisory body to the government in matters of legislation) and the other half to the Cour de Cassation (France's highest jurisdiction for the private sector).
11. Jacques Chevallier: Le service Public-Dossier—Themis. P.U.F, 1971.
12. See *Les Grands Arrêts de la Jurisprudence Administrative* (Long, Weil, Braibant), the Terrier decrees (1903) and the *Societé des Granits porphyroides des Vosges* (1912).
13. See decree relating to the *Societé Commerciale de l'Ouest Africaine* (1921) in *Les Grands Arrêts de la Jurisprudence Administrative*.
14. *Le Monde*, 12 August 1976.
15. See R. Laufer and A. Burlaud, *op. cit.*

Chapter 3

Counting—from a Symbolic Procedure to a Pragmatic Procedure

Say it with numbers.

Before turning to the analysis of the role of counting in modern society in the fields of business, politics and public administration, it is necessary to consider first the way in which counting and legitimacy are related.

To raise the problem of legitimacy is to raise the question of the source of the sovereign's right to act. To raise the problem of action is to raise the question of its ends and means.

Every system of legitimacy is founded on the dissociation of the order of ends—defined by the source of power—from the order of means, within the limits defined by the source.

Thus, charismatic power identifies God as its source, his reign as its purpose and the prophet as the instrument for revealing his word in the world. The power of the prophet is therefore uncontestable and unlimited for it is the direct expression of God's will. Traditional power identifies history as its source and the perpetuation of history as its end; it calls for a human knowledge of the past, through the interpretation of tradition, which is the business of those whom the tradition designates as its repositories (priests) or its historical embodiment (the prince); their exercise of power is restricted to the spheres of jurisdiction that are granted to them by respect for tradition and the duty to perpetuate it. Rational–legal power, finally, identifies nature as its source and human reason, which is itself natural, as the instrument for the interpretation of ends; every reasoning being possesses all of the power except inasmuch as he is required to abandon part of it to maintain the conditions of natural order. Even so, he dispossesses him by an act of reason and delegates his power of constraint to a subordinate body in strictly defined spheres and forms.

Every system of legitimacy thus distinguishes between the ultimate subject of power (God, tradition, nature), its representatives, the social subjects

33

of government (the prophet, the prince and the priests, the individual), and the objects of this government (believers, "subjects," those governed). The second group are the custodians, under the eye of the source, of the formidable right to designate these objects of power and to *count them*, to "account for" the things to be administered. One of the operations necessary in bringing about the real order of the world consists in delegating the task of counting to the administration. For the first task, as every human group learns, is that of counting resources—men and things—in order to distribute them. But this is a formidable operation for it assumes a distinction between the categories that must be counted and the others, that is, it assumes that the meaning of the world is to be developed by designations. Hence we should not be surprised[1] if the order to conduct a census comes from the God of the Old Testament and not from David, just as it comes from the Legislature of the democratic society and not from its government. It is for God to count his people, he is the source of all knowledge; any enumeration that he has not ordered can only be the work of Satan. We can see why Saint Ambrose and Saint Augustine in the Middle Ages were still condemning David for his vainglorious enterprise, and why, even in the 18th century, Saint–Simon was condemning those "impious censuses" which had always "enraged the Creator, causing him to stretch forth his hand and meet out exemplary punishment to whoever had ordered such censuses to be conducted."[2] What God condemns is not census–taking as an act of administration but the implicit assertion behind this act, that His creature is the object of the administration of men. What God punishes is David's usurpation of His symbolic function, who sets himself up as the subject, beyond the limits that He has assigned to him.

Categories

The first prerogative of the subject of power is to *designate*. Marcel Granet tells us that in an age when the decline of the Chinese feudal system disturbed the traditional bases of the representation of world order, there flourished two schools of thought:[3] the school of Names and that of the Legalists. They undertook the task of "re–establishing proper order by the correct use of language," as Granet puts it. The former school sought to do so by establishing a fixed tradition. Thus when Tsu Lu asked Confucious: "If the Lord of Wei left the administration of his state to you, what would you put first?" the Master replied: "If something has to be put first, it is, perhaps, the rectification of names. . . . When names are not correct, what is said will not sound reasonable; when what is said does not sound reasonable, affairs will not culminate in success; when affairs do not culminate in success, rites and music will not flourish; when rites and music do not flourish, punishments will not fit the crimes; when punishments do not fit the crimes, the common people will not know where to put hand and foot. Thus, when the gentleman names something, the name is sure to be usable in speech, and when he says something, this is sure to be practicable."[4] The Legalists sought to achieve their program by resorting to the power of the written word, to the law. The Emperor Shi Huang-ti decreed the official dictionary, standardized the writing system and engraved on his steles: "I have brought order to the multitude of beings and put actions and realities to the test: each thing has a name that fits it."[5] For both schools, it was the "correct" value of words, their *common meaning* that had to be fixed so that their usage could not be perverted to "embellish injustice and trouble the multitude." Thus it was necessary to guarantee the invulnerability of meanings, the value of words as a *common measure*, as an instrument of truthful communication and, hence, the order of the world "for names control social behavior because the name calls up the reality."[6]

Categories bring order to the world because they refer in a stable way to the source of truth. Thus the word of the charismatic guide is guaranteed by God, that of priests and the prince by custom and by the interpretation of tradition, that of the legislator by nature through the voting procedure. This is why the word is equivalent to the thing. When the source dries up, the meaning of the world and the stability of categories are threatened. Every *likely* organization of meanings becomes a possibility; rhetoric, the task of persuasion concerning the validity of any one of these meanings, enters the scene.

This is what happened in fifth-century Greece; it is also what is happening in the marketing society. The unique discourse of truth is replaced by many possible variations in a world that, for having ceased to acknowledge a referent, is becoming relative. The persuasive person, the one who most skillfully organizes the resources of argument, is the most successful at creating the illusion that the meaning he proposes is the real one, is the one who will win.

Counting

Administration consists of the totality of the concrete tasks required to keep the world in order.[7] These are executed according to the orders of the subject of power, according to "correct designations." It represents the management of things, profane or mortal, in order to maintain or achieve the order of the world, sacred or eternal.

Counting is one of the first universal instruments of administration.[8] Census-taking allows the subject of power who proclaims the census[9] to

gain awareness of the concrete state of the world; it qualifies resources—
men and things, men as well as things—by their numbers.[10]

Administrative counting is a practical operation. It should therefore not
be confused with measurement in the classical economic science, whose
theoreticians, as it happened, had only contempt for pragmatic figures.
They dismissed statistics enthusiasts as so many antequated "collectors"
and even worse, accused them of endangering the order of the world by
trying to replace nature's work of regulation.[11] There was mutual in-
comprehension here since the latter, for their part, denounced the lack of
practical utility of the flourishing science of economics.[12] The problem was
that the economists claimed to be practicing the science of nature, the
source of harmony in human relations through the medium of things,[13]
while the latter maintained that the proper order of the world could not do
without the supporting hand of man, that is, without the administration of
men and things. Administration, for which counting was necessary, had to
be reduced to ensuring that civil society functioned properly, that is, it had
to be satisfied with managing the limited but irreducible sphere that lay
outside the rule of natural laws because it had no exchange. This was the
justification of administration and the basis of its subordination to politics.
Every intervention of man outside these limits could only be damaging to
the natural achievement of equilibrium. The ills and sufferings that makers
of statistics claimed to treat by the empirical counting of the social realm,
beyond the boundaries of administration, were themselves only a painful
but necessary expression of the natural order. Placing them in the care of
administration could only engender worse ills.[14]

The use to which the classical economists put measurement was quite
different: for them mathematics (and no longer arithmetic) made it possible to express the natural relationships between men by the intermediary
of things. It was through economic exchange (and deliberation, seen as
political exchange corresponding to that part of activity that lay outside the
market)[15] that the natural harmony of interests"[16] was established. For the
market was the *common place* of all communication among men. It was
through exchange that the natural equilibrium price was to be established.
Thus the free-market society attached a central value to price as a means of
communication. Price was the common measure among men;[17] it was
endowed with a value that was no longer pragmatic but symbolic. The
market enabled society, composed of an aggregation of individuals, to
communicate naturally, without any other language than that of price. In
spheres where exchange was impossible, that is, for matters that came
under the heading of administration, the language of categories was still
needed. But the definition of the relevant designations for use by the administration was subordinated to the political sphere, ensuring the depend-

ence of culture on nature; for as we shall see later, politics was itself seen only as the cultural detour needed by the representatives to express natural categories when the absence of the market made economic exchange impossible.[18]

The belief in the source of truth that founds the symbolic order in a liberal democracy defines the purpose of the world (natural progress through production and exchange) and the means to achieve it (compliance with the conditions for attaining equilibrium on the market); weaken this belief and words and figures lose their value as a common measure, a natural instrument of communication between men. They become shadows of themselves, the prey of rhetoric that plays on all the registers of the lost referents of tradition or reason. By dressing themselves up as expressions of the traditional or natural order of things, the cultural operations of designating and counting appropriate the persuasive capacity that comes with using the image of eternal truth.

From Nature As the Measure to Man As the Measure

In every system of legitimacy, the source of power defines a criterion which is the *yardstick* of truth in the symbolic order, and the foundation of the measurements taken by its agents in the practical order.

In the model of free-market society, nature supplies the criterion of truth; science is the means to reveal its laws, reason is its method. This model thus adopts a homogeneous system for representing the world, and a principle for splitting it up into economic, social and political spheres.[19]

The universe of free-market society consists of entities—individuals—characterized by their desires. Interaction, exchange are made necessary by the effort to satisfy these desires in a universe of scarcity; they are made possible by the capacity of each individual to order his preferences according to the usefulness, in terms satisfying his desire, of the goods he seeks, and according to their cost on the market. This market is the pure expression of utilities, that is, one from which all viscosity is excluded, where the price expresses only the relative scarcity of the article, where time and space can therefore be calibrated according to the scarcity of the useful goods that they provoke.

In a free-market society, everything makes for science: nature is the measure of all things. Society is reduced to exchange. It is nothing but the meeting of desires ordered by the reason of those autonomous atoms, the individuals: individuals acting as producers, consumers, voters in a homogenous and fluid time–and–space universe. The territory is the Nation-State and time is purely mechanical.[20] Under these conditions, society functions according to laws whose model is provided by rational physics. In the long term, the equilibrium of the system optimizes the satisfactions of everyone and minimizes scarcities. If the conditions for reproducing the model are assured—through autonomy and free competition—nature takes things in hand since, with the help of the "invisible hand," which is a sort of natural Holy Spirit, it converts the confrontation of individual and selfish interests into group harmony and progress.[21]

This requires two conditions. First, the State must guarantee the conditions of a peaceful and industrious life: external defense, internal policing, the exercise of justice, without intervening in the workings of civil society. This function is fulfilled by administration, seen as a necessary evil because it deals with all that lays outside the market in the life of a society, that is, all that eludes the benevolent action of the "invisible hand," but an acceptable evil inasmuch as it acts under the permanent supervision of civil society or its legitimate representatives and within the bounds of the jurisdictions they assign to it. Second, the individual must be truly autonomous, that is, free and the equal of all. Established as a subject, freely exercising his reason to make choices among his preferences, the individual being can be made object by no one—except by administration within the bounds of what is strictly necessary for the survival of society.

Man exercises his reason on the market of economic goods as a buyer or seller; within this area of activity, exchange qualifies him as *homo economicus*. He communicates by means of the price–equivalent. But he also exercises his reason to discover, in nature, the laws that should govern the relations among men in all those exchanges that do not occur in the economic market. In this area of his activity, exchange qualifies him as *homo suffragans*. . . . In the "political market," in the legislative sphere, he communicates through the vote–equivalent. Outside these qualifications, he is of no interest to the physical science of society, political economy, to which political theory may also be linked. Upstream of the market, the shaping of his preferences is part of his innermost consciousness, that is, the unfathomable essence of his being; downstream of the market, when he dispossesses himself of his labor power by contract, he barters his freedom and equality for renumeration for the duration of his contract. Outside the market, in his relations with the administration, he is subjected to the authority of the Garrison–State, as a *bounden subject* or *constituent*. If the natural criterion on which the order of the world is based is weakened, the liberal model of representation goes into a crisis. For nature is no longer the yardstick of truth. Without a point of reference, man remains alone in a universe from which meaning has been withdrawn while science has lost its absolute value (see "Pragmatism, Cybernetic Ideology and Marketing Society"). *Homo suffragans*, dear to the ideologists of the Enlightenment, is now annihilated by his incapacity to *state* the world through the rational procedure of the search for truth as constituted by the vote. What remains is the voter who is assailed by the opinion poll (See "From the Vote to the Poll"). The rationality of the free–trader, *homo economicus* beloved of the classics of political economy who only follows his own need, is replaced by the irrationality of the consumer, the "object" of marketing, and the "limited rationality" of the manager, whom H. Simon[22] describes as seeking solutions in a complex, uncertain and changing universe by using limited knowledge. It becomes impossible to regard the market as a self–regulated mechanism and, hence, the "invisible hand" as a sufficient instrument for satisfying needs and for economic and social regulation. The entrepreneur becomes a manager, a man of foresight, a strategist in a now structured universe (see "From the Market Price to the Product Image" below); by a reverse and complementary process, public administration seeks to make good the inadequacies of the market and thus steps out of its legitimate function of distribution and policing to assume a role of entrepreneur and macro–economic regulator (See "From Bureaucratic Counting to Social Indicators"). Having entered a crisis of legitimacy at the same time as the model of representation of the political order to which it is subordinate and of the economic order whose conditions it is supposed to preserve, having therefore lost its political moorings in a source of legitimacy, the administration no longer finds any justification for its action other than in the *fact* of its own practice, nor any argument other than persuasion.

To persuade man that his needs are such and so and that a certain product, politician or administrative act is necessary for their satisfaction is the purpose of the rhetoric that develops in the marketing society (See "The Method of Discourse"). This rhetoric addresses the whole man and no longer that abstract entity of classical economics, the free–trader, endowed with reason. Does this mean that rhetoric has rediscovered *human nature*? Nothing is less certain, for there is no guarantee that abandoning distinctions between the various symbolic orders leaves any capacity to distinguish something that might be called the individual in the classical sense of the term.

Notes

1. Unlike J. Hecht in his article "L'idée du denombrement jusqu' à la Révolution," in *Pour une histoire de la statistique*, tome 1, Paris, INSEE 1978, p. 23 ff.
2. *Mémoires* of the Duc de Saint-Simon, quoted by Hecht, *ibid.*
3. Cf. Marcel Granet, *La Pensée Chinoise*, Albin Michel, coll. l'Evolution de l'Humanité, 1934, p. 431. This is why the act of labelling plays a primordial role: it is the guarantee that the traditional order of the world is preserved.
4. *Ibid.*, p. 446. Our italics.
5. *Ibid.*

6. *Ibid.*, p. 448. Many interesting reflections on the relationships between language and the legitimacy of domination can be found in F. Raison–Jourde's article, "L'échange inégal de la langue," *Annales E.S.C.*, May 1976 which superbly shows how the preparation of a dictionary in Madagascar at the start of the 19th century simultaneously created and reinforced a new logic of domination.

7. The words "administration" and "minister" are derived from the same root, meaning "service," "servant"; cf. G. Duby, *Les Trois Ordres et l'Imaginaire du Feodalisme*, Paris, Gallimard, 1978.

8. J. Goody in *La Raison Graphique*, Paris, Editions de Minuit, 1978, recalls that writing was probably invented for purposes of enumeration (see especially chapter V). The census is seen in all States whose size entails problems of distribution. It is taken charge of by specialized bureaucratic institutions.

9. It is God, the prince or the representative assembly, who commands the administration to conduct a census.

10. In *Le Règne de la quantité et le signe du temps*, Gallimard Paris, 1970, R. Guénon shows that matter is related to quantity and mind to quality. Nature is quantitative, culture is qualitative. To qualify men by their number as a resource is to assign them a nature within the framework of the (cultural) designation.

11. J-B Say illustrates this accusation: "When I see that there is no destestable operation which is not supported and determined by arithmetical calculations, I rather believe that it is figures that kill states," in C. Menard, *op. cit.*

12. This is what F. Bédarida shows with respect to Great Britain in "Statistique et société en Angleterre au XIXème siècle" in *Pour une histoire . . ., op. cit.*

13. Adam Smith's famous "invisible hand," "the natural harmony of interests" of Mandeville's *Fable des abeilles.*

14. This was an argument constantly developed by the tenants of free-market and democratic society against the expansion of administration. See for example Paul Leroy–Beaulieu in *L'Etat Moderne et ses fonctions*, Paris, Guillaumin, 3rd ed., 1900. (See also ch. 6 below.)

15. See ch. 5 below.

16. According to Mandeville who first used this expression.

17. See ch. 4 "From the Market Price to the Product Image."

18. See ch. 5.

19. Rosanvallon, *Le Capitalisme utopique*, Paris, Seuil, 1979.

20. Mechanical time is the time of the clock, abstract time, as opposed to natural time, the value and uses of which are governed by natural or traditional rythms (such as the rythms of a "naturalized" society). See *Approche socio–culturelle du problème de l'organisation du temps*, SORADE, French Department of Tourism, Vol. I, 1976.

21. Mandeville B., *La Fable des abeilles ou Les vices privés font le bien public*, Paris, Vrin, 1974; L. Dumont, *Homo equalis* Paris, Gallimard, Bibliothèque des sciences humaines, 1976. See E. Halévy's seminal work: *La Formation du radicalisme philosophique,* Paris, Alcan, 1901-1904, 3 vols.

22. H. Simon, *Administrative Behavior*, New York, Macmillan, 1957.

Chapter 4

From the Market Price to the Product Image

The law of supply and demand states that the value of a thing increases all the more as demand overtakes supply. So much so that a thing may gain value by the sole fact of being very much in demand. This is a universal law. In science, for example, there are fields like the social sciences where the demand for knowledge is far greater than the supply. So much so that the smallest supply of knowledge acquires immense value by the simple fact that it is in demand. Thus, for instance, the law of supply and demand . . .

The Firm in the Free-Market Society an Archetype

As treated by classical political economy, the firm had no existence as a human community or as an organization. It was thought of as a point in the infinite space of the market. It was one dimensional. It was entirely identified with the entrepreneur.[1] Its activity amounted to the combination of production factors, whose prices were defined in the different markets of capital, materials and labor; its purpose was to produce for sale in the market place.

The entrepreneur's activity was entirely immersed in nature: the demand that he sought to meet by his supply was determined by buyers' desires and by the choice that defined for them the relative utility of goods at different prices; the scarcity of supply demand determined the sales price. The sanction—loss or profit—lay in the difference between cost price and sales price, both of which were established naturally in the markets, independently of the action of the producers. On the competitive market, an intangible place, there was instantaneous exchange (since any delay comes down to an additional cost) of perfectly fungible materials which entered into the combination of factors, or of products, graded by the price that constituted their common measure (quantity of the product, amount of time, amount of worker or machine energy).

41

As both buyer and seller, the firm or entrepreneur, a social atom, was seen to be both all powerful and essentially powerless in that market. Since he was a subject, he was all powerful in his choices: he decided what products he intended to put on the market, and he selected what he considered to be the most reasonable technical combination of factors. As a solitary atom in the infinite universe of the competitive market, however, he was powerless: he was incapable of modifying the face of the market by his action: he could neither provoke a demand nor hinder other producers nor ally himself with anyone. His sale price was dictated to him by a market over which he had no individual hold and whose shape depended on the aggregation and immediate confrontation of the behaviors of suppliers and demanders. The market regulated his activity by the sanction of profits and losses, by the mediation of price fluctuations. His action therefore was limited to proposing his products to those other free, solitary and rational individuals, the buyers.

The sole instrument of his blind and selfish quest for profit was the knowledge of the existing conditions of supply and demand. The idea of a strategy had no meaning in this universe which had neither history nor structure. The meeting between the selfishness of other sellers and buyers and the selfish action of the entrepreneur was supposed to produce, in the long run, natural harmony and progress.[2] For the equilibrium price would correspond to the optimum satisfaction of the individual desires of the buyers and the remuneration of the production factors without loss or profit. As for progress, it would be a natural result of entrepreneurs' renewed search for profit, and would culminate in the renewal or extension of production and the satisfaction of the other desires of potential buyers.

The entrepreneur was therefore a passive being. "Success in business meant rapid and intelligent adaptation to events occurring outside, in an economy shaped by impersonal, objective forces that were neither controlled by the businessman nor influenced by his reaction to them. . . . Even if he was not considered a parasite, his contributions were seen as purely mechanical: the shifting of resources to more productive use."[3]

The Work Factor

None of the production factors that the entrepreneur combined had any special character: the work factor, in particular, occupied no special position among them. Within the walls of the firm, the worker had no existence whatsoever as a human entity. By the work contract, he had sold his labor force, which the entrepreneur exploited. The remuneration of work was identical to the purchase of a quantity of mechanical energy expended by the firm. Outside the firm, the worker might be seen as being fully human, that is, capable of exercising his reason as a buyer or seller of his labor force.[4] He was himself an entrepreneur when he entered into the contract; but no sooner had he entered the firm than he was reduced to a potential quantity of energy.

Only exceptionally was the worker an object of interest or solicitude as a laborer. People examined his fate[5] only when he threatened public order outside the firm. In seeking to preserve "public morality," the civil society, through charitable associations, ensured the conditions for the reproduction of the worker's labor force. The State administration, for its part, contributed to the maintenance of social peace by investigating the condition of the laboring classes, suspected of being dangerous, by suppressing disorder and by administering justice.

Price As Language in the Market and General Accounting

The firm was at one with the classical entrepreneur's innermost consciousness. Its natural place of expression and communication was the market. "The concept of the entrepreneur merges into that of the trader."[6] The entrepreneur could apply his intelligence only to the task of reasoning on his *purchases* and *sales*, that is, at those points where production factors and products are exchanged.[7] His language was the language of price. His communication was completely natural. All his activity was reduced to the operations described in general accounting. The law obliged him[8] to keep accounts in the form of business registers, admitted as proof in litigation. In this role, accounting functioned as "a certifying machine."[9] The firm was held to be at fault when it presented share–holders with inexact books or published such books, that is, when it attempted to falsify its conditions of natural *communication* with the outside world, thus disturbing the openness of entrepreneurial activity.[10] We can see why it could assert in all seriousness that "For government, order in accountancy is the sacred law."[11] The point was that general bookkeeping was the symbolic procedure by which the actual firm could become one with the way the free-market society saw it as an atom in the structureless social space by claiming that the "unique economic operation (was) the purchase and sale of an exchange value or utility, that is, exchange according to natural law."[12]

An instrument of natural communication, that is, not subjected to manipulation by man, translating the natural movement of the costs of production factors into figures, general bookkeeping became incapable of expressing concretely the inner spirit of the firm as the latter grew and diversified. At this point, its symbolic value and the conditions of its maintenance were firmly reasserted: "We believe profoundly that the expressions of bookkeeping are mathematical in nature, to such an extent that it is possible to attain the rigorous certitude of an equation ... bookkeeping equations are like mathematical equations ... this is why there are so many *false accounts*, because *false–accountants* or *administrators interpret* and change the *immutable* factors of the bookkeeping equation and its basis: the *cost.*"[13]

Thus spoke a defender of classical entrepreneurial theories who felt the dangers inherent in modern administrative practices, which imperilled their instruments of symbolic communication. But he was already out of date.

The Big Firm in Conflict with the Free Market

Let price cease to be regarded as the natural expression of the combination of production factors or the meeting of a supply and a demand in the market—in other words, let it only be acknowledged that the entrepreneur has a power to fix price—and the classical conception of economic exchange is threatened. The image of the entrepreneur can then no longer be limited to that of the free trader. It becomes no longer possible to "reduce industrial life to simple applications of natural law."[14]

The Emergence of the Worker and the Problem of the Boundaries of the Firm as Organization

It was indeed this kind of change that the growth of big industry and of the multi–product firm brought about. The competitive market lost its credibility as the place where the firm was to act; the firm lost its unidimensional character. The growth of the big firm led to a contradictory development within the enterprise: in order to set up the worker as a source of purely mechanical energy justifying rational quantitative management, it was necessary for the worker as seller of labor force to be truly dissociated from the worker as purely labor force. A rational actor before he entered the factory, when negotiating the work contract, and a rational actor afterwards, as a buyer, he became quite simply an ox[15] supplying mechanical energy within the walls of the firm for the duration of the job. Such was the two–headed monster the classical economists created as soon as Taylor attempted to put the inferences of this vision into action in order to rationalize the activity of the big firm. The dissociation was theoretical, and was not free of practical problems since it meant acquiring technological mastery over the human body and being on guard against any properly human activity, on the part of the worker in the firm in order to eliminate all *imponderables*. It assumed that work, in the concrete sense, went into the worker as a man of flesh and blood.[16] And in fact Taylorism required a substantial portion of management resources to be devoted to training workers in the "perfect movement" considered to be *the one best way.*

The entrepreneur was thus forced to practice what had been unthinkable in the classical economic model, namely company activities that were neither purely productive nor related to trade. To develop the scientific processes by which he could treat factors of production as materials from which "chance and whim have been eliminated,"[17] "the worker must become, he has become, an automaton adapted to the automatic movement of the machine and complementary to it. His personality and initiative must disappear."[18] Paradoxically, this meant training men into a state of inhumanity in the firm. According to Taylor, the ideal worker was uniformly christened John. He was passive, without desires, sexless, always in good shape, dumb, friendless, nameless, classless and without a past. He was the unit of accounty. But he was an individualist as soon as he left the premises of the firm. His motivation was purely economic. What he desired most was to maximize his salary, to build (outside working hours) a home where he could have a family and reproduce his labor force. Henceforth the firm employed workers who were not directly productive, it had a supervisory staff, a training staff and a measuring and time–keeping staff.

It had to develop a new language—of management—for communication among its different members. This was the first intrusion of the social and psychological element into the firm in the guise of a psycho–technique. Thus within the firm grew up a set of tasks, derived from the necessities of production; the organization of work and the division of activity between tasks of conceptual organization and productive tasks produced a *hierarchy* and an *administration*; training qualified certain workers for industrial work. Workers were no longer interchangeable. The firm could not waste the capital that it had incorporated in the worker by subjecting him to a breaking in and training process. Henceforth it had to find the means to keep him. It paid him a bonus to reward a *quality* that had no *common measure* with the market, since it was the value of his attachment to the firm; and above all, it created the conditions of his dependence while creating the conditions of his reproduction as labor force outside the firm. Fordism and all forms of paternalism organized, around the firm, living conditions that gave Taylor's worker, John, a life in keeping with his image. They built workers' cities, organized social life into clubs, associations, trade unions, schools, going so far as to duplicate, on their own territory, the tasks that the traditional small firm had left to State administration.[19] To be the place where production factors were combined in all their purity, the firm had to develop company patriotism and a hold over a territory that extended well beyond the factory walls.

To get the utmost out of the mechanical inhumanity of the worker in the workshop, it had to manage his humanity outside it. It sought to resolve the problem of the real man through a spatial distribution of the various functional emoluments that it gave him. Therefore just as it took on substance and acquired an interior[20] and an exterior, the firm, for the first time, willfully blurred this demarcation: with *scientific management*, the human factor remained at the door of the workshop but had to be administered outside the workshop. A little later, human relations specialists were to attempt to solve the problem in reverse by bringing the human factor into the workshop, taking no further interest in it on the outside, and moving from a psycho–technique to a social psychology of organization. From 1920 on, attacks against Taylor's *one best way* grew more pronounced. This became the subject of American[21] and British[22] work on industrial psychology. In 1924, Myers asserted that henceforth, it could be considered that Taylor's methods, based on the calculation of time, were without any scientific, psychological or social foundation.[23] Workers were fully human, including in their working life. Their motive for working therefore could not be reduced to an economic one; it was also psychological and social. From there, there remained only one step to making the work group the focus of social life in the factory, to whose harmony the worker's efficiency would be subordinated, and the school of human relations[24] did not hesitate to take this step around the mid–thirties. The crucial position in the firm then became that of the managers, the organizers of an "adaptative society."[25]

Having brought humanity into the workshop, the school of human relations took virtually no further interest in it on the outside. And that is why it was unable to resolve the problem of the firm's limits, since it brought in not only the worker as total man, but with him all of society. From this moment on, the firm could no longer be the simple site for the combining of production factors; it had to take the social variable into account in a pragmatic way. The singular nature of the work factor was stressed. But the specificity of the activity of work in the firm was lost and, by the same token, so was the *measure* of the firm's activity. The entrepreneur's action was no longer natural. He had already partially lost his legitimacy. However he still had some arguments left: although he was no longer a free trader, he was still an owner. He defended his right to enterprise in the name of the right to private property.[26] But because his leadership was no longer "natural," the only criteria of his authority became pragmatic ones. If he was not "boss by divine right,"[27] he would be a manager. He would have to prove his competence empirically. He would be judged on his results. However, these results were no longer the effect of nature, assisted by his intelligent passiveness, but really the consequence of his action in the firm and on the market. For, on the inside, he had to manage: organize, calculate and plan without the support of any transcendental criterion;

and, on the outside, he had to keep and win markets without the aid of the "invisible hand"—now incapable of harmonizing interests because the conditions of the free, competitive, transparent, fluid, non–structured and infinite market had disappeared.

"Talking Organization": Cost Accounting, the First Managerial Language

The task of the manager as the head of the firm was no longer restricted to combining production factors, since there now existed non–productive administrative tasks. These activities entailed organization costs, overheads and indirect costs, which were only indirectly productive and which bore a multifunctional relationship to production. Thus the problem arose of assessing these expenses and charging them to the costs of production. General bookkeeping could not provide a solution here. It was no longer possible merely to take note of the naturally established prices of products; decisions had to be taken on where to charge indirect costs, without the aid of a natural criteria for charging costs. Accounting *categories* had to be created. General bookkeeping, however, continued to be the only accounting system that was legal, the mark of the firm's autonomy but also, by this very fact, the sign of its loss of transparency. For as a symbol this accounting system was a mere shadow of itself; it no longer represented the atomicity of the firm in any way but fictitiously. It was unsuited to indicating the prices of factors and hence to playing its role as a means for setting cost prices naturally, through simple addition based on market prices.

The accounts that were made public were obtained by *totalling* internal accounts (symbolized by the *ledger*), which, for their part, received no publicity. Their existence proved the existence of the firm as organization; but the secrecy that veiled them was a reflection of the fact that, by principle, its innermost recesses were to remain unfathomable. The firm alone judged what portion of internal information should be divulged to the outside world.[28] No doubt, what it revealed was not the full or exact reflection of its inner life, which—for strategic reasons—it might not wish to lay open to every gaze. A point illustrated by a joke among chartered accountants: "A balance sheet is an accounting document generally drawn up in three copies which are very different from one another: (in descending order of profits) the first is intended for the board of directors, the second for the internal revenue authorities and third for the share–holders."[29] In the relations between the firm and the market, the natural price no longer fulfilled its function in the accounting of purchases and sales; within the firm, price had no theoretical existence—the draft of the accounting plan made it clear that it was a cost. Not only did the firm incur administrative costs but also, having become multi–productive, it had internalized entire sectors of the market. By manufacturing its own use values, it had deprived itself of market assistance in setting prices as "exchange value." However, the assessment of the production costs of each article was a vital operation from the strategic viewpoint that the firm adopted as soon as it became large enough to gain a hold over the market. By assessing these costs in its own system of categories, the firm could determine its cost prices and sense the direction of profit.

Cost, an empirical indicator, became the firm's compass. Quantitative measurement was no longer the natural expression of a naturally self–regulated exchange; it became an empirical process of knowledge, organized culturally: cost and price became pieces of *information*. As early as 1938, an innovator in the field of accounting techniques wrote: "We are convinced that accounting, considered with a scientific mind, does not constitute a goal in itself, as certain legislation and jurisprudence would suggest, but a proper resource placed at the disposal of entrepreneurs to inform them of what happens in their business and enable them to take it into account in the future."[30]

This was the purpose of cost accounting (also called industrial book–keeping and internal management accounting), which emerged in the big firms around the thirties.[31] Its advocates saw it as the extension of the rational processes of *scientific management* to administration. "We are at this very moment witnessing, with our own eyes, the birth of a new period, that of organization, which might also be called the period of administra-tion: the scientific method, which had conquered the workshop, but was restricted to it, is henceforth penetrating the offices, and especially the offices of management. . . . The positive method, long universally accepted in the technical field, is now reaching into administration, commerce and distribution. It is no longer enough to produce, it is now necessary to distribute, that is, to administer. . . .

It has become impossible to manage a big firm without an advanced system of bookkeeping, without a system of information–gathering, fore-casting, comparing and sampling that is as rigorous as a science."[32] Once accounts were treated as information, it was possible to measure and there-fore "eliminate chance and whim to the maximum extent." Cost account-ing thus extended and transformed the field of action of company accoun-tancy. From an instrument of *a posteriori* evidence, used for the unambiguous determination of a cost price sanctioned by the market, it became an instrument of *a priori* knowledge that acquired meaning be-cause the firm became the object of management and because en-trepreneurial choices became decisive for the firm's power over the market. From the passive record of the entrepreneur's action, it became an active instrument for the manager's planning and control. The cost price was no longer unambiguously determined. Its amount, for a given product, depended on the decision to distribute indirect overheads among cost units [33] arbitrarily defined as homogeneous, on the basis of the need to establish *accounting units* for the firm. The chief accountant was given the task of establishing "bases of distribution." The arbitrariness of the distribution was objectified in the accountant's categories.

Fixing the cost price henceforth implied two major "cultural" operations: defining entities and defining a standard of comparison. In addition, it assumed that a set of conditions for spreading cost over a period time could be determined; and this depended on the manager's assessment of the prospects for the sale of the product.[34] This was a novelty since, in the classical economic model of the firm, prices had always been set instantaneously or in the very long term, that is in the eternity of nature, and without the entrepreneur's having any power to intervene. To sum up, the fixing of cost prices implied administration of costs. Cost accounting was an active operation for a second reason: the practical knowledge that it acquired was aimed at modifying production goals on the basis of a comparison between the profits brought in by different products. In other words, it was an integral part of the firm's *policy*,[35] at the technical level (the supervision of manufacturing from the cost standpoint) as much as the human one (examining employees' results).

"The Dialogue with the Market": The Birth of Marketing

On the outside, there was the problem of keeping and winning markets. As output increased with technological progress and mass production, the multi–product firm finally emerged (after the First World War) from the age when Ricardo could claim that nobody produces without intending to consume or to sell, that desires are restricted only by limits on the means to purchase.[36] And von Wieser declared as early as 1913 that consumption as such was not at all an economic act. Goods, he said, acted as a medium of material pleasure, but it was not the function of economic theory to show how they should be accomodated. It was the adepts of the practical art of living (the moralists, doctors and artists) who were qualified in these matters.[37] The problem of consumption, which until then had been carefully avoided by classical marginalist political economy, now appeared clearly. Abstract political economy was caught in the problems of concrete economy, that is, in the problem of outlets. Demand constituted a problem. It no longer followed the expansion of supply. The entrepreneur had been a trader; now he had to become a salesman, that is, he had to intervene in a concretely identified market, which, by every token—and the crises of overproduction provide a dramatic demonstration of this—could no longer be conceived of as being self–regulated, a market in which identifiable competitors clashed, for they now became increasingly large in size and small in number. The pragmatic view of consumption as a social phenomenon came into the practice of the firm.[38] Henceforth, it had to take *the measure* of the market by seeking information from it. This is the role of marketing and of the notion of the share of the market, which developed in the United States in the aftermath of the First World War.

The first market surveys were carried out by Procter and Gamble between 1924 and 1929. And by 1946, marketing activity absorbed the efforts of a third to two–fifths of the employees of big firms.[39] To keep one's share of the market, or to increase it, henceforth implied gathering information on the market and forming a market: this was to be the object of advertising with a view to shaping the consumer, and the object of the organization of distribution circuits with a view to creating the conditions for conveying products to the consumer. The market was no longer the spontaneous meeting ground of supply and demand. Winning and keeping a market implied a duration and a cost: the workings of the market were no longer open or perfectly fluid.

Scientific management had attempted to reconstruct the worker in the image of the role assigned to him by classical economic theory. It was to the same theoretical sources that marketing first applied. For it was thought in the twenties that the outlet crisis was related to the loss of the market's traditional features: in particular, its size had made it lose its fluidity, and the novelty of products its transparency. The remedy for the former ill lay in distribution and, for the latter, in informing the consumer. Unable to count on the spontaneous infinity in time and space of the classical free market, the initiators of marketing set about, in a pragmatic way, to establish the conditions of communication and information with which demand could be met. This was an operation that entailed a fixed time and given work, that is, an administrative cost and a policy. From the outset, marketing was company policy even when it was still confined to problems of salesmanship.[40] The idea was to *take the steps* needed to know the market—not the laws of the market—to better anticipate its approval and rejection, for the production process used *precious time*, which would soon spell the death of any firm that waited for the sanction of demand before launching its production plans. The whole policy of the firm was conditioned by this awareness.

The fact that the market could be studied as an object meant that it was seen as an *entity*, "a real, tangible and definite"[41] thing, something that could be counted and administered. The market was localized by a demand, which precedes the organization of production and sales. All the early works on marketing[42] put their main emphasis on the importance of distribution.[43] The point was not to provoke demand but to adjust the production and distribution of the product to the *a priori* nature and distribution of the demand. The "potentialities of the market" had to be known in order to satisfy "human wants."[44] The term *need* did not appear, so to speak, and was entirely conditioned by that of the consumer's *will*, that is, the conscious expression of need.

Measuring the characteristics of the markets meant locating them, describing the organization of relationships between buyers and sellers; it therefore amounted to considering that the market possessed *attributes* which had an evenness, which *structured* it. Just as the firm was structured by its need to organize production, so the market was structured by the organization of marketing.

Knowledge of the market was an indicator of the space available for the product, a space the firm would occupy by advertising and choosing of the most appropriate distribution circuits, a space that defined the welcome given to the product. Since demand was seen as the welcome afforded the product, and since demand was seen as a *datum*, to know the market was to describe it quantitatively and objectively: where were the buyers?, how many were they? what were their means? what *objective* qualities of the product did they appreciate? what products did they want? Already, a record was being made of the socio–economic variables that affected the consumption of the product, but the main purpose of this was to set up the "average customer," "a fiction created to typify the demand coming most often from the most people."[45] All the measurements made in marketing research still referred to a conception of the rational consumer who was thought to judge products according to the knowledge he might obtain of their existence and true qualities, whose purchasing behavior was uniformly that of *homo economicus*, confronted with the truth of the product, which he sanctioned by the "dollar vote."[46] The firm might conceivably change production the better to meet demand; but a given product was defined objectively by a set of qualities that constituted its *truth* and which the firm could not modify.

The function of advertising was to inform and educate the consumer, taking into account the objective character of his needs and of the products. To inform meant to proclaim the truth about hundreds of articles,[47] to reveal their objective qualities. To educate, hence to fulfill a useful task, meant providing for the most *intelligent* choices by preparing the consumer for the various goods and qualities available.[48] These would be the most intelligent choices because, while the consumer had the last word in determining the type of product he wanted and its quantity, the appearance of new products, without altering his needs, gave him new ways to satisfy them. Advertising educated inasmuch as it made it possible to change outmoded and perhaps harmful "habits": "Advertising has probably done more for the Nation's teeth than the personal advice of hundreds of dentists."[49]

The problem of outlets was sharply revived by the crisis of 1929. The innovations of Keynesian economic theory as well as entrepreneurial techniques led to greater attention being paid to the consumer[50] at the same time as the development of the big firm led—as we have seen above—to the birth of an interest in the working man. Social psychology was sailing before the wind. Henceforth, it was not enough simply to meet demand. Demand had to be anticipated. While production remained paramount for the post–crisis firm, the idea emerged that its survival depended on action for creating demand. There was an imperceptible shift from the old view, according to which the consumer was allowed to buy, to the new idea that the consumer was sold to.[51] Consequently, to succeed, the successful businessman had to be consumer–minded.[52] The quality of the product began to appear to be constituted solely by the consumer's desire.[53] Success in business henceforth depended on the talent with which one managed correctly to interpret demand.[54]

Market research was no longer to be content with defining what people wanted, where they wanted it and in what quantities: it was to deal with the problem of *why*. Why did people want certain things and not others?[55] It was during this period that the first in–depth studies of *buyers' motivations* appeared. Experimental research was conducted in big firms on this subject.[56] The role that habits, customs, fashions, knowledge, education, imitation, profession, climate and religion played in buying practices was analysed.[57] The consumer's desire was uncontestably shaped by various influences. The term "consumer" began to acquire meaning, one which was quite distinct from the *homo economicus* of economic theory. The buyer was born to his humanity at the same time as the worker. Henceforth, all books on marketing devoted their first chapters to this consumer, who was wholly absent from previous works. The door was opened to subsequent developments by which marketing was to break with the rationality of the theoretical buyer and rely upon the irrationality of the real consumer. This point had not yet been reached on the eve of the Second World War. The consumer's desire was then still broadly seen as being objective. People spoke of "stimulating demand" rather than of discovering or revealing it. Need remained objective. The "potentialities" of demand were examined and product surveys sought to determine the tastes of the customers. But the idea was growing that, however objective they may be, needs were not all conscious. There were also "dormant" needs. The sovereignty of demand did not mean that the sole responsibility of companies was to determine what the existing and conscious demands were: in addition to conscious and clearly stated demands, the sales activity of businessmen had to bring dormant needs to the surface in the consumer for the greater material profit of both the producer and the consumer.[58] Advertising was henceforth assigned the role of making products more attractive so that the buyer might awaken from the slumber of his consumer habits and become aware of his latent needs for products he would never, until then, even have dared dream about.[59] Thus advertising was to be successful when it matched a basic social trend of needs.[60] The purpose of advertising was no longer limited to the function of informing or educating. Its role also became one of seduction, in order to bring out dormant buyers' motivations which could not be awakened as long as the article that could satisfy it was not proposed.[61]

From Natural Price to Price Policy

Through the development of cost accounting, the change in the relation of the entrepreneur to his internal environment challenged the view that the cost price was the natural result of exchange in the market. It led to the search for new sources by which to legitimize the action of the entrepreneur as organizer. This movement entailed the growth of the pragmatic use of figures in the firm, thus confirming the loss of the symbolic power of the figure as a means of natural communication. The same change took place in the relationships between the entrepreneur and his external environment—through the appearance of price policy—and challenged the notion of the sales price as an equilibrium price ensuring natural communication between supply and demand." In a situation of competition, prices tended in the long term to coincide with production cost, provided that disturbing forces, such as monopolies or government action, did not come into play. These two conditions had become so decisive in the fixing of prices that there could be doubt about the validity of the theory of prices, as commonly accepted, which used cost as its basis."[62] If cost was no longer the natural basis of price, the idea that it would ever be possible to fix the *true* cost price and the *true* sales price had to be abandoned, in other words, the natural order could not be relied upon for this operation. Everything then became a matter of assessment: "In the course of time, a notion of equitable, honest or just price has developed. Many people proclaim that prices are fixed by competition and that ethical considerations have no effect on their value. . . . Perhaps this is true, but let us say that there are many exceptions to this rule. . . . The idea of 'excessive profit' is related to the feeling that cost or investment brings more than a reasonable reward to whoever undertakes it."[63]

But what is a reasonable assessment? "The normal price resembles a moving target that slides from top to bottom, perhaps moving, in a particular direction under the effect of some predominant current like the Gulf Stream. It is impossible to determine the exact position of the target at a given instant. However, it is essential to know that there is a target and that its approximate position is known."[64] Such statement tells us very little about empirical price–setting procedures in this new situation. If the determination of prices was not a natural process, it could only be a cultural one, that is, it could only follow government injunctions which defined a sort of official morality of prices (against *dumping* for example) and/or responded to the firm's sales prospects. Prices were no longer set by natural interaction in the market but by negotiation and after studying the state of the market. Prices became the object of a sales strategy within the limits of State regulations. They were based on the results of studies and of the firm's long–term policy prospects, and not on costs of the moment. All available information on the competition, buying habits and the reputation of the product was taken into account, and the long–term margins were calculated. The customer came first, profits afterwards; to make the customer happy meant, first of all, discovering his desires, finding out what he wanted to pay, getting what he needed and offering it for a price that he was disposed to pay. The firm had henceforth swung from nature to culture: in a related development, figures lost their symbolic value and became pragmatic information. The period following the Second World War, with the emergence of new theories of the organization of work and marketing, saw the outcome of these developments.

The Reign of the Big Firm and Man as the Measure

The classical economists had a unitary conception of the firm. The firm was made up of an economic man, the entrepreneur, and inert production factors. The firm was transparent for the entrepreneur equipped with his accounting books, in which he could, like anyone else, read the immediate nature of the productive activity: a purely natural combination of productive factors.

Scientific management threw this conception into training to bring the worker willy–nilly into the category of (natural) factors of production. The school of human relations managed merely to shift the contradiction by moving a little further towards culture. It restored to man the totality of his psychological being inside the firm, but, in gaining the diversity of motives, it had lost the sense of his being anchored in the activity of production. It had recognized, in opposition to the school of *scientific management*, that when one hired a worker, one always hired a man who, contrary to any other resource, had absolute control over his decision to work or not to work (and who, for this reason, always had to be motivated in his work).[65] It had recognized that "work was not an article of commerce," and the worker was not a "slot machine."[66] But, for want of an analysis of the relationship between the worker and his work, the school of human relations lapsed into ineffectual talk about the need to give "the worker a sense of responsibility," that is, into a new form of paternalism that was barely credible, "a pleasant tranquilizer for fractious children."[67]

Throughout the period of big firm development, the effect of this contradiction had been to dissociate the management of men from the management of things: on one side, cost accounting with its function of distributing quantities, which assessed units linked to products; on the other side, a special consideration for men, shown by training them into the state of a production factor, along with a purely formal attention paid to a very real humanness.

MBO* and Management Control as Attempts at Synthesis

It now appeared that the starting point of the theory of human relations had been correct. But by stressing the psychological dimensions of motivation, it overlooked the influence exerted by the specific character of work on the nature of motivations. It therefore forgot about both the social and the economic factors that determine diligence in work. From the fifties onwards, people became reticent about theories[68] that defined the worker as an indolent being, passive, lacking ambition, self–centered and resisting change. These attitudes toward work sprang, according to the post–war writers, from the relationship that the organization had created with its members. The human relations school had produced passiveness because it had talked a lot about "the sense of responsibility" without giving the worker any of it, because it had spoken emphatically of the "feeling of importance" the worker needed without giving it to him. It was necessary to give up these so–called "X theories" for the "Y theories" according to which the performance of the members was related to their perception of the importance of their task. Consequently, employers had to structure organization so that their goals and those of their employees coincided: this had to be done through job enrichment, participatory management and the decentralization of power.[69] The firm had to create "an aggressive *esprit de corps.*"[70] Once it was acknowledged that the economic motive was not enough to explain motivation, it became possible to channel the motivations of workers towards a common objective, that adopted by the firm as the best possible one. "In each firm, every job should be oriented according to the goals of the firm taken as a whole. . . . The manager should know and understand what the goals of the firm require of him in terms of perfor-

* Management by objectives.

mance and what his superior asks and expects of him; he should be assessed from this point of view. . . . Every worker, from the top to the bottom of the hierarchy needs clearly defined goals."[71] All these principles called for new means of action: these were to come from management by objectives, backed up by budget accounting and management control. Budget accounting, "the estimated forecast of all the elements corresponding to an operating hypothesis for a determined period, an estimated programme for short–term action,"[72] is constructed on the basis of data furnished by cost accounting. Management control enables each person to compare his results with his goals by comparing the differences between the two. Thus MBO attempts a synthesis between scientific management and human relations. It seeks to reestablish the totality of man from the viewpoint of the goals of the firm conceived as an organization in its own right. Like scientific management, it seeks to integrate the nature of the firm into man. But the nature of the firm is henceforth social: it is defined by its goals. Inside the firm, the members of the organization seek personal human fulfillment in their productive action, outside the circulation of products that contribute to betterment. The firm takes the variety of motivations into account, as do human relations, but integrates them by turning the total man into "the organization man."[73]

The Language of the MBO and Management Control

To achieve this twofold objective, MBO needs a language that ensures communication within the limits of the "social nature" it defines. This language is precisely that of the measurement categories it adopts in budget accounting. Like every language, this one must be sufficiently natural and sufficiently cultural at the same time: it is cultural because it results from the permanent encoding that the firm carries out on itself through its categories; it is natural as well because it defines itself, in relation to the (social) nature of the firm organized on the basis of its goals, as a set of "measuring instruments, . . . clear, simple, . . . relevant. . . . And they have to be, so to speak, self–announcing, understandable, without complicated interpretation or philosophical discussion."[74] This is the language in which the firm "speaks of itself": it expresses its general objectives for all its members and translates them into "personalized" goals so that each person internalizes its overall mission and his specific task. The firm thus simultaneously provides a general motivation and an instrument which monitors specific results in the light of specific and overall goals. The language of management by objectives thus makes it possible to "substitute management by self–control for management by domination."[75] By this process, each member constantly incorporates the entire firm by internalizing all its motivations and goals at his level. The firm builds motivation by negotiating it concretely with its members on the basis of its goals. It recognizes the completeness of this motivation which cannot be reduced either to salary or to the fear of losing a job: it goes so far as to consider its employees as entrepreneurs, self–managed through management by objectives. They can use the goals that the firm gives them to regulate themselves just as the market price enabled the entrepreneur of the liberal economists to regulate himself. But each "employee–entrepreneur" is interdependent with every other entrepreneur in the organization. The firm defines itself as a *system*. Thus management control has lost its specialization; it becomes multifunctional. It is the central regulator of the firm as a whole.

Management by objectives and management control achieve the permanent, renewed synthesis between the real and the encoding of the real. For the organization man, the whole reality of the firm is reduced to the encoding of the real by the firm, for it is this encoding that organizes categories relevant to his action. The language of MBO and management control is hence a circular, systemic language by which facts are controlled by men and men by facts.

In this language, man produces standards—with or without figures—by which he regulates himself. Every man, every total man, is an organization man, that is, *social by nature*, engaged in a special social relationship that defines his ends and motives. By these means, management by objectives creates a confusion between nature and culture by taking the organization as nature and the organization man as an element of the firm's social system.

Marketing of Subjective Need

The nature of the organization is defined by its goals. The firm ultimately asks marketing to set its goals. Consumer analysis becomes central. Business is based on the consumer. The future of the enterprise depends upon what he considers valuable. He alone provides jobs, "There is only one possible definition of the firm's objective: to create a consumer."[76] The marketing function becomes of primary importance. As in the earliest days of the firm in the classical economic theory, the market is at the very center of the firm's life. But from one model to the other, there is the same distance that separates nature from culture, the autonomy of *homo economicus* as seller or buyer from the interdependence of firms and from the dependence of consumers. Henceforth, markets are created neither by God, nor by nature, nor by economic forces, but by businessmen.[77] This means that market research becomes essential, for the motivation of the consumer is not directly and naturally decipherable, any more than is that of the worker or the entrepreneur. It has lost all *common measure* with the market: "What the consumer calls value is so complicated that it can only be answered by the customer himself. Management should not even try to guess at it. It should always try to go to the customer in a systematic search for the answer."[78] Marketing has to put all the resources of psychology and the social sciences in general to work in defining managerial strategies. The policy of the firm becomes one of targets and images. From now on, consumers are described as being "irrational at least as often as rational, motivated in large degree by emotions, habits and prejudices; differing widely in personality structure, in aspirations, ideals and buying behaviors." It is therefore "important to research the basic reasons for buying behavior, the underlying motivations, attitudes, feelings and group norms."[79] The strictly quantitativist point of view is discarded for experimental, clinical in-depth study[80] If the consumer is irrational, his needs are only what he thinks they are: they are subjective. It is therefore not only the intrinsic qualities of goods that determine his purchases by the image that he develops of the products. Henceforth, the firm's strategy comprises a product-image policy that includes the firm's policies on prices, trade mark and image, "everything that can take the place of the (lost) criterion of rationality" for the consumer. But while it is possible to analyze the psychological and social consistencies[81] that are the source of irrationality in consumer choices, it becomes necessary to work out sales policy on the basis of the expectations of different publics: that is, to allow for the fact that the clientele is segmented and to align the product with its target.[82] Marketing makes it possible to define products and targets, and to analyse the image of the products in each of the targets.

The visibility of the firm increases with its size and the extension of its powers over the universe of powers, the firm has lost the innocence that classical economic theory conferred on it. The nature of modern enterprise "imposes upon the business and its managers a responsibility that not only goes far beyond any traditional responsibility of private property but is altogether different. It can no longer be based on the assumption that the self-interest of the property owner will lead to the public good, or that self-interest and public good can be kept apart. . . . It requires of the manager that he assumes responsibility for the public good. . . .[83] Henceforth, "the manager is no longer only the creation of the economy, he is also its creator."[84] His sources of legitimacy in the free market are now exhausted: he must rebuild them from elsewhere by managing his image, that is, not only the image of his tangible products but also that of his social products,[85] the image that circumscribes his "personality." The firm is thus led to expose its innermost workings, that sacred and unfathomable region of the firm in classical economic thought.

*Wherein the Firm Has no More Limits. Public Relations and Social
Accounting*

The firm profoundly internalizes the market by establishing an organic
link between management control and marketing from the standpoint of
the definition and operationalization of objectives. At the same time, it
turns toward the exterior as it develops a public relations policy which, in
its comprehensiveness, goes far beyond advertising policy in the strict sense
of the term. The most recent works on marketing present this policy as "a
fundamental mental attitude, . . . a philosophy of management."[86] For public relations policy aims at giving the firm a good image, at creating the idea
that it is conscious of its responsibilities and accepts them in the collective
interest. Thus the multinational and national firms take out full page advertisements in the newspapers, in which they vaunt their work organization, the promotion and salary prospects of their employees, the social
utility of their production and the support that they give to non profit–
making cultural activities. Marketing furnishes the complex of these images to the firm which internalizes them, along with its traditional images,
in defining the MBO's goals in order to readjust policy.

The public is the set of groups that may, in an interdependent environment, have a (positive or negative) feedback effect on the firm.[87] From this
point of view, the workers are also a part of the public since they participate
in the construction of the firm's image and themselves react, in their working behavior, to this image. The firm projects an image to itself as it does to
its customers and to the organizations that surround it. It internalizes the
market and externalizes management.

This twofold development can be seen in the interest shown everywhere
in Europe[88] in the *social balance–sheet* and in the fact that it has been
enshrined in French law since 1977.[89] The activity of the firm can no longer
be expressed by financial ratios alone. Giving an account of the firm's
action also means giving the measure of its organic relationship in every
sphere with man and the environment, "for its responsibility is all-embrac-
ing and concerns the economic as well as the social sphere, that is, all that
has a bearing on life in society."[90] To the economic balance–sheet, must be
added a social balance–sheet, which assembles a set of qualitative and
quantitative indicators[91] on the life of the firm as organization. The social
balance–sheet becomes an instrument for creating the organization's image
among its members and in the public outside. It becomes a language of
communication among various social actors, both within and without. It
fills the vacuum, created in the ideological realm by the failure of general
book–keeping to account for the inner life of the firm ever since the latter
acquired substance, that is, an administrative and social dimension. The

firm is no longer naturally transparent. The social balance–sheet renders the internal and external images of the firm homogeneous and permanently retroactive, management control tends to increasingly internalize external costs. For the growing size of the firm forces it to consider its own physical, psychological and social impact on its environment as an integral part of its costs. Thus the task of public relations not only constitutes one of the elements in forming the image as a means of action on the environment, it should also and ever–increasingly be regarded as an element in management control.

Cost (internal) and sales (external) prospects tend to be identified with each other, and finally lead to marketing control of management. The homogeneity of internal and external publics, identical work on images, fusion of the viewpoints of costs and sales—all this shows that, at the very moment the firm fully becomes an organization or a system, it has to consider itself an element of a vaster system onto which it opens and with which its differences are less and less sharp. In all of this, the figure has lost its symbolic value. From a natural regulator, it has become a cultural indicator of the self image that the firm projects, for its own use and for the use of others; from the expression of a natural relationship, it has become an instrument for entering cultural entities (categories) into accounts, that is, it has become a pure simulacrum of the objectivity of nature, providing a representation of the order of the world from the standpoint of organizational categories.

Notes

1. 19th century French literature is marked by it. See for example, Honoré de Balzac's *Father Goriot*.
2. Cf. Louis Dumont, *Homo Equalis, op. cit.*
3. P. F. Drücker, *The Practice of Management*, London, Heineman, 1955, p. 23.
4. Even if his position, in terms of reason, remains ambiguous inasmuch as his capacity to exercise his reason is subordinated to private property. Cf. chapter 5.
5. L. Chevalier, *Classes Laborieuses, Classes Dangeureuses*, Paris, Plon, 1969.
6. Drücker, *op. cit.,* p. 23.
7. The terms "input" and "output" would be unsuitable here since this firm is devoid of depth.
8. The commercial law of 1807; cf. for example, L. Batardon, *Doctrine et Technique Comptable*, Paris, Dunod, 1953.
9. As M. Mareuse aptly puts it in *Le Contrôle de Gestion dans les Entreprises*, Paris, Dunod, 1938.
10. An executive order dated 8th August 1955 gave the balance sheet the role of "making known the real state of the firm," thus adopting this principle, bringing it up to date in form, but not in essence. For it sanctioned not the drafting of an inexact balance sheet, but its *publication* or its *presentation to shareholders*. Cf. Batardon, *op. cit.*

11. Letter to Savary, 29th Floreal, Year VII, quoted by Batardon, *ibid.*
12. R. Delaporte, *Concepts raisonnés de la comptabilité économique*, published by the author, 1930.
13. *Ibid.* Our italics.
14. Marx.
15. "One of the very first requirements for a man who is fit to handle pig iron as a regular occupation is that he shall be so stupid and so phlegmatic that he more nearly resembles in his mental make–up the ox than any other type." F. W. Taylor, *The Principles of Scientific Management*, New York and London, Harper & Brothers, 1913, page 59.
16. Taylor is said to have told workers that they were not supposed to think since there were people paid to think for them; cf. M. Rose, *Industrial Behaviour, Theoretical Development Since Taylor*, Harmondsworth, Penguin, 1978.
17. M. Mareuse, *op. cit., p. 4.*
18. Merrheim, in *La Vie Ouvrière*, 5th March 1913 quoted in CGT research document *Des Manufactures à la Crise du Taylorisme*, November 1978.
19. Gramsci well describes this preoccupation of Ford's; "in America, rationalisation of work and prohibition are undoubtedly connected. The enquiries conducted by the industrialists into the workers' private lives and the inspection services created by some firms to control the morality of their workers are necessities of the new methods of work," Antonio Gramsci, *Prison Notebooks*, London, Lawrence and Wishart, 1971, pp. 303-304.
20. This is the birth of the firm as an organization, illustrated by the emergence of organization charts and company rules.
21. Cf. L. Baritz, *The Servants of Power*, New York, Wiley, 1965.
22. We refer here to work developed subsequently to Myers, *Industrial Psychology in Great Britain*, Cape, 1924, within the framework of the Industrial Fatigue Research Board, set up in 1918, and the National Institute of Industrial Psychology set up in 1921. On this subject, see M. Rose, *op. cit..*
23. C. S. Myers, *op. cit., p. 83.*
24. As Rose points out (*op. cit.*), (p. 11), to speak of the "school of human relations" and to organize it around a leader like Mayo, is "a grotesque distortion of reality, but an excellent myth. . . ." Since we are concerned here with managerial ideologies and not with the history of industrial relations, the myth naturally serves our purpose.
25. E. Mayo, *The Human Problems of an Industrial Civilization*, Boston, Harvard University Press, 1946. This solution to the problem appears necessary only to a conservative philosophy, namely one that attributes social disintegration to the movement of ideas and not to the relations of production, one therefore, that locates the restauration of harmony in human relations and not in social confrontation. This point is stressed by M. Rose.
26. Pierre Bourdieu clearly shows that, as the distance from property grows, other sources of managerial legitimacy are increasingly resorted to. Thus, in fact, the educational qualifications of a manager increase conversely to the degree to which he is an owner. Cf. "Le Patronat," *Actes de la Recherche en Sciences Sociales,* No. 20-21, March – April 1978.
27. We should rather call him "a proprietor by natural right" if we are willing to accept that "natural right" is to capitalism what the "prince by divine right" is to feudalism.
28. It must be noted that cost accounting is not always obligatory. The accounting

plan lays down a model of transcription which provides coherence between cost accounting and general accounting. But it postulates the singular nature of each firm and hence the incompatibility with one another of various cost accounts whose final form depends solely on the firm: "the operational cost accounting of a firm must be exactly suited to its organic structure and to its special operational activities. It follows that, although the rules of cost accounting concern firms as much as those of general accounting, their presentation is different. Those of cost accounting comprise a range of solutions from which the firm must make choices and combinations on the basis of its specific features." *Projet de Plan Comptable Général*, appended to the executive order of the Minister of the Economy, *Journal Officiel*, 15th June 1979, Chapter III, "Comptabilité Analytique d'Exploitation," p. 257. This really implies that cost accounting is a matter of the *culture of the firm.*

29. Batardon, *op. cit.*, p. 31.
30. Mareuse, *op. cit.,* p. 53.
31. Historically, the development of cost accounting is related in a concrete way to the growth of the big firm and of scientific management. But developments in accounting came very late. On this subject, see R. H. Parker, *Management Accounting, An Historical Perspective*, London, Macmillan, 1969.
32. A. Siegfried, preface to Servoise, *L'Etude Scientifique des Marchés*, Paris, PUF, 1944.
33. Cost accounting defines cost allocation units called "sections": a section is considered to be homogeneous in terms of production and hence identifiable with a single-product firm; whence the definition of the production unit to which is allocated a part of the indirect costs assigned by management norms. Whence, the simulation, within the firm, of the market exchange which is supposed to take place among all the single-product firms corresponding to all the sections. The distinction between fixed and variable costs emerged in theory only in 1830 and in practice with the "break-even chart" in 1903. Cf. Parker, *op. cit.*
34. This idea was developed, among others, by J. M. Clark, *Studies in the Economics of the Overhead Costs*, Chicago, University of Chicago Press, 1923; but for a long time it had no effect on accounting practice.
35. So true is this, that, in the Soviet Union, the accounts manager is the third most important person in the enterprise after the general manager and the engineering manager. See R. Ghez, *La Comptabilité, Langage du Management*, Paris, Cercle du Livre Economique, 1969.
36. David Ricardo, *Principles of Political Economy and Taxation*, quoted in P. H. Nystrom, *Marketing Handbook*, New York, Ronald Press Company, 1954.
37. Von Wieser, Social Economics, quoted in Nystrom, *ibid.*
38. Just as it came into the practice of States, practically with the New Deal and Welfare policies, theoretically with Keynes, who gave the practice of state *dirigisme* its titles of nobility.
39. Converse and Huegy, *Elements of Marketing*, New York, Prentice Hall, 1946, 3rd. ed.
40. The term "marketing" appeared in its present meaning after the First World War. Its definition was established in 1931 by the American Association of Teachers of Marketing and Advertising. According to the definition given by Theodore N. Beckman, Harold H. Maynard and William R. Davidson, marketing "embraces the entire group of services and functions from the producer to

the consumer...excluding only operations relating to changes in the form of goods" in *The Principles of Marketing*, New York, Ronald Press, 6th ed., 1957, p. 3.

41. P. White, *Market Analysis*, New York, McGraw Hill, 1925, 1st ed. 1921.
42. Cf. Maynard *et al, op. cit.*; White, *op. cit.*; Converse and Huegy, *Elements of Marketing*, New York, Ronald Press Co., 1932, 2nd ed.
43. So much so that, in its initial usage, "marketing" was employed to designate problems of distribution; cf. Maynard *et al, op. cit.*
44. Converse and Huegy, *op. cit.*
45. White, *op. cit.*
46. In certain respects, the vision of the consumer put forward by these first hesitant steps of marketing is even more rational than that of nature since it implicity assumes that the previous behavior of the consumer was related more often to tradition than to reason; in a market in which there was no innovation, reason could coincide with tradition (since tradition is nothing but the repetition of an initial rational act in an unchanged universe); this could not be so in a shifting environment.
47. Maynard, *op. cit.*
48. *Ibid.*
49. *Ibid.*, p. 429.
50. Cf. chapter 9.
51. P. H. Nystrom, *op. cit.*, p. 150.
52. Converse and Huegy, *op. cit.*, p. 1-3.
53. *Ibid.*, p. 36.
54. Maynard, *op. cit.*, p. 56.
55. Converse and Huegy, *op. cit.*
56. Maynard, *op. cit.*
57. These are recurring themes in present-day books on marketing.
58. Maynard, *op. cit.*
59. *Ibid.*, p. 14.
60. *Ibid.*, p. 84.
61. *Ibid.*, p. 71.
62. *Ibid.*, p. 618.
63. Converse and Huegy, *op. cit.*, p. 131-132.
64. Holtzclaw, *The Principles of Marketing*, Cromwell Company, 1935.
65. Drücker, *op. cit.*, p; 219.
66. *Ibid.*, p. 323.
67. *Ibid.*, p. 336.
68. McGregor, *The Human Side of the Enterprise*, New York, MacGraw Hill, 1960.
69. Cf. M. Rose, *op. cit.*
70. Drücker, *op. cit.*, p. 323.
71. *Ibid.*, p. 156.
72. *Projet de Plan Comptable Général, op. cit.*, p. 351.
73. After W. H. Whyte's famous work, *The Organization Man*, Simon and Schuster, 1956.
74. Drücker, *op. cit.*, p. 162.
75. *Ibid.*
76. *Ibid.*, p. 51-52.
77. *Ibid.*, p. 77.
78. *Ibid.*, p. 78.

79. P. Martineau in "It's Time to Research the Consumer," *Harvard Business Review*, July-August 1955, stresses the need to train engineers and statisticians, the usual partners of marketing men, in the social sciences. This injunction became widespread in books on marketing from the fifties and sixties onwards. See also the very fine declaration by A. P. Sloan, then ex–chairman of General Motors, in a letter to the shareholders quoted in P. H. Nystrom ed., *op. cit.*: "To regard Consumer Research as a functional activity would be an error. In its broadest implications, it is a philosophy of action. . . ."

80. For example, B. B. Gardner and S. J. Levy, "The Product and the Brand," in E. C. Bursk and J. F. Chapman, *Modern Marketing Strategy*, Cambridge, Harvard University Press, 1964.

81. R. Toubeau, *Psychologie du Marketing*, Paris, Dunod–Economie, 1970.

82. Either the product exists and a search is made for the most suitable target (the market is "segmented") or the target is fixed and a search is made for the product (the product is "positioned").

83. Drücker *op. cit.*, p. 454-455. See also, for example, P. H. Nystrom, *op. cit.*

84. Drücker, *op. cit.*, p. 23.

85. Cf. for example, Nystrom, *op. cit.*

86. Nystrom, *op. cit.*, p. 537, quotes a list of "musts" in public relations defined by Wright in *Public Relations for Business*.

87. Influential groups, consumers, suppliers, shareholders, employees, competitors, government, press, media. Nystrom gives full vent to his lyricism: Let the oil of human understanding lubricate the relationships of the firm with the community. . . ." *ibid.*, p. 548.

88. *Rapport Sudreau*, Documentation Française, 1975.

89. The Law of 12th July, 1977.

90. A. Maggio, J.-J. Pascaud, R. Penalva, J. Pruneau: "Le bilan social des entreprises," *Droit Social*, No. 5, 1977.

91. Jobs, wages, ancillary expenses; hygiene and safety conditions, other working conditions; training, professional relations, other conditions relating to the firm.

Chapter 5

From the Vote to the Survey

Consensus: The last common place.

The Vote As the Basis of the Democratic Political Order

The Fundamental Equation of Political Democracy

"If there were a people of gods, it would govern itself democratically" said Rousseau.[1] It is a people of gods that philosophy of the enlightenment intended to make of men, relying on the idea of the sovereignty of the subject liberated from divine authority in this world.[2] It was really democracy that it sought to provide as natural government to the individual invested with omnipotence and, in particular, invested with complete power to express the natural laws that were the basis of the world's new order. A people of gods who would govern itself according to the laws of nature: everyone agreed that the first item on the agenda of democracy should be the quest for means to ensure the legitimate expression of the will of all in order to achieve the Common Good and Natural Law. The vote was chosen as the means of achieving this, with certain conditions as to the voters. But first of all, what was the Common Good? There was unanimity on this point: it was the realization in this world, by Reason, of the Law of Nature, the generator of Justice, Harmony and Progress. Locke proclaimed: "The state of Nature has a law of nature to govern it, which obliges everyone, and Reason, which is that law, teaches all mankind who will but consult it, that beings, are equal and independent, no one ought to harm another in his life, health, liberty or possessions."[3] Montesquieu took up the same point when he wrote that "the legislator's role would be to promulgate and thereby make positive the (natural) relationships of justice, which the reason of each individual could not fail to perceive, were it not for special interests likely to muddle their perception."[4]

How was one to discover Natural Law? Through the exercise of reason.

Only lawful subjects had the power to express the common good because they alone entertained a relationship with Truth. Thus, for Voltaire, "it was those devoid of prejudices, enlightened people, philosophers who should seek to intervene in the lawmaking process. They had to exert their influence on those who were there to govern the people. The supreme magistrate was the enlightened people. Gradually, philosophers had to gain way over public opinion. They had to try and make people think for themselves."[5] Since the exercise of reason was required of responsible voters and candidates, all those who were deprived of reason by their condition would be automatically disqualified. Thus, to the extent that the exercise of reason depended on a vested interest in property, the lower orders were kept from active participation in democracy. "But immediately, another question comes up. For as long as we were confined to the question of who was to be entrusted with the task of making the best laws, it was easy to reply: enlightened people. But at present, . . . we want to know *who* has the *right* to make the law . . . there is no longer any question of deciding which is the best of laws but of giving the law a legal basis. Since, by nature, any man who has reached maturity may not be made subject to the will of another . . . he cannot let others prescribe for him laws in which he has not collaborated personally or through his representatives".[6]

It is a widely held idea that man should conduct himself by the exercise of his own reason and that the Nation should submit itself to the exercise of the reason of its citizens: "A Nation should make its own laws because it is made up of intelligent beings, to whom God has given reason with which to judge what suits them. They say that only children and madmen should be guided by the reason of another. They say that nature lays down the same duties for all men, and that it endows them with the same rights . . . society can flourish only insofar as its citizens care for to Public Affairs, and they care only insofar as they obey laws of which they are the authors."[7] "Public Opinion,"[8] everyone agreed, had to be be responsible for legislative power.

The search for the Common Good through reason was based on deliberation among all beings of reason. This principle was consecrated by the French Revolution. Siéyes stated "the necessity of recognizing the common will only as being the opinion of the plurality." For him, "this maxim is uncontestable,"[9] for deliberation is itself a reasonable method: "How are the shadows of error to be dissipated if not by the light of truth? Why ask a blind man to lead another blind man? . . . If the ignorance of a sovereign is rightfully feared, why would it be absurd to share the sovereign power in such a way that nothing may be ordained without first having been carefully discussed?[10]

Moreover, the exercise of reason should not be clouded by "the influence of (particular) interests, passions, corruption and error"[11] which hinder the declaration of the Common Will "not only by enfeebling the understanding of the voters but above all by setting up other than disinterested relationships between them."[12] This was really the fear expressed by people like Mercier de la Rivière, who saw the *Assemblée de la Nation* as a meeting where "each one brings his personal opinions, his arbitrary claims and the firm resolution to make them prevail."[13]

For the sovereign expression of the people, by whatever means it was manifested, to be capable of leading to the Public Good in civil society, the political system had to function in the manner of economic exchange. For it was on this condition alone that deliberation among free, equal, independent and reasonable beings could yield its fruit: the Truth of the Natural Law. The fundamental equation which stated the legitimacy of the French democratic political organization could be deduced from these assumptions:

— The Common Good is the expression of Natural Law;
— The Common Good is the expression of the Common Will;
— Hence, the Common Will, the Common Good and Natural Law are one and the same thing.

It was on this basis that the Constitution of the Year III built its definition of the law as "The General Will, expressed by the majority of citizens or their representatives."[14]

This definition raised two problems for theoreticians: the first concerned the justification of the "dictatorship of numbers" in the law of the majority, the second concerned the delegation of power to the representatives of the people.

The "Dictatorship of Numbers"

The principle had been stated by the founding fathers. Thus Locke declared that he had already shown how the majority could express itself in the name of all. He even thought that it was unnatural, hence pernicious that the body politic should take a decision that it had not been asked to take by the broadest consent, namely the consent of the majority. In other words, he felt that the majority, when in action, could take the measures of governance that suited it, and these measures would represent the highest authority that could be claimed by a model of government.[15]

In revolutionary France, everyone agreed that the Common Will was expressed through the vote and the rule of the majority both when representatives were appointed and when these representatives voted the law. However, there were voices raised against the dangers of this procedure:

"Those who oppose this law are fascinated by a sort of dread aroused in them by the idea that the most important questions should be decided by a single vote. But let them make no mistake about it; it is not this or that vote that decides the matter, it is the comparison of the sum of those who say yes with the sum of those who say no."[16]

The objection was a weighty one, and Mirabeau's argument would have seemed quite weak if it had not been assumed that the rule of the majority was the instrument of the Common Good, i.e. that the rule of numbers made it possible to attain to Natural Law. Condorcet tried to give the assumption a mathematical basis. He related the pragmatism of probabilism to the metaphysics of Natural Law. He made the vote the instrument of the True, that is, the central symbolic procedure of democratic political life, the *common measure* between the Common Will and the Common Good.

Condorcet pointed out that legislators, far from being "creators" of the law, were its "discoverers." Through the virtues of deliberation and the alchemy of the vote, the majority opinion was supposed to be transmuted into an expression of Natural Law. The deliberators, as a body, revealed the law.

On the basis of Locke's doctrine of the social contract and a philosophical interpretation of probabilities (the theory of the "motive for believing"), Condorcet established his mathematical conception of society, formulating a theory of decision compatible with democracy, and one that might be considered as the ideal of all democratic societies.[17] In Locke, he found the conception of man as a reasonable and free individual, equal in rights to all other individuals insofar as he met the conditions for belonging to the body politic: namely, that he was enlightened and that he was responsible. Between individuals, politics represented "an ontologically marginal addition according to the philosophers of the Enlightenment,"[18] an artificial construction but necessary for the permanent renewal of the contract which was the condition for maintaining life in society through the formulation of law. The procedure by which law was formulated was of capital importance. On it depended whether life in society was pure artifice without any natural guarantee or the attainment of Natural Law, the condition of harmony and progress. Was it possible to conceive of a natural procedure that managed to reconcile the will of the Nation, expressed by the Assembly, with the Common Good or Natural Law? Yes, replied Condorcet, if we accept, according to the *theory of the motive for belief,* "the general principle that natural events are governed by constant laws, since we can base our opinion only on the observation of the order of past events and on the assumption that the same will hold for future events."[19]

Thus the motive for belief appeared "as an available means for deciding among various judgments and opposing opinions. It is a rule for choosing and a means for deciding, and not only the property of a judgment or of a relation between two propositions."[20] If the elected representatives abided by the motive for belief, that is if, freed from passions and interests, they actively sought the Truth, it might be reckoned that there would be an even probability of their making decisions in accordance with the Truth. If these very elected representatives were truly free, equal and independent (according to democratic theory) it might be deduced that the variety of their opinions (with respect to the Truth) would be quite entirely governed by chance. The divergence between the standpoints of representatives would be very similar to "a statistical error," that is, to the effect of the multitude of mutually independent causes implied in the liberty of the subjects; the vote of the representatives would be distributed according to Bernoulli's law. Then, according to the theory of probabilities, one might compare the Truth to the mean distribution or to the majority. As a graduated measure of the motive for belief, the vote made it possible to reveal Natural Law, for which the deliberating elected representatives were the "tools of interpretation." On the condition, of course (and this was another way of stating the problem of the elected representative's independence), that the mandate was not an imperative one, that is, that variations in opinion were independent of any cause other than the exercise of the individual freedom of judgment. In this way the vote made it possible "to reconcile the established rule calculating probabilities with the feeling and conduct of reasonable and prudent men, in most instances where this rule initially appeared to run contrary."[21] In French democratic thought, the vote assumed practical value, but it first had symbolic value: it ensured agreement between nature and society in the political realm, as did market price in the economic realm. The shift that the French version of democratic philosophy brought about in the role of the vote will be better appreciated by comparing it with the role given by a traditionalist like Burke, the sworn opponent of Condorcet, in whom he saw concentrated every defect of French intellectualism. Burke agreed that the representatives had to be men of superior wisdom and capacity since their function was essentially one of deliberation. However, he felt that deliberation did not establish the laws of nature but the laws of God, and of nature under cover of God, that is, the order of tradition. The way to attain to these laws was not through intelligence or abstract knowledge, but experience, good judgment, virtue and wisdom. Parliamentary deliberation performed, at an accelerate pace, the work of time on opinions. The representative was thus dissociated from his constituent whom he did not have to consult. He was elected, but that was no more than a "convenient procedure" which could be replaced by any equally efficient artifice. The vote had no symbolic value but a pragmatic one. Elected representatives were chosen from among the members of the natural aristocracy whence they derived experience and conformity of interest with the State, for a true natural aristocracy was not a special interest group in the State; it was not distinct from it.[22] Burke therefore established a common measure between the interests of the Nation and the decisions of the representatives, but this common measure dispensed with the expression of the Common Will, for the people were not the subject of the law. This common measure, rooted in Burke's model of legitimacy, is called *tradition.*

The Dignity of the Representative

There remained the problem of the appointment of representatives, a sore spot for the founders of representative government in France. Since the size of the Nation did not allow for the direct expression of the individual will, the continuity of legislative action made it necessary to elect representatives. Many solutions were proposed to restrain their power, among these, obligatory mandates and the restriction of their task to formulating and discussing certain projects to be submitted for the approval of the people by referendum. However, in the end it had to be accepted that they were to be entrusted with full legislative power. But "the people continued (under the French Revolution) to have a certain distrust of their deputies. . . . As for the deputies, they never stopped wondering if they were sufficiently impersonal, if they were truly worthy of representing the National Will; they realized that they needed a constant moral rigor to attain the level that the people expected of them."[23]

This problem, so knotty in reality, was but a very secondary one from the standpoint of theory. Indeed it was rarely dealt with and, when touched upon, it was to the effect that, since all individuals of reason were equal, appointment by lot should suffice. For Montesquieu, "suffrage by lot is as natural to democracy as sufferage by choice is to aristocracy. Suffrage by lot is a method of electing that offends no one, but animates each citizen with the reasonable hope of serving his country."[24] If, however, emphasis was laid on "choice by suffrage," it was because all were not equally reasonable among citizens. The true reason for which electors were required to be qualified in terms of property was to exclude those whose condition was so mediocre that they might be deemed to be lacking in self-will.[25]

Montesquieu confirmed this view: "Yet as this method (suffrage by lot) is in itself defective, it has been the endeavor of the most eminent legislators to regulate and amend it"[26] and a little later: "The great advantage of representatives is their capacity to discuss public affairs. For this the people collectively are extremely unfit. . . ."[27] Holbach went further: "To maintain the harmony that should always subsist between sovereigns and their peoples, to shelter both from the outrages of bad citizens, nothing would be more advantageous than a Constitution that enabled every citizen to be represented, to speak in assemblies whose object is the General Good. To be just and useful, these assemblies should comprise those whose possessions make them citizens, whose condition and enlightenment make them fit to know the interests of the Nation and the needs of peoples; in a word, it is property that makes the citizen; every man who has possessions in the State has an interest in the good of the State, and regardless of the rank that is given to him by special conventions, it is by virtue of his possessions that he must speak and that he earns the right to be represented."[28]

Property–based suffrage on the one hand, and an act of candidacy on the other, for legislative action would be pursued with all the greater diligence if it were entrusted to those who would bring the most devotion to it.[29] But all these measures were not conceived as a means of restricting the right to vote or be elected to a group of unchanging men, as the aristocracy had been.

"All those who do not possess their independence are excluded *de facto*, and *de jure*, from the political public realm. ... Culture is the first condition to be met by whoever wishes to belong to this realm, the second condition being Property. ... The restriction of the right to vote is not tantamount to a restriction of the public sphere itself so long as it remains the mere political ratification of a status acquired on the economic plane ... by the private man, both as a cultivated person and as a proprietor. ... Everybody will be a voter, when economic and social conditions grant every individual the same possibilities of fulfilling the criteria that give access to such a status."[30]

Universal suffrage was, in a way, the vanishing point of property-based suffrage, to be attained when all men had become property-owners, that is, when the democratic society had been reached. This is why universal suffrage could be adopted in 1848 without changing the dogma of political democracy: it sufficed to replace the criterion of capacity by property by that of capacity by vocation.

Thus was the underlying principle of French parliamentary democracy established: the Assembly stated the law (invented it but did not create it). The positive law that it brought to light was not distinct from Natural Law. The legislative body chose, from within, an executive organ, a government that it controlled. This government set up a totally subordinate administration which managed matters of State, that is, ensured the conditions for the proper functioning of exchange in the civil society: peace (national defence), spatial fluidity (civil engineering), the guarantee of the means of transaction (national mint) and the guarantee of contracts (the administration of justice).

The Crisis of Democratic Political Thought

The Second Republic granted universal suffrage, which was immediately confiscated by the "servile democracy"[31] of the Second Empire. The Third Republic finally restored the liberal democratic form as it had been conceived by the doctrinaire theorists of the French Revolution, and set its latent contradictions in motion. For the Revolution had planned on fulfilling the Enlightenment by the representative system but simultaneously called for its prerequisite: the active promotion of the Enlightenment among all citizens[32] through the intervention of State administration beyond the limits assigned to it by the theory of democracy.

Radical Contradictions

What historians call the radical Republic took up the dual task left to it by the Revolution: this led it to develop an unstable and contradictory doctrine. As an individualistic Republic, it preached the fulfillment of the republican and national ideal through the universal suffrage of abstract citizens even when, in line with the science of its time, it affirmed the fundamentally social nature of the real man. "Despite a good many defects, universal suffrage retains an essential advantage derived from its flexibility; it eliminates class categories and distinctions; on one point at least, it achieves equality. It remains the essential instrument of this French unity which we do not wish to sacrifice."[33] Later, others were to try to absorb the contradiction by calling for the elimination or transformation of the representative regime to the benefit of real groups.[34]

Since the time of Auguste Comte, society had been considered as being governed by a new law of organic Progress,[35] which required solidarity in the civil society as opposed to individual selfishness,[36] and the development of State assistance as opposed to laissez-faire non-interventionism. The radical party took on the task "of organizing society politically and socially according to the Laws of Reason, that is, with a view to the all-around development of the human person."[37] The party placed its work under the patronage of science, the place of the meeting of minds: "Science and science alone must create the new France."[38]

Fighting the effects of this modern rationalism, which justified the expansionism of the Welfare State,[39] the democratic neo-theoreticians sought to absorb the contradiction by reducing the representative system to its purest form.

In the face of the contradictory nature of the situation illustrated by Radical doctrine, and of the pragmatism of its exercise of power which earned it the name of the "golden mean policy," thinkers and polemicists themselves became pragmatists. Confronted with the same difficulties, they sought to deduce the necessary reform of the political system from the analysis of inadequacies in the application of doctrine, or the reform of the doctrine from the analysis of its actual inadequacy. In both cases, what preoccupied them, as well as their philosophical mentors, Comte, Durkheim, Renan, Taine or Maurras, was actual society. In the great wave of positivism and experimentalism, the socio-political "reality" was analyzed, and an attempt made to discover social laws. Tardieu expressed this when he announced the plan for his work *Le Souverain Captif*: "If I may be permitted to make a bold comparison, I would say, taking inspiration from the memory of Claude Bernard, that I am writing an 'Introduction To Experimental Politics'."[40] And Aldo Dami, among many others in the journal *Esprit*, says the same thing: "Our century will set against the concept of the citizen that of the producer, and against the abstract and juridical man, the real man. The present crisis is above all a crisis of adaptation. Institutions no longer correspond to facts."[41] What was discovered was an opposition that enjoyed considerable success in the thirties: the opposition between the "legal country" and the "real country."

Sociology: Reality Versus Utopia

Desacralizing the elected representative. It was shown first of all that the elected representative did not fulfill the sacred mission that he thought. The member of parliament was not that disembodied being who was supposed to place his reason at the service of the Nation. He exercised a specialist's activity, an occupation that called for special know-how, a trade and not a supreme duty. "There is no mistake about it: to be a representative is not a ministry, it is an occupation with its customs, methods, channels and, almost, its hierarchy. No great civic virtues are needed, but there must be order, know-how and willingness."[42] The elected representative was a specialist, the specialist in negotiation and mediation between his fief and Parliament: he was "the travelling salesman of the Republic."[43] Far away indeed was the injunction laid down in the Constitution of 1791, according to which "the deputies appointed by the departments (shall not be) the representatives of a particular department but of the entire Nation,"[44] the expositors of civic wills and not the agents of the demands of the real people. It was as far from the mind of the voter as it was from that of the elected representative: "the deputy ceases to be a proxy and becomes an obligee. . . . He no longer represents a political program but only friendships. . . . The voter finds it natural that the one he has made a representative should make him a member of the Academy."[45] "Desacralized" as it was, the occupation continued to be useful: "the voter . . . has to entrust a professional with the task of regulating interests for which he does not himself have the feel. A representative is chosen as one chooses an attorney, because one does not know the law."[46] As with every professional body, the representative was recruited within his own group, among the managers of political organizations, the parties. The relationship between these professional politicians and the voters was a mediated one and this was in the nature of things. As Thibaudet tells us: "Experience proves it," "this is a common-sense distinction . . . there is only a minority of citizens who are normally called to deal with public affairs. . . . (In the present democracy) active citizens are those who take an interest in politics of themselves, that is, those who are active by vocation."[47]

Political professionals depend on the powers of finance. The period between the two World wars saw a revival of the accusation against "these little empirical dictatorships"[48] which spell the death of great principles, these feudal systems in which everyone, depending on his own bias, saw the hand of freemasonry, the parties, Jews and trade unions. There was enough here to "obscur the General Will" as Condorcet might have said.

Suffrage is not universal. As for universal suffrage, it was more theoretical than real. Tardieu, in an authoritative demonstration of empirical sociology, proved, figures at hand, that out of the forty million individuals in the Nation, " to express universality, 25 percent of the total seemed meager (to represent the Nation) and that it would not correspond to the scaled-down map of the country with which Mirabeau was satisfied." He added: considering that women of majority age were not entitled to vote, that abstentions, in the best case, amounted to forty percent of the electorate, "what we call the General Will is nothing but the will of ten percent of the nation."[49] If it were added that "thanks to carefully preserved artifices" (the demarcation of constituencies and balloting procedures), the majority vote was never reflected by a majority in the Assembly, his charge led to the observation that "the allegedly arithmetical law of popular sovereignty expressed by number founders on the schemes of men. Sovereignty suffers along with equality. But scheming triumphs . . . what it is called the sovereign people is only a part of the people and is not sovereign."[50]

A nation is not made up of individuals. If the observer turned his gaze from the painful spectacle offered by the representatives and concentrated on analyzing the real society, what would he discover? That the real society was formed not of individuals but of groups. In other words, society was the product, not of a contract but of History; consequently, Natural Law was not the immutable law of Nature that had to be read, but the social law of Human Progress which had to be deciphered (by scholars) and, if possible, accompanied or facilitated by suitable measures.[51]

By entrusting the invisible hand with the task of harmonizing the selfish interests of every individual by natural means, the classical laissez-faire and democratic conception of the individual had freed society from the imperatives of morality and language. The conception of the real man, governed by the laws of history and of the group, reintroduced the necessity of a morality and a language. A language which was still restricted to expressing the nature of society, a language of science, whose preparation had to be entrusted to learned people. As the interpreters of social law, they would thus receive the supreme power to name the world, that is, to interpret its orders in realms laissez-faire and democratic thought had left to nature to regulate: the economic and social realms, where the specialist was assigned the role of stating collective needs[52] (here was the birth of public service and macro-economics); the realm of justice, where legislative power was no longer qualified to reveal Natural Law naturally[53] (here was the growth of the historical school of law).

If groups were the basis of social order, they could be represented politically. One would then be building on the real society. Perhaps the solution to the "moral crisis" looming up at the start of this century was to be found there. In any case, this is what many sociologists and historians of the day believed.[54] The alternative lay in a rigorous application of the democratic principles of political representation." Jaurès, contemplating the French people on an election day, said with irony: "It is an assembly of kings. Perhaps, but do nothing kings in that case. . . . It is a captive Sovereign, who is forbidden to ask if the regime satisfies him, who is forbidden to express himself directly on the essential problems of national life."[55] The Nation is governed in the name of the people, without their being truly consulted. Far from being the means to define the Common Good, the vote becomes a procedure wherein special interests confront one another.

Was this procedure still legitimate? After the two great crises of parliamentary democracy in France, Boulangism and the Dreyfus affair, two contradictory responses emerged, two denunciations of the great crisis of democracy after 1930. Both agreed on the overall analysis of the situation. They saw a structured and non-atomized society, an inadequate political representation. Both called for moving towards a situation where representation would be real and no longer fictitious. But they parted ways on the definition of remedies for they could not agree on the *entity* they represented.

For the neo–democrats like Tardieu, the model was a good one and the solution to the problem lay in "remaking the Revolution";[56] for the others, the philosophers of the organic society, the true children of Auguste Comte and Emile Durkheim, of Taine and Renan, the model itself was bad. Another one had to be constructed: "The utopia of democracy was to despoil man of his tangible qualities, reduce him to the abstract condition of citizen. Of the real man of flesh and blood, possessing a trade, an environment, a personality, it made an unreal being, an allegorical character living outside time and space, identical on every level of society. Neither worker nor peasant, neither industrialist nor merchant, from neither north nor south, neither learned nor ignorant; a theoretical man."[57]

The Way Out of the Contradiction

Make the doctrinal model work? For Tardieu, the ills of democracy stemmed from the gap between the practice and the model. Suffrage was only allegedly universal, the Assembly was made over to special interests and the vote was co-opted by a few: "From the standpoint of theory, the law expresses the General Will of the Nation. In point of fact, it is voted by elected representatives who represent neither the majority of the Nation nor the majority of voters. The Law is, for the minority, the means to sanctify its will. . . . Once the form of the law is correct, it can do what it likes as far as the essence is concerned. . . . The law can do everything. . . . A vote can render legal that which is unjust."[58]

Administration encroached upon areas of social activity that did not fall within its theoretical juridiction, thus giving all power to the State. As R. de Jouvenel was saying already in 1914: "Power corrupts and absolute power corrupts absolutely."[59] The corrupt State lost its authority for it had lost its credibility. The State was ill because its principles were corrupt: "If it is true that the decadence of regimes begins with the corruption of their principles, this regime must be quite ill."[60]

For these ills, two types of remedies were proposed: democracy had to be seen as a system of controls; the existence of small groups had to be acknowledged and fostered as checks on power. The conception of an Assembly's tasks had therefore changed: the House was no longer the organ by which Natural Law was discovered. It had become an organ of decision under the supervision of citizens or groups. What then became of the significance of the vote, asked Tardieu: "National sovereignty is exercised by universal suffrage, that is, by the law of numbers. . . . What are numbers? . . . A proof? No. A simple superficial characteristic, a transposition of force. But what does that show? What proves that the majority is necessarily right? That the opinion of twenty million men is closer to the truth than that of two hundred thousand? That numbers give a total of individuals virtues that each one of them lacks? That a million individual mistakes can be equal to a truth? . . . Are they righter? No, but they are stronger."[61] Was it enough for a government to be based on numbers for it to be right? Was politics nothing but arithmetic? The response was a pragmatic one. The majority vote acquired its significance, not because it produced truth, but because it expressed the opinion of the greatest number of persons. "Opinion" came out rather diminished from this operation: it was no longer the *great* deliberating "Public Opinion" of the century of Enlightenment. The "Majority" lost its letters of nobility: the doctrinaire theorists of the Revolution had indissociably identified the "Majority" with "the greatest number" and the "majority of reasonable beings"; henceforth it was reduced to quantity. The democratic maxim atrophied into a bland utilitarianism, quite remote from the metaphysics of utility of Bentham and James Mill, for whom the majority decision drew its legitimacy[62] from the law of nature by ensuring the "greatest good of the greatest number."

For Tardieu and the neo-democrats, democracy was first of all the true representation of the country: for the justice of equality assumed that everyone could make his voice heard. In a way, parliament had to become the reduced model of society.[63] The choice of representatives by vote was legitimized solely by the representation of interests. This was the pragmatic consequence of the democratic principle. It could very well have been replaced by casting lots—some thought of this[64]—if deliberation had not become the business of specialists of representation and of public affairs: everyone was the judge of his own interest, but there were persons more qualified than others to express common interests because they had received suitable training and because they had the leisure for it. It was not enough to be reasonable, wise and "enlightened": it was necessary to possess specialist know-how, which was a knowledge of the modes of negotiating public business, knowledge of the population that one represented and a cultural capacity for mediation between the central power and the voters; the knowledge of the negotiator and interpreter; the knowledge that founds the power of local leaders as professionals of politics. Representation split away from any reference to the national group and led to the idea of the imperative mandate.

In that case, suffrage had to be truly universal, so that all interests could be represented in reality. Tardieu campaigned in favour of women's suffrage and for the referendum which, he felt, ought to become a normal procedure of consultation on major questions: "Had the French possessed the referendum, they would have been spared many abuses that now burden them: the proliferation of public functions, monopolies and offices, inquisitorial taxes and the laws dictated by the State on workers' retirement, social insurance and education would have come up against the common sense of the masses."[65]

True universal suffrage finally presupposed the assurance that the ballot papers represented something other than "anonymous letters of social life," that is, that the State returned within its bounds. Tardieu's renewed democracy was far from representing the "return to the principles of 1789" that he claimed to propose. To him the vote expressed force rather than reason. He did away with what had formed the "common measure" between Common Good and the Common Will; the fundamental equation of classical French democracy was destroyed. If this was so, it was because the representation of the vote as an expression of force followed logically from the new conception of society as a structure and no longer as an atomized universe. A structure where particular wills clashed and negotiated. In the "sociological society," the Common Will had disappeared. Politics, aided by specialists, could adopt the task of improving the conditions of confrontation by perfecting procedures; it could not abolish them.

In 1935, it was no longer possible to ignore the deep-rooted influence of positivist thinking. Although the idea of a Common Good remained (as indicated by the national and centralizing conceptions of the democratic reform tendency and above all by the *de facto* actions of administration), it could no longer be formulated in the political sphere. Where could this be done then? Those who argued for a renewal of democracy and laissez-faire explained that "to seek social security is to find the authoritarian State."[66] They demanded, though in a fainter voice than before, that the administration return to its traditional jurisdiction. In the name of democratic principles, they favored direct control by the political sphere over the administrative one. Thus, on the one hand they claimed a task for politics—the definition of the Common Good—while, on the other, they admitted their incapacity to make politics fulfill this task.

Overthrow the doctrinal model? Those who have been called "the non–conformists of the thirties" found a common ground, beyond the clash of their political preferences, which ranged from Christian humanism to fascism, in the observation that "modern man has lost the measure of what is Human."[67] More precisely, they ought to have said that man had lost one measure of what is human, the one that made nature the criterion of legitimacy in the philosophy of the enlightenment. "The century of reason has collapsed into chaos; into it are piled the ruins of the faith the new idol sought to destroy, as well as its own ruins which were unable to withstand self–criticism. Never has man been so deprived of support, he no longer knows."[68] "The eternal bases of man"[69] had to be rediscovered if the foundations of a new social order were to be laid.

The problem could not be resolved by the simple manipulation, however artful, of the procedures of representation. "The dictatorship of the majority" was detestable not because the procedures were imperfect but because the vision of social organization that produced it was mistaken. "Laissez-faire capitalism has delivered democracy to the oligarchy of the rich by using the very formulas and weapons of democracy. Capitalist democracy is a democracy that gives man a freedom, while capitalism deprives him of its use."[70] Democracy and laissez-faire camouflaged capitalism in its unrestrained form. The idea of representation that was derived from this was only a lure: in the name of a disembodied freedom, it sacrified persons to the interests of "capitalist powers."[71] "The individual votes, the person works, thinks, loves and feels hungry. The individual is the imaginary sovereign of a world founded on numbers; the individual is only the millionth of a State, a numerical participant in the national community, a sorry unit without hope and without flame, awaiting salvation from others. The person has a family, he exercises a trade, he pays taxes, he fights, he has precise needs, heartfelt enthusiasms, both just and unjust ones; he is subject in the flesh to all the ills that beset man: hunger, anxiety, death and despair that no words can express."[72]

By artificially dividing up natural social groups, the product of a shared history and a shared present, into undifferentiated individuals, liberalism created a theoretical liberty without a practical purpose. By depriving persons of their natural social environment, it despoiled them of every authentic framework for thought, hence of every defense against those opinion-manipulating forces, the press and Parliament, the means of expression of "capitalist powers." The individual of the philosophy of the Enlightenment, far from being "something very simple, an obvious fact, a kind of commonplace . . . (is a man) without a place, reduced to an arithmetical unit."[73]

The weakness and timidity, the irresponsibility of the elected representatives were only the expression of the fictitious character of the political representation that followed from these principles. The elected representative "represented" abstract beings who had, nevertheless, the collective power to dismiss him.[74] It was necessary to put an end once and for all to these "logical graveyards" which tended to "standardize the abstract,"[75] to this "scholasticism of pedants," the product of this revolutionary government which was the "triumph of pure reason and of practical unreason";[76] it was necessary to recognize, first of all, that social groups" possessed the natural right to govern themselves, for they were facts of nature. All that they lack today is what has been taken from them.[77]

It was necessary to reform the State by recognizing that it was not a collective person, endowed with an autonomous will, but "an arbiter between collective and individual persons." The State therefore had to return to its most traditional functions, "specialize" in the political sphere, that is, in matters common to all groups in the nation (Defense and Currency), and in the "automatic, public services such as the mails."[78] The legitimate functions of the new State coincided with its traditional functions as stated by democratic theory. But their meaning was not exactly the same. They formed by far the greatest common denominator of the interests of the members of the national community, but these members, the elementary units of society, were no longer individuals: they were "groups" (according to the right-wing) or "persons" (according to the personalists, the *Esprit* group), that is, "total men," the irreducible products of social history and of nature. The locus of the initial transcendence was no longer the Nation but the "natural group," guild, family, etc. Only here could a common measure be found, a common natural language among persons. There lay the only possible source of any representation.

Two problems arose at that point, for which it was necessary somehow to find a solution: the first concerned the procedures for appointing the representatives of the natural group, or the persons intended to become its spokesmen at the State level. The second problem concerned communication between these representatives, since what had been their common measure appeared to have been lost. There was only one way to elude these questions. This was to take a pragmatic view of the political sphere (that of the emulators of Christian personalism) and reduce politics to problems of management, make decision a matter of knowledge and method, not one of legitimacy, in other words, rely entirely on specialists who, knowing the methods for discovering the laws of nature, would place humanized reason at the service of man. Thus the idea of a "sobered," "de-dogmatized" reason led to the question of the legality of decision-making procedures and that of the technical competence of the decision-makers. It was symptomatic of this approach that the personalists as well as the various humanist reforming tendencies (for example, the *X-Cris* group or the *Esprit* group) bothered little about questions of legitimacy, while right-wing thinkers were obliged to found their idea of a new social order on a different type of approach.

To the first question (on procedures for appointment), the answers were as varied as the ideological inclinations that produced them, and were drawn from the complete "repertory" of legitimacy. Some (the fascists) proposed the natural selection of charismatic leaders, others (royalists, Maurrasians) were for appointment by tradition, and others again (defenders of certain forms of occupational and regional corporatism) were for a pragmatic electoral procedure, that is, one stripped of the democratic "mystique of figures." But all were agreed in considering that the natural groups and corporations had to be the masters of their procedures for appointment.

As for the practical criteria for recognizing "natural" groups, and the problem that the various levels of a person's membership (occupational and regional, for example) would probably overlap, their views generally remained vague or confused.

The second question—concerning communication—received two types of answer: if universal reason was no longer guaranteed by individual reason, two possibilities remained. It might be considered that the groups only needed to work together in a restricted sphere called "the political" sphere: in that case, they needed to share only a specialized language which had no claim to universality. Hence it was necessary that the "politician should no longer dominate the professional."[79]

The other type of solution consisted in identifying communication among natural groups with a community of destiny of a superior type. It should not be surprising then that corporatist philosophy often went along with nationalism, which helped to reconstitute what had been lost through corporatism, namely a common measure between the will of the groups and the Common Good. What remained to be found was the medium of national expression. This could only be a charismatic leader or one appointed by national tradition. The solution with the widest currency in France was undoubtedly the latter one, expressed by Maurras, who pleaded for the restoration of monarchy, for a return to traditional legitimacy rooted in the history of the nation. It was not that he believed in the "divine right of kings" but, to him, "the monarchy, within the framework of a natural policy" was the best embodiment of national continuity. He suggested placing "at the head of the State, not entities born of numbers but a person, that is, a man framed by his family, the basic social unit, by his profession, the profession of King."[80]

In every instance, at the level of groups, of "re-humanized" persons, or of the Nation, what everyone rejected violently was the dictatorship of figures, the symbol of abstract reason, the carrier of "democratic decadence, daughter of numbers and quantities."[81] This story, which culminated with the disaster of the Second World War, but which lingered on throughout the period of the Fourth Republic, tells of how the French classical democratic doctrine fell into contradiction in the political sphere, just as it did in the economic one. Like price, the vote here lost its symbolic value. Just as the laissez–faire representations of the economic sphere could not withstand the growth of the big firms, so the doctrines of political democracy could not withstand the power of interest groups and the development of the Welfare State.

An Attempt at Synthesis: Representing the Vote, the Opinion Poll and Politics "In Representation"

Radical Socialism: Another Try

General de Gaulle's access to power in 1958 marked the real end of the Third Republic. Its extension, the Fourth Republic, had tried, in the aftermath of the war and in the face of corporatist philosophy, to restore democracy in line with the thinking of critics like Tardieu. At the same time, it had laid the foundations of a new pragmatism soon to be called technocracy, in the name of a humanistic economic philosophy, derived from the X-Cris group and the *Ecoles des Cadres d'Uriage* and, beyond that, from the Mendès–France interlude.

The Fourth Republic had given women the vote. It had established proportional representation, which was the perfect achievement of the idea of sociological representation, but had also led to the development of the state administration. Thus the Fourth Republic had deepened the radical-socialist contradiction without being able to resolve the problem of legitimacy that it posed from the standpoint of democratic doctrine. General de Gaulle's access to power constituted the second attempt to resolve the problem that had been formulated between the wars.

De Gaulle or Representing Power

The meaning of the vote underwent a radical change under Gaullism. National legitimacy, a tradition embodied in a man, existed before the vote. Charisma and tradition were the two pillars of Gaullist legitimacy. "Under the monarchy, by virtue of a traditional principle acknowledged by all, including those who rose in revolt, heredity made the king the sole source of powers, even when he conferred rights or delegated powers. But in my case, it was without hereditary right, without a plebiscite, without an election, but simply in response to the silent but imperative call of France, that I had formerly been led to take the reponsibility for her defense, her unity, and her destiny. If I have now assumed the country's highest office, it is because, since then, I have come to be accepted as its final refuge."[82] From this viewpoint, the vote was the procedure by which the people gave and renewed their ovation to the one who embodied the nation: ". . . because my office, as now constituted, is the product of my own initiative and the sentiment which existed towards me in the national consciousness, it is essential that a fundamental accord should exist and be maintained between the people and me."[83] Whence the idea of electing the President by universal suffrage. Whence the referendum whose approval the historic leader needs to pursue his mission.

The legitimacy of the leader called for permanent confirmation, for he was the embodiment of tradition by his charisma, not by hereditary right. From this point of view, de Gaulle's preferences were highly Maurrassian as a man of the hour, he did not enjoy a permanent legitimacy on which national institutions could be based. This was the problem that he expressed at the end of his last book: "All this raised in the most disturbing way the question of what would become of the country when I disappeared, and with me, the phenomenon consisting of an effective authority at the head of the State, legitimized by events and identified with the faith and the hope of the French people."[84]

Without the permanent legitimacy entrusted or codified by tradition, the election of the President by direct universal suffrage and the referendum acquired an important symbolic value. They were the elements that confirmed the charismatic leader in a society that was profoundly steeped in the idea that the people were the ultimate judge, expressing themselves naturally by the vote, the objective instrument of democracy: "Now while I was convinced that sovereignty belongs to the people, provided they express themselves directly and as a whole, I refused to accept that it could be parcelled out among the different interests represented by the parties."[85]

In this sense, it may be said that the conception of representation brought into play by de Gaulle was a "feudal" one: "it deploys the public sphere (by linking it) to the attributes of the person, to insignia . . . to a style, . . . an attitude, . . . a type of rhetoric, in a word, to a strict code of "noble" behaviour. . . . The people are not totally excluded, they are constantly present in the streets. Representation is addressed to an entourage for whom it is deployed."[86] The Gaullist conception no longer had much to do with the classical democratic doctrine in which the impersonal law of nature was supposed to be realized through the vote; but it was related in many ways to the Medieval and traditional view of representation as the embodiment in one man of the higher principle of legitimacy which he displayed physically by his tangible attributes. "Words like Greatness, Sovereignty, Majesty, Glory, Dignity and Honour seek to designate the singular nature of this being, capable of providing a representation."[87] The pomp with which General de Gaulle surrounded himself, and which caused both amusement and irritation can be understood in this light.[88]

The private and public domains, so carefully segregated in the system of representation of the bourgeoisie, were intermixed throughout the development of the State, to the point where state encroachment on the private domain was violently denounced by all.[89] From then on, there could no longer be any question, unless it was to perpetuate the crisis of legitimacy, of justifying the State by its subordination to the political sphere, which was overwhelmed from all sides. The omnipotent State had need of overall recognition. The State was legitimate because it belonged to the "intendancy" of the Prince invested with legitimate omnipotence.

The constitutional consequences of the embodiment of national will. We know the contempt in which de Gaulle held politicians and fancy talkers, "the jugglers with doubts and reservations, the conjurers of the lecture hall and the editorial column, the acrobats of demagogy."[90] whom he lost no occasion to needle. This contempt was inherited directly from the Maurassian conception of power, which saw the Assembly as nothing but pantomime and vested interests. Bearing this in mind, the three types of complementary positions that he adopted towards political life become perfectly clear.

He rejected the idea that the Assembly could constitute the "sociological representation" of the country. He therefore abandoned the pragmatic point of view which the neo-democrats had thought might bring the crisis to an end. For General de Gaulle felt (as the dying Third Republic found out to its sorrow), that the national will cannot be divided. Any such attempt and it disappears to the benefit of negotiation among special interests. The national will was embodied in the person of the President: "The President guarantees national independence, territorial integrity, the observance of treaties and, by his arbitration, the smooth working of the administration and the continuity of the State: this simply expresses the vital role that I play in my eyes and in those of my fellow-citizens."[91] He was the sole master, overseen by the people, of the definition of the Common Good reconciled with the National Will which he incarnated. He was the common measure that the Third and Fourth Republics had lost.

From the vote as an instrument for the designation of representatives, he did not seek political legitimation, which he found elsewhere, but a pragmatic means to relay his personal action to the country." There is a government that 'determines the policy of the Nation.' But everyone knows and expects it to proceed from my choice. Of course there is a Parliament, but the mass of the nation sees nothing there to limit my responsibility."[92] He would always be a firm supporter of the two-round majority voting system which strengthens majorities and dispossesses minorities ("In order to have a majority, one needs an electoral system that will produce one.")[93] For this reason he did not oppose the administration in its meaner tasks of gerrymandering.

The second position, which was always to be his stumbling block, was drawn directly from the ideas that had shaped him: the replacement of party representation by that of "the vital forces." He adopted the idea of work councils and called for their creation; he championed associations,[94] the idea of participation, of economic management by planning, and made himself the inventor of the Economic and Social Council, which he never managed to substitute for the Senate as the Upper House.

The third position concerned his relationship with technology and science. It throws light on the stand he took on the other two points and complements it: de Gaulle thought he could rely on those he called the technicians, that is, especially those senior civil servants, specialists of the general interest, whose role in the ministries grew during this period to the detriment of the "politicians."[95] They were competent people, trained in public disinterestedness by the schools of administration. He placed them at the head of ministries and, in so doing, accentuated the presidential character of the regime which was endowed with an "Administration" increasingly composed of civil servants. An ever smaller proportion of ministers came from the Assembly, and all they found in election was additional of symbolic power. Political personnel became more technical and less "representative." The technical ministries grew considerably. They took charge of economic and social interests that could not be represented *per se* at the political level. De Gaulle thus covered the entire achievement of the projects put forward by this school of thought, which had grown in the thirties with the *X-cris* group, was taken over by the *Ecole des cadres d'Uriage,* and which had given the technicians power and consideration after the war, when parliamentarianism was crumbling.[96]

The departure of this charismatic, tradition-backed personality inexorably brought back the earlier problem: the dual incapacity of political democracy, in a clearly bureaucratic society, to found the legitimacy of power on the impersonal truth of Natural Law and to justify the ubiquity of the bureaucracy.

The "Neo-democratic" Answers

The new princes tried to meet the renewed crisis of democratic political philosophy by coming up in one fell swoop with all the answers that had hitherto been seen as contradictory; the political philosophy of representation tried to meet the renewed crisis of political legitimacy by the simultaneous use of all the available resources of legitimacy.

Representation. The first type of response comes from a context of the type of democracy Tardieu had advocated. It adopted the argument, already rejected by the General, that the nation's political representation is nothing more than the sociological representation of the country. It questioned the extent to which elected representatives were a faithfuly reflected the votes cast. Giscardian democracy thus proposed a variety of measures: making the age of legal majority the same as the legal voting age; increasing the number of women in government; establishing proportional representation in towns of more than 30,000 inhabitants to "ensure greater participation of the citizens in the management of their cities."[97]

Participation and communication. However, the world had changed since Tardieu's time, and it seemed difficult to give up the view of man that had been emerging for a century. Valéry Giscard d'Estaing renewed the profession of faith in man as a totality. "Democratic doctrine does not take contemporary social reality into account ... it gives a partial representation of human nature . . . man engaged in economic and social life is not just a one-dimensional robot with material interests in a narrow sense. Similarly, the citizen engaged in public life is not just a Sleeping Beauty who wakes up every five or seven years to give or withhold his ballot."[98] The theme of the "society of communication and participation" in a "community of free and responsible men"[99] with a view to "individual fulfillment" led Mr. Giscard d'Estaing into a series of brilliant analyses which recalled those produced by the language of MBO in the firm: "At this stage of its development, French sociey should be organized with Man as its starting point and for Man . . . the option in favor of the individual should be compatible with the construction of a society of participation and communication . . . the common denominator is the idea of autonomy and responsibility."[100] The total man could not be reduced to the abstract entity represented by the vote; his autonomy and responsibility made it necessary for him to express himself personally; the ideal of participation required permanent and direct consultation; the notion of sociological representation called for the statistical representativity of the population that was consulted.

The new sovereign public opinion. There was only one solution to the continued participation of the whole man: he had to be constantly questioned by opinion polls which were henceforth seen as a necessary and virtually sufficient condition of democratic expression. For the opinion poll provided an exact statistical image of the country. In any case, it could do this, and this is what was asked of it.[101] Thus by exposing its methodological rigor, it easily persuaded its audience of the validity of its conclusions. The opinion poll provided for a circular relationship between the ruler and the ruled, by which the former could keep before the public eye his osmosis with the latter; this is what the governor called opinion and claimed as the source of his legitimacy: "the impulse and the sanction are to be found in opinion. It is opinion that decides where freedom ends and where disorder begins. Its orders are sovereign."[102] Here then was the end of the road that led from the vote as the common measure of *homo suffragans*'s reason, to the opinion poll as a pragmatic means to count the opinions of persons who had become the sole measure of all things.

When political man was now polled, it was no longer his reasons but his sensations and instincts that were of interest. The whole man was a being whose sociology and psychology had to be taken into account. If political discourse no longer had any common measure with reason, the politician looked for a common ground with his audiences. He found them all the more easily as the technical conditions of political communication through the media gave him a spectacular place on the stage. Because his visibility increased, he was exposed to fresh perceptions. He now delivered not only his speech but his whole personality (his manner of being, his look, smile and carriage) to the intellectual and instinctive[103] sagacity of his audience. No longer did the audience assess first of all the credibility of his speech *per se*; rather it assessed the credibility of this particular speech, coming from this particular man. "Speaking to the people without an intermediary, he must of course have the attitude, but also the profound nature, that the people expect of their leaders, for television does not tolerate dissimulation for long."[104] The art of politics thus became, more than ever, a Sophistical art, a body technique as much as a verbal one.

Legitimacy crisis, instinct and consensus. Henceforth, the appeal was as much to instinct as to reason. Unlike the democratic mode of argument, the new ones did not appeal to the reason of public opinion, it sought its resources in matching the conformity of the meaning of its action with public opinion. This was called the "search for consensus." But it is precisely here that it diverged fundamentally from charismatic adhesion: the charismatic leader asks for the ovation of the crowd but does not ask it what he should do. Charismatic adhesion is taken to be spontaneous. Directly invested with power by God and tradition, hence necessarily just, the leader limits himself to ascertaining that the crowd still follows him, and resigns if this is not the case (or establishes a reign of pure force); the leader by consensus probes the heart and minds of his public to read the desire he has helped create by previous action and which he claims to restore in his policy. The leader by consensus, who is none other than the Bureaucrat Prince, is a social psychologist and a showman: his capacity to create a consensus depends on his knowledge of the public and his power of seduction. Hence it is not surprising that the order of cause and effect is of little importance to him, since, henceforth, no one can say which comes first, seduction or public opinion, polled opinion or defined policy.

Since he is no longer sanctified by God, Reason or Tradition, the Bureaucrat Prince's only resource is his capacity to seduce the public by drawing upon all the power of evoking legitimacy by using the methods available to him. Evoking democracy as a tradition is, without doubt, the most efficient of his rhetorical devices.[105] In the opinion poll, he can simulate a vote from which he can extract a simulation of public opinion. He thus constructs his own "consensus" as a simulation of democratic consent; the result of the opinion poll, as our journalists never fail to point out, "is only an image of opinion at a given moment"; the vote was the sanction of a deliberation ordained by reason informed by knowledge. The opinion poll gives the sum of the impressions and instincts shaped in irrationality; the vote conveyed the truth by an act of political reason *par excellence*.

Opinion polls. The image given by the opinion poll is the image of opinion. It reflects to the perception of the politician a symmetrical image of the political activity that shapes it. As a consumer seduced by the images of products in the economic world, the man whose opinion is polled is also a consumer of images in the political sphere, which he regurgitates in the form of answers to survey questions.

"Justice at your service."[106] Thus a French Minister of Justice was seen to defend a plan for judicial reform against the wishes of the judicial profession,[107] using the argument of the mass and the majority in the following terms: "My bill is not made for five thousand judges but for 53 million French men and women."[108] Ruling out technical discussion with the specialists, he related the meaning of his project to French opinion: "Justice is rendered in the name of the people. It cannot be cut off from the deepest sentiments of the French,"[109] Whatever the relation of this opinion to objective fact may be: "Of course, the statistics reveal that the real increase in violence is more pronounced in delinquency than in violent crime. Nonetheless the spreading feeling of insecurity reflects a profound reaction on the part of our fellow-citizens."[110] Consequently, he adopted the goal of "restablishing the equilibrium of the collective conscience shaken by the horror of crime," of "keeping social cohesion intact by increasing punishment of crime."[111] He hoped to protect or rebuild the popular consensus by reacting to the feelings of insecurity as revealed by the opinion polls.[112]

The opponents of the reform replied that if the feeling of the population was to be respected, a complete analysis would show that out of the 81% of the French who felt that violence was on the increase, only 16% of them attributed it to the clemency of the judges, and 55% to the rise in unemployment. Furthermore, these opponents thought the feeling of insecurity largely resulted from a strategy designed "to sell a bad legal product to public opinion, as one would sell any product."[113] In other words, they accused the Minister of Justice of making skillful use of demagogy, of doing good marketing for what they deemed to be a bad product, conceived against the opinion of competent people. They judged the argument that the *vox populi* derived from the opinion poll should be respected to be a fallacious one. They cited another current example in which the death penalty had been abolished in many countries by an act of sovereignty, in spite of unfavorable polls.[114] They inferred from this that the real purpose of the Ministry's action was not the one that was explicitly presented: the real purpose was to get a product accepted by presenting it as reflecting a consensus that had been constructed beforehand through massive advertising directed at opinion so as to attain a threefold goal which had become the political one: "to sell" its product—in this case major (and to them disturbing) innovations in penal repression—, to manage the consensus and to improve its own image with the public. Adopting the language of marketing, these opponents of the bill said: "In reality the victims, and undoubtedly the real targets, of those who framed the bill and of their master, are . . . those poor wretches who have been skillfully driven into panic for the past three or four years with a heavy dose of advertising . . . and once fear has been struck into their hearts, they are told 'Now look at me, I am here, I will save you'."[115]

Although always available as a tool for persuasion, the opinion poll as permanent referendum is not always used—especially when it is unfavorable. Thus, while the Minister of Justice argued with every appearance of conviction that his bill reflected the insecurity felt by the French as revealed in opinion polls, the Prime Minister affirmed its unpopularity, in the name of his own scientific competence and of the unreliability and irrelevance of opinion polls. These arguments would seem contradictory only to those looking for a common relationship to a truth revealed by opinion polls instead of seeing them as an effect of the ever-active pragmatism of the Bureaucrat Prince.

Political marketing. The reign of direct communication between rulers and the ruled transformed the art of government into one of consensus-management; management which implied that opinion was probed and informed in a circular process. The media reconstituted audience accessibility. Henceforth, the politician had no longer to convince opinion of the universal value of his discourse but to seduce by his representation, in which what he actually said occupied only a very limited space. Politics was becoming a show because it was, more than ever, the art of seduction, of persuasion by gesture and speech, the Sophist's art. The politician was a product at the same time as he was the medium of a party brand image.

As such, he of course puts himself in the hands of technicians of political marketing, specialists of opinion polls and market studies. Parties want to be informed about their public (its composition, tastes and expectations); they ask the specialist to define those segments of the population that might be added to their public if they make certain adjustments in behavior or position, to analyze the perception of their "image," the acceptance of a new product, man or program, to find the best "sales talk" and the best man for a given public.

Or, they ask the specialists to prepare suitable images for their products: the visibility provided by the media and by the institutional rules is such that it is at least as necessary for a "party firm" to work at preparing a good label for the party and attractive features for its representatives[116] as it is to proclaim its "objective" qualities. Hence, the rating of politicians will be measured;[117] emphasis will be on the characteristics likely to make up a good profile, and his image will be periodically readjusted to changes in the temperature of public opinion and to the goals in view.

Some will water down their proposals, others will improve their diction, others again will exchange their green eyes for softer, grey ones; and it is said that some even file down their teeth. The image of the party and of its popularity is also polished, for example through galas and rallies. Finally (and in terms of competition this is a big advantage from which French law and professional ethics exclude business firms) "a contrario" arguments may be used: pointing out the ugliness or inefficiency of the other party's "product"; the incapacity of its "salesmen" and the bad reputation of the adversary "firm."

Slips are to be avoided. For in marketing, it is as bad to go too fast as it is to go too slow. Herein lies all the utility of market studies. Thus if a President provokes the ire of the voters by hasty innovations, overlooking the fact that tradition is not yet wholly moribund, and that the enthusiasm of the French for modernity is still fettered by inevitable "sociological sluggishnesses," he must not hesitate to cast off his "relaxed" pull-over for a dull checked suit, bring back Armistice Day celebrations after having over-hastily consigned them to oblivion, and restore the Bastille Day parades to their rightful place, leaving proletarian manifestations to their own legitimacy. In short, to the slightly scandalized question asked in a recent television program:[118] "Can you sell a politician like a packet of washing powder ?" It would seem that the political class, for its part, has replied with a resounding: "Yes."

Notes

1. J.–J. Rousseau, *The Social Contract*, Book III, Ch. IV, Democracy.
2. A process begun much earlier by Duns Scotus and Ockham; cf. for example P. Chaunu, *Le Temps des Réformes*, Paris, Fayard, 1975.
3. J. Locke, *Essay on Civil Government*, quoted in Vachet, *L'Ideologie Libérale*, Paris, Anthropos, 1970, p. 203.
4. Montesquieu, *The Spirit of Laws*, Book I, ch. 1.
5. B. Groethuysen, *Philosophie de la Révolution Française*, Gonthier 1966, p. 99.
6. *Ibid.*, pp. 100–101.
7. Abbé *Mably, Doutes proposés aux philosophes économistes sur l'ordre naturel et essentiel des sociétés politiques,* La Haye, Paris, 1768; in Mably, *Sur la théorie du pouvoir politique*, Editions sociales, Les Classiques du peuple, 1975.
8. In the powerful sense that the term had in the 18th century; cf. for example, J. Habermas, *Strukturwandel der Offentlichkeit*, Hermann Luchterhand Verlag, 1969. Abbé Sieyés, *Qu'est–ce que le Tiers-Etat?* Paris, Société d'histoire de la Révolution française, 1888.
10. Mably, *op. cit.*, p. 173.
11. Condorcet, quoted in R. Rashed, *Mathématiques et Société*, Paris, Herman, 1974, p. 76.
12. R. Rashed, *op. cit.,* p. 77.
13. Mercier de La Rivière, *L'Ordre naturel et essentiel des sociétés politiques*, quoted in Mably, *op. cit.*, p. 165.

14. Constitution of the Year III, article 6.
15. J. Locke, *Second Treatise on Civil Government*, quoted in W. Kendall, *John Locke and the Doctrine of Majority Rule*, Urbana, University of Illinois Press, 1941.
16. Mirabeau, speech on 19th July 1789, *Oeuvres*, Paris, Lecointe et Pougin, 1834.
17. These observations are based on R. Rashed, *op. cit.*, and Condorcet, *Esquisse d'un tableau historique des progrès de l'esprit humain*, Paris, Editions sociales, 1966.
18. *Ibid.*
19. *Encyclopédie méthodique*, article on "Probability," p. 651, quoted in R. Rashed, *op. cit.*
20. *Ibid.*, p. 59.
21. *Ibid.*, p. 46.
22. *Burke's Politics*, Appeals p. 397, quoted in H. F. Pitkin, *The Concept of Representation*, Los Angeles, University of California Press, 1967.
23. B. Groethuysen, *op. cit.*, p. 210.
24. Montesquieu, *The Spirit of Laws*, Book II, ch. II, Of the Republican Government and the Laws in Relation to Democracy.
25. Sir W. Blackstone, *Commentaries of the Law of England*, I, p. 171, quoted in Pitkin, *op. cit.*
26. Montesquieu, *op. cit.*
27. *Ibid.*
28. D'Holbach, article on "Representatives" in the *Encyclopédie ou Dictionnaire raisonné des sciences, des arts et des métiers*, 1751, in *Morceaux choisis*, Editions sociales, Les Classiques du peuple, pp. 219–220.
29. This idea subsequently acquired a great deal of importance. Benjamin Constant expressed it, arguing that the reduction in political importance with the size of the country, the loss of leisure activities linked to the abolition of slavery and to the regularity of commerce restricts the exercise of democracy by "ordinary" individuals to supervision over an active political body. In so doing, he brings out the terms of a contradiction which we shall develop in the second part of this chapter: if politics implies a specialization of activity, then it needs special qualifications which will weaken the possible relation between the representation of the elected representative as a person with the qualities of *all* the individuals in an accomplished, liberal society and the sociological reality of this representation. It is into this abyss that all of political philosophy in the early 20th century was swallowed up. Cf. B. Constant, "De la liberté des anciens comparéeà celle des modernes," speech delivered at the *Athénée royal de Paris* in 1819, in *De la liberté chez les modernes*, Paris, Librairie générale française, Pluriel, 1980, pp. 491–515.
30. J. Habermas, *op. cit.*, pp. 65 and 95.
31. F. Furet, éditorial in *Le Débat*, 1st November 1979.
32. F. Furet and J. Ozouf, in *Lire et écrire*, Editions de Minuit (coll. Le Sens commun), 1977, show this with respect to educational policy under the Third Republic for example.
33. E. Herriot, *Créer*, Paris, Payot, 1920, vol. II, pp. 183–184. See S. Bernstein, *Histoire du parti radical*, Paris, Presses de la FNSP, 1980. Herriot is favorable to the de jure equality of citizens, transcending material differences and individual inequalities, and this makes him the direct heir of the *doctrinaires* of

the Enlightenment. He gives primacy to the political realm, in which he sees the indispensable arbitration among categories in the name of a national will. In this respect, as in many others, he is opposed to corporatism.

34. See below in this chapter.

35. See Chapter 8.

36. On the *solidariste* doctrine, see for example *Essai d'une philosophie de la solidarité*, lectures and discussions prepared by L. Bourgeois and A. Croiset, Paris, Alcan, 1902.

37. This definition is given by L. Bourgeois in his preface to F. Buisson, *La Politique Radicale*, Paris, V. Giard, 1908, quoted in A. J. Tudesq, *La Démocratie en France depuis 1815*, Paris, PUF (coll. L'Historien), 1971.

38. Herriot, *op. cit.*, Vol. I, p. 14, quoted in J. T. Nordman, "Le radicalisme, créature d'Edouard Herriot," in *Edouard Herriot, études et témoignages*, Paris, Publications de la Sorbonne, 1975. For Herriot, "only science will be able to preserve the reconciliation wrought by patriotism among the French." *Ibid.*, I, p. 14.

39. Herriot says, for example: "It now seems certain that a great country like France can no longer be satisfied with permitting the play of free competition, a point that was, for a long time, the economists' ideal." *Ibid.*

40. A. Tardieu, *La Révolution à refaire, le souverain captif*, Paris, Flammarion, 1936, p. 119.

41. A. Dami, "Crise de la démocratie et réforme de l'Etat," *Esprit*, No. 22, July 1934, quoted in J.–L. Loubet de Bayle, *Les Non–conformistes des années 30*, Paris, Seuil, 1970.

42. R. de Jouvenel, *La République des camarades*, 1914; Geneva, Slatkine Reprints (coll. Ressources), 1979, p. 37.

43. *Ibid.*

44. Constitution of 1791, chapter III, section III, article 7.

45. Jouvenel, *op. cit.*, p. 41.

46. *Ibid.*, p. 42.

47. A. Thibaudet, *La République des professeurs*, 1924; Geneva, Slatkine Reprints (coll. Ressources) 1979, p. 162; cf. p. 92, n. 2.

48. Tardieu, *op. cit.*, quoting Auguste Comte, p. 238.

49. *Ibid.*, p. 217.

50. *Ibid.*, p. 219.

51. But opinions are divided on this point. Comte recommends action where Spencer does not see the possibility of it, for, to him, the movement of progress is ineluctable and independent of human action.

52. This, for example, is Durkheim's point of view in the preface to the second edition of *The Division of Labor in Society*, New York, Free Press, 1964. "A moral or juridical regulation essentially expresses, then, social needs that society alone can feel; it rests in a state of opinion, and all opinion is a collective thing, produced by collective elaboration. For anomy to end, there must then exist, or be formed, a group which can constitute the system of rules actually needed. . . . Neither political society, in its entirety, nor the State can take over this function; economic life, because it is specialized and grows more specialized every day, escapes their competence and their action. An occupational activity can be efficaciously regulated by a group intimate enough with it to know its functioning, feel all its needs. . . .

53. See Chapter 7.

54. Thus Durkheim says: "What we especially see in the occupational group is a moral power capable of containing individual egos, of maintaining a spirited sentiment of common solidarity in the consciousness of all the workers, of preventing the law of the strongest from being brutally applied to industrial and commercial relations," p. 10, and further on, "There is even reason to suppose that the corporation will become the foundation or one of the essential bases of our political organization . . . the elementary division of the State, the fundamental political unity," *op. cit.*

55. Tardieu, *op. cit.*, p. 211.

56. *Ibid.*

57. Lagardelle, *Plans*, No. 1, January 1931, quoted in Loubert de Bayle, *op. cit.*

58. Tardieu, *op. cit.*, p. 226.

59. Jouvenel, *op. cit.*, p. 37: "One is an agent of the people as one would be an agent of a business."

60. Tardieu, *op. cit.*, p. 276.

61. *Ibid.*, p. 100.

62. J. Bentham, *Collected Works*, London, Athlone Press, 1968. It should not be here forgotten that Bentham was made a French citizen by the Convention and that he corresponded with Condorcet, L. Reybaud, *op. cit.*, vol. II, p. 202.

63. This point of view was expressed during the Revolution, among the Physiocrats for example, in the words of Mirabeau: "In its whole as in its parts, the copy should retain the proportions of the original," speech to the *Etats de Provence*, 1789. This view was also widespread in England and the United States. Cf. J. Adams, Letter to J. Penn, Works, Boston, 1852–65, IV, p. 205, quoted in Pitkin, *op cit.*.

64. Pitkin, *ibid.*

65. Tardieu, *op. cit.*, p. 211.

66. *Ibid.*, p. 210.

67. D. de Rougemont, *Politique de la personne*, new edition, Paris, "Je sers," 1946, in Loubet de Bayle, *op. cit.*

68. J. Touchard, in *Esprit*, No. 18, April 1934, *ibid.*

69. These were "the family, the vehicle of a living tradition; the *commune*, a territorial location; the profession; the native region to which is attached the irreducible sentiment of belonging to the land." *Ordre nouveau*, No. 9, 1934, *ibid.*

70. E. Mounier, Letter to P. Archambault, *L'Aube*, 27 February, 1934, *ibid.* The "anticonformists" of the thirties shared a common opposition to free-market society which led some (the reactionaries) into a sharp form of anticapitalism (calling for a return to the land, traditionalism) and others (the *Esprit* and *X-Crise* groups, those who were to found the *Ecole des cadres d'Uriage*) to the idea of a reconciliation of classes through industrial control in the service of man.

71. La Tour du Pin, *ibid.*

72. J. Maxence, *Demain, la France*, Paris, Grasset, 1934.

73. A. Dami, *Esprit*, No. 21, quoted in Loubert de Bayle, *op. cit.*

74. For example, T. Maulnier in *Reaction*, No. 1, April 1930, *ibid.*

75. The latter expression is that of Daniel–Rops, *Ordre Nouveau*, No. 1, May 1933, *ibid.*; the former is from Mounier, *Esprit*, March 1934, *ibid.*

76. Taine, quoted by Loubet de Bayle, *op. cit.*

77. L. Salleron, *Naissance de l'Etat corporatif*, Paris, Grasset, 1942, quoted in S. Berger, *Les Paysans contre la politique*, Paris, Seuil, 1975.

78. E. Mounier, *Esprit* No. 19, April 1934, quoted by Loubet de Bayle, *op. cit.*
79. "Elected by the representatives of all the professions, the deputies cannot devote themselves to the defence of a particular profession and must seek compromises capable of satisfying everybody. So long as this is the case, so long as the politician dominates the professional, our grievances, our action, the displays of our sufferings will come up against the walls of this palace," Guébriant, *Ar voor goz*, 1st January 1935, quoted by S. Berger, *op. cit.*
80. *Revue du XXème Siècle*, No. 3, June 1933. From the teachings of modern biology, the knowledge of the laws of natural selection, Maurras claimed to derive a condemnation of egalitarian democracy and the fact that the king is the person who, by his education and family history, is most "fit" to represent the nation.
81. T. Maulnier, *Reaction*, No. 1, April 1930, "Manifesto."
82. Charles de Gaulle, *Memoirs of Hope: Renewal and Endeavour*, New York, Simon and Schuster, 1971.
83. *Ibid.*
84. *Ibid.*
85. *Ibid.*
86. Habermas, *op. cit.*
87. *Ibid.*
88. Every individual or group who embodies national sovereignty must *represent* it. He can do nothing but this, as in a constitutional monarchy or as under the Fourth Republic in France. The crisis of the U.S. presidency, in recent years, has been seen to be accompanied by a desacralization and simplification of presidential rituals. One of Ronald Reagan's first acts as president–elect, which symbolically reflected his intention to restore the authority of the presidency, was to require visitors to the White House to wear ceremonial dress.
89. See Chapter 6.
90. De Gaulle, *op. cit.*, p. 140.
91. *Ibid.*, p. 284.
92. *Ibid.*
93. *Ibid.*, p. 38.
94. *Ibid.*, p. 114–115.
95. V. Aubert, "Les spécifiés du personnel politique français," mimeographed, CNRS–Sorbonne, May 1980.
96. See Chapter 6.
97. R. Barre, asked to reflect on this point by the French President during his press conference on 14th June 1978, in an interview with *Le Progrès*, Lyon, quoted in *Le Monde*, 16th April, 1980.
98. V. Giscard d'Estaing, *Démocratie française*, Paris, Larousse, 1977.
99. These are chapter headings from V. Giscard d'Estaing, *ibid.*
100. *Ibid.*, Preface to the second edition.
101. It has often been noted that all the discussions on opinion polls which, among other things, have led to ad hoc supervisory commissions, have centered not on the nature of the political expression permitted by the poll but on the technical validity of the sampling and questioning procedures. See for example P. Bourdieu, "Questions de politique," *Actes de la recherche en sciences sociales*, No. 16, September 1977.
102. V. Giscard d'Estaing, *op. cit.*, p. 158. Our italics.
103. This is a social instinct, of course.

104. G. Pompidou, *Le Noeud gordien*, Paris, Plon, 1975.

105. But the argument of tradition can still be used: for example by stressing one's noble origins, as Louis XVII did when he retrieved the Capetian lineage, going beyond Napoleon the trouble-maker to join up again with the pre-eminent legitimacy of blood, beyond bourgeois democracy. If this argument makes little impact, it is undoubtedly because the French tradition is at present more republican than it is monarchist. Similarly, deprived of personal charisma, one might try to emphasize one's contact with the charismatic leader. The argument has little weight for the nature of charisma is precisely not to teach. Furthermore, if the competition is weak in the former register, it is sharp in the latter.

106. Badge distributed by the French Ministry of Justice in 1979.

107. Among those who condemned the project: the Syndicat des éducateurs (teachers' union), the Grand Orient of France, the bar council, the federation of young lawyers, the magistrates' union and the prosecutors' union.

108. Quoted in the *Journal du dimanche*, 8 June 1980.

109. Letter dated 23 April, 1980, presenting the project to the lawyers.

110. *Ibid.*

111. Explanation of reasons for the *Securité et Liberté* (Safety and Liberty) bill put forward by the then Justice Minister, Mr. Alain Peyrefitte, in 1978.

112. For example the Figaro/SOFRES opinion poll of 30 April, 1980, from which the figures that follow are taken. In an interview with *Le Point*, Mr. Bonnet stated that, while petty crime was on the increase, the rate of major crime had remained stable: "The number of murders is decreasing. It is smaller today than in 1930." In Paris, between 1978 and 1979, crimes and offenses fell by 0.9% and serious crimes amounted to 4% of the total number of crimes and offenses. *Le Point*, 2 June 1980.

113. Casamayor, *Libération*, 12 May 1980.

114. Thus the death penalty was abolished in Germany even though 67% of the population declared to be in favor of it. The corresponding figure in France was 58% in the early eighties.

115. Casamayor, *op. cit.*

116. For example, "French Democracy" or the "Fight for Jobs," etc.—all these are labels that correspond to the idea the "target" has of what would make the candidate attractive.

117. In market research for a "product," everything is designed to attract. The pragmatic value of the figure for the pollsters matches its rhetorical value for the polled. The former involves a play on public opinion by projecting its image, constructed by aggregation, on public opinion; it involves rhetorical value because it produces effects which, while they are themselves difficult to measure, are no less certain for all that. These are known as the "bandwagon effect," the "withdrawal effect," the "underdog effect," etc.

118. French television program, *Les Dossiers de l'écran*, 23 September, 1980.

Chapter 6

From Bureaucratic Counting to Social Indicators

It is not because a social indicator is sound from a methodological point of view that it will be accepted, it is because it is accepted that it will be considered sound from a methodological point of view.

Administration in the Age of Liberalism

The laissez-faire principles included the necessity for the State to maintain the work and the public institutions that an individual or a small number of individuals would have no interest in maintaining, or the profit from which would not cover expenditure.[1] The State was the necessary evil of the democratic stand in civil society. Evil because it eluded the natural regulations of economic exchange. Necessary because it guaranteed the workings of exchange in the civil society. The administration was the sole institution in which man defined empirical procedures in order to collect and distribute resources. As the only social institution with an organic character and pragmatic ends, it was always suspect. For its complexity could easily hide a power which could escape the checks of legitimate power. Insubordination was a permanent risk in this set of institutions which derived their legitimacy solely from their submission. The administration was the mechanical arm of the civil society in spheres where the natural force of exchange failed as the regulating mechanism of nature.

In the relation of the administration to the civil society, the potential insubordination of the former might lie in the improper exercise of the power to constrain which it received from the political realm, for the purpose of collecting resources in order to carry out communal tasks; in the internal organization of administration, insubordination might lie in irregularity, that is, in non-compliance with standard procedures of action established by the law of the sovereign authority. Administration had the

97

power to enforce the law, and the administration itself had to apply the law. As an instrument of social order, it controlled civil society by the organization of the police, justice, the army and finances. By the force of public power conferred on it, administration could objectify the subjects of power whenever and to whatever extent they permitted it to do so. "The police department is instituted to maintain civil order, liberty, property, individual safety. Society taken in the mass is the object of its solicitude."[2] Administration named and counted in order to act, but it did so at the behest of the citizens or their representatives. The collection of taxes was decided by a law; census was organized by a law; a law again made it possible to raise armies. In the theoretical framework of the democratic principles, the administration was overseen in each of its acts by the civil society. Moreover, the civil servant was the emanation of the political sphere and was to remain so, in theory, until fairly late in the nineteenth century.[3]

But in practice, as administration became organized, as it acquired complexity, the injunctions of political authority had to be relayed by regulations that were seen as extensions of law. Inasmuch as the civil servant received a *delegation of power*, the rules had to be formalized in such a way that it was possible to work out the legality of his acts as well as to verify them. Thus, in the course of the nineteenth century, the rules began to be framed by which the administration could account for its activity to the legislator publicity and the verification of consistency were the first experiments in administrative law. Both were cultural procedures that sought to restore the openness of the democratic administration. For nothing was more foreign to democratic principles than the notion of administrative secrecy—the spectre of the *Ancien Régime* and the *lettre de cachet*—and nothing was more difficult to uphold than the readibility of administrative acts. A retired senior civil servant put it well at the turn of the century: "the country no longer wants ... masters who order and decide everything arbitrarily. It wants leaders, chosen solely on merit and for the services that they are capable of rendering. ... (It is necessary to replace) shadows by light, mystery by publicity through the organization of the only control that is truly efficient, the control that is organized with the fairly won co-operation of the interested parties."[4]

Counting and Distributing

From this viewpoint, numbers were a way to ensure simultaneously the knowledge of things (with a view to action) and the accountability of acts. The administration counted in order to distribute the men and values that it had collected; it counted in order to distribute its resources among various allocations necessary for upholding social order and the functioning of the markets. It gave an account of the regularity of distribution procedures by means of public accounting, which was gradually developed during the century.

Its search for information, like its activity, stopped here. Its power to objectify subjects was strictly subordinated to its pragmatic prospects. The State administration counted men in order to raise the army and goods and to levy taxes. The counting permitted by the law enabled the administration to collect resources in the civil society by constraint, but did not permit any action *on* the civil society: the State was neutral. It had no inherent economic or social effect. Budgetary distribution was the result of a political negotiation. Taxes depended on the State's needs for resources; the State was the necessary instrument for supplying the budget by a collection based on things and not men: "It is property alone that is charged with the contribution, and the owner is only an agent who pays the contribution for it."[5] The information collected in order to define the amount of the tax also related to "external signs" and not to persons. It was from this viewpoint that the *Constituante* (i.e. the constituent assembly of 1789) conceived the land register, which was implemented from 1807 onwards, to ensure the justice of taxation in the name of the principle that "no property should be exempt from the salutary law of equality."[6]

The administration was therefore devoid of any inherent capacity for action: it represented the *immediate* instrument by which the proper functioning of the civil society was guaranteed. It was not the *manager* of civil society. Moreover, this would have been inconceivable in a doctrine which did not regard the civil society as an organic entity and which therefore could not regard it as the object of management. The information that the administration collected on civil society represented knowledge at a certain point in time. It was unaware of its relationship to the ends of civil society because it was in the hands of the political body. It was the "knowledge of facts without a knowledge of the relationships" that held them together. It was merely the "undigested knowledge of an office clerk."[7]

On the Impossibility of the Concept of an Economic Policy

Because it could not master the relationships among its objects, the administration was unable to take a common measure of things: it counted within the natural and obvious boundaries of each of its spheres of action: men, materials and values, as the case may be. By the mid–nineteenth century, Vivien was to condemn the practice of administrative statistics, which had begun to overflow the limits and modalities assigned to it by the principles of democratic rights. "Statistical research should be circumscribed within the ambit of official, authentic and uncontestable facts that can be verified. ... Draw up judicial statistics, statistics on prisons, on charitable establishments, no one will utter a word against them; but if you claim also to record industrial and agricultural production, to point out the causes of population movements, you will gather only hypotheses."[8]

The democratic system of liberties repressed the idea of calculating national wealth. This idea had been the grand project of the Physiocrats and came back as the grand project of the postwar planners. Under the *Ancien Régime*, "State counsellors (thought that) the concept of value provided an answer to one problem of the Prince: the assessment of national wealth."[9] In the democratic view of society where every citizen was a king, and therefore all–powerful, but equally powerless because of the omnipotence of his fellow citizens, pragmatic counting of power had lost its earlier purpose. For the way to achieve the good society lay no longer in the *voluntary action* of the Prince in culture but in the *natural conjunction* of all the individual omnipotences in the market through the natural medium of communication, money. The market was not the site of the purposeless counting of the power of actors who had no strategies, but the place of exchange between these actors freed of all social ties. It was only much later, in the mid–twentieth century, that these individuals were to be economically reintegrated into society and become the agents of national accounting.

For the time being, nothing was more foreign to democratic thought about exchange in civil society and management than the idea of counting power, and that of organizing it through economic policy. This would have been an *abuse of power*. J.–B Say said as much when he suggested that "the ideal government is a government that costs little and acts little."[10] Politics could not be economical: the economy however was political. It governed the political sphere. In concrete terms, it was the economy that forced the State administration to make the financial adjustments that resulted from its functioning.

The only interventions that remained legitimate were those that could be likened to police regulations and enactments. In the economic sphere, these amounted to the suppression of practices that hindered the unhampered formation of prices [11] and caused excessive price increases.[12] In the social sphere, they related to those tasks on which communications depended (standard public works and installations such as those relating to land management, the highways system) and the setting of standards (codes and regulations, weights and measures).

The Nature of Information

The intervention of the State in civil society, the knowledge that it is allowed to acquire about civil society were limited to the strict needs of national defense and the enforcement of civil order: for national defense, the census of men; for collecting State resources, the census of things; for civil order (the action of the police in its narrow sense), records on hiring, strikes, crime and vagrancy.[13] Quite naturally, the gathering of these various types of information came under the Ministry of the Interior.[14]

Immediately after the Revolution, the Encyclopedist thinkers of the Enlightenment had thought that they could appropriate this information for the purposes of gaining scientific knowledge about the world, but Napoleon's administrative organization—with representatives of the state or prefects in each administrative area—was soon to prevent them from doing so.[15] The prefects rejected offers of collaboration from learned societies and, furthermore, emphasized the pragmatic nature of their interest in statistics by substantially restricting its fields of study to those areas that were directly useful to policing tasks.[16] Thus economic information was totally absent from the State's spheres of interest except as an indicator of social peace.[17] Moreover, for the first six decades of the nineteenth century, it was restricted to information from private sources.[18]

Similarly, the State lacked social data.[19] Social statistics were gathered by sources other than the State: chambers of commerce, statistical and philanthropical societies.[20] For, as a moral obligation, charity belonged to the private sphere: it was a duty of individuals and not a right of persons receiving public assistance. The "great transformation" introduced by the free-market system, brought about a radical difference in the treatment of poverty.[21] Thus the social statistics of the State were restricted mainly to prisons, justice and the indicators of public peace.

This was to be the main tenet of laissez-faire ideology up to the end of the nineteenth century even though, beginning with laws (on labor regulation), the interest of the State in social matters[22] began to be manifested in an ever-increasing number of ways. This tenet stated that poverty was a necessary evil, the sanction of competition and of liberty in the market. Quételet asserted that when "states wish to regulate charity and formulate laws on it, they are heading straight for a goal opposite to the one that they wish to attain."[23] The echo of this concern was to be heard at the end of the century among tenants of laissez-faire ideology, Leroy-Beaulieu, for example, who attacked the assuming of social problems by the State, which he accused of undertaking "a task of deplorable social disintegration by replacing the duty of the rich by the alleged right of the poor."[24]

The Administrative Routine

To accomplish these limited but indispensable tasks, an administrative *organization* was needed. This was dangerous because it threatened to conceal within its depths deviations from its appointed task. It was dangerous because it eluded the natural regulation of civil society. Thus it could act only under the close control of the political sphere, as regards its fields of action (against the excesses of power) and procedures (against irregularities). "Democracy is distrustful," Vivien was to say.[25] It sets up principles of vigilance.

With regard to the decision–making process, the administration gradually organized its own routine. For, in the abstract order of democratic principles, the tasks of administration were immutable. Only the cases to be dealt with, the specific situations, changed. Thus the idea of an administrative norm was conceivable. The administration was immutable because its problems were immutable. It could establish the eternity of an impersonal rule that matched the natural eternity of the market. Supervising the administration thus came down to ensuring the impersonal nature of the application of rules, eliminating the subjectivity of officials in the exercise of their functions, just as making the free-labor market work came down to stripping men of all their humanity once they crossed the threshold of the workshop. The civil servant was not asked to think but to apply the rules. This movement gradually led to the pragmatic formulation of an internal rule of conduct for civil servants, which was to be formalized only at the end of the century.[26]

Administrative routine, far from being abusive, thus rendered administration acceptable to democratic ideology from the moment that it acquired a certain complexity. Adam Smith had already said as much with regard to the affairs of big firms, when he wrote that they must obligatorily be conducted by agents and that this require that their duties be clearly set out and defined so that the partners would not lose all control over them.[27]

Accounting Controls

Organizing controls meant organizing the memory of administrative acts. If there was one field in which the problem was a crucial one, it was that of resource distribution: "He who has the right to vote taxes necessarily has the right to examine whether he is being asked for the needs of the State, to check these needs, the expenditures and their motives, to supervise the use of funds and to see to it that they have not been diverted from the ends to which they were granted."[28] Thus the establishment of the rules of public accounting and the rationalization of its connection with budgetary procedure were to be among the major tasks of the first half of the nineteenth century. With the unification of accounting rules,[29] the return to the division of labor in budget matters between paymasters and accountants,[30] the growth of the corps of comptrollers and inspectors[31], and the creation of the rule of annual recurring budgets,[32] the State acquired a set of coherent instruments for the organic financial control of administration. Responsibility for actions could be assigned by analyzing conformity between ministerial accounts and general accounts; a detailed account of each ministry's expenditure was made public before Parliament by the report of the *Cour de Comptes* (the National Audit Office) established in 1807,[33] and by budget discussion, when large sums of money were involved. Thus the rule by which "nothing that is public should be exempt from the regulation of public accounting"[34] was put into practice.

The legislature was to verify that the administration had properly abided by the orders that it had given in voting the budget and by the procedural rules for distribution. It was the *regularity* of the action, and not its efficiency, that was subjected to scrutiny. Just as the notion of economic policy managing civil society was inconceivable, so the notion of "administrative management" was meaningless, since the administrative act was limited to the application of procedures.

So long as democratic principles remained credible to account for the administration's role, numbers retained then descriptive character in it. They were the essential characteristic of categories. A privileged characteristic, because they were evident and natural. Numbers were what made the observations of the administration natural. They represented *information* gathered and read with the prospect of action (of collection and distribution) and *a posteriori* control (of regularity). Administrative numbers were a *cultural* entity. They were a social instrument and not a natural medium of communication.

Public Service

The Golden Age

"Instead of the six ministries of 1790, there are now ten; there have even been twelve for some time. And nothing proves that matters will be stopped here, since several members of the far left were proposing the creation of a Labour Ministry some months ago."[35] Thus spoke, in scandalized tones, the Vicomte d'Avenel, who was the author in 1891 of yet another addition to that (already large) body of works entitled *Administrative Reform*. What best characterized the administration, from the end of the nineteenth century, was undoubtedly the extension of its field of action. Yet it had not ceased to grow since the French Revolution, and especially after the major turning point of the 1848 revolution. After 1914 it grew constantly. Budgetary expenditure, assessed at 15% of national income in 1914 (which was at the time poorly known) amounted to 45% in 1945. In the immediate aftermath of the First World War, this extension already led some people to expose the fiction of Parliament's sovereignty with its incapacity henceforth to propel and to control such a huge machine.[36]

Intervention and general interest. The extension of the State's functions was matched by changes in the discourse that accounted for administrative action: from a language of repressive order, it became a language of prevention. The Garrison–State turned into an interventionist State. Herein lies the whole story of the development of social legislation [37] at an increasingly sustained pace, from the first laws on child labor in 1841 to the creation of the Labour Ministry in 1906. A story that includes all of Jules Ferry's laws of the 1880's on free, compulsory and secular education.[38] Similarly, in the economic sphere, the State took an interest in specific endangered categories of producers. The Ministry of Commerce and Crafts was established in 1880; the Agriculture Ministry may be said to have been truly born in 1881. The granting of public service concessions (railways in 1842, urban transport and telegraphy in 1848) by the State was stepped up. The State developed economic regulation.[39] So striking was this development that H. Spencer, that champion of the free-market society, reported the astonishment of the English delegates to the 1883 Trade Unions congress at the extent of French economic regulation, which they deemed to be "a shame and a monstrosity for a republican nation."[40]

The social sphere, which liberalism had been unable or unwilling to see as more than a residue, acquired a place of its own. In the realm of political discourse, the development of the so–called theory of solidarity[41] also reflected the extension of administrative intervention. However, at this time when a new, organicist conception of society was flourishing in France, the economy had not yet come to be seen as a State matter. It had been pre-eminently the realm of the civil society, and so it continued to be. The State was not invested with power to make *economic policy*. It did not represent itself as a *guide*; at most it was a protector when it used the law for the symbolic maintenance of competitive conditions or when it made good the failings of private enterprise. It even had to guarantee that the extent of its actions did not in any way weaken the "leading role" of civil society in the economic field. Thus, significantly, the principle of the neutrality of public finances was reasserted, by which the State budget was supposed not to have any inherent effect on the economic. Reasserting the strictly political character of the budget debate, the State sought to avert accusations of misuse of power. It was only from the twenties onwards, and especially after the crisis of 1929, that taxation came to be seen as more than a simple financial instrument, that it came to have a new role, in the management of the production, circulation and distribution of goods.[42]

It could henceforth be said that "in the theories of social economy that are gaining favor, established power ceases to be considered as a natural enemy; it appears increasingly as an indefatigable and benevolent auxiliary, as a supporting guardian. There is recognition that it is called upon to guide society towards good and preserve it from evil, to be the active and intelligent promoter of public improvements.[43] Through these developments there emerged a new conception of the role of the State and, concomitantly, of the status of the individual in civil society. The idea emerged that the administration alone possessed the vision of the public good in the long term and that, for this reason, it had a normative role and the monopoly of the search for the general interest beyond special interests. Hence, in support of the growing activity of the administration, there re–emerged a key idea which the free-market social model had got rid of: the idea of the antagonism between special interests and the general interest. The administration henceforth took charge of defending the general interest, of correcting what might be bad in "social nature," of satisfying social needs. In the administrative sphere, there also grew up the notion of social interdependence. The general interest was identified with the satisfaction of collective needs and hence with the regulation of social matters by society. Attaining of the ideals of the French Revolution, liberty and equality, henceforth implied active intervention, and this was not to come about without creating formidable contradictions.

Needs and administrative legitimacy. To begin with, intervention justified the choice of themes by the administration in the name of its knowledge of society's needs. For the administration had already exceeded the limits of the task entrusted to it by the liberal body politic and threatened to elude the supervision which was the condition of legitimacy. This implied that it had to gain knowledge of needs by increasing its means of observing the objective features of social life. This was the condition on which the administration could close the legitimacy gap that it had created by its excesses: by guaranteeing its objectivity, that is, by justifying its acts directly by its knowledge of social *nature*.

Quantification, an expression of the positive scientific method applied to the reading of social facts with a view to pragmatic use, was to play a major role in the service of this task. The quantitative data on which the administration relied were the measurements of positive social laws. If society could be objectified by statistics, this was because it was an objective phenomenon ruled by natural laws. Progress was the product of social laws. What statistical knowledge contributed was still knowledge for action. But the nature of the action had shifted: it has lost its atomistic character. It was no longer just a matter of repression and collection. Like the society on which it worked, it had become total. The action had become that of prevention, promotion and distribution. Statistical information revealed the natural, objective and unambiguous norms of society itself; it provided scientific evidence about the nature of the general interest, for social facts could be dealt with "like things."[44]

From the mid-nineteenth to the mid-twentieth century, the instruments for collecting statistics in the service of administration were developed and refined. For example, while the first reliable data on public education appeared in 1829, it was only in 1876 that a statistical *system* of education began to prevail with the establishment of a "standing committee for statistics on primary education" in the Ministry of Education.[45] Similarly, 1874 saw the adoption of a law that laid the foundations of the Inspection du Travail (Labor Inspectorate) and entrusted it with a set of statistical tasks. The Supreme Labor Council was established in 1895. The explanatory statement on which the law was based stated that "absolute theories are daily losing credit. All countries which are concerned that struggles between capital and labor should be resolved peacefully are striving to gather precise information on working conditions."

Consequently, the law gave this office the mission of "collecting, coordinating . . . and publishing all information that relates to labor and concerns . . . the organization and remuneration of labor, it relations with capital, the workers' conditions."[46] It was on labor that the greatest effort of information gathering was concentrated.[47] In the economic sphere, the means for gathering statistical information in France remained very limited until the eve of the second World War. The first great decennial survey on farming was launched in 1852.[48] It was not until the middle of the July Monarchy (i.e. the period covered by the reign of Louis-Philippe from July 1830 to January 1848) that industrial statistics (in the form of annual data on the mining industry), which had been given up since 1789 made a timid reappearance.

Then came the industrial surveys of 1844-45 and 1860.[49] There was just one production census in 1861-65, which covered industrial activities. There was also an enumeration of establishments as a by–product of the population census; finally there was some information on farm and industrial production, routed through administrative channels at the municipal level and through professional bodies. After the failure of a survey in 1932, which was attributed to 'dogmatic free-market principles'[50] and the lack of attention to facts, it was finally decreed in 1938 that occupational groups and firms would be required to send certain statistical data to the administration.[51]

The need for systematic information in the social sphere gradually separated data collecting from the tasks that were delegated to administration by political authority. It was henceforth necessary to assemble data on subjects such as labor as exhaustively and as systematically as possible. The administrative tasks of information gathering tended to become autonomous at the level of each ministry. However, no *overall* coherence was as yet sought. The links became weaker between the collection of data and the precise orders from the political authority on action to take. The justification of information systems was related to the need for *a priori* knowledge of the social needs that had to be satisfied.

The preventive state and status of the citizen. The administration moved from a repressive to a preventive view of its relation with civil society. The consequences of this shift were profound. First because it shifted the centre of gravity of power. The individual earlier defined as a *subject of law* became a *subject of need* for the administration: it therefore had to be treated as an object of study and a consumer of services. The free–market theoriticians were to say that the State was trying to do him good "in spite of himself." He was denied the full autonomy of decision which had been the very source of the representation of power in a democratic and free-market society. The administration infiltrated the private life of citizens. "It is the citizen who is enlighted by reason, who is guided by his own interest, who is cautioned by the law; it is the citizen who is suspect. It is the government which can be led astray by so many illusions, which can have only general views and which is in no condition to enter into purely private matters with clear–sightedness and solicitude, which is entrusted with conducting the business of the citizen."[52] As the object of administrative care, the citizen ran the risk of abdicating his responsibility as a subject of the law. "For public authority, there is no greater cause of weakness than the exercise of prevention. It becomes responsible for everything in which it has had a hand, . . . the object of all complaints and the presumed cause of all sufferings. Permission is seen as a guarantee of success and the administration is accused of miscalculations that it could not have forseen . . . for their part, citizens lose the habit of self-reliance . . . they depend on public power, which has become the dispenser of industries and rights."[53]

The relation of the citizen to the State was altered. Since the administration thereafter adopted *social need* and no longer the *legal norm* as its criterion for action, nothing could stop its intrusion into the civil society: "It is not enough for a thing to be recognized as good, or even excellent, by the social body for the said social body to place it freely at the disposal of all its members, and even less for it to force them to use it. Ordering compulsory education is like ordering compulsory cleanliness, or compulsory gymnastics as in Sparta; for agile and strong citizens are no less useful to the State than educated citizens. Once such a road is embarked upon, there is no longer any reason to stop."[54] It was indeed improper intervention by the administration that was being called illegitimate: "The consequence of the entirely preventive (new State system) is to increase the powers of the public authorities ... the old repressive system needed only judicial authority. ... Between these two systems, the choice could not be in doubt. Only the latter satisfied human liberty and dignity ... the dominant feature of the preventive system is mistrust, a sentiment that is injurious to those who cause it and humiliating to the people whose legislation is inspired by it. Mistrust directed against individuals leads to absolute confidence in the government. On what is this confidence based? Might it be true that wisdom, foresight and enlightenment exist only in the repositaries of public power? There is a curious contradiction here."[55]

Public service actors. A curious contradiction indeed from the standpoint of the philosophy of the Enlightenment, but one that is absent from the philosophy of the social realm that flourished in the mid-nineteenth century. In this philosophy, the administrators were supposed to be "trustworthy" for the simple reason that they were considered to be the impartial experts of the General Interest.

Indeed, the development of public service was corollary with the principle of the neutrality of its civil servants. If the administration was to be seen as the instrument of society, acting beyond the direct control of the political authority, its agents had to be independent in the exercise of their functions from the pull of private interests, and absolutely dependent on the administrative institution. The entire hierarchical and centralized organization of work, as well as the whole system for training and sanctioning members of the civil service were designed to this end. They sought to ensure the ethical neutrality of civil servants so they could be defined as simple instruments for applying the orders of the hierarchy according to the proper rules.[56] In this context, civil servants acted in line with the General Interest by following general instructions originating in the political sphere, and by specifying the particular instructions that these implied. For henceforth the latter had to be conceived at the double levels of law and of regulation: "Let the law not neglect a single social interest but let it not descend, with respect to anyone, to the level of secondary details; this is its true mission."[57] For while administration was at the service of the public, the benefits of its action depended on the speed of its intervention and the suitability of the answers that it gave to the problems it had to solve. Consequently, "questions that need technical competence should be passed on to be dealt with by regulations; seconded by skilled advice from the scientific organs of the highest standing and devoted to the practical matters of business, administration can fathom every difficulty, penetrate every secret, and give satisfaction to every interest."[58]

Thus the civil servants found justification for their power as specialists of the General Interest in the service of the governed; they found legitimacy for the autonomy from the political sphere that the breadth of their task gave them, an autonomy in the operationalization of ends[59] and in the definition of means. This was a new division of labor between law and administrative order, between legislator and civil servant. However, the viewpoints of both were reconciled in theory for both abided by "social law" which was a "law of purpose. Every purpose is legitimate when it conforms to the social law, and every act accomplished to attain this goal has social, i.e. legal, value."[60] Thus for Durkheim's friend, Duguit, defender of the notion of *objective law*, as for the men of the positivist age, the theoreticians of democratic society had missed the point: social need had not replaced the legal norm, it *was* the legal norm. "Objective law is born of social reality, and public service has grown out of this positive reality": the notion of public service replaced the concept of sovereignty as the basis of public law.[61]

The repercussions affected the way in which the duty of the State was conceived. For the founders of the theory of public service, who inaugurated a brief but famous golden age of administrative law, the obligation of the State was to keep the public services running, public services being "every activity whose performance has to be ensured, regulated and supervised by the rulers because the performance of this activity is indispensable to the achievement and growth of social interdependence and because its nature is such that it can be fully developed only by the intervention of the governing force."[62] The State was no longer a power that commanded; it was a process of cooperation among government departments. The notion of public service became the fundamental criterion of administrative law. The State's sovereignty was limited by individual liberty, the safeguard of which implied submission to the principle of public service. For the law was not a creation of the State. The law was evident to the State as it was to individuals since it was the social norm itself. Law was objective and governments had to implement it in order to organize and supervise the functioning of their departments.[63]

Thus legal order was guaranteed to both governors and the governed. The administration remained subordinate in theory, but in a new way: subordinate to the political authority, from which it received its general instructions, it was also subordinate to nature since it obeyed the "natural laws of society." In following the disinterested advice of science, it no longer asked the sovereign legislative assembly for the entire "revelation" of these laws. It sought this revelation from specialists in the social sciences as well.

This transformation modified the character of administration for, to accomplish its mission, it henceforth had to be animated by an active philosophy and could no longer be restricted to the passive execution of orders received from the political realm. Thus it justified its opacity and its independence from the political authority: the fact is that expertise called for secrecy, and social action for strategy. Consequently, the art of the civil servant called for the obligation of secrecy and the independence of those whose task was the "conscientious and disinterested study of public need and of the means to satisfy it."[64]

Controls. While the rules of internal controls remained similar to what they had been, the supervision of regularity became more difficult since, henceforth, the extension of the administrative domain effectively removed the presupposition on which this control had been based, namely the idea that the administrative order was immutable. Thus it became increasingly difficult for the administration to account for its acts.[65] Leroy-Beaulieu, among others, criticized the difficulties of supervising public expenditure attributing them to the increasingly heterogeneous nature of administrative tasks.[66] Moreover, the methods of supervision were increasingly unsuitable; the rules for the formal verification of the regularity of procedures were not applicable to sanctioning the administration's new responsibility at the level where it was henceforth exercised: namely that of matching actions to objective social needs.

Having extended the range of its activities on the one hand and strengthened its defences on the other, the pre–Second World War administration had become the many–headed monster that both defenders of free–market society and theoriticians of the corporation, and even civil servants themselves, condemned. Postwar theories sought to restore the administration's weakened legitimacy by reorganizing the way it represented its relations with the political realm and with those whom it governed.

In the aftermath of the Second World War, nationalization, planning and the growth of State economic management extended the administration's field of action in a decisive manner. Henceforth, the administration intervened at the heart of the area in which discourse on the free market had located the very source of society's natural order: the economic sphere, the market. This came about at the cost of extending the discourse formulated in the preceding period and of making it systematic. The idea of interdependence was extended to the economic sphere, and, at once, the sphere of public service was broadened.

More than ever, the administration was faced with the contradictory task of reconciling the democratic conception of its role with the leadership that it exercised. When it sought to do so, the spread of the idea of public service—as disinterested service in a general, objective interest—deepened the contradiction. The notion of public service reached its peak at the same time as it went into crisis. For, in a situation where a view of society as an organic whole ruled by laws was triumphant, only those who specialized in identifying and implementing these laws retained the capacity to identify the general interest. In other words, the specialist tended to become the sole competent mediator between the natural laws of society and the definition of the ends and means of social action. Only he could define the *true* social and economic needs, while more completely eluding political scrutiny. As a result, the legitimacy of the administration hung by a thread. First of all, because its subordination to political authority remained the primary theoretical condition of this legitimacy. At the same time, the dramatic extension of administrative action made the formal procedures of supervision ever more fictitious, while the political sphere itself lost some of its legitimacy[67] and, its approval therefore lost some of its power of legitimation. This is shown, in the legal field, by the so–called crisis of the criterion of administrative law. The legitimacy was also fragile because there was only one condition on which the inherent legitimacy of the agents of public service, as scientists and technicians, could fill the vacuum created by the loss of legitimating power by the political sphere. This condition was the maintenance of belief in the disinterestedness of the specialists and in the scientific character of their methods as means for defining and pursuing the collective ends that represented the general interest. But, as the meaning of the general interest became less and less evident and the center of the system of interdependence gradually shifted as a consequence of the internationalization of the economy, the conditions for maintaining this belief were eroded, and with them, the capacity of the national specialists to regulate the economy. From 1960 on, the crisis was an open one and democratic discourse could reply only by seeking to reconstruct the initial conditions of administrative legitimacy, namely transparency. Since the administration could not be brought back within the bounds of action that ensured transparency through supervision of the rule, the idea developed of a direct relation between administration and politics, administration and the public: first the technique of "rationalization of budgetary choices" (RCB), then public management tried to resolve the crisis set off by the contradiction of public service. Unable to anchor its legitimacy in politics or social law, the administration sought to ground it on matching its products to the desires of society members.

The Spreading Concept of Public Service and its Crisis

"The shift in attitudes."[68] Rarely did the ends of national economic activity seem more generally self-evident than in 1945: reconstruction was the key word of the period. Under the weight influence of the history of this century, this task was handed over to State administration. In recent times of war past, it had already taken charge of the management of scarcity. On this occasion, the real interdependence of the economic agents had only reinforced the organist view of society which emerged in the social thinking

of the first half of the twentieth century. Furthermore, the 1929 crisis had caused the idea and fact of *economic policy* to spring up on the terrain of classical economy. Although the work of Keynes and the policies of the New Deal were as yet little known in the France of 1945,[69] they had already given rise to books with evocative titles like *Organization in the Firm and in the Nation*[70] published by men who were to play an active role in planning.

Reconstruction: the nature of the task was as obvious as the choice of its organizers. To reconstruct was to rebuild production capacities; this was the work of specialists in the service of the Nation. The growth rate of the Gross National Product—which remained to be calculated[71]—(or of the National Income, the first aggregate figure to be estimated) thus expressed the General Interest unambiguously, in the form of a number. This step acquired meaning only within an organicist conception of society. From this point of view, the assessment of national wealth, taken from Quesnay's project for an economic input–output table (the creators of national accounting quoted him as their authority), was to be to the Nation what cost accounting was to the firm. Its value lay in providing an instrument for gaining concrete knowledge of economic interdependencies with a view to action. The purpose of action, to increase national wealth, was to the Nation what striving for profit was to the head of the big firm. Agreement on ends at the national level defined the general interest as a function of collective utility: the *law of value* applied to the Nation as it did to the firm.

In these circumstances the Nation could be managed like a firm. Moreover it *had* to be managed: its goals had to be formulated explicitly and its resources had to be organized in an optimum way for the group. Defining ends and identifying economic resources became decidedly cultural tasks. The economy was no longer a state of nature. Economic policy became a national concern.[72]

Formulating coherent goals was the business of the *concertation* organized by means of the Plan between those who represented the "vital forces of the Nation" and the specialists. Defining optimum resources was the business of specialists on the basis of the knowledge that national accounting would provide.

This was truly a "shift in attitudes." For the old free–market principles of the autonomy of economic actors in an abstract market, already quite damaged by the practice of firms[73], was replaced at the centre of economic theory and administrative practice by the concept of the interdependency of economic agents in concrete markets. Observation showed that although they could achieve points of equilibrium, there was no natural necessity by which markets tended towards long–term equilibrium. The founding axiom of classical economic thought, the principle of the natural harmony of interests, was overthrown. The invisible hand was powerless to regulate the market.

Quite the contrary, the multiplying and accelerating effects[74] of decisions by economic agents, together with the forecasts that they made,[75] amplified imbalances over a period of time if forecasting tools were not actually created. The state had to take over the task of visible hand, acting on the behalf on growth: regulating, compensating, stimulating, it could leave no stone unturned, to "fill the gaps and correct the flaws of the spontaneous evolution of the economy[76] in order to "master" the growth of its action.

The role of the state was to stimulate productive investment directly or indirectly, by subsidies, credit,[77] nationalization[78] and economic guidance, planning. Its role was to assist firms faced with the uncertainty of real markets. A favored tool for this was the Planning Commission (*le Plan*), the first of the *administration de mission* (task–oriented administrative bodies),[79] "the effective substitute for an illusory shadow, the real model of an unachievable mechanism,"[80] a "reducer of uncertainty," the purpose of which was to restore economic openness by producing "a vast market study on a national scale."[81] "Without going so far as to say with Keynes that the data available to the investor amounts to little, sometimes to nothing, it must be acknowledged that the isolated firms lack serious bases for calculation. For no generalized markets exist. . . . The guiding idea of planning is to integrate all these effects of interdependence by extending the technique of the commercial agreements of private law . . . to the entire nation. . . . The Plan is thus a substitute for the generalized market.[82]

The role of the state was to organize the conditions for efficiency of action, which would be the contrary of the "ill–regulated State control of the pre–war period."[83] Thus the collective definition of ends became crucial to the justification of action.

For the first time the administration was to draw its legitimacy directly from the public. Discussion on the Plan was to take place, on the one hand, in the Economic and Social Council, between the national representatives of the "social partners" and, on the other hand, within the framework of the Planning Commissions, between representatives of sectors to be planned and specialized technicians of planning.

"Since the execution of the Plan calls the cooperation of all, it is indispensable that every vital element of the Nation participate in its elaboration."[84] The theme of concertation on the objectives of the Plan, through deliberation and consent, brought, for the first time, into the sphere of economic ends, the idea of direct relationships between the administration and its public, the idea of a form of "direct democracy" outside of the mediation of political body. The other source of the legitimacy of this new form of intervention was, as before, the specialist's knowledge: specialists who were entrusted with preparing the draft Plans which the Economic and Social Council would discuss; specialists who prepared economic and social information for this purpose; specialists who were present in the Planning Commissions, the role of which was to translate overall ends into operational sector–based ends, that is, simultaneously to accept the means and the ends of action. Specialists, moreover, who were so certain of the "reasonable" and economically "optimizing" nature of their project that they did not hesitate, on occasion, to make up for the inadequacies of their data by "bits of sleight–of–hand"[85] in order to convince their various partners. F. Bloch–Lainé, (a well–known senior civil servant who was one of the initiators of national accounting in France), put it bluntly when referring to an administrative meeting in October 1947: the participants, he said, had been "completely taken for a ride by the planners." But, he added, this had been a major psychological and political step because "it was the first time that a practice had been based on reasoning of this sort."[86] Etienne Hirsch, Jean Monnet's successor as head of the Planning Commission went so far as to lay down the following maxim for his first colleagues: "Our best weapon is our tongue."[87] The specialists justified these short cuts in the name of practical urgency. Contrary to the theorical economists, exemplified in particular by reviled university men,[88] the initiators of the Plan and of national accounting claimed to be servants of the Prince. This position was plausible the reversal of the viewpoint on the economic reality that they brought about by generalizing and formalizing the model of social and economic interdependence. From the specialists' viewpoint, this conception was enough to ensure the rightness and efficiency of the reasoning to which it led for which the new servants of the Prince pleaded more than the details of the information that was the go into it. This conception had no meaning unless it was shared by the political sphere, that is, unless it modeled the future action of the Prince. It was therefore a political conception that was ill–concealed under technical appearances. Thus Simon Nora saw national accounting as a "commando operation in the machinery of the administration ... producing a fundamental step not only in thinking but in the coherency of administration in this country and in the pre–eminence of the public over the private."[89]

The means: State stimulation. The primary criterion of these new specialists of the General Interest was that of pratical efficiency in the service of growth. The Planning Authority was an instrument for action as were the other administrations de mission then being set up. "The planner is responsible for preparing, with the greatest economy of resources, stage of development coherent with the directions that correspond to the preferences of the nation."[90]

Therefore, every State action related to economic planning had to be directed by a united political will. Financial intervention by the State had to be the central to mechanism. Its propulsive power was played up while the old theory of the neutrality of public finances was cast away all the more easily as financial equilibrium no longer appeared to be the sacrosanct mark of a healthy economy.[91] The Finance Ministry came under the Economic Ministry in 1934. A shining symbol, as Pierre Mendès-France stressed: "To bring finances under control is to put an end to the State as the mere guardian of the rules of the free-market game. The economy dominating finance is tantamount to the Plan dominating the market."[92] Financial practice became one of the elements of economic policy.[93] Thus, from 1957 onwards, an economic report was to be appended to the Finance Bill, and the national accounts were routinely presented to Parliament from 1960. The nationalized firms, for their part, played a leading role in defining wage policies and stimulating production. Stimulation by the State could go so far as to encourage the free-enterprise sectors to develop ideas on competition and technological development: the "productivity missions" to the United States, organized just after World War II by Monnet, then head of the French Planning Commission, were probably the most striking example of this development. The Plan was more than an instrument of distributing scarce resources; it was an "arrangement" of resources aimed at a desirable future result.

To reach this objective, planning needed organic information as did the economic system that it claimed to stimulate. Therefore, it had firstly to build a framework for data–gathering and, second, to collect data which would fit it.[94] If it was allowed to perform this task, if it even had to perform it, this was because "the new State is not an economic actor like another . . . it is set up over the economic parties of which it is the protector, arbiter and regulator."[95]

The means: accounting frameworks. The first instruments that the planners acquired were quite naturally accounting systems. To estimate the wealth of the nation and, above all, to organize its growth, the administration had to count it and understand the connections between its various constituent elements. In the task of collecting information, defining the accounting matrix came first: the essential part of the work done by the national accountants and by the INSEE (the national statistical institute) during the initial years of reconstruction was to be methodological. They constructed categories and codes. This was a vital task, for it established the framework of the intelligibility of society for economic and social administration. Thus the administration began comprehensive encoding of the world and very rapidly extended it. Henceforth, to be effective, communication had to be expressed in these categories.

The accounting framework henceforth called for information to be collected. Since the nation was meant to be organic, and action required the forecasting of the effects of interdependence, the reference tool to the man of action had to be the full matrix of these interdependencies. The instrument of action led to constructing what were later called "information systems." By giving rise to the view that collecting information on society was one of the normal tasks of administration, the imperative of efficiency in the service of an organic view of economic life forced administration in every sphere to exceed the limits that democratic and free–market principles had set on its investigation of the civil society. Thus Saint–Simon's project came to be partially implemented: "There, it was no longer owners or isolated capitalists who regulate the choice of firms and the destiny of workers. A social institution is invested with these functions so badly fulfilled today; it is the repository of all the tools of production, it presides over all material exploitation . . . it can therefore account for general needs and individual, convey hands and instruments where the need is felt, in a word, direct production, bring it into harmony with consumption."[96] The matrix of national accounting was to be the overall economic matrix (*tableau economique d'ensemble*) which, descending directly from Doctor Quesnay's matrix, gave an organic description of national wealth. Two additional instruments, the input–output matrix (*tableau d'echanges interindustriels*) and the financial matrix (*tableau des operations financieres*) were used to keep track of the volume relationships and value flows by which the "state of wealth" could be established at a given moment. Hence, the planners were able to predict the future state of economic matters on the basis of probable or planned changes in the level of interdependencies and flows.[97] Even before the growth of national accounting, an initial balance sheet had been drawn up in 1947; the first macro–economic agregate figures had been published in 1945.[98] Although an account by profession, the planner was an accountant of a new type within the framework of the State: he no longer considered his accounts as the means for a posteriori observation established by the administrative custom of enumeration; he now considered them as the macro–economic instrument for managing the nation as a whole. The planner's national accounting thus became to the nation what cost accounting was to the firm: at once an instrument for observing, supervising and forecasting. "People were excited not about making beautiful accounting instruments but about preparing decisions in a more rational way."[99] Since the generalized market was now seen as fiction, since interdependence appeared to rule every level of economy and society, the problem of the goal–setter was to work out sound strategies for the future. Although model–making and simulations were as yet barely developed,[100] forecasting was making great strides as can be seen in the volume of literature on this subject that flourished in the early sixties.[101] The administration became "future–oriented."[102]

The means: economic information. To succeed, the administration had to gain knowledge of the objects of its action, it had to read and interpret the world.

To the very sparse economic data that had been traditionally collected by the State apparatus—almost solely the opinions of entrepreneurs on short–term business movements, known as "advanced indicators" and the few indicators mentioned earlier—were added, objective indicators such as production and price indices and agregates such as the GNP. The task was a huge one, for economic information in particular was very incomplete at the end of the war. Thus one of the earliest planners recalls: "We were asked to supply information, and this information did not exist. We had a little information for 1938 but after 1938 nothing at all. So we looked for figures really everywhere: from employers' associations, ministries . . . it was not really statistical work; it amounted practically to a police inquiry based on a few contrivances; it was a make-shift affair."[103] Data–collecting organizations were created or perfected. In 1947, the financial studies and statistics bureau of the Finance Ministry, which later became the SEEF (the department of economic and financial studies), created the Statistics Committee whose task was to "gather information from every corner of the financial and administrative apparatus."[104] The INSEE (the national statistical institute), set up under the 1946 finance law, had its tasks increased, renovated and organized along with the development of the data–collecting machinery needed for national accounting.[105]

The system for gathering information from companies was in place. When the Vichy regime's professional committee organization (which had been set up to cope with wartime scarcities by organizing production and distribution) were dissolved in 1946, the tasks of distribution, based on full and detailed statistics of physical quantities, were entrusted to employers; organizations; in 1951, provisions for branch by branch investigation, which was still professional to a great extent, were made. Firms were obliged to reply to these inquiries; starting from 1960, surveys were prepared and carried out in industry, transport, distribution and services. From 1964, the INSEE carried out an annual study on companies to supplement studies by branch and inquiries into the state of business.[106] The basic elements of the machinery for gathering routine, objective information on the postwar economy was henceforth in place. As early as 1945, the extension of administration's powers had provoked what has been called "the crisis of the public service criterion" at the juridical level. The reason being that it was becoming more and more difficult to make a legal definition of public services as the State overflowed into every area of social life. However the legitimacy of administrative action was never directly challenged until nearly the sixties. Of course, customary proposals for administrative reform flourished but the phenomenon was more than a century old; of course, the inefficiency of the administration was exposed, but the purpose of the attacks was also to justify the growth of *administration de mission* which, in turn, only aggravated the legal crisis. For, in the name of the general interest, they dealt with problems that were "non–standard" with "para–administrative" staff and experts recruited for their competence in the "para–public" sector. In a word, they eluded the controls on regularity since the fields they covered were not regulated by procedures; or perhaps the control procedures had become so complex and restrictive that these bodies were simply exempted.

However, for as long as the obvious character of the general interest could survive, along with the qualification of specialists to reveal and pursue it, the administration could seek resources of legitimacy—as it had done previously—in its contribution to the satisfaction of collective needs. But once the ends could no longer claim to be evident for everyone, the legitimation of administrative action had to be achieved in other ways. This is what happened at the start of the sixties, under the effect of two combined phenomena. On the one hand, the internationalization of capital, the opening of the European market, brought into question the relevance of the national framework as the place in which to define the system of interdependence. In other words, it brought into question the validity of the Plan as a reducer of uncertainty and, more generally, the validity of national models of interdependence. On the other hand (and this is how the problem was framed by the Planning Commission itself), the major expansion that came during the first fifteen years after the war forced a reconsideration of the nature of national goals that began with the Fourth Plan. More generally, it broadened the range of alternative options. The French administration entered its present crisis of legitimacy when the Fourth Plan raised the question, "Growth for what."[107] At that point, the chosen ends, the methods by which they were defined and the means used to attain them all had to be justified.

From the Multiplicity of Objective Ends to the Subjectivity of Need

The problem remained a limited one so long as there was agreement in recognizing the objective character of need. It was then merely a matter of justifying the ends chosen among all the objectively acceptable ones, that is, of justifying the procedure for acquiring knowledge and choosing between alternative options. Quantitative data then took on their full importance as practical indicators. Method constituted the grounds for rationality. It was decided to gather objective indicators of social needs; methods for alternative model–making and aids to decision–making were perfected.

As for the legitimation of the means used to reach these ends, the problem was to replace the now inoperative view of external controls on procedures by a notion of internal controls on efficiency. From the model of private business organization, emerged the idea of administrative responsibility with respect to its objectives. This was the movement towards rationalizing budgetary choices. But as needs changed from being numerous but objective to being numerous and subjective, the legitimation of the ends selected by the administration became more of a problem. For, if need was subjective, then each person in the Nation was the only specialist of his own need. The very existence of collective need was thrown into question. Individual needs had lost their common measure, and it became impossible to establish priorities among them. The administration therefore had to assert the importance of suiting ends, means and results to the subjective demand of each individual. Every available rhetorical resource had to be mobilized: when tradition could be used to emphasize a need as being an objective one or shared subjectively by all, an educatory stance would be adopted; if not, it would be pointed out that the means and ends defined resulted from the aggregation of the subjective needs expressed by public opinion; freedom of the market or the process of democratic consultation would be simulated. Legitimacy would constantly have to be renewed through market research, opinion polls, the marketing and managing of its own image.

Arbitration Among Objective Ends

"Growth for what?" The Fourth plan called for establishing "our choices for the future" on the basis of "a less partial idea of man."[108] The Fifth Plan brough an initial response to this question by emphasizing the interdependence of the social and economic tasks of the State, laying the stress on economic planning. The state replied: growth for full employment and the promotion of "certain collective values" through transfers of resources, public installations and an income policy.[109]

These values were claimed to be obvious, shared by the entire national community. At their center, growth appeared as the uncontested condition for the achievement of all the other values. But a fresh problem arose, derived from the new awareness that the economic and social spheres were largely interdependent: while growth was the necessary condition for the achievement of group values, every goal of expansion that made for their

achievement did not equally promote the pursuit of growth. It was therefore necessary to arbitrate between the various options that had to be
assessed and whose effects had to be compared. The multidimensional
nature of political and social goals no longer provided justification for the
ends selected on the basis of the evident optimum, to which they would
lead. And so the choice of the best ends lost its obvious character. Hence,
policy–makers developed short–term and medium-term projecting techniques in order to simulate alternative futures under different assumptions.
For the first time, the Fifth Plan submitted a report to Parliament broadly
setting forth the medium–term economic and financial prospects on the
basis of three alternative growth options; from then on, this became a
required procedure. Indicators were included in the definition of the Plan.
Their purpose was to correct orientations in reaction to the possibly unex-
pected and harmful effects of economic and social changes: in the Fifth
Plan techniques assumed that society was a vast system integrating the
economic and social dimensons. The sectorial variability of the economy
was matched by the sectorial variability of the social sphere. Defining a
social policy therefore amounted to identifying priorities among objective
social needs, under economic constraint. The Sixth Plan was to identify the
"target groups of public action," relating the variability of the social sphere
to the psycho–sociological characteristics of the population. The definition
of objectives in their new form called for the emergence of a common
measure of social and economic activity, a standard that provided for this
way of making choices. This was a real difficulty since, as the Sixth Plan
noted, "in the social field, the theory of value has still to be invented."[110]

The quantitative—production, investment, consumption, growth—had
been quantified; now the qualitative—the social—was to be quantified in
the form of indicators. Here were the beginnings, starting with 1968, of
social indicators, "which include all categories of affairs to which our fellow
citizens attach value, and which they aspire to or wish to avoid."[111] Indicators of condition or impact, indicators of results, indicators of means,
helped prepare bureaucratic information on social needs. Indicators armed
the administration with all the power of figures and the rigor of measurement. It provided a language with which it could "talk" about society in the
same terms as it had been doing about economy, a language which would
allow it to relate economic and social data. This language assumed that the
relationship between the nature of the social service provided and the
satisfaction of objective need was unequivocal. In this sense, it was a language of objectivity.

This new view entrusted the administration with the role of arbitrating
among various ends for various groups whose respective needs were defined by their economic and social attributes. Thus social groups emerged

at the very heart of macro–economic models. The Sixth Plan had a project to prepare national accounts of households by social and occupational categories in order to throw light on "the reverse side of macro–economic projections."[112] These accounts, which are being prepared now in the early eighties, will provide for detailed projections of household consumer needs, employment needs in terms of education and sectors of activity, housing needs, etc.[113] Here the administration of the Plan, the institution that had symbolized consultation at the national level, acknowledged the growing difficulty of defining a collective social and economic scheme, a General Interest distinct from the sum of the interests of particular groups.[114]

Finally, the techniques of aids to decision–making (operational research, cost/benefit analysis, multi–criterion analysis)[115] were developed to amplify the technical instruments available to specialists. Specialists could now take refuge behind the objectivity of their data and their computing and decision–making techniques. They could separate objective calculation from political decision. As experts in method, the former was theirs by right. The latter was the business of legitimate, decision–making bodies, who had to choose from among the reasonable ends identified by the specialists. Thus the administration seemed desirous of returning to its pristine virginity: it rejected the idea it would usurp the power to define ends. It reasserted its technicist will, but its technique absorbed the whole process by which objectives were formed, excluding only the final decision.

The efficiency of administration as a means of legitimation: the language of RBC (Rationalization of Budgetary Choices). The administration was induced to legitimize its ends by rationalizing the means that it used to determine reasonable goals. It was also led to assert its ability to achieve them. Now, neither its very incomplete subordination to the political sphere nor its subordination to social laws, which vanished as the notion of the General Interest was obscured, could ensure that the ends would fit the means. Nor would these forms of subordination provide for supervising the proper execution of means. Controls on regularity had lost their credibility because they had lost their relevance, therefore the administration grew even more opaque. It could seek to rebuild its legitimacy by putting forward another criterion of control, hence another criterion of the transparency of its action. This solution came in the shape of efficiency checking measured by the relation between the goals assigned to the organization and the results obtained. By substituting the discourse of efficiency for that of legality, the administration borrowed the method and the discourse on method from private firms. In so doing, it totally reversed the discourse and claimed to sanction irresponsibility as the source of inefficiency, instead of sanctioning illegality with respect to procedural routine.

This trend began immediately after the war, when "administration and methods" cells were created. The *Comité central d'enquête sur les coûts et les rendements des services administratifs* (Central committee of inquiry on administrative costs and efficiency) was established in 1946. Starting in 1952, "a new school of administrative reform" sprang up, giving "priority to questions of output, method and efficiency, taking inspiration from the general movement for work organization which had been transforming the world for 50 years."[116] A *Comité exécutif de la réforme administrative* (Executive committee for administrative reform) was set up in 1953. Its purpose was to take an inventory of services and to reflect on methods for calculating cost prices. The SCOM (*Service central d'organisation et méthodes*—Central organization and methods department) appeared in 1959. These developments led to the emergence, in 1967, of the "RBC movement"[117] (rationalization of budgetary choices) which provided the most complete and systematic discourse ever held on administrative reform. It claimed to represent a "scientific and extensive search for all procedures and methods that would make for improving the relevance, coherence and efficiency of public decisions or procedures and methods backed by budgetary resources or whose effect could be seen in the budget."[118] Though it was never entirely put into practice and is today largely abandoned,[119] it was effective in the 1970's. As a comprehensive discourse on the rationality of administration's technical activity and its subordination to political decision, it claimed to restore the threatened legitimacy of the administration by applying the criterion of rationality. This ensured transparency and the possibility of supervising its action by creating new modes of subordination.

First, it claimed to subordinate the administration to the political sphere for the definition of ends: the autonomy of the administration stemmed from the fact that the political authority found it impossible to control the allocation of budget credits, a fact that was due to the way in which the budget procedure itself was organized. Of course, it fell to Parliament to vote the yearly ministery budgets. However, this power was to a large extent a fiction, since the carry-over of previously voted credits (which formed the essential part of their resources) counteracted, in the name of the continuity of administration, the effect of any stimulation by the political sphere. Moreover, although the economic importance of the budget had been recognized since the end of the Second World War, the budget document itself did not show the allocation of public funds, which alone could make it possible to assess the costs and advantages of each action. The budget document was simply a mode of presenting expenditure, an *a posteriori* document of allocations, whereas it should have been the technical instrument for programming, the means for forecast-based management by the administration. Therefore the RBC movement invented the "program budget" as an instrument for allocating resources and checking results. It proposed abolishing the distinction between "voted credits" and "new credits" in order to counter the institutionalization of resources which hampered stimulation and sanction by political power. Only program budgets were to see the light of day in every ministry from 1977 onwards. But as formal instruments they remained without legal value and without any practical value other than that of a mode of presentation to Parliament.[120] The ultimate purpose of RBC— "to invent and establish a fuller, more flexible and more efficient budgetary discourse"[121] that would account for the real interdependence of expenditures, which is fragmented by conventional budgetary procedures—, was seriously compromised.

While following the injunctions of political power, the administration also had to lend an ear to the public that it served. Centralized, hierarchical organization, routinely condemned by all as a source of bureaucratic sluggishness and rigidity, had to be replaced by a decentralized system whose decision-making units would never be solidified and would be built around the targets of the programs described in the budget documents. Thus the RBC procedures would reorganize the allocation of funds, the responsibility of administrative entities and controls—of efficiency—over the use of resources, in sum the transparency of the system.

What remained was the internal organization: if the principle of organizational responsibility was to work, each decision-making unit had to be able to be inspected and made responsible for its performance. This was the language of MBO (management by objectives) within the framework of the administration. This form of supervision (the self-supervision of performance for internal use, an instrument of observation and sanction for external use) meant developing information of a type as yet foreign to administration, an equivalent of private cost accounting, which was to be called "program accounting." Program accounting made it possible to charge each expenditure to its related program. It has remained in an experimental state until the present day. Undoubtedly for technical reasons (the specific difficulty of where to charge the common expenses of the administration, the problem of defining production), but above all for a fundamental reason that applied to the entire RBC undertaking. It came up against the mass of operating criteria of that routine organization, the administration. On the financial controls side, RCB was intended to renew accounting procedures where the only legally valid rules for charging expenditure remained the unchanged rules of public accounting. On the side of the organization of human resources, it upset the whole concept of public service, on which the role of the State's agents had been based. RBC proposed to "deTaylorize the administration,"[122] that is, to do away with the idea of civil servants as simple mechanical instruments for the application of rules under the supervision of the rule. Making civil servants responsible amounted to withdrawing them from a general task in order to re-attach them to a special function, "using them no longer as elements of an apparatus that was the repository of certain tasks, but as elements of mission costs,"[123] an idea that was opposed by the whole corps of the civil service.

RBC tried to reconcile on a microsocial basis rationalizing, through technicization, the administrative processes and restoring overall decision-making power to the political realm. It also appeared as the discourse of individual responsibility within the framework of a system of total interdependence. "The task-oriented public offices, initially considered as intruders in traditional bureaucratic structures, could become the triumphant model of the renewed organization of administrative tasks were RBC to reach its goal. Efficiency would have provided it with new sources of legitimacy. Thus the most revolutionary technique, . . . that of the economy of entreprise, would have been implemented in the administration."[124] The whole concept of RBC aimed at reconciling the latest modes of legitimation (by method serving efficiency) with the oldest modalities by defining objective ends with the help of specialists of the general interest in the service of representative power. Since the method proved to be unrealistic, and the specialists' ability to define objectives uncertain, a new relationship legitimating ends and means remained to be invented. Public management retained the power of legitimation by methods but gave them a practical efficiency; it gave them a new pattern of legitimation by ends since it made it possible to determine them methodically.

The Subjectivity of Ends and Public Management

To the question of the Fourth Plan: "Growth for what?" the Seventh Plan replied that "instead of asking what to make of growth, it is necessary rather to start with what society wants to do and look for the corresponding growth."[125] Growth as an end was no longer self-evident; it was no longer the obvious sign of Progress. The Plan, which represented the State's discourse on economic and social practice, henceforth adopted the slogan of "zero growth"[126] and denounced of the "havoc of growth."[127] If indeed there was a consensus (the possibility that a virtue was being made of necessity matters little here), it was an embarrassing one from the standpoint of the legitimation of administrative action. For it dissociated progress from the standard that had served it as an uncontested measure since the Second World War. Henceforth, everyone was entitled to his own idea on the question. There was only one way left to define collective ends: that was to make them the sum total of individual ends. The "general will" of the "national community" and the "science of well-being" of the specialists of the "general interest" were disqualified. All that remained was to ask "society" as a collection of persons to say "what it wanted to do." For want of a common measure of collective ends, "man became the measure of all things." He alone could define the need that he felt and what would satisfy it.

As the administration had extended its field of intervention, it had lost the source of legitimacy provided by its submission to political authority. It had then developed the principle of public service, which, in turn, proved to be ineffective. If it could no longer gain legitimacy by obedience to the civil society via its submission to political power, it could still make the point that its actions matched the wishes of the users. In a word, it could try to detect, create and maintain the consensus of the public on the relevance of its ends and on the value of its results.

The problem that it now faced was similar to that of large private firms: its survival depended on its capacity to produce actions that were acceptable to the public of users, just as the survival of the firm depended on its capacity to produce goods acceptable to its clients. The administration entered the age of marketing. In order properly to fulfill this task of growing importance, it had to gain knowledge of the psycho-sociological characteristics of its public or publics. Opinion polls, survey research and market studies were to provide for defining the targets of administrative action and the proposals related to each of these targets. They were to provide the arguments by which the public or publics could be led to recognize the new language of administration as their own: they were to give the measure of their subjective needs and satisfactions. Henceforth, systematic encoding by the administration was no longer restricted to the definition of "objective" economic and social indicators.[128] The administration undertook to assemble subjective indicators which alone could account for the subjectivity of need and its satisfaction.[129]

The administration now tried, Godlike, to assume the absolute power to objectify things and men. Under its gaze, men were no longer the irreducible beings of the philosophy of the Enlightenment, but composite entities constituted by bureaucratic categories.[130] Maintaining the consensus meant stressing how adapted the products were to public demand. The information gathered made it possible to use every available means of persuasion and, in particular, every means with which to evoke the lost legitimacy of market and democratic society and of the general interest. The administration sought to persuade the public that the forms of behavior it urged them to adopt were in the interest of all or of a whole segment of the population; it presented its actions as a simulation of the free market; it increasingly consulted the public. In the end, as a big organization, it could not uphold the consensus without managing its own image.

It had to adapt to its public, or rather to its publics: it had to define the products that it offered in relation to what made these products acceptable, to modulate its actions according to the needs and inclinations that it identified in each segment of the population as revealed by market research, to advertise the virtues of the action that it proposed. In a word, it had to make marketing a central element of its activity. As we have said, the Sixth Plan was the first to reveal this trend in administrative practice. By defining "target groups of development,"[131] it had officially undertaken to differentiate the real relationship between the administration and the "users, those strange, mixed beings"[132] who replaced the "administrated" with whom its relations, until then, had been merely legal ones. It automatically threw a central element of the democratic representation into crisis: as it no longer provided a uniform and continuous service to every citizen, it could no longer be seen as the "common property" of a unified civil society. By moving from "an overall view of social solidarity and collective need to a selective view in the American style,"[133] it struck a blow against the principle of the equality of the governed in the eyes of the public service, which had been one of the tenets of the French Republic.

The administration was forced to abandon its attitude of lofty solicitude for the governed, which had been associated with the practical developments of the theory of public service. Henceforth it had to print up the qualities of each product as it came out. The administration was on its way to becoming France's biggest advertiser. Thus, the specialist of the general interest was unseated by the "specialized professional" as the unilateral definition of society's real overall ends was supplanted by the bilateral relationship of seduction through which the administration sought to win acceptance for its products. The specialists of tooth decay, engine spark plugs, road safety and lung cancer became the instruments by which the administration related its activity to the interest of each.

Education. Once it had become an educator, the administration could no longer be content with laying down the norms of an interest that it declared to be a common one: it had to use all the persuasive power it could draw from the backing of scientists to bring about the effects that it hoped for. In so doing, it took over one of the prerogatives of public service. But the form of intervention had changed. Through advertising, the administration displayed its interest in citizens' health (by reminding them to get their flu vaccinations or to brush their teeth), their safety (by asking them to fasten their car seat belts), the fulfillment of their duties (by reminding them to register to vote), the improvement of their leisure time, their wallet, etc. In each case, the administration highlighted the individual advantages derived from its measures. The collective benefits and social utility remained in the shadows or, at best, were presented as the aggregate of individual benefits: assuming responsibility for "high-risk categories" was depicted as the effect of the State's maternal solicitude for its members before appearing as an element in reducing the social costs of road traffic and health: energy savings were lauded as a means of individual savings and when civic virtues were called upon, they were presented not as the duty of a national community sharing the same "collective consciousness" but in terms of the individual benefits that would result from this nation-wide policy.[134]

In the period when the notion of public service was triumphant, collective ends could simply be declared by the specialists of the General Interest to be socially and humanly worthwhile. This rhetoric no longer worked. First, because, in a society that now acknowledged the psycho–social specificity of needs, what was good for one person could no longer be assumed to be good for another; second, because the administration had to get each of its actions accepted since it could no longer presume any comprehensive mandate on political pretexts apart from certain very limited sectors of its activity.

Simulation of the market. It was again an idea of legitimacy, evoked this time by the theories of the free market, that the administration drew upon in other spheres where it had become a simulator of the market. In losing their objective obviousness, the ends lost their specialists; or rather, each member of society once again became the sole specialist of the definition of his personal ends. When the administration could not warrant its action by the need of each as revealed by science, it could resolve the problem of ends by giving users the responsibility for defining their demand. Thus, for example, assistance in building construction was supplanted by assistance to the person[135] through the technique of vouchers, "a method that re-placed subsidies for public works by individual rights granted to citizens, who would make their applications according to rules resembling those of the market."[136] The administration appeared then not as an entity external to the market but as its substitute in the public goods sector, a sector where market rules were inoperative.

The market it simulated in that way was restricted to a single product, provided with a "specialized currency" that had no common measure with the currency of other markets or substitutes. It depossessed money of its essential role as a means of universal communication in the generalized market through which the freedom of autonomous beings could be expressed. It restricted communication to spheres defined by the intervention of the administration.[137] In other words, it was a very special type of market according to the conceptions of classical economics.

The identification of target groups, the definition of users' categories and the characterization of the subjects of the voucher policy called for collecting information on the public; its success depended upon the information of the public. The constant creation of new products in conjunction with the increasing differentiation in users greatly heightened the risk of misinforming potential users. It was no longer enough for the governed to be aware of an unchanging and uniform procedure; advertising had to meet a permanent need for fresh information. In addition, it provided an image of the administration's solicitude for the user and thus fulfilled the dual function of a means of information and a means of managing the image of the organization.

Participation. Finally, the administration professed to be participatory. Each person was to define his own ends, thus the participation of all was required to define legitimate common goals for the administration's action in view of the good of each. The theme of participation was present in planning from its outset. But the actors changed. In the immediate postwar period, society was seen as a tangible nexus of social forces identified by their relations to each other: trade unions, employers, specialists, such as they appeared in the planning commissions and the Economic and Social Council. The relevant entities of national deliberation were the "vital forces of the Nation." Concertation ended in agreement on true, objective and common ends, and on appropriate means to attain them.

In the conception of participation as it developed from the early sixties onwards, the actors were more willingly defined as "users," "consumers," "customers" and the "public." The administration became consultative. "Through the representation of the interested parties and the adoption of the rule of unanimity, agreement was reached among executors, administrations and private persons on the level of the consultative function. The project is a work performed in common, and thereby its execution is ensured. The force of constraint no longer results from the legal formulation of the decision, but in the very terms of its elaboration ... at the outside limit, the decision that takes on the force and form of law is no longer needed, for it no longer adds anything. It is even theoretically irreconcilable with the effective decision contained in the act of consultation, in the sense that rigidity (which characterizes the law) does not go well with the flexibility needed to implement such a decision. Even when established, the traditional elements of the legal act no longer constitute the true mainspring of the act. This mainspring is located in the active adherence of the governed at the very level of its elaboration."[138] Seeking to legitimate its choices by consultation, the administration first had to prove that it adhered to the decisions of those whom it consulted. It sought to do so in two ways: first by turning for help to the opinion poll as an evocation of the vote, that is, by making the most of the idea that, as the equivalent of a majority vote, the opinion poll could truly represent a reduced model of the wishes of the population.[139] The variables that defined the resemblance between two individuals were the same as those by which the public could be segmented according to the psycho-social identity of its members: age, sex, social group, income, dwelling, etc. Thus defined, the public amounted to something quite different from "social partners"; it was the sum of agents, capable of being aggregated, determined by various psycho-sociological condition, whom it would be improper to identify with the actors of classical economics.

A second form of participation developed at the very heart of the institutions set up by the public authorities:[140] namely the consultation of users' committees and of associations of all kinds. As far as we can see, this practice left the problem of representativity more or less unresolved as is evidenced by the fact that many decisions taken by the administration on the pretext that the users were in agreement were contested on the grounds that the associations consulted were non-representative in character.[141]

Image management. The last point of the programme for the permanent management of administrative legitimacy was image management, in particular by the mediation of relations with the public. The image of administrative solicitude and efficiency in the service of the various publics deflected the problem of the administration's transparency, which RCB had left unresolved, by playing up the image of its transparency. In 1953, a "bureau of public opinion" had already been set up to "ascertain the needs, habits and claims of users and civil servants." It very quickly came to an end.[142] In 1959, the Rueff-Armand report not only recommended the rationalization of methods but also the development of the administration's public relations by every means liable to promote the idea that the public services were *at the service of the public.* In particular, it called for the personalization of relations with the public so that the civil servant no longer appeared as an "abstract partner." It suggested that the administration should explain the aptness of its decisions to the public. It held up the example of American administration.[143]

But it is only in the course of recent years, and after the failure of RCB, that the importance of this aspect of things has become clear. As the bilateral *de facto* relationship of administrative agents with the users gained on the unilateral relationship of law with the governed, it became necessary to explain procedures to the public (in offices set up to receive the public); it became necessary, as far as possible, to make it easier to settle disputes outside the rigour and complications of the law (through the institution of ombudsmen); it became necessary to bring out the utility of the administration for each individual (by advertising measures taken: "the administration is there to serve you"). In other words, it was necessary to personalize the relationship with the public. All this highlighted, once more, the profound change in the theory of the relationship between the administration and civil society. Old practices, founded on an essentially uniform and impersonal relationship, were replaced by relationships that relied on the idea of a necessary humaneness in contacts between the administration and the public. The legal point of view, on which the democratic construction of the administrative edifice had relied, was swept away.[144]

Henceforth, the activity of the administration, the political authority and the firm all followed the same path of management and marketing: the boundaries were blurred in and between each of these sectors, which had been separated by the democratic free-market vision of the world. The relations of exclusion and subordination that had been established were destroyed by new practices. These relations had been founded on the distinction between the market and the firm, the governor and the governed, the citizen and the body politic, as well as the distinctions between the entrepreneur, the politician and the administrator, all of whom sought information on the publics in order to define their products. All used the weapon of seduction through advertising. All, finally, were similarly concerned with managing their "manufactures" and "sales" as well as their image.

Notes

1. Adam Smith, quoted by H. Laufenburger, *L'Intervention de l'Etat en matière économique*, Paris, LGDJ, 1939.
2. Articles 16 and 17 of the Code of Criminal Law (Code des délits et des peines) 3rd Brumaire, Year IV. There were six essential ministries in 1791: Justice, Public Taxes and Revenue, War, Navy, Foreign Affairs, Interior. See P. Legendre, *Histoire de l'administration*, Paris, PUF (coll. Themis), 1968.
3. Under the provisions of a rule established as of 1789 and 1790, the elected administrator of the *départements*, districts and *communes* could be prosecuted in a civil or penal court for deeds relating to his function. This rule was very quickly modified by article 75 of the Constitution of 22 Frimaire, Year VIII, which decided that no prosecution could lead to a government agent being sentenced for deeds related to his functions without prior permission of the *Conseil d'Etat*—and such permission had to be ratified by the head of the government. Cf. C. Durand, "Une application de la (garantie des fonctionnaires) sous le Premier Empire," *Annales de la faculté de droit d'Aix–en–Provence*, new series, No. 39, 1946.
4. E. Aimés, *La Réforme administrative et le favoritisme, 1887E,* quoted by G. Thuillier, *Bureaucratie et bureaucrates en France au XIXème siècle*, Geneva, Droz, 1980.
5. General instruction on the land tax, November–December 1790, quoted in H. Laufenburger, *Histoire de l'impôt*, PUF, 1959.

6. Quoted in P. Legendre, *op. cit.*
7. J.–B. Say, "Discours préliminaires," quoted in C. Maynard, "Trois formes de résistance à la statistique: Say, Cournot, Walras," in *Pour une histoire de la statistique*, Paris, INSEE, 1978.
8. Vivien, *Etudes administratives*, Paris, Cujas, 1859, 3rd. edition.
9. F. Fourquet, *Les Comptes de la puissance*, Paris, Encres 1980.
10. J.–B. Say, quoted in Laufenburger, *op. cit.*
11. The French penal code.
12. Law of 22 July, 1791.
13. C. Paradeise, *La Criminalité à Paris au début du XIXème siècle*, mimeographed, University of Michigan, 1970.
14. *Pour une histoire de la statistique, op. cit.*
15. M.–N. Bourguet, *Déchiffrer la France, la statistique départementale à l'époque napoléonienne*, Paris, Editions des Archives Contemporaines, 1988.
16. J.–C. Perrot, *L'âge d'or de la statistique régionale française (An IV-1804)*, Paris, Société des études robespierristes, 1977.
17. Starting with the Constituent Assembly of 1789, measures were taken to re-establish official market price–lists. From 1811 onwards, the prefects had to prepare monthly situation reports on the mains items of farm produce. Cf. B. Gille, *Les Sources statistiques de l'histoire de France,* 1964; S. Woolf, "Towards the History of the Origin of Statistics: France 1789-1815," typed, 1980.
18. P. Legendre, *op. cit.*
19. M. Perrot, "Les premières mesures des faits sociaux; naissance de la statistique criminelle en France" in *Pour une histoire de la statistique, op. cit.*
20. B. Lecuyer, "Médecins et observateurs sociaux," *ibid.*
21. See, for example, R.H. Tawney, *Religion and the Rise of Capitalism*, West Drayton, Penguin Books, 1948.
22. M. Bargeton, "Historique des ministères du travail, de la santé publique, des affaires sociales; la formation des ministères," *Revue Française des Affaires Sociales*, January–March 1971; *Questions Sociales*, French Economic and Finance Ministry, vol. I, 1975.
23. Quételet, quoted in P. Legendre, *op. cit.*
24. P. Leroy–Beaulieu, *L'Etat Moderne et ses Fonctions*, Paris, Alcan, 1890, quoted P. Legendre, *op. cit.*
25. Vivien, *op. cit.*, p. 115.
26. C. Fourrier, *La Liberté d'opinion du fonctionnaire; essai de droit public comparé*, Paris, Librairie Générale de Droit et de Jurisprudence, 1957.
27. Quoted in McCulloch, article on "Companies" in *Dictionary of Commerce*, 1834, 2nd edition.
28. Comte Roy, quoted in P. Legendre, *op. cit.*
29. Ordinance dated 14 September 1822, decree dated 31st May 1861.
30. H. de Montcloux, *De la comptabilité publique en France*, Paris, chez Bossange, 1840; G. Devaux, *La Comptabilité publique*, 2 volumes, Paris, PUF, 1957.
31. *Ibid.*
32. Law of 22 Thermidor, Year V.
33. On the latter two points, see H. de Montcloux, *op. cit.*
34. G. Devaux, *op.cit.*, vol. I, "Les Principes."
35. This prophecy was to come true in 1906. Cf. Vicomte G. d'Avenel, *La Réforme administrative*, Paris, Berger–Levrault, 1891.

36. Cf. Chapter 5.
37. M. Bargeton, *op. cit.*
38. F. Furet, J. Ozouf, *Lire et Ecrire*, Paris, Editions de Minuit, 1977.
39. J. Chevalier, D. Loschak, *La Science Administrative*, Paris, LGDJ, 1978.
40. Quoted in P. Legendre, *op. cit.*
41. Cf. Chapter 5.
42. H. Laufenburger, *Histoire de l'impôt, op. cit.*
43. M. Chevalier, *Cours d'économie politique*, quoted in Leroy–Beaulieu, *op. cit.*
44. Emile Durkheim, *Les Règles de la méthode sociologique*, Paris, PUF, 1947 (1st edition 1885).
45. A. Ziegler, "Historique des ministéres du Travail, de la santè publique, des affaires sociales les structures administratives," in *Revue française des affaires sociales, op. cit.*
46. Bargeton, *op. cit.*
47. J. Martinez, *Quantification sociale et langage; les enquêtes ouvrières en France*, 1848-1891, DEA dissertation, Université de Paris–VII, June 1980.
48. G. Garnier, "Les enquêtes agricoles décennales au XIXe siècle, essai d'analyse critique," in *Pour une histoire, . . . op. cit.*
49. T.J. Markovitch, "Statistique industrielle et système politique," *ibid.*
50. M. Volle, "Naissance de la statistique industrielle en France, 1930-1950," *ibid.*
51. P. Dubois, "Le système public d'information statistique sur les entreprises," *Economie et statistique*, No. 79, July 1976.
52. Vivien, *op. cit.*, p. 48–49.
53. *Ibid*, p. 50.
54. Vicomte d'Avenel, *op. cit.* p. 330. A statement echoed almost a hundred years later: "Let us refuse to fasten our seat belts. Today the belt and tomorrow the muzzle. Are we to see the State force us to wear underclothes in winter on the grounds that we might catch a cold?" (On the Swiss referendum on the compulsory wearing of seat belts, *Le Monde*, 16th November 1978).
55. Vivien, *op. cit.*, p. 48.
56. An important element in this ordering is the idea of the civil servant's status on which an article by Georges Demartial in the *Revue du droit public,* 1907, which aroused widespread interest (according to Guy Thuillier): "De l'opportunité d'une loi sur le statut des fonctionnaires." Later Demartial was to present a bill on these lines. In G. Thuillier, *op. cit.* See also C. Fourrier, *op. cit.*
57. Vivien, *op. cit.* p. 12.
58. *Ibid*, p. 10–14. The first work with "civil service reform" in its title that we were able to find in the library of the Institute of Political Science in Paris was published in 1822. Since then, there has been no end of complaints about the cumbersome nature of bureaucracy and the need for reform.
59. L. Duguit, *L'Etat, la loi objective et la loi positive*, quoted in E. Pisier–Kouchner, *Les fondements de la notion du service public dans l'oeuvre de L. Duguit,* doctoral dissertation, Paris, Faculté des sciences économiques, 1970.
60. L. Duguit, *Les Transformations du droit public*, 1913, *ibid.*
61. *Ibid.*
62. J.-L. de Corail, *La Crise de la notion de service public en droit administratif français*, Paris, LGDJ, 1964.
63. Vivien, *op. cit.*
64. Whence the importance of professional ethics as a code of socialization in administrative practice, as the guarantee that the corps is socially constructed in order to control its members.

65. P. Leroy–Beaulieu, *op. cit.*
66. See Chapter 5.
67. This was the main theme of the Fifth Plan.
68. F. Sérisé; quoted in F. Fourquet, *op. cit.* p. 189. In this section, we have made extensive use of the mass of data assembled in this work.
69. F. Fourquet, *ibid.*
70. A.L.V. Vincent, *L'Organisation dans l'entreprise et dans la Nation*, Societé industrielle de l'Est, 1941, quoted in Fourquet, *ibid.* p. 395.
71. This was to be accomplished in 1947; *Estimation du revenu national,* Commissariat Général au Plan, March 1947.
72. For example the interest that General de Gaulle showed in these problems from the start, as of course did the politicians of the Left who later presided over the early days of the Fourth Republic.
73. Cf. Chapter 4.
74. J. M. Keynes, *The General Theory of Employment, Interest and Money*, London, Macmillan, 1936, Book II, Chapter X.
75. *Ibid.*, Book II, chapter V.
76. P. Massé, *Méthodes et doctrine de la planification française*, Documentation française, 1952.
77. The reorganized Finance Ministry plans and finances investment with the FDES (*Fonds de dé*veloppement *économique et social* – Economic and Social Development Fund) up in 1948 and the SEEF (*Service des études économiques et financières*—Department of Economic and Social Studies set up in 1952. Concomitantly, there has been a shift to a productivist view of the Treasury. Cf. F. Fourquet, *op. cit.,* p. 184.
78. Nationalization is justified by (1) the dominant position of the firm which is nationalized in order to ensure that the national interest is served; (2) by the character of a given industry which shows diminishing returns but whose preservation is necessary for all; (3) the indivisible character of the goods produced which necessitates a takeover by the State on the basis of non–economic criteria.
79. The massive extension of the administration has been achieved to a great degree by the creation of administrative institutions which do not come under the rules of traditional administration. These are the so–called *administrations de mission* or "administrative task forces." Their temporary character (some have become permanent since 1960) is in contrast with the permanent character of the former: the recruitment, training and status of the members also follow different rules: "The task should have a volume, a complexity, an urgency that remove it from the ambit of traditional administration and warrant the creation of autonomous organisms endowed with legal status and equipped with a programme budget. We might add that it should be defined in time, space and the field of technology." E. Pisani, *Revue française de science politique*, Vol. VI, No. 2, April–June 1956.
80. P. Massé, *op. cit.*
81. P. Massé, *Le Plan ou l'anti–hasard*, Paris, Gallimard, Coll. Idées, 1965.
82. P. Massé, *Méthodes . . . , op. cit.*
83. S. Nora, in F. Fourquet, *op. cit.,* p. 180–186.
84. Général de Gaulle's instructions to Jean Monnet, 10th January 1946.
85. Bloch–Lainé in F. Fourquet, *op. cit.* p. 91. Thus Fourquet notes that the first effect of national accounting was to provide an argument in favour of the

special taxes which were raised in 1947. Hirsch makes this comment: "Uri conducted the matter brilliantly. It was something of a hustling operation, but if you want to get something out of the government, hustling can be useful. From the scientific point of view it could probably be challenged somewhat, but the essential point of the matter was to get a result," *ibid.*, p. 83.

86. Bloch–Lainé, *ibid.*, *Commission du Bilan* (Accounts Commission) was set up in 1947 in order to draw up the first national accounts.
87. Hirsch, *ibid.*, p. 63.
88. *Ibid.* The creators of national accounting and planning rejected the following categories *in toto*: university academics, the statisticians of the INSEE (the French national statistics institute) to which the early Statistique Générale de la France had just given birth and the financial experts of the Finance Ministry, *ibid.*, p. 254.
89. Simon Nora, *ibid.*, p. 181.
90. Massé, *Le Plan . . . . op. cit.*
91. Growth can be buttressed by a budget deficit policy designed to stimulate consumption and provoke a revival in growth through the multiplier and consumption effect. Keynes said so, and social welfare policies proved his point. Cf. F. Fourquet, *op. cit.*, ch. V.
92. R. Schumann: "Restoring economic equilibrium through financial practice was one of the purposes of the inventory," in F. Fourquet, *op. cit.*
93. Cf. Fourquet, *ibid.*
94. In fact, these two operations were handled separately so that it was possible to argue for economic policies in the name of the accounting framework, even though it was empty or filled with extremely whimsical figures, as the authors themselves admitted. Cf. F. Fourquet, *ibid.*, ch. VII.
95. F. Grünig, *Le Circuit économique*, Paris, Payot, 1937.
96. *Doctrine saint–simonienne*, Paris, 1854; new edition, Paris, M. Rivière, 1924
97. The overall economic table presents the balance sheet of economic activity by type of "economic agent" (non–financial undertakings, households, administrative bodies, financial institutions, etc.) and by type of "operation" (relating to goods and services, distribution, finance). The activity of each agent is entered in terms of five accounts (production, operation, allocation, capital and financial accounts). The table of inter–industry exchange (*tableau d'échanges interindustriels*), derived from Leontieff's input–output matrix, provides for planning in volumes. It gives the branch–by–branch distribution of the total output by source of intermediate consumption, and makes it possible to deduce the added value of each branch. The table can be used to calculate the technical coefficients by branch, that is, the ratios between the intermediate consumption of the various products that go into the input of the branch and the total output of the branch. The financial operations chart assembles all the financial operations or all the financial accounts of the agents to describe the debt and credit variations for each agent. Cf. for example, F. Fourquet, *op. cit.*, p. 413–422.
98. *Point économique*, No. 5; cf. F. Fourquet, *op. cit.*, p. 396.
99. A. Vanoli, *ibid.*, p. 136.
100. There is a technical reason for this of course, but also a theoretical one (the consensus on ends) to which we shall return below.
101. Some examples: B. Jouvenel, *De l'art de la conjecture*, Monaco, Editions du Rocher, 1964; Club Jean Moulin, *L'Etat et le citoyen*, Paris, Seuil, 1961; G. Deferre, *Un Nouvel Horizon, le Travail d'un Equipe,* Paris, Gallimard, 1965.

102. L. Sfez, *L'Administration prospective*, Paris, A. Colin, Coll. U., 1970.
103. P. Gavanier, quoted in F. Fourquet, *op. cit.*, p. 84.
104. The SEEF was set up in 1952 and was replaced in 1961 by the *Service de la prévision* (the forecasting service). At the time, it brought together all the chief promoters of planning and national accounting in the Ministry of Finance. It is therefore a crack in the bastion of liberal financial tradition that is represented by the ministry. Furthermore, the entire operation was conceived with this end in view. Cf. F. Fourquet, *ibid.,* p. 180 ff.
105. The INSEE succeeded the *Service national de la statistique* (National statistical department), created in 1941, which itself resulted from the merger of the Demographic Service, created in 1940, and the Institut de la conjoncture. The latter, in turn, succeeded the *Statistique générale de la France* in 1939. Cf. Fourquet, *ibid.* p. 426; F. Volle, *Le métier du statisticien*, Paris, PUF, 1980; A. Desrosières, J. Mairesse, "Les temps forts de la statistique française depuis un siècle" in *Pour une histoire de la statistique, op. cit.*
106. P. Dubois, "Le système public d'information statistique sur les entreprises," *Economie et statistique*, No. 79, July 1976; for the prewar period, cf. J. Caumartin, *Les Principales Sources de la documentation statistique*, Dunod, 1935.
107. *IVe Plan de développement économique et social*, Paris, Documentation française, 1962.
108. *Ibid.*
109. *Rapport sur les principales options du Ve Plan*, Paris, Assemblée Nationale; 1964.
110. *VIe Plan de développement économique et social*, Paris, Documentation française, 1971, 3 vols.
111. Delors, J., *Rapport du Groupe de Travail sur les Indicateurs Sociaux*, ENA, 1968.
112. Cf. R. Laufer, A. Burlaud, *Management Public, Gestion et Légitimité*, Paris, Dalloz, 1980.
113. The Sphinx model, which is aimed at analyzing measures to reduce inequalities, uses these accounts. Cf. P. Kaminsky, "Perspective de Développement des modèles à moyen terme d'étude des inégalités," CRNS – Paris X, June 1979.
114. It was in this period that planning lost some of its importance: this spirit, this mystique, that carried an entire team from various horizons, died out from 1960 onwards, L.P. Blanc in F. Fourquet, *op. cit.*, page 257. Paradoxically, it was the weakening of planning that led Général de Gaulle, who had initiated it in 1946, to develop the theme of planning as an "ardent obligation."
115. M. Guillaume, "Les méthodes d'évaluation," in P. Huet, J. Bravo, *l'Expérience Française de la RCB*, Paris, PUF, 1973.
116. E. Bonnefous, *La Réforme Administrative*, Paris, PUF, 1973.
117. P. Huet, J. Bravo, *op. cit.*; see also L. Sfez, *L'Administration Prospective, op. cit.*
118. Definition in P. Huet and J. Bravo, *op. cit..*
119. At least in its ambitions and in its initial philosophy.
120. R. Laufer, A. Burlaud, *op. cit..*
121. P. Huet, J. Bravo, *op. cit.*, p. 80.
122. Gélinier, O., in Peyrefitte, *Décentraliser l'Administration*, Documention Française, 1976.

123. A. Cottereau, "Les Techniques Nouvelles, Mythes et Réalités" in *L'Administration*, 1970.
124. Bloch–Lainé, F. *L'Economie du XXe siècle*, Paris, PUF, 1961.
125. *Rapport sur l'orientation préliminaire du VIIe Plan*, Documentation française, 1975.
126. The theme became one of current interest when the Club of Rome started publishing its work. Cf. D.H. Meadows et al., *The Limits of Growth*, New York, Universe Books, 1972.
127. This is the revealing title of a work published by the CFDT *Confédération, Les Dégiricale du Travails Française du progrès*, Paris, Seuil, Coll. Points, 1977.
128. Cf. the studies made by that highly reliable organization, the CEREBE (*Centre de recherches sur le bien-être*—welfare research centre). For a more extensive development of the notion of subjective indicators, cf. R. Laufer, A. Burlaud, *op. cit.* p. 123–140.
129. See Chapter 10.
130. *VIe Plan, op. cit.*
131. Largeault, *op. cit.*
132. Y. Weber, *L'Administrative consultative*, Paris, LGDJ, Bibliothèque du droit public, 1968.
133. J. Fournier, N. Questiaux, "Les politiques sociales et l'évolution du capitalisme," *Journées d'économie sociale,* CNRS–PARIX X, June 1979.
134. We are referring here to advertisements on radio and television.
135. This measure flowed from the reform of the housing assistance system under a law dated 3rd January, 1977.
136. R. Laufer, A. Burlaud, *op. cit.*
137. It is in this sense that we can speak of the "refeudalization" of society by the administration. See for example, Université de Vincennes, *Le Nouvel Ordre intérieur*, Paris, Albin–Moreau, 1980.
138. Y. Weber, *op. cit.*
139. See Chapter 5.
140. For example, the commission of users in the plan for reform of local government in France. This trend is not restricted to the French administration. Thus, in 1980, the U.S. administration recruited nearly 7,000 volunteers to participate in the administrative inspection of the safety of products. See *Le Monde*, 27th November, 1989.
141. On this point, cf. the debates reported in the French press.
142. E. Bonnefous, *op. cit.*
143. *Rapport sur les obstacles à l'expansion économique*, Paris, Imprimerie nationale, 1960.
144. It is true that the relation of law has undergone similar changes. Note the tendency now to replace the adage "ignorance of the law is no excuse" by the precept according to which "everyone is supposed to be ignorant of the law." Cf. colloquium on relations between the administration and the administered, Jouy–en–Josas, CESA, 1979.

Chapter 7

Rhetoric: The Method of Discourse

Rhetoric deals with the visible side of what is beyond our control.

Democracy, Free Market and Truth

When the conditions of democratic and free–market exchange are achieved, communication among men is entirely ensured by common measures provided by nature—through the price and the vote. Exchange expresses the natural law in the economic market by setting the price at a level where supply and demand reach an equilibrium and in the "political market" by designating the law voted by a majority of representatives as the right law.[1]

The Language of Nature

In classical economic theory, the notion of the *true price* took the place of the old, medieval concept of the *just price*. Henceforth, price established itself in nature and no longer in society. The medieval *just price* was the monetary expression of the material or psychological service rendered by a given item to an individual, assessed independently of the appreciation of those who were materially engaged in the exchange. It was set by theologians as the legitimate interpreters of God's design, to give a person, in a determined situation, the "means to achieve the ends proper to his nature . . . by the possession of a given piece of goods."[2] The market or competitive price (*communis aestimatio fori*) did not result from the application of the divine plan but from the supply/demand ratio. It could not be likened to the just price (*communis aestimatio*) unless it represented a "normal competitive price," that is, a price that was supposed to express the real value of the goods; it left no room for a subjective element of appreciation except on the part of the seller. When the competitive price was very different

137

from the stipulated just price, the seller could be condemned for usurious practice by the interpreters of God's word, the ecclesiastical judges.

For the idea of a *just price*, set unequivocally and rigidly by God and interpreted by his priests through a legitimate social procedure, the notion of *true price* substituted the idea of price set naturally and unequivocally at a level that varied according to the relationship of the moment between supply and demand in the act of exchange. The *true price* was justified by nature as the *just price* was justified by God. Interpretation became unnecessary. Nature expressed itself directly. Price was the language of natural truth, shaped in an impersonal way in the market. As such, it was the prime medium of communication among individuals who were otherwise withdrawn into the inner recesses of their private lives.

In the area of legislative decision, the vote fulfilled the law of nature by the intermediary of representatives. Thus Montesquieu could identify physical law with law as it emerged from human legislative action.[3] In so doing, he reconciled, under the rule of Natural Reason, what the tradition of natural law had divided into immutable natural law, accessible by revelation,[4] and "arbitrary" *positive law*. As he put it in a famous formula: "Laws, in their broadest sense, are the necessary relationships that derive from the nature of things; and in this sense all beings have their laws, intelligences superior to men have their laws, animals have their laws, man has his laws."[5]

Positive laws were similar to physical laws, even if they did not have the inflexibility of the latter. The exercise of reason had to prevent positive laws from transgressing the laws of nature. It had to seek to found the rights of people on "true principles," that is on the recognition of "relationships of equity anterior to the positive law that establishes them."[6] "The law in general is human reason inasmuch as it governs all the peoples of the earth; and the political and civil laws of each nation should be only specific instances in which this human reason is applied."[7]

The Usages of Language

Under these conditions, rhetoric had no place because there was no place for language.[8] The latter's mediation was indispensable however, in two circumstances: first for naming the categories of good administration; second for allowing the deliberation needed to illuminate reason by publicizing knowledge of nature.

The lexicon of administrative categories was conceived as the language of nature provided by the law. It was a language of truth constituted by the true categories of objective knowledge. All knowledge of nature resolved into statements of non-ambiguous facts. Language was without ambiguity.

Administrative categories represented the means needed to objectify individuals within the limits of the organization of State resources. Because they were binding, these categories had to be used in limited fields, and under the strict control of the political authority. They were restricted to the observation and control needed for the proper functioning of the civil society.

Because these categories had to be defined by law, language was to be used in deliberation, in conditions where one might say with the philosopher Perelman that "the real dominates."[9] In this case, there was no real basis for rhetoric since deliberation was not aimed at persuading the undecided but at leading to the rational evidence of the relationship between means and ends through the unambiguous exercise of reason. "If the truths taught are such that it is enough to believe and to know them, giving one's assent implies nothing but the knowledge of their truth."[10] In other words, the argumentation was aimed not at persuading but at demonstrating. What was called deliberation was more like the explanation of knowledge, which ensured the proper functioning of the assembly as a "political market." Whence the importance of publicity, provided in particular by the press and the salons, in educating public opinion.[11] Language had lost its role as cultural medium by which through scholastic interpretation and commentary God's purposes were expressed, to the benefit of those of his clerics.

Natural truth found its own expression through the vote. Deliberation worked like a logical syllogism.[12] The premises were posited as being natural; the rules of discussion were consensual; they aimed at the common goal of the search for truth, that is the search for "the true principles of law" through the exercise of reason. Finally, the variety of individual opinions thus shaped by deliberation guaranteed the majority opinion as truth and not as simply the mean opinion.

Lastly, language was used for administering justice, the task of which was to state the law in each specific case on the basis of the general rule. In this view, jurisprudence itself was not interpretative but deductive. This was stipulated by the law of 16-24 August 1790: "The courts can make no rules, but they shall apply to the legislative body whenever they believe it necessary either to interpret a law or to make a new one."[13] The role of the judges was thus reduced to the minimum. Their "power will only be that of applying the letter of the law to special situations through a correct reduction and without resorting to interpretations that might deform the will of the legislator."[14] For their part, jurors as the citizens' representatives, were assigned the same deductive task. From 1790 onwards, they had to listen to the following text when they retired to deliberate: "The law in no way asks the jurors to account for the means by which they have been convinced. It does not prescribe any rules on which the fullness and sufficiency of a proof should depend. It enjoins jurors to question themselves in silence and meditation and, in the sincerity of their conscience, seek out the impressions made on their minds by the proofs brought against the accused and the means of his defense. The law in no way tells them: 'You shall hold to be true every fact attested by such and such a number of witnesses"; nor does it tell them: 'You shall not consider any argument, not formed by so many elements, so many witnesses and so many clues, as being sufficiently established'; it asks them only one question, which contains the full measure of their duties: 'Have you an intimate conviction?'"[15] This conception of the judge as a simple "administrator of justice," was perfectly coherent with the principles of a democratic philosophy of law. It was to prevail in theory until the 1880s.

For the law to be purely deductive, there must be a rule of law for every type of situation. This quest for the "system of perfect law" was undertaken by the members of the "exegetical school" during those years. They sought to frame all possible judgments so that they could be derived by syllogism constructed by reason on the basis of law. In such a system, the judge was only the hand that brought sovereign power to its application at the conclusion of a purely impersonal operation of deduction and of "weighing" the crime on the scales of the legal norm.[16]

But the practical impossibility of the theory had appeared much earlier: "It is impossible for the legislator to provide for everything . . . a host of things are necessarily left to the realm of practice, to discussion by educated men, to arbitration by judges . . . in the absence of precise texts on each subject, constant and well-established usage, an uninterrupted sequence of similar decisions, a received opinion or maxim take the place of the law."[17] Thus the Napoleonic Code stipulated early on that "the judge who refuses to judge on the pretext that the law is silent, obscure or insufficient may be prosecuted for denial of justice."[18] In this way the judge was to acquire prerogatives that were no longer those of mere certification and application of the law. The code opened the way to *de facto* interpretation by judges even when legal theory remained entrenched in its previous positions.

The Rhetoric of Need

In a previous chapter, we noted that the emergence of specialists in connection with the development of organizational management, struck a blow at the legitimating power of the free-market and democratic representation of the world constructed by the Enlightenment. In every sphere of society (political, economic, administrative and juridical) there was a widening gap between theory and practice.

This transformation challenged the obviousness of the relationship between individual ends and social means. The market price could no longer be conceived as the immediate expression of the order of individual preferences since, in the daily practice of the enterprise and that of the buyer, the market was no longer atomized, fluid or perfectly informed. This indeed was why the techniques of management developed inside the firm, and those of marketing outside it. Price was no longer a universal medium of communication, a language that provided for the equilibrium of exchange. A sales function slipped in between supply and demand. "It no longer suffices to be able to produce in order to become an entrepreneur; one must also be able to sell."[19] The firm had goals—self–perpetuation and profit—and organized the means to achieve them. But, somewhere between the entrepreneur and the consumer, the common measure of price had been lost. In other words, there was no longer anything to provide the *a priori* certitude that the goods produced by the entrepreneur would satisfy the consumer's demand, since the natural long-term mechanism for suiting supply to demand had been lost.

The administration had conquered new fields of action: Specialist corps had sprung up: specialists in the management of public firms and administrations, specialists in the interpretation of laws as the judges had become. The fact that laws were put to a vote which, in the former conception, had assured natural mediation (delegation and sanction) between the representatives (hence the citizens) and the administration, was no longer enough to justify the growth of administrative action. Whether in the political or the economic sphere, the invisible hand, which provided for the natural harmony of interests between individuals, had disappeared. The ends of the consumers or citizens and the means to satisfy these ends were defined by organs that acquired theoretical and practical existence as organizations. From the standpoint of the economic and political doctrine, nothing any longer guaranteed that communally organized supplies would satisfy each individual demand. And, as it happened, there was no lack of attacks on the excessive power of the administration and big firms.

The rhetoric of needs was harnassed to the reconciliation of ends defined by organizations and individuals. Society was ordered by ends that could not be achieved naturally, either immediately or in the long term of the free market, but which had to be achieved culturally over a span of time, within society. Therefore, it became necessary to discover the natural laws of social history that define the legitimate ends of society and make it possible to bring them about.

The satisfaction of individual needs remained the primary social law;

but the need was no longer capable of finding natural unspoken expression. It therefore had to be read and stated: consumer's need, group need, social need, such were to be the key words of a society that accorded itself a full existence. It no longer considered man as a being of pure, abstract reason, lost in nature, but as a tangible person naturally imbedded in society which molded him.

Individual Need

The big firm was to legitimate its production and business choices by the consumer's need, in the same way as it was to legitimate its increasing dependence on advertising. It was open to the charge that it disposed of useless products by blotting out the consumer's critical faculties with the enticement tactics of advertising, with the sole objective of profit. It could be accused of taking advantage of the vacuum the market's imperfections created in communication to impose its own "commercial propaganda." Anticipating these objections, the early marketing specialists[20] likened advertising to an act of informating and educating the consumer on the true qualities of the product. This trend was to lead to the concept of the "consumer-king" in as early as 1930-1935. The argument went as follows: a set of new products had become available in an innovative, tangible market. These products fitted the objective needs of the consumer, which were so obvious that it was not even worth the trouble to describe them.[21] However, the principal interested party, the consumer, did not have the means to know about the availability of these new products. To inform him through advertising was to enable him to make more intelligent choices. Moreover, advertising was a means to educate the consumer.[22]

The argument was to change as the rhetoric of need was developed. In its initial form, it relied on a vision that was as yet still steeped in free-market philosophy; it was merely a matter of replacing the market where it had lost its openness with respect to information. Reference was made to a truth of the product, to a need whose origins were not really questioned. Thus the notion of the market's being segmented was still absent. Advertising was addressed to an "average consumer" who might be a "*homo economicus* made real." Need was a matter of individual preference. The argument of education was becoming ever less credible inasmuch as advertising aimed increasingly at selling a brand and not a product in a universe of monopolistic competition. Therefore, by returning to the sources of need, and especially by reflecting, through the practice of advertising, on the innate or created character of need, this argument came to be discarded for the one that said, need changed with society. And so a new product that some might call useless, created to satisfy a need that some might accuse the firm of having invented, in fact fitted (according to marketing theory) the law of social change. Consequently, the firm was permitted not only to identify existing needs and meet them but also to reveal "dormant" needs. Similarly, it did not have to know about the real or imaginary nature of the consumer's need, for it would then have usurped the right to intervene as a moral power. Marketing theory thus tended to center increasingly on the consumer and to move from a viewpoint of objective need to one of subjective need. Simultaneously, it moved away from the view of the consumer as a rational buyer. The analysis of buyers' motives referred less and less to reason and habit and more and more to the effect of "social laws," like the law of "conspicuous consumption" identified by Veblen.[23] Of course, in the end, all were agreed that the consumer was king, but, as Clémenceau said of the people in a democracy, he reigned but did not govern.[24] The consumer was seen as a "Supreme Court," who judged in the last resort but could not devote all his time to "fruitful reflexion on the nature and distribution of a single article."[25]

The satisfaction of needs was hence beneficial both to the producer (who achieved his goal of profit) and the consumer (whose well–being increased). The ideal for the firm would be to obtain information through market analysis in order to anticipate demand so as to place the ideal product in the market at the very moment the consumer's desire was awakened. The question of a possible antagonism between these two poles of the commercial relationship was resolved by this discourse which displayed its new pattern in a harmonious light. Every product corresponded to a need. Furthermore, by making it possible to pursue productive activity, profit met an essential societal need: by ensuring the perpetuation of markets, it made for the survival of the entrepreneurial system as a whole, and hence of the free society.[26]

Collective Need

The same type of argument developed in the administration when it set out after the general interest through public service, in particular by seeking to satisfy collective needs by itself or through policies that guided, stimulated or discouraged private initiative. In itself, every act of public service thus defined was excessive from the viewpoint of the democratic conception, which gave the legislative assembly alone the legitimate power to define the interest of all. This was an abuse of power in more ways than one: first because it meant denying the role of reasoned deliberation among the people's elected representatives in defining the general interest; second, because it meant neglecting the fundamental principle of individualism, according to which the achievement of the social optimum, identified with the maximization of the satisfaction of one and all, was subordinated to the free expression of individual preferences in the market. Now, as Condorcet had shown[27]—and the demonstration was to be repeated later by Arrow[28]—it was impossible to define a coherent collective order by which all individual satisfactions could be simultaneously maximized. In other words, it was impossible to construct a function of collective well-being that would be compatible with all the functions of individual utility, and would respect the preferences of one and all. Every function of collective well-being—which the administration identified with the general interest—was therefore very likely to be coercive for some people, unless they were incapable of seeing their true need or unless the goods in question were indivisible.[29] It was in the name of economic and social needs for goods that they considered to be useful or necessary for the well-being of some or of all, and which for various reasons were inaccessible in the private market,[30] that the agents of public service justified their concern with the general interest. Thus the rhetoric of need legitimated direct intervention by the State with a view to satisfying a supposed demand, and hence its entry into the field of producing and providing services, which went well beyond its traditional boundaries.

Somewhat later the rhetoric of need also strove to justify the state's economic policies: for example, if the equilibrium of full employment was defined as a function of collective well-being, every action of the state that sought to solve unemployment was legitimate.

The notion of need thus made it possible to reinterpret all the classical responsibilities of the state—defense met the need for peace, the police met the need for security, the civil engineering department the need for communication, etc.—as well as its future actions. So the administration lisped the first words of the new language in which it was to address its public. Since it would be acting henceforth to satisfy needs, it quickly had to subordinate performance to identifying the effective wants of those whom it addressed. It had to draw the consequences of the fact that while certain needs were identical for all (for example, those related to indivisible goods like defense), other needs were felt unequally, depending on the socio-economic characteristics of the beneficiaries. This was true for most of those to whom the new administrative services were directed. Just as the firm, in its real practice, tended to dissolve *homo economicus* and turn him into an irrational being determined by his social attributes, so the administration tended towards variable treatment for the governed metamorphosed into *user*.

The Guarantee of the Specialist

Trying to understand need meant trying to clear up something that had lost its clarity, namely the link between a collectively defined end and individual satisfaction. It meant creating a language for social mediation, which was made necessary by the loss of the natural medium formerly provided by price in the classical free market. It meant legitimating the product by the interest of the consumer and administrative decision by the general interest. Because this operation implied acquering empirical knowledge about the consumer's and the user's innermost feelings, it endangered the very conception of the individual, for it made an object out of what the philosophy of the Enlightenment had made the subject of power. It besieged that innermost recess, whose integrity guaranteed the qualities of the individual. He who studies needs divides man. Yet "man cannot be divided" for to divide him is to dissolve him, to make him "a system of interaction, a product of force, an anthropomorphism." Exploring man's psycho-sociological characterics deprived the individual of his essential attributes: equality, independence, omniscience, omnipotence, autonomy. Since a power was exercised (the power to promote a purpose or product to the detriment of other purposes or products) on the pretext of "need," it could not be done without a guarantee.

This guarantee was provided by nature, wherein the discourse of need was firmly anchored, through the intermediary of science and its specialists. The specialist was the necessary mediator for the expression of need. He endowed the categories that he constructed with objectivity, for he confined himself to noting their existence in physical or social nature. The definition of ends and the decision remained the business of the political sphere. But the precise designation of needs as categories of language concerning social nature, and the means to satisfy them, as rational methods, were the function of the specialist. For the public in general was incompetent to identify its own collective needs. Only the specialist could judge which method could be used to satisfy a need, assess the effects of an innovation, the consequences that might be expected of measures that transformed those at whom they were directed (education for example). Because the specialist defined and applied categories by the irreproachable method of scientific reasoning, he guaranteed the natural and objective existence of need.

Unlike the political authority and the free-market entrepreneur, unlike the administrator of the democratic doctrine, the specialist had no mandate to do so. He had to derive all his sources of legitimacy from a discourse of truth, based on his competence as a specialist, namely on the power of science to convince. His independence guaranteed above all the disinterested nature of his analysis of reality by ensuring the impersonal nature of his approach and, consequently, the objectivity of the categories that he constructed and the honesty of the use he made of them. This was the function fulfilled by the discourse that separated the scholar from the political realm.[31] It was also the function fulfilled by implicit or explicit control by peers, as symbolized in the drafting of codes of professional ethics[32] against an "equitable" definitions of the product's price and deceitful or improper practices.

The Specialists of Law

This internal guarantee was reinforced by external guarantees provided by law. For, among specialists, jurists played a very special role. In the public domain, they no longer simply guaranteed the legality of public practices by their approval. They had to create the means to judge the fitness of public decisions made on behalf of ends in the general interest.

Thus, after the thirties, new forms of administrative controls of results were gradually set up alongside conventional controls of procedures. Henceforth, administrative justice needed the assistance of a specialized language. For it had not only to compare the legal and actual spheres of administrative intervention in order to decide whether or not it had sinned by overstepping its power. With increasing frequency, it had to judge in the light of administrative ends and, more recently, on the validity of the decision taken. The judge used to be a specialist of law. He used to decide between right and wrong. He now had to become also a specialist of management or accounting, to decide between what was efficient and inefficient.[33]

In the private sphere, the abstract nature of the traditional view of the law was also criticized. It was seen to prevent the real nature of the misdemeanour from being taken into account, unless the interpretation of the law itself were replaced by the interpretation of the intent behind the law. This search for the legislator's intention became "all the more necessary as, with the passage of time and with social and technological change, the means given in the codes seemed all the more frequently unsuited to the ends pursued."[34] In analyzing the conditions for creating the law, an attempt was made to find the original need the legislator had intended to meet, and to fit the interpretation to current conditions. The law was no longer an autonomous system. It was what the legislator provided himself with to serve an end. The end, not the system, had to serve as the criterion of the legitimacy of judgment.[35] It is in this sense that the "functional" (or "historical" or "sociological") schools were to attack the idealism of the classical view of law from the 1880s up to the Second World War.[36] For them, it no longer sufficed to start from concrete experience in order to interpret an abstract law. The situation had to be corrected where it had come wrong, that is, at the root. The problem had to be dealt with in the framing of laws itself. Duguit, like Barthélémy, went so far as to reject Parliament's right to legislate, on the grounds of its being incompetent.[37]

Against Parliament's preeminent function as defined by classical democratic thought, they were to argue the need to entrust this task to those who know. Those who know first of all that the law was not an immutable abstraction but an objective social rule, normative certainly, but evolving. That is, those who would know how to relate scientifically their knowledge of society with their knowledge of the constraints of the legal system; those who would therefore be able to found the legal norm on the social norm. Thus natural law and positive law, which the movement of society had dissociated, would be reconciled: the spokesman for nature, the translator of natural law into positive law had changed. The "jurist–sociologists" of the late 19th century wished to replace the sovereign assembly that had founded positive law on the revelation of nature, by the specialist who would found positive law on the revelation of social nature by science. For them, the Assembly was unfit to tell the Truth by the deliberation of Reason because it was incapable of doing so. The Truth of Enlightment Reason, the conception of which had presided over the constitution of the Assembly as the legitimate place of revelation, was succeeded by the Truth of specialized Scientific Knowledge. Having lost its capacity to tell the former Truth, the Assembly did not acquire the ability to reveal the latter. The intuitive knowledge of universal Reason was unseated by the experimental and specialized knowledge of positivist Reason.[38] Thus, the nascent crisis of political power found its expression in the area of legal theories.

The Rhetoric of Opinion: The Rhetorical Empire

The boundaries of the domains that determined the conception of the world held by the Enlightenment (the frontiers of the firm, the line of demarcation between the private and public sectors, the boundaries between the political and bureaucratic spheres) were blurred. Social ends had lost their transparency; quantitative growth was no longer the uncontested sign of progress. The age of the assessment of "qualitative need" had begun. Since the criteria were no longer unequivocal, this assessment could no longer be anything but an attempt to measure subjectivity. The expert appraisal of need had lost its meaning when need lost its moorings in nature. In all fields, expertise in the measurement of subjective needs henceforth came to the fore.

The debate on ends developed everywhere, in the administration, associations and professions, without it being possible to relate the expression of the needs of each to a measure, unless it were the measure of the number of persons sharing the same feeling. And since this feeling was based on no criterion that could claim superiority or truth, it could not hope to be shared by others through reasoned deliberation. In order to be shared, it had to rely on the methods of persuasion.

To persuade and to be persuaded that a need existed, to persuade and to be persuaded that the means of satisfaction proposed were the most fitting ones meant guiding the other person towards the feeling that one had or wished to make him have, in particular by persuading him that others shared the same feeling. Evidence was no longer anything other than the evidence of the senses. The satisfaction of each could no longer be reduced to a common measure. Therefore, to persuade someone that a point of view was shared meant holding up this point of view as the reflection of the view of each or of the greatest number, as a conjunction of the particular perceptions of the world; it meant making man the arithmetical measure of all things, the only possible common measure in a world of beings whose opinions were irreducible to one another.

As it happens when society loses all the criteria founding the obviousness of its order, Sophism triumphed.[39] Deprived of a source of truth, and hence incapable of demonstration but capable of argument, stripped of proofs but full of persuasive talent, deprived of an objective standard for measurement but taking man for all measurement: such was the Bureaucrat Prince in his Kingdom.

In the empire of rhetoric, the only criterion was the pragmatic one of efficiency. The Bureaucrat Prince used every weapon at his disposal: if he could not convince by reason, he would persuade by seduction; if he could not demonstrate, he would argue. Since he was in no condition to prove his truth, he sought emotional adhesion.[40]

The development of an emotional, irrational relationship, the play on the implicit, on images, on connotations: these were the means by which the Bureaucrat Prince sought to "intensify adhesion to values, without which the discourse on action could find no lever to move and affect its hearers."[41] The consumer, the user, the polled man was not a partner but a spectator. The new Prince's method consisted in the manipulation of opinion in its modern form of marketing. His instruments were all the means that evoked the legitimacy of his person and his actions: charisma, tradition and, above all, reason and competence (in its dual meaning of knowledge and delegated power), the attributes by which the society from which he sprang was bound to its criterion of truth: Nature.

The Argument: Method

Foremost among argumentative resources was the rhetoric of scientific rationality. A rationality whose image was reduced to respect for procedure, since a science without criterion, hence without any *a priori* object, could not legitimately ask any questions other than empirical ones, by any means other than "operational" concepts (that is, concepts organized with a view to their practical effectiveness in culture).[42] The Bureaucrat Prince made the most of the fact that it was commonly accepted that compliance with method was a pledge of the neutrality of the constructed object and of the disinterestedness of its constructor. Method became the sign of the natural truth of the constructed object, hence of the scientific character of the approach. Compliance with method became the central argument of the rhetoric of reason. Here we can recognize the characteristic structure of the technique that the rhetoricians named enthymeme, wherein "the purpose of argumentation, unlike that of demonstration, is not to prove the truth of the conclusion from that of the premises, but to transfer to the conclusion the adhesion granted to the premises."[43]

Numbers, symbolizing the rigor of the procedures, acquired central value in the application of this technique. Irresistibly evoking reason at work, they legitimated the person or organization who used them or calculated them. "Say it with numbers" is the motto of the Bureaucrat Prince: the use of numbers means that scientific reason has been employed somewhere, hence that those speaking are reasonable, namely, that they know what they are talking about; hence that the results they put forward are reliable. The number is the residual emblem of nature, and the concept is but the suspect sign of culture.

The Goal: Consensus

Using numbers also provides a measure that evokes the assent that is at the source of political legitimacy. In a world with no common measure other than man, counting is the most powerful rhetorical instrument for simulating what nature achieved in the democratic doctrine, namely agreement among the members of society, "consent" being the assent of the "Majority" of "Public Opinion" at the end of the deliberation of Reason sanctioned by the Vote. "Consensus," on the contrary, is the adhesion of the "silent majority" of public opinion as expressed by the summing up of spontaneous, individual opinions[44] gathered in the opinion poll. A specialist put it this way: "Consensus is the state of opinion when a substantial part of the population answers "yes" to a question of the poll."[45]

The consensus expressed by this percentage is the Sophist's *commonplace par excellence*, from which every undertaking aimed at efficient persuasion must start, and to which it must always return. The problem of the Bureaucrat Prince is to "manage consensus," the common ground between his own conviction of the pragmatic value of the ends and means as he designates them and the conviction of everyone that they will find in it there own advantage (which each shares with many others). The passage from consent to consensus, and from common measure to common ground is a passage from rational to irrational. The abstract, rational and autonomous individual becomes a tangible human being, moved by the irrational impulse that is triggered by the evocation of tradition, habit or even the charisma of his leaders. The ideal rational individual chose his ends and means in a universe without structure; the irrational, tangible man of the marketing society adheres to ends in a society endowed with a structure of power, and hence of influence. But the totality of what the opinion poll reveals with regard to the opinion expressed in it is precisely what it conceals in its rhetorical use of the poll as a *simulacrum* of the democratic vote. For here it presents the results of its probe into the irrational depths of the unconscious, shaped by tradition, charisma and all the tricks of influence, as an image of agreement among autonomous consciousnesses.[46]

The Argument: Categories

Managing consensus means using arguments that work. A vital factor in the power of argument is consensus on the meaning of words. But, while the order of the world does not yield itself of its own accord, consensus management assumes that the instruments that the Bureaucrat Prince uses to order the world are also his common ground with his subjects. Name everything in order to count everything, since nothing is any longer left out of culture, since there are no longer any essences that yield themselves, but only existences that are to be interpreted.[47] Count in order to govern everything: this is the Bureaucrat Prince's dual task of management.[48]

In a society of evolving practical needs, the building of new categories is a permanent process.[49] The job of the category creator is of two orders: creating categories for action, and naming these categories. Creating good categories provides an efficient tool for action, one to which legitimizing rhetoric may be applied. Naming these categories well means taking, from the traditional resources of language, the images which will reinforce the legitimacy given by the mode in which the categories are built. They will therefore provide the common ground that has all the appearances of the preeminently natural and social common measure: language. Thus the most ordinary words might be rehabilitated or renovated, as old houses, whose outside walls are kept as a sign of tradition while the interiors are renovated for modern use. Seen in this light, it will perhaps be easier to understand the strange social path taken by a word like "poverty," which fell into administrative disuse in French in the postwar period, but has now regained currency.[50] In the vocabulary of voluntary growth, it was deemed appropriate to speak, on a comparative scale, of "underprivileged social groups." No doubt this was meant to signify that the condition was not beyond cure, in contrast with the connotations attached to the poor and their abjection, who bear the shame of being an unchanging element in a society of progress. Yet the poor are with us again, entirely rehabilitated, rebuilt from within by the aggregation of statistical categories, rigorously manufactured by the intersection of a battery of economic and social variables, categories in which the informed eye cannot fail to recognize the old target groups of development, only slightly reshuffled.[51] Does this mean that the condition of poverty is once again to be considered as matter of fate? Certainly, considering the fact that the common administrative treatment of all the categories grouped under the same notion charts a common destiny for all its members in spite of their obvious differences. This destiny is marked by a common downgrading, control and services, in a word by an identical form of State intrusion into what used to be considered as private life.[52] It might be said that the come-back of poverty is modernity under cover of tradition.[53]

The Statisticians' War of Religion

Constructing categories is a necessity of action. The category is the clearest operational concept. Thus, after the shaky attempts of as yet uneasily installed bureaucracies, we might conceive of current procedures for the routine creation of categories: action will then be legitimated by the presumption of truth conferred on the category by the "rational" procedure that has created it. This is how things stand for all the "types" and "factors" that are created by standard statistical routines for the organization of a set of heterogeneous "variables." These types and factors are usually treated as so many natural entities. They are named as if the objects they designate were not themselves constructed by the cultural selection of variables, by computational procedures[54] and the interpretation of results.[55] Measurement creates something that remains to be designated. The rhetorical effect begins when this "something" is endowed with a quality of essence, that is, when its reality is postulated by the mere fact that it has been produced by measurement.

But rhetorical facility goes hand in hand with difficulty. For since the categories are no longer moored in nature, they can no longer ensure the separation of subject and object: they are always relative to " who is speaking and to what purpose." The guarantee of the neutrality of categories is related to procedure. But when many procedures back their rhetorical power with the same argument (that of statistical rigour, for example) they enter into competition with one another. For statistical procedure provides for the methodologically faultless creation of as many objects as it has shapes. Consequently, the categories that designate these objects are revealed, no longer as instruments of intangible communication founded on social nature itself[56] but as the pragmatic instruments of groups with hegemonical designs. For it is a vision of the world that is conveyed in a word. Whoever has the power to name and the power to construct the content of words holds the world in his hand, for he possesses the rhetorical means to impose his action as one imposed by the order of the world, by the "nature of things."[57] Constructing categories in a bureaucratic society thus becomes an important element in the stakes of power.[58] Gramsci put it simply: "The supremacy of a social group is shown in two ways, as 'domination' and as 'intellectual' and moral leadership."[59] Imposing the dominant language is an instrument for universalizing the interests of the naming group for it catches every speaker and every hearer in the trap of its presuppositions.[60]

This is the statisticians' religious war in which cost–of–living indexes computed on different items by rival establishments are confronted;[61] where insults are traded over employment and unemployment figures, over growth and inflation rates. This war feeds the media, which in turn develops debates and commentaries on the methods or results of these calculations. Indeed this topic is like a bottomless pit: no criterion makes for a final decision, since all adversaries venerate number and method, the two totems of universal reason. Totems whose witch doctors are the statisticians, the specialists of empirical counting, whose interpretations depend on what they are counting for. Because these new specialists are subordinated to a pragmatic purpose when constructing their categories, they do not offer any more than a rhetorical guarantee of the "truth" of numbers. A guarantee that is all the more precarious as the stakes are of greater importance and, consequently, the results more contradictory. There no longer exists any internal guarantee of the discourse on the order of the world. But what, then, about external guarantees? Alas, the external inspectors, the private and, above all, administrative judges, have been reduced to the same fate: that of judging pragmatically.[62] Thus the most sophisticated methods for building consensus (like the DELPHI method[63]) have tried to combine all the evocations of legitimacy: the science of specialists, democratic deliberation, the quantification of the qualitative.

Catch Words

When one has a good catch word, one does not need to change it with the necessities of action; it is enough to shift its content by means of a rhetorical device that validates its new meaning. Thus in recent years we can trace the ups and downs of the bureaucratic use of the term "unemployed," whose substratum seems to vary according to the necessities of administrative management (in terms of social costs) and the management of the politicians' images with respect to public opinion.[64]

A catch word is a word or phrase that confers its own obviousness on the category that it covers. The choice of a catch phrase, of a catchy symbol in general, assumes "the capacity to analyse the mental dispositions, implicit knowledge, habits and even instincts that determine the association of speech, acts and thoughts with words and, more generally, signs, an association that confers on them the possibility of logical or performative use (related to) what they connote and what they denote in a manner whose universality and certainty are variable."[65]

A catch word is a phrase "that works." And the phrases that work are those that evoke a legitimate tradition. Words that work are those which, in a general fashion, miraculously resolve the problem of legitimacy (such as "public opinion" and "consensus") or abolish a contradiction between a de facto reality and a legitimate aspiration (such as the "silent majority" or "mass culture"). Words that work also provide new sources of legitimacy by drawing upon neighboring sources (for example people depending on social workers will be called "clients" instead of "users"; conversely, firms will offer "services" to customers rather than sell "products"). Words that work may also be those that symbolically paralyze the adversary: "democracy," which the French right wing has appropriated throughout the 20th century is one of these.

Words that work induce action in the manner desired by their promoters. In general, words that work are good labels that adequately fulfill an intention. A catch word is managed like a brand name: this is the task of political marketing as it is the task of commercial and administrative marketing. The marketing of words accentuates and accelerates a mechanism by which meanings and values are constantly dispossessed and, therefore, the available rhetorical resources of legitimation are gradually exhausted.[66] Words, like any product, are henceforth subject to the law of obsolescence. Thus, once they have been created or recreated, words not only have to be promoted but also maintained. The word–product has all the resources of marketing at its disposal: creativity, market research, opinion polls, segmentation, etc. . . . Politicians as well as administrators and even judges have taken up work on signs and the image of signs, following in the steps of advertizing men. This is an authentic work that includes analyzing the conditions for making the message function. For, as Perelman has shown,[67] once rhetoric is victorious, language can no longer be separated from action. Discourse can no longer claim impersonal validity; it may use artifices to secure belief in itself, but the credibility of these artifices is related to the personality of whoever uses them. The value of the word depends on its bearer. It is therefore a task of fitting not just the right sign to the right target but also the right sign to the right bearer. Thus it induces a veritable re–personalization of power. We can now explain the importance for the administration of making its relationship with the users more human, the importance to the politician of staging his actions and the importance to the firm of managing its public relations. For it is through this set of signs that consensus is constructed and made visible. It is on this set of signs that the Prince in search of legitimacy constantly and repeatedly feeds; to renew his existence by simulating his relationship to an essence—such is the rock that the new Sisyphus is condemned to roll.

The Media

The Bureaucrat Prince abandons the guarantees of Reason and Science to seek his categories in the shifting world of appearances. This procedure uses up, one after another, all the common grounds that tradition has bequeathed to the power of the new Prince. Soon, there is only one common ground left, namely, the idea of a common ground called consensus.[68] By studying the market, the Bureaucrat Prince takes words from the mouths of those he addresses, and these words soon give way to a silent majority and a dumbstruck opposition, which seeks to express itself by violence. Any word spoken by some member or other of the public can be picked up and returned to him in the shape of a product or service offered by the Bureaucrat Prince. To escape the words–trap, many then turn towards the ineffable experience of mysticism. There they discover that even silence and its mysteries can be organized bureaucratically.

Notes

1. Cf. Chapter 3.
2. J. Largeault, *Enquête sur le nominalisme*, Paris, 1977, pp. 255-256.
3. V. Goldschmidt, Introduction to Montesquieu, *L'Esprit des lois*, Paris, Garnier, 1979.
4. Or by reason according to Domat, *ibid.*
5. Montesquieu, *The Spirit of Laws*, book I, chapter 1.
6. *Ibid.*
7. *Ibid.*, book I, chapter III.
8. C. Perelman, *L'Empire rhétorique*, Paris, Vrin, 1977.
9. *Ibid*, p. 38.
10. Saint Augustine, quoted by Perelman, *ibid.*, p. 26.
11. J. Habermas, *Strukturwandel der Offentlichkeit* Herman Luchterhand Verlag, 1962, Paris, Payot, 1978, Chapter I,3.

12. C. Perelman, *Logique juridique*, Paris, Dalloz, 1976, p. 24. We are greatly indebted in this chapter to this work and to *L'Empire rhétorique, op. cit.*
13. *Ibid*, p. 16.
14. *Ibid.*
15. Art. 342 of the French Code of Criminal Procedure, quoted by Perelman, *ibid.*, p. 27.
16. C. Perelman, "Droit, logique et épistemologie", in *Le Droit, les sciences et la philosophie*, Paris, Vrin, 1973.
17. Portalis, *Discours préliminaire*, quoted in Perelman, *op. cit.*, p. 17.
18. Napoleonic Code, art. 4, *ibid.*, p. 16.
19. P. Doré, *Concepts de Base du Marketing*, Paris, Nathan, CIFG, 1973, p. 12.
20. Textbooks consulted: M.T. Copeland, *Problems in Marketing*, Chicago, N.Y., A.W. Shaw, 3rd ed. 1927; H.H. Maynard *et al*, *Principles of Marketing*, Ronald Press Co., 1st ed., 1927; H.F. Holtzclaw, *The Principles of Marketing*, N.Y., Th. Y. Crowell, 1935; P. White, *Market Analysis*, New York, McGraw Hill, 1921; E.P. Learned, *Problems in Marketing*, New York, McGraw Hill, 1936; D.M. Phelps, *Marketing Research, Its Function, Scope and Method*, Ann Arbor, University of Michigan, 1937; L.O. Brown, *Market Research and Analysis*, 1936.
21. The earliest textbooks do not use the *notion* of need in the same way.
22. See Chapter 4.
23. Veblen T., *The Theory of the Leisure Class, An Economic Study of Institutions*, London, G. Allen and Unwin, 1949.
24. Clémenceau, quoted by Tardieu, *Le Souverain Captif, op. cit.*, p. 268.
25. Maynard, *op. cit.*
26. See for example Drücker, *op. cit.*
27. Condorcet, "Essai sur la Constitution et les fonctions des assemblées de province", *Oeuvres*, Vol. VIII, Paris, 1947–1949.
28. K.S. Arrow, *Social Choice and Individual Values*, London, J. Wiley, 2nd ed., 1951.
29. See Chapter 6.
30. The most famous development of this thesis can of course be found in Max Weber, *Politik als Beruf*, Munich, Duncker und Humbdt (1st ed., 1919).
31. Cf. Max Weber, *ibid.*
32. Significantly, it would seem that codes of professional ethics are being drawn up at a time when the objectivity of the specialists and of science is no longer an evident fact. Thus the profession as a body culturally takes over the role abdicated by nature in the legitimation of specialists.
33. *Cahiers de l'IFSA*, Cujas, 1978, No. 16.
34. See for example the development of the theory of *manifest error* in public law. Cf. IFSA colloquium on "The discretionary power of the administration," *Cahiers of l'IFSA, op. cit.*
35. The new school of social defense, although it came later than the functionalist school, was to encounter this difficulty. Cf. for example, *La Défense sociale nouvelle; Un Mouvement de Politique Criminelle Humaniste*, Paris, Cujas, 1954.
36. With jurists like Durkheim's friend Duguit, or Barthélémy. On this subject, see Perelman, *Logique juridique, op. cit.*
37. Pisier–Kouchner, *Le Service public dans la théorie du droit de Léon Duguit*, Paris, LGDJ, 1972.

38. Cf. chapter 8.
39. C. Perelman, *L'Empire rhétorique, op. cit.*, p. 175.
40. *Ibid*, p. 35.
41. His discourse belongs to the *epidictic* mode, to use the terms of rhetoric: "In the deliberative mode, the orator advises in favor or against, and his concluding opinion is for what seems to him to be the most useful response; in the judicial mode, he makes an accusation or a defence with the purpose of deciding what is right; in the epidictic mode, he expresses praise or blame and his discourse is related to the beautiful or the ugly . . .; his action is aimed at a heightened communion around certain values for which he seeks to win acceptance and which should guide future action", *ibid.*
42. Cf. Chapters 8 and 9.
43. Perelman, *l'Empire rhétorique, op. cit.* p. 35.
44. C. Buci–Glucksman shows a drift in the interpretation of "consensus" from the liberal sense of "consent" ("the force that moves an association by the consent of the individuals who make it up"—Locke), based essentially on the contract, the state of law and all the mechanisms by which the will of the majority is expressed, to another meaning related to the investigation of social–psychological processes, to irrationality, and this is the meaning of "consensus" as it is used today. It is thus that Gramsci noted the sociologically illusory character of "consent" ("numerical consent, which would have it that every voice is equal, is systematically falsified by the inequality of wealth . . . and the existence of organized centers of education and persuasion") and showed that the technique of consensus is a technique of domination. Cf. C. Buci–Glucksman, *Pouvoirs*, special issue on "Consensus," October 1978.
45. P. Favre, *ibid.*
46. See for example, P. Bourdieu, "Questions de politique," *Actes de la recherche en sciences sociales*, No. 16, September 1977. Durkheim defines the collective consciousness as a "silent and spontaneous agreement among various consciousnesses which . . . vibrate in unison." The collective consciousness, in which the entire school of Durkheim took such a lively interest, is nothing but the consensus reviewed in sociological perspective. In other words, the consensus is the collective consciousness when it is presented as an agreement among the autonomous consciousnesses of liberalism and not as a culturally constructed agreement. E. Durkheim, *Textes*, Paris, Editions de Minuit, coll. Le Sens commun.
47. The naming of essences is necessary only "to do"; God "is," and is by essence indescribable: what could be done with Him?
48. See Chapter 10.
49. A revealing title: G. Ardant, *Codification permanente des lois, réglements et circulaires*, Paris, LGDJ, 1951.
50. For example, several seminars on *poverty* were held in Paris since 1980. Several research projects on poverty have been funded in recent years, especially projects to define the categories of the poor.
51. These categories are the unemployed, the physically and socially handicapped, shifting manual laborers, unqualified workers in the secondary labor market, etc.
52. On this point, cf. Chapter 10 below.
53. Bentham expressed it in a felicitous turn of phrase: "We think that we understand what is usually spoken of precisely because it is usually spoken of. Be-

tween words and things, there is such a connection that one is often led to take the one for the other; when one has words in the ear, one willingly believes that one has ideas in the mind . . . this long habit we have of using such and such an expression suggests that we have ascertained its value. This is precisely the role of customs officers who, after having sealed certain goods, consider themselves to be dispensed from having to ascertain their nature again," Quoted in L. Reybaud, *Etudes sur les réformateurs contemporains*, Paris, Guillaumin et Cie, 1841, Paris, Geneva, re–ed. Ressources, 1979, vol. II, chap. IV.

54. See for example the difference in results (in regression analysis) induced by the choice between "least error squares" and "absolute distance."

55. To readers looking for a comical example of this, we would recommend the article by J. Scott–Armstrong, "Tom swift and His Electronic Factor Analysis Machine," *The American Statistician*, 1967.

56. P. Bourdieu, L. Boltanski, "Le fétichisme de la langue et l'illusion du communisme linguistique," *Actes des la recherche en sciences sociales*, No. 4, July 1975.

57. P. Bourdieu, "Questions de politique," *op. cit.*

58. Cf. for example L. Thévenot, "Les fonctions sociales du flou et de la rigueur dans les classements," *Actes de la recherche en sciences sociales*, Nos. 26–27, March–April 1979; M. Cézard, "Les qualifications ouvrières en question," *Economie et Statistique*, April 1979; P. Bourdieu, "Classement, déclassement, reclassement," *Actes de la recherche en sciences sociales*, No. 24, November 1978.

59. *Quaderni del Carcere*, Grulio Einaudi, editore, 1975. And well before him, of course, the Sophists, for whom language, since it opened out on to nothing, could be nothing but the instrument of existential relationships, which were never relationships of knowledge but those of power as we showed in Chapter 1. A word may be applied to things that already exist, do not yet exist or have ceased to exist. The creation of words is wholly related to the "de–naturing" and "re–naturing" of nature and this "re–naturing" is nothing else but the cultural operation by which the decision is taken to designate that which will henceforth be called "nature." Thus threatened categories are offered a certificate of existence and promised treatment. Thus, under the impact of bureaucracy, nature and the society of the past are themselves "embalmed" and rendered "quaint." "Ecological museums" and "natural parks" are created. Nature is placed in the museum, wherein culture assigns it the characteristics (authenticity and eternity) that endow it with its new (cultural) value. To preserve, to restore becomes an imperative of this prince who is deprived of the support of legitimacy, of the referent, of time, of the concept and who must, rhetorically, find the guarantees that the existence of a nature and a tradition bring to the preservation of the stability of the world.

60. P. Bourdieu, "L'économie des échanges linguistiques," *Langue française*, May 1976.

61. H. Picard, "Elaboration et calcul de l'indice des prix à la consommation," *Economie et statistique;* J.–L. Moynot; "Le nouvel indice des prix de la CGT," *Le Peuple*, No. 888, 1978.

62. This is shown, for example, by the growth of the theory of manifest error in administrative law.

63. The purpose of the DELPHI method is to give a quantitative weighting to the qualititative variables of a decision–making model: A group of experts is

brought together from every relevant field. The model is presented to them and they are asked to name the variables for which quantitative weightings should be made, and to define these weightings. Each expert is then left to ponder the matter, and at the next meeting he gives his weightings and justifies them. The mean weightings are established, and the experts go their separate ways. In the final series of meetings, a consensus is sought on the weightings, each expert having in the meantime pondered the distance between his own weighting and the mean value.

64. Cf. *Cahiers IFSA*, No. 16, *op. cit.*
65. J. Poirier, preface to Largeault, *op. cit.*
66. J. Habermas, *Legitimations probleme in Spätkapitalismus*, Suhrkamp Verlag, Frankfort, 1973.
67. C. Perelman, *L'Empire rhétorique, op. cit.*, p. 177.
68. M. McLuhan, *Understanding Media: The Extensions of Man*, New York, McGraw Hill, 1964.

Chapter 8

Pragmatism: The Formation of the Cybernetic Ideology

Speaking about language is but another manner of speaking.

Cybernetic Ideology and Pragmatism

Pragmatism and cybernetics can be understood in two different ways. Pragmatism in a broad sense means judging an activity by its results. In late nineteenth century philosophy it was given a more rigourous, restricted, meaning in the works of William James and Charles Sanders Pierce.

Similarly, cybernetics can be defined as a technical term designating a scientific procedure widely used by a variety of specialists. It can also be considered in a broader perspective as a way to look at any phenomenon be it natural or cultural. Its development can be traced back to the seminal works of Ludwig Von Bertalanfly and Norbert Wiener.[1]

The argument of the present chapter is that the link between these broad notions and their more technical manifestations can be related to the history of the systems of legitimacy in such a way that it is possible to argue that modern times are dominated by cybernetic ideology which is nothing other than the expression of the modern form of pragmatism.

This form of pragmatism differs from the one defined in Ancient Greece in that the definition of goals and the evaluation of results are not primarily defined in terms of the individuals rather than in terms of organizational entities. In other words in modern pragmatism individuals are simulated in the same way as other entities due to the "general" nature of systems theory and the way in which cybernetics makes "human use of human beings."

The tendency of modern pragmatism to replace man by a model is well illustrated by how successful the concept of Artificial Intelligence is. Its success is so overwhelming that some may consider it has outmoded the very notion of cybernetic model. However there is a distinct advantage of sticking to the notion of cybernetics before discarding it for a futuristic view of generalized artificial intelligence: the first notion is well defined and actually constitutes the basic model of management and consequently of marketing whereas the second notion has not yet been clearly defined. Its scope and potentialities are the objects of intense debate its use in management is still very limited.

For the time being, we prefer to consider artificial intelligence as the latest form the question of the epistemological foundation of action has taken. As such we try to show that A.I. does represent the most pragmatic form epistemology can take. We must now locate the common link between Sophism, marketing, pragmatism, cybernetics and the crisis of legitimacy.

Sophism, Marketing and Pragmatism

If Sophism and marketing are the worst forms of invective that philosophers can trade with one another, it is because these names designate the contrary of philosophy. But the contrary of philosophy has yet another name: pragmatism. The easiest way to demonstrate that philosophy and pragmatism are opposites is to note that each may be defined (hence represented, seen) only by being placed for a instant on the grounds of the other.

To the question, "what is philosophy?", the high school teacher replies: "Philosophy is what we do when we ask this very question." This definition evokes pragmatic theory (the definition of a concept by action) and Sophistical technique (what I offer you is the answer to your question).

If the philosopher cannot define philosophy except pragmatically, the pragmatist cannot define pragmatism except theoretically. For, in its radical form, pragmatism must be defined as that which eludes all definition. If the philosopher objects that this is in itself a definition, the pragmatist will have no way out but to take the point as proof of the decidedly paradoxical nature of reality.

Some will object that it is not proper to make pragmatism the opposite of philosophy and the synonym of Sophism when, since the end of the 19th century, there has existed a school of philosophy which claims direct kinship with pragmatism. But this would be to overlook the point that Emile Durkheim made in 1913, in a lecture entitled "Pragmatism and Sociology"[2] namely that one of America's earliest pragmatists, F. C. S. Schiller, claimed kinship throughout his work with Protagoras. The fact, said Durkheim, is that Sophism and pragmatism run contrary to the whole philosophical tradition by denying the necessity of statements of truth. For them "the mind remains free with respect to the true,"[3] "man is the measure of all things." These propositions are enough to prevent the constitution of well–formed legitimacy systems.

Crisis of Legitimacy and Pragmatism

Any well–formed legitimacy system implies a representation of the world, or a cosmology in which the world is divided into two places, of which the first (the sacred, nature) is the source of legitimate power and the second (the profane, culture) is the place where this power is applied.[4] Therefore, every system of legitimacy assumes a representation of the world that exists prior to the acts that take place in it: this representation will be said to be true.

A specialist is needed to state that a truth exists prior to the person who enunciates it; the ordinary man, lacking in faith or reason does not see the obvious character of truth. This is why philosophers must bear witness: what they see can be seen by others equipped with the same philosophical system. A well–formed system of legitimacy therefore assumes a cosmology (a representation), a faculty of perceiving (reason) and a specialist (the philosopher) who connects cosmology to the human faculty so that each bears witness to the truth of the other. The crisis of the legitimacy system therefore implies the crisis of the cosmology, the crisis of the faculty of perceiving and, consequently, the crisis of philosophy. The crisis of philosophy is the triumph of the most extreme pragmatism.

Degrees of Pragmatism

If a reference must be made to "the most extreme" pragmatism, it is because there are degrees in the opposition between pragmatism and philosophy, which we must try to define. An action is a change in appearances inasmuch as it is ascribed to a cause. The least pragmatic way of defining the legitimacy of action consists in stating that this action is legitimate if its cause may be attributed to the source of legitimate power (the sacred, nature). In this case, the act is legitimate regardless of its effect. To make this system work, it is enough for everyone to have access to the faith or reason through which the cosmos can be seen. If cosmology, which makes it possible to isolate the site of legitimate power from the place of its application, suffers a crisis, one will be led to legitimate the action by its result: that is, by a judgment made on the changing of appearances. This pragmatism, however, has degrees.

A moderate form of pragmatism will refer the assessment of results to a norm accepted by all. This assumes the existence of a hypostasized authority (God, the God—Progress). As this authority cannot express itself directly, it will do so through interpreters (specialists, priests or philosophers) who pass practical judgment on actions and their results. To make this system work, there must be a hypostasis, specialists and a public that acknowledges the role of the specialists.

An extreme form of pragmatism will consider the assessment of results as an action which itself cannot be assessed except in relation to its own consequences. This action will be legitimate as it possesses the wherewithal to appear as legitimate. In its most extreme form, pragmatism joins Sophism. To make this system work, there must be a specialist in beliefs (the Sophist, the marketing man), who studies the public to see what might appear to it as legitimate.

When a "radical" pragmatist considers the systems of the true, he sees them as simple systems of shared beliefs, ideologies. The triumph of the marketing society and of the pragmatism that characterizes it will therefore furnish both confirmation and an explanation of that end of ideology which has been proclaimed for some time now. At most, it might be said that these defunct ideologies have been followed by the age of Pure Ideology, where rhetoric and empiricism exert themselves in a universe without structure, marketing being the pre-eminent technique for the research, the production and the definition of a sort of ideology with "no obligations or sanctions."

However, far from marking the end of ideology, the marketing society is characterized by the almost absolute triumph of a specific ideology. And if an ideology should triumph in this age of pragmatism, that is because it is nothing other than the systematization of this very pragmatism. Its domination extends from physics to psychology, from technology to sociology, from sociology to administration. Nothing escapes it. In this world of uncertainties, of appearances and confusion, an ideological structure is necessary: its name is cybernetics.

How can an ideology be established when the distinction between the sacred and the profane has long been abandoned as a principle and when, as we have seen, the distinction between nature and culture has become unclear and is vanishing in its turn. This is possible only because cybernetics is precisely the ideology that corresponds to the confusion between nature and culture. After all, did Herbert Simon not define cybernetics, or the science of systems, as the science of the artificial, the only science by which the "architecture of complexity"[5] could be grasped? Now, the artificial is precisely that space between the natural and the cultural which can be attributed to neither of these fundamental orders. The artificial is the product of human action considered in the place of its genesis: to anyone who takes a look at the earth from the cosmos, it appears as a concretion of nature; to anyone who tries to grasp the project that guides human action, it appears as the product of culture.

This view of the contact and intertwining of the natural with the cultural evokes the illegitimacy of incest. Legitimacy is disturbed if it cannot ascribe a fact either to nature and the legitimate tyranny of nature's laws or to culture and the accepted meaning of its customs. Herbert Simon himself notes all the pejorative connotations attached to the word "artificial": "(My dictionary) proposes the following by way of synonyms: affected, factitious, fabricated, feigned, simulated, falsified, unnatural; by way of antonyms, it gives: real, true, honest, natural, authentic, unaffected. Our language seems to reflect man's profound distrust of his own works." Are these not the very connotations of the words Sophism and marketing?

Curiously, for Herbert Simon the opposition between artificial and natural corresponds to the contradiction between complexity and simplicity. The purpose of the science of nature is to bring out that which is simple behind the appearance of complexity, the purpose of the science of the artificial is to account for complexity and for its architecture. This complexity is the expression of that which cannot be articulated: the incestuous confusion between the laws of nature and those of culture. Systems analysis may be defined as the technique that consists in describing a complicated (complex) reality by circles and arrows. Cybernetics provides a more precise definition of these systems when the circle under consideration has a reverse arrow by which it can check the effects of its action on its environment (which itself is described by circles and arrows).

Contradicting the statements of Herbert Simon, a Nobel prize winner in economics, we must quote the proposition of a Nobel prize winner in physics, Ilya Prigogine,[6] that complexity is produced directly by nature as order. Let it suffice here to point out that, if cybernetic ideology is really the characteristic of the marketing society and, hence is an important component of what we have come to consider as the modern equivalent of Sophism, it is normal to rediscover in it two tendencies which already opposed each other in ancient Greece: the champions of the *nomos* (of the law) the champions of the *physis* (of nature). No one should be surprised if an eco*nomist* defends the former view while a *physi*cist defends the latter.

From Natural Law to Nature Denatured

Free-market ideology may be summarized thus: individuals interact freely in the economic sphere; the resulting situation conforms to the laws of nature, on the one hand and, is in a state of harmony on the other. The history of ideas which leads to this definition should consider each of its terms in relation to its antonym. We shall consider the following pairs in succession:

1. economy/politics
2. individualism/holism
3. harmony/chaos
4. nature/culture[7]

We have frequently had to distinguish the realm of government, of final ends, from that of administration, which is subjected to it. In the beginning, the economy rightfully belonged to the realm of administration, since *oikos nomos* signifies the art of the proper management of a household. To be separated from the political sphere, economics first had to appear in the realm of government. Among the mercantilists we find an initial state of the development that changed economics from the most subordinate, even the most obscure, of activities to the most important institution of social life. For it was the mercantilists who stressed the essential importance of wealth for a government, and it was they who began to create what was to become the science of economics.

Although economics became a preoccupation of government, it continued to be formulated essentially in the categories of administration. The Prince, to whom the economy was totally subordinated, could not conceive of occurrences in his kingdom being formulated in the same categories as occurrences in relations among kingdoms. The internal and external economies were dissociated; economy could not yet be thought of as being autonomous.

It is to Quesnay that we owe the advent of economics as a total system submitted to its own relationships of equilibrium, which he summarized in his famous table.[8] According to the social anthropologist, Louis Dumont, such a vision "could not be achieved at the inception of the economic viewpoint—to the extent that this viewpoint can be considered to have existed before Quesnay's invention—but had to be derived from the exterior, had to flow, so to speak, from the projection, onto the economic plane, of the general conception of the universe as an ordered whole."[9] Beginnings are places of paradox. When Quesnay was unifying economics, he asserted the primacy of the whole over the part and of the community over the individual, placing himself, by this latter proposition at the opposite pole from the democracy that he made possible through the former. In particular, he subjected the economy, thus delimited, to the Prince, who became responsible for creating the conditions for the proper functioning of the system. In this, Quesnay remained attached to a profoundly traditional vision of the opposition between nature and culture. On the side of culture, tradition assigned the Prince his singular place in the economic system of action (in particular, taxes were conceived in terms of rent, the fees paid by the serf to his lord).

Three stages remained logically necessary to arrive at a complete formulation of the liberal ideology. First of all, economics had to be emancipated from the primacy of the collective over the individual and/or to take up Dumont's formulation, it had to move from holism to individualism. The notion of the natural harmony of interests, without which individuals, left to themselves, would fall into chaos, was to provide for this transformation. Then, it was necessary to emancipate the economy from the traditional power of the Prince: it was the concept of utility that assumed this task by using the model of physics to describe the mechanisms of the economy, thus replacing the will of the Prince by the laws of Nature. Finally, it was necessary to abolish the favoured status of land in the economy by replacing the idea of a traditional nature, owing its wealth to itself, with the idea of a nature whose wealth proceeded above all from the relationships of exchange between men. The triumph of the notion of exchange value over that of use value was to put an end to the excessively tight linkage between wealth and land.

The flowering of individualism meant above all the abolition of all hierarchies and organization among men, conceived as being equal and free. It escaped no one that this could be synonymous with anarchy and chaos. Such an awful fate was to be averted by the notion of harmony. The idea of moral harmony became the basis of Locke's optimism. It enabled him to develop a view of society which at that time was already very close to democracy. "With Locke, politics as such is reduced to a simple addition to morality and economics. Morality and economics provide, in the law of nature, the foundation on which the political society should be built. "Man's freedom could not harm society since it consisted in "obeying the law of Nature."[10]

Moral harmony made it possible to emancipate men from hierarchy and constraint: all that remained to make them totally subject to the laws of nature and to these laws alone was to emancipate them from morality itself. This is the step taken by Mandeville in the *Fable des Abeilles*, whose sub-title, "Private Vices and Public Benefits," is a revealing one. This new recipe for harmony made the selfishness and immorality of individuals compatible with the well-being of society, which was reduced to the "mechanism by which interests come into harmony with one another."[11] Thus the principle of the invisible hand came to be set out: it would come into full play only when it was recognized as the expression of the laws of nature. For it was said, henceforth, that nature followed laws that science made it possible to discover. The day was gone when the practice of physics entailed the risk of the gallows, and it would seem that Newton developed a spiritual view to justify his work more from personal need than social obligation. For science in this period was above all physics, and it was on this model that the new science of economics was to be built.

Physics used the concept of force; economics was to use utility. Utilitarianism is the name of a principle as well as a school of thought. The principle stated that man sought the greatest possible happiness. It gave the free-market ideology an objective definition of the force that animated human nature, such as it was expressed in economics. Political economy could then rise to the status of an objective science, since it was freed of all morality: *homo economicus* was guided by none other than the natural force that impelled him to seek his own interest. Neither pragmatism nor social psychology was involved here since both assumed that the subject of discourse was concrete man, whereas it was only the "reasoning being" as expressed in his economic behavior. Far from calculating his preferences in order to forecast his behavior in the market, utilitarianism adopted the market as the site where these hypothetical preferences would be revealed. In this sense, what was implied here was truly a principle, which could found a symbolic order. The utilitarian school, for its part, from Jeremy Bentham through James Mill to John Stuart Mill, stated, developed and then defended the principle of utility thus taking on the pious task of upholding one of the fundamental concepts of free–market ideology.

The principle of utility made possible an economic science designed on the model of the natural sciences. To be permanently rid of Quesnay's model, all that remained was to rid economics of the traditional conception of agriculture and land as sources of wealth. This was an important stage: it was the only one that could completely free political economy from the logic of authoritarian distribution which might require the intervention of a prince. Political economy could become the science of scarcity only at the cost of concealing it behind market mechanisms. If prices could not be used to attain the equilibrium of transactions, if two men could claim one and the same material good with the fierceness of two mothers claiming one and the same child, then Solomon had to be called in. Yet it was use value that made goods incomparable and, hence, made competition for goods impervious to reasonable, or rational, mediation.

The liberal society needed a prince, and got the invisible hand: it needed a judge and it produced exchange value. Exchange value produced that miracle wherein man (homo economicus) encounters man only through the mediation of things. Thus was abolished all that remained of direct interpersonal relationships in the economic relationship. In feudalism, the relation of "cultural" men to concrete things (use value) induced concrete relations among men which called for the establishment of hierarchies through violence, tradition or the intervention of the judge. In the free–market system, the relationship of "natural" men to abstract things (exchange value) introduced relationships between men which could be entirely mediated by the exchange of things.

The need for an "abstract" definition of exchange value in free–market ideology can be seen from the fate of the concept of labor value. It was Adam Smith who put forward simultaneously the concepts of exchange value and labor value. It is undoubtedly for this reason that he must be regarded as the true founder of modern, free–market political economy. However, his proposition only imperfectly resolved the problem of legitimacy for the free–enterprise system.

While the concept of exchange value made it possible to resolve the problem of economic relations among men, the concept of labor value once more created the possibility of a direct, unmediated conflict as the well-known, long drawn out debate on surplus value shows. So true is it, that no sooner is a substantial content given to what is exchanged than there is a growing danger that civil conduct will no longer prevail. In replacing land value by labor value, Adam Smith asserted himself as the economist of the modern industrial world but, in doing so, he did not completely achieve the ideological coherence of the free–market system legitimacy, which is self–contained in the exceptional use that it makes of tautology. This is why Leon Walras'[12] representation of political economy by a system of equations can be considered to be the complete form of the representation sought, where the tautology is expressed directly by the "equals" sign. Reason is binding on everyone because its law is laid down by logic; and logic as we all know is merciless with contradictions. Hence free–market ideology was to rid itself of other possible approaches to economic facts. We have dwelt on the reasons why free–market ideology had to rid itself of its Physiocratic origins and especially of Quesnay's work. It also had to put aside the work of Malthus.

The story of the legitimacy crisis of free enterprise can be traced through the resurgence of the modes of thought of these two authors.[13] With them, a little holism is mixed in with nature's workings, a little use value is mixed in with exchange value, even a little chaos is substituted for harmony. At least the harmony is no longer preestablished; it requires the intervention of a prince as an arbiter among men. The traditional prince was a feudal lord, the prince of the world of science was to be a bureaucrat. And we have already named the organizing principle of his fiefs: cybernetics.

To continue with this story, let us project the cybernetic model onto free–market society. For the most part (namely in the economic sphere), we find an infinite quantity of atoms exchanging data, thus achieving a constantly renewed state of equilibrium. This description confirms something that we knew already: the application of the cybernetic model to free-market society is useless. At every stage in the degradation of the free-enterprise system of legitimacy, this model is modified and becomes ever more necessary.

This process can be described in three stages: the Garrison State, the Welfare State and the Omnipresent State. If we agree to call communication a piece of information exchanged between two agents, we may describe the economic system of the Gendarme State as the result of a mass of communications: the infinity of economic agents freely exchanging information with each other. With the Welfare State, the State became a direct regulator of this mass of communications: it is by the action of the State that the mechanisms of the market result in a state of equilibrium, full employment. Hence, the mass of communications (the market) was now subjected to mass communication (the State) and the cybernetic model started becoming a useful description of the Keynesian system. Finally, with the Omnipresent State came the big organizations that dominated the market, mass communication and, with it, the marketing society, were triumphant: political economy tended to become one with cybernetics.

Let us continue down the road that leads from the free–market system to the cybernetic world. We have already had many opportunities to see the efforts made by the Welfare State to twist the invisible hand. Thus put to the challenge, economic theory was to take up the gauntlet and put it into the hands of the new Prince. It is to Keynes that we owe the complete formulation of macro–economic theory which was to give the State's interventionism its credentials. With his theory, he made it possible once again to consider the economy in the form of a table as did Quesnay. A major practical consequence of Keynes' work was the establishment of national accounts, the logic of which (the definition of agents, economic aggregates and balances of flows) can already be seen in Quesnay's work. Thus a holistic view of the economy was restored, and free exchange became accountable to the government for the way in which economic equilibrium was established. If such a government was necessary, it was because it had become impossible to expect a satisfactory equilibrium to be re–established over the long term. Short term imbalances were no mere viscosities in the adjustment of individual utilities and disutilities; they resulted from the collective behavior of groups of economic agents.

Taking up Malthus's theories on the difference between effective and real demand, Keynes gave wide currency to the notion of anticipation, thus introducing social psychology into the heart of economics. What came into play in the interval between *ex ante* and *ex post* equilibrium was unemployment, which resulted not from idleness but from the establishment of an equilibrium of under–employment through collective (macro–economic), hence holistic, phenomena.

While analyzing the causes of under–employment required introducing a minimal social psychology of unemployment, studying its remedies was to necessitate the development of a social psychology of demand, that is, the introduction of the notion of need, especially the need for public service, since the equilibrium of full employment was to be ensured through investment by the Bureaucrat Prince. However, the legitimacy of public expenditure did not depend on the legitimacy of needs: even if public works were confined to digging holes merely to fill them up again, the equilibrium of full employment would be ensured. All the same, no one could object to the notion that public expenditure had to strive to meet socially acknowledged needs by developing public services.

Political economy thus went beyond the realm of natural laws. Cultural man made a fresh appearance in economic choices. If Providence no longer fulfilled its role, the State would take its place. What made this vision of the providential Welfare State possible was the idea of unlimited economic progress.

Although economics, in its submission to the hegemony of politics, accepted the re–emergence of a traditional, holistic view of culture, it still believed that it could do without the traditional view of a limited nature which was the source of all wealth. It was when it came up against this limitation that economic power (which we have just examined in its transformation from an atomized power to a guaranteed concentrated power) was to shift from a guaranteed concentrated power to a concentrated power without guarantee.

The work of the Club of Rome and its success mark the curious return of the traditional view of nature. For its essential message is that natural resources are limited. Here we can recognize the Physiocrats' attitude to the natural wealth of the soil and even more Malthus's reflections on the demographic principle which "states the problem of scarcity more particularly from the standpoint of food resources."[14] This notion of limited resources reiterates the economic problem from the standpoint of rationing and distribution and brings the confusion between nature and culture to its peak.

We have seen that cybernetics is the ideology corresponding to the effort made to account for complexity (the nature/culture confusion) by means of a new form of model. It was really systems analysis that the members of the Club of Rome used to make their forecasts. Their results were the subject of heated discussion. Everyone who knows the mechanics of these simulations is aware of the arbitrariness that governs their construction and the art that is needed to produce a satisfactory contrivance. This is but a further sign that cybernetics does not provide any well-constructed symbolic guarantee. This is why the debate on the truthfulness or the falseness of the Club of Rome's forecasts is secondary to the recognition that the chosen method of representation is a fitting one. The confusion between nature and culture leaves room only for representation by the science of the artificial, namely cybernetics, the modern ideological form of pragmatism, which is used in an attempt to describe the architectures of complexity. And if additional proof were needed of the link between cybernetics and the marketing society, it might be said that the Club of Rome's model owes much of its validity to the wide hearing it received from the media. Henceforth, economics is cybernetics plus advertising.

Thus the loop is completed and the shift made from economics to ecology, that is, from the proper management of the household to the management of the world as the home of men. Kenneth E. Boulding founds his unified theory of the economy on the fact that reality in its quantitative aspect has to be seen as a population system. Populations act and react to one another and the equilibrium size of the whole population is a function of the size of all the others. Boulding notes that while there does not appear to be a name given to the general study of the equilibrium and dynamics of populations, this study has probably reached its highest level of development in the biological studies known under the name of "ecology."[15]

From Natural Science to Cybernetic Science and to Artificial Intelligence

What distinguishes pragmatism from well-constructed legitimacy system is the rejection of any distinction in principle which is not itself constantly legitimated by its goals. Cybernetic ideology is the modern name for pragmatism. The free–market system distinguishes between nature and culture, cybernetics merges them into the single category of the artificial; the free–market system is founded on science, cybernetic ideology itself performs science. The science which founds the free–market system separates subject from object in order to ensure its objectivity, cybernetics simplifies them under the common category of the system, whose degree of openness depends on the goal pursued by the user of the model. Cybernetic ideology is the ideology of model and simulation; all the more reason that it should be built in the image of a well-constructed model, namely the free-market ideology. Like the free-market ideology, it draws its legitimacy from science. The confrontation with science could have been fatal, for the objectivity of the science of nature could have destroyed the illusion represented by the subjectivism of the science of the artificial. However, no such thing happened for, since the end of the 18th century, the evolution of science itself has strangely paralleled that of society; to the disappearance of the distinction between nature and culture corresponds in the ideology of science, the dismantling of the barrier that separated the subject of knowledge from its object culminated in the cybernetic representation.

In calling itself a science, cybernetics was unable to legitimate itself in a symbolically satisfactory way. In becoming cybernetics, science lost any right to criticize cybernetics on this point. Hence, to understand the strength of cybernetic simulation, it is necessary to retrace the legitimacy crisis of the history of the science, which is the crisis of the gradual alteration of the distinction between the subject of knowledge and its object.

Clearly, the separation of subject from object is essential for guaranteeing the objectivity of science. It is this objectivity that turns the results of science into binding laws. Thus, when God has departed from heaven and kings from the earth, there remains one source of legitimacy binding on all, capable of providing legitimacy to symbolic systems that might have need of it. But to confer the legitimacy of science on political power, it is necessary to contrive conceptual constructions. Their engineers are the philosophers we shall now see at work.

The Science of Nature: Kant

The most radical and most exact expression of the principle of the separation of subject from object may be attributed to Descartes. Since extent is strictly separated from thought, Descartes relies on the intervention of a good spirit to ensure that the same things are inscribed in both, and that the great book of the world, written in mathematical language, can be read with eyes closed. The reassuring function of the good spirit must have shared the soporific virtues of opium since it took nothing less than Hume's radical empiricism to awaken Kant from his dogmatic slumber, as the latter himself put it. For it is to Kant that we owe a theory of science capable of founding the political legitimacy of a modern democratic system. It founds this legitimacy by showing how it is possible to know eternal nature and its laws within the limits of reason without the intervention of God and the Devil.

Knowledge is the result of contemplation or action. If knowledge is contemplation, if contemplation is not action, if it is the search for already existing, ordered representations, then the representation is guaranteed only by faith in its truth and in the God that this faith assumes. If knowledge is action, then subject and object cannot be dissociated. Knowledge is restricted to the random subjectivity of each person and bound by his pragmatic interest. Kant does not wish to choose between Descartes and Hume, theoreticism and empiricism, dogmatism and skepticism.

The subject of knowledge should not be God, for if it were the world order would remain subordinated to the hierarchy of the sacred. The subject of knowledge should not be the psychological subject, man, or else the world order would be governed by disorder and the arbitrariness of subjectivities. Knowledge should be an action (this enables man to accomplish it and thus to be the sole source of the authority that he discovers and to which he submits) but knowledge should preserve the separation of subject from object so that man can discover the laws of eternal nature, the source of all legitimacy.

That science, philosophy and politics are related with one another has been clear ever since Galileo had to retract his views in order to avoid the fate of Giordano Bruno, so great was the clash between scientific truth and the authority of the sacred when the image of a closed world, ruled by heavenly emanation, was transformed into an infinite universe that challenged man's central position and God's supremacy. Descartes's task was to found the philosophy that would authorize Galileo's physics. His enemy was scholasticism for which the source of knowledge was Holy Writ, not the book of the world written in mathematical language. To introduce the science of nature into the culture of the 17th century, he had to abandon politics to those whose concern it was and even invoke the aid of the deity to guarantee a body of knowledge which could have very well done without the divine. A century later, Kant could allow himself the use of Newtonian physics, by then accepted, to found a philosophy of knowledge that needed the intervention of neither good nor evil spirits. His enemy was no longer scholasticism but Sophistry. Man had become the sole guarantee of knowledge but he still had to be prevented from becoming the measure of all things. Thus, the history of the philosophy of sciences since Kant can be seen as the establishment and gradual alteration of a separation between subject and object, a separation that made empiricism possible while shielding it from subjectivity.

The way Kant ensured the action of knowing while at the same time respecting the separation of subject from object was by bringing division into the heart of the subject and object. Thus the subject of empirical knowledge (understanding) is separated from the subject of thought (reason); and the object of empirical knowledge (the phenomenon) is separated from the unknowable thing–in–itself (the noumenon). The subject of knowledge grasps the phenomenon through the a priori patterns of knowledge (time and space) and knowledge avails itself to measurement in these categories. Thus the action in which the subject constitutes its knowledge of the object by subordinating it to these categories leaves unscathed and face to face the transcendental subject (which sees without being corrupted for having seen) and the object, the thing–in–itself (which is not altered by the gaze of the subject of knowledge).

To protect this construction, ramparts have to be built against the return in force of appearance. Now, appearance can come in either by the effect of an interrogation on the immediate data of the consciousness (logical patterns or sensations) or by the effect of ideas leading to confusion where careful philosophical work had patiently plotted boundaries, separations and demarcations.

Logical error was quickly ruled out: "Logical illusion, which consists merely in the imitation of the form of reason (the illusion in Sophistical syllogisms), arises entirely from a want of due attention to logical rules. As soon as this rule is applied to the case at hand, the illusion totally disappears."[16] Kant then had to abandon the use of psychology as a mode of questioning knowledge. Not that he was unaware of the questions raised by dreams or the hallucinations of madmen and visionaries. He even devoted three works to these subjects: *Dreams of a Spirit-Seer illustrated by Dreams of Metaphysics*, *An Essay on the Maladies of the Head* and *Anthropology from a Pragmatic Point of View*. In explicitly empirical and pragmatic form, these works analyzed the concrete functioning of specific individuals "who have joined the game" of the world, which is examined, at a distance from the theory of reason itself.[17] It was in the form of the possibility of some rational psychology that the question was to be taken up in the *Critique of Pure Reason*, with the affirmation that no general knowledge of the modes of thinking, being and knowing could be deduced from the affirmation "I think." "There does not then exist any rational psychology as a doctrine furnishing any addition to our knowledge of ourselves. It is nothing more than a discipline, which sets impassable limits to speculative reason in this region of thought."[18]

Ruling out the questioning of logic (and logical error) and of psychology provides the critical method with immediate data in good working order. The fact remains that the functioning of reason itself is not immune to Sophistical arguments. For, through transcendental ideas, reason produces objects of which it is not possible to have any (empirical) knowledge but only a "problematical conception"[19] with which it is possible to go astray in one's reasoning. Here again Kant was aiming at the Sophists and their formidable art of contradictory discourse with his "antinomies of dialectical reasoning."[20]

Just as the Sophists in their *dissoï logoï* developed a thesis and its contrary to the full extent, so Kant developed four series of contradictory theses, two on mathematics (the finitude of the world and the simplicity of the world) and two on dynamics (the existence of a free cause and the

existence of an absolutely necessary thing). The solution to the mathematical paradoxes lay in showing that they consisted of propositions which
were all false, for they spoke of the world and of matter as things–in–
themselves and not as objects of knowledge. Hence, in mathematics, the
principle of non–contradiction is upheld.

The solution to the dynamic paradoxes consisted in showing that they
were all true depending on the viewpoint adopted, the viewpoint of understanding (that of the knowledge of the world) or the viewpoint of reason
(that of the freedom and autonomy of human action). In dynamics, the
notion of causality or necessity introduces the idea that there might exist
propositions which are contradictory and true. Thus no sooner does time
intervene than a breach is created in the beautiful ordering of the *Critique
of Pure Reason*, for the flow of time forces man to situate himself in
relation to it and to take sides against knowledge in the name of the interests of reason.

The science of Newton had no need of Kant's philosophy to be legitimated as science: the philosophy of Kant, however, needed Newton's science in order to define a legitimate philosophy founded on the notion that
natural laws exist. And it was as a lawgiver that Kant organized the human
faculties (understanding, reason) as the powers of the State were to be
organized, seeing to their separation by a constant care to respect the
boundaries of each institution of power that participates in the elaboration
of the law. Kant's philosophy plots the boundaries of the sciences and of the
use of measurement just as the democratic State plots the boundaries
between the attributes of sovereignty. It is law that makes it possible to
discover the law of nature in whose image the laws of society are created.
And just as the legitimacy of democracy lies in the manner in which the law
defines the source of power, so the legitimacy of Kantian science lies in the
ways that the powers of the mind have obeyed the laws that command their
use.

The Newtonian "world system" is the contrary of the cybernetic world
because it reveals the simplicity of natural laws behind the complexity of
appearances, instead of trying to mask it by models and imitations. Thus
we can understand the celebrated *hypothesis non fingo* which Koyré translated as "I do not feign a hypothesis," meaning "I use no fiction and no
false propositions as premises and explanations."[21] For what Newton
aimed at and achieved was not a plausible representation of the world, but
the very truth of its laws. The pragmatic use of hypotheses was rejected and
so was the pragmatic meaning of the world as revealed by science. Thus
Koyré wrote; "there is something for which Newton should be held responsible, or to put it better, not Newton alone but modern science in general,
namely the division of our world in two. I have said that modern science

has torn down the barriers between heaven and earth, that it unites and unifies the universe. This is true, but, as I have also said, it does so by replacing the world of qualities and sense perceptions, the world in which we love and die, by another world, one of quantity, of deified geometry, a world which has room for everything but no room for man. . . . In reality these two worlds are daily united by praxis. From the standpoint of theory, they are separated by a gulf."[22]

If we want to look at the Newtonian system as being either open or closed, let us then say that it is the most open system of all, open to the infinite and offered up completely to God's gaze alone. And nothing that could be assumed to be human subjectivity can come under its laws. Thus, the idea that time is irreversible could only occur to mortals: physics was to be the theory of reversible phenomena. Thus the idea that an event can occur by chance is incompatible with divine omniscience: physics was to be the science of perfectly determined phenomena. If Kant, who had Newton's knowledge available to him, needed no divinity to found his own conception of science, Newton, without access to Kant's philosophy, had to resort to divinity to dare produce Newtionian physics. In science, too, the passage from Newton to Kant marked the shift from a world dominated by the opposition between sacred and profane to one characterized by the opposition between nature and culture. The disappearance of God to the benefit of scientific truth marked the passage from the religious to the metaphysical state, as Auguste Comte put it.

The Science of Positivism: Comte

In establishing the free–market ideology, the paradox of the metaphysical age lay entirely in its capacity to reconcile revolution with eternity: the gods fell but nature remained. The new political order would have its eternity. The latest revolution rejected history, which threatened it in turn. The Hegelian view of truth unfolding in history thus came up against the idea of an eternal truth capable of founding a political order. Subject and object were no longer separated; the dialectic ceased to be the logic of appearance that it was in the *Critique of Pure Reason* and became the logic of the emergence of the true. Although Hegelian philosophy was to have a powerful influence on political and theological thought, it was never to control the idea of objective knowledge, which dominated the 19th century. To be compatible with the progress of the sciences, history had to be made into the history of progress. This is what Auguste Comte did when he defined human history as the succession of three states: the religious, the metaphysical and the positive.

Despite Newton's victory, the beauty of the Kantian edifice could not disguise the fact that it had been quite overtaken by the scientific project of the Encyclopedia. Scholars' desire for knowledge and the initial technical concerns of the engineers overran all barriers. Science embarked resolutely upon uncharted spaces. Just as the legitimacy of society would have to abandon the security of the "Garrison–State" for the promises of the Welfare State, so the legitimacy of science was to set aside the stern rod of critical philosophy for the promises of positivism. The metaphysical age that August Comte himself called "legalist" was replaced by the "scientific and industrial age." In this new age, society's goals, Order and Progress, legitimated the pursuit of the special ends of each individual independently of any (metaphysical) guarantees of the absolute. Man engaged in becoming chooses the positive, namely (following Auguste Comte himself, who declined all the possible meanings of this term), the real, the useful, the certain (as opposed to the undecided), the precise and the relative (as opposed to the absolute).[23] The pragmatism of the positivist orientation is evident in the very manner in which the philosophy of a science develops out of its results. "These rules, these methods, these artifices comprise, in each science, what I call its philosophy."[24] We are indeed at a remove from Newton's *hypothesis non fingo*. Far from being rejected, fictions became the very stuff of which positivist philosophy was built. But the positivist was not left to himself or, worse, to the mercy of his imagination. For Auguste Comte, the end of the metaphysical age meant also that the egoism of "I think" had given way to the "we" of society, for "if the idea of society still appears to be an abstraction of our intelligence, it is above all because of the old philosophical order, because a characteristic such as this really belongs to the idea of the individual, at least in our species."[25] Teaching, by lectures and catechism, was the favored means of communicating those collective truths, the results of science, to individuals, and this would be all the easier as "the true nature of positivist speculation has often led us (Comte) to verify the fortunate and basic harmony between healthy scientific contemplation of every sort and the spontaneous workings of public reason."[26] Moreover, it was among the public that the positivist school was to find its greatest support: "The positivist school can find no general resource other than to organize a direct and sustained appeal to universal good sense by striving from now on for the systematic propagation, in the active masses, of the principal scientific studies capable of forming the indispensable basis for its broad philosophical elaboration."[27]

However, the criterion of scientific truth was not left to the achievements of science and the approval of common sense. What Auguste Comte established was a new system of the legitimacy of science founded on the goals pursued. The functioning of this system can be compared, point by point, with that of the Welfare State. Both are oriented towards progress; both define it through a succession of fields all of which are opportunities to participate in the advent of progress: to the diversity of public services corresponds the diversity of sciences. Both have recourse to nature to define the particular ends of social action. Positivist philosophy "naturally" found itself "divided into five fundamental sciences, whose succession is determined by a necessary and invariable subordination, founded, independently of any hypothesis, on a simple, extensive comparison of corresponding phenomena: these sciences are astronomy, physics, chemistry, physiology and, finally, social physics."[28] It was natural needs that determined the public services, for which the State had to ensure their equal sharing and continued distribution. The ordering of the sciences, from the simplest to the most complex, from the inorganic to the organic, ranging from the oldest to the most recent, showed the progress to which the positivist age bore witness. In the same way, the public services, in developing from assistance to security, from instruction to education, from culture to leisure, revealed the march of social progress.

Each field of science was developed by specialized scientists just as each public service was managed by a qualified corps of professionals. Like the civil servant, the scientist was enlisted in the service of the public. "Thus the universal propagation of the major fields of positive study is not intended today solely to meet an already manifest need among the public, which increasingly feels that the sciences are no longer reserved exclusively for scientists but that they exist above all for themselves. By a fortunate, spontaneous reaction, an intended purpose such as this, when suitably developed, should radically improve the present scientific frame of mind by removing the blind and dispersive quality of its specialization so that it may gradually acquire the true philosophical character indispensable to its principal mission. This path is indeed the only one, in our day, which can constitute, outside the speculative class as such, a vast spontaneous tribunal, as impartial as it is unimpeachable, made up of the mass of sensible men, in whose presence many false scientific opinions would irrevocably vanish: opinions, which viewpoints characteristic of the preliminary elaboration of the past two centuries must have mixed profoundly with truly positive doctrines, which they shall necessarily alter for so long as these doctrines are not finally subjected to universal good sense."[29]

A final obstacle impeded the advent of this universal common sense: the "excessive specialization of individual research"[30] the product of scientific progress, could end in disorder and anarchy if specialists of a new type, namely "the specialists of generalities," were not added to the castes of specialized scientists. The business of the students of generalities would be "to take the respective sciences as they are, determine the spirit of each, ascertain their relations and mutual connection, and reduce their respective principles to the smallest number of general principles, in conformity with the fundamental rules of positive method."[31] These principles would then be taught to scientists in specific disciplines who, in return, could keep the "specialists of generalities" informed of changes to be made in these disciplines; thus a body of rules for scientific method would be established, somewhat as the *Conseil d'Etat* (France's highest administrative jurisdiction and advisory body to the government in matters of legislation), acting as a "specialist of generalities" in the administrative sphere, had been able to produce the principles of public service management which were, as was only right, incoporated into the programs for training specialized corps of civil servants.

What remains to be considered is the body of doctrine thus produced, which comprises the principles of the scientific method. We have seen that Kant did not challenge the evidence of logic. Similarly, Auguste Comte distrusted "an abstract theory of numbers and an arithmetic taken in itself; he ruled out the idea of a mathematical logic when it was presented in the form of a general theory of signs or a project for a universal language; exaggerated abstraction, formalization, are revolting to the positivist spirit."[32] This concern with not disturbing what is evident by an excessively detailed consideration of the immediate data of consciousness can be found in Auguste Comte's condemnation of "the deplorable psychological mania that a famous Sophist momentarily managed to inspire in French youth."[33]

Thus, so that science might exist, Kant and Comte discovered a common enemy: the self. Auguste Comte's statement that "the famous theory of the self is essentially without any scientific purpose, since it is designed solely to represent a purely fictitious condition"[34] echoes Kant's ironic observation on the affirmation that the self exists as the only dogmatic assertion supported by the Sophists,[35] since their relativism stopped at the point where they had to define a subject capable of supporting it. Although Kant and Comte were at one in rejecting logical and psychological questioning, they differed on at least three other points. While, for Kant, science was one, and was limited to measuring time and space, for Comte it comprised various regions, each endowed with its measurements and principles and strictly separated from the others by the rejection of all interdisciplinarity. Thus, while for Kant astronomy took in the infinite universe, for Comte the only subject of astronomy could be the world of man, the world limited by the planets around the Sun: "The last outer planet encloses a stable, independent, circular, oscillating field, constitutes the home where mankind prepares its conditions of existence, which provides for his needs and forms the ground for the exercise of his means."[36] By separating the "solar point of view" from the "universal point of view,"

Auguste Comte was safeguarding for humanity the perfect model for all science. This distinction nonetheless seemed to Comte to be an indispensable condition "in order to clearly separate that part of science which contained a complete perfection from that which, without its being conjectural, appears fated by its very nature to remain always in its infancy, at least as compared to the former.[37]

At the same time, this boundary made it possible to assert the practical purpose of science: " . . . we need to know only that which can act on us in a more or less direct manner and, on the other hand, by the very fact that such an influence exists, it becomes sooner or later a means of knowledge for us."[38] This pragmatism of Auguste Comte's positivist philosophy is found in the status granted to mathematics. While Kant made mathematics the model of science, to the point where he identified it with physics, Comte made it the means, the tool of all sciences to such an extent that it does not itself appear in this list of sciences. For today, mathematics "is of less value for the learning of which it is made up, substantial and valuable as that learning is, than as the most powerful instrument that the human mind can employ in the investigation of the laws of natural phenomena."[39]

From Kant and Newton to Auguste Comte, something of cybernetics, and above all pragmatism, entered science. The entire work of dividing the faculties and limiting them was intended to make knowledge independent of the interests of reason, the latter guiding the former from a distance great enough to avoid destroying its objectivity. For Auguste Comte, on the contrary, knowledge existed only to meet the needs of society, the philosophical distinction between between reason and understanding being replaced, in a way, by the social distinction between the specialized scientist and the specialist in generalities. To this pragmatism of ends corresponds the pragmatism of means. For Kant, mathematics were indissociable from physics, they were the very structure of reality; for Newton, there was no question of feigning hypotheses but of attaining the True. For Comte, on the contrary, mathematics were a means, a tool whose only advantage was that it was more powerful and more efficient. Hence we should not be surprised to see him include, under positivist philosophy, the "artifices" by which the sciences had progressed.

Positivist science did not shy away from choosing man himself as an object of knowledge. Although introspective science was left out of the list of positivist sciences, social physics or anthropology, was included. Kant would have ruled it out: "anthropology seen from the pragmatic viewpoint" by the very fact that it was pragmatic, could not claim to be a part of scientific knowledge.

However, we are not yet in the science of the artificial here, nor for that matter are we involved with a form of unlimited pragmatism. For Auguste

Comte, the useful was subordinated to faith in the movement of history. Collective growth was what gave meaning and objective necessity to individual research beyond the psychological satisfactions of the illusory "self" of the scientists. "Science is the product of the mind as mind: since the sciences have a history, the mind itself is a history, and this history of the mind coincides with the history of sciences. Thus three obvious points are established beyond discussion: a functional view of the spirit, the identification of the spiritual and the intellectual, and the introduction of the historical point of view into the definition of intelligence."[40] The encyclopedia of positivist knowledge, the history of the mind, evokes Hegelian philosophy, but with a more sober Hegel, whose dialectic, leveled by the law of the three estates, enables the positivist age to work out its development in the reassuring categories of growth and perfection. Thus, by the skillful use of periodization, Comtean philosophy was shielded, on the one hand, from the wholehearted pragmatism of those who were ignorant of history and, on the other hand, from the absolute power of history, which would deprive pragmatism of its whole foundation. What positivism offered was a moderate, well-tempered and classical pragmatism. In the criticist outlook, the subject was separated from the object by a double theoretical rupture, one which isolated understanding from reason and another which separated the phenomenon from the thing in itself. Henceforth, the subject was isolated from the object by a practical device: science was the study of closed or isolated systems, like the bottles and sealed boxes that the scientist handles in his laboratory or the lid that Auguste Comte put on the infinite universe in order to make a palatable doctrine of the science of the world.

The scientist was the new demiurge with his experimental apparatus. He could create the categories by which he would measure phenomena. *The noumenon* ceased to be inaccessible by principle. However, at the very moment when the thing–in–itself opened up before the scientist, it showed itself dressed with the garment that the scientist had tailored for it. If it was to be decent, this garment had to resemble the model left by Newton in physics and chemistry. Force in dynamics corresponded to attraction and repulsion in electricity, affinity in chemistry and even the repulsive force of heat, which accounts for the phenomena of expansion and dissolution. In each field, there was an attempt to define a relationship similar to that of (kinetic and potential) energy in dynamics or the conservation of mass in chemistry. In each field, full knowledge of the initial state of the system would make it possible to determine all subsequent states in a way that excluded chance. In each field, the phenomena studied were to be reversible as they must be if the laws of nature were to have the shape of eternity.

School children would be shown the experimental apparatus, the measuring instrument that corresponded to it and thus "the chosen phenomenon would be presented to the public."[41] Alone before his box, the scientist could not resist the temptation to break the isolation in which nature was contained. To produce, science needed an art. "The experimental approach is an art, that is, it relies on know how and not on general rules, and is consequently without guarantee, exposed to triviality and blindness."[42] The result of this art is the artifice by which the scientist conceals the effort needed to maintain conditions at the boundaries of the system supposed to be isolated, an artifice whose final form can perhaps be found in Carnot's machine. Since it is impossible to build a reversible heat engine, its ideal model is conceived as functioning between a heat source and a cold source. The slight–of–hand lies in the fact that no one will ask how their temperatures remain constant without a *deus ex machina* to keep the boiler stoked.

Thus the simulated isolation of the system can conceal the irreversibility inherent in heat phenomena. Fourier's law predicts that if two bodies of different temperatures are placed in an isolated system, their temperatures will equalize at an intermediate level. This time, the isolation of the system unrefutably reveals an irreversible physical phenomenon. But what was recognized as such in England was to be concealed in France by the way in which Auguste Comte legitimated directional time in physics as long as its direction was that of order and equilibrium.[43] And what could be a more harmonious ideal than lukewarmness?

While order, equilibrium and progress make it possible to legitimize experimentation in physics, their intervention is even more necessary in biology, for the conditions of the experiment provide an imperfect guarantee of its "complete rationality." For, according to Auguste Comte,[44] "the complete rationality of a particular artifice and its undisputable success" rely on conditions which "the nature of biological phenomena must make almost impossible to achieve to an adequate extent."[45] This would not prevent biology from being the very model of positivist science, just as it saw the organism as the very model of society. Far from the notion of order, equilibrium and progress being necessary to legitimate life, it was life that showed what order was through the work of scientists. And this was so true that the cellular theory was rejected by Auguste Comte, who held it to be "a fantastical theory and, moreover, one that obviously comes from an essentially metaphysical system of general philosophy."[46] For "Comte does not admit . . . that the life of an organism is the sum of particular lives any more than, contrary to the philosophy of the 18th century, he admits that society is an association of individuals."[47] Following the work of the French anatomist and physiologist, Marie François Bichat (1771-1802) in this respect, Auguste Comte rejects, along with the cellular theory, the use of the microscope.

After the infinitely big (the sidereal spaces), the infinitely small was banished from science. In this way, the scientist, and through him society, would be protected from the fear that gripped Pascal in presence of "the eternal silence of those infinite spaces."[48] Far from man's being "a mean point between all and nothing,"[49] something lost in the universe, the universe proved to be man's milieu, that is, according to Auguste Comte, "all the circumstances needed for the existence of each organism."[50] And the presumption of positivism went so far as to grant man, and man alone, the capacity "through collective action" to act on this milieu. The problem of the biological dimension was thus stated in functional terms: "given the organ in a given environment, find the function and vice versa."[51] The history of the human species evokes Lamarck's tranformism. Depending on circumstances and surroundings, the needs of animals lead them to develop suitable organs by which they can adapt to their conditions of existence. The milieu then becomes the truth of the space whose progress it determines, nature defines the needs that the species strives to satisfy. And if the community of men acts on the milieu, the confusion between the subject and the object of science in biology becomes such that the legitimacy of biology can have no guarantee other than the ends pursued, namely adaptation and progress.

From Neo-Positivism to Cyberneticized Science and Artificial Intelligence

The method of Auguste Comte's system, which was supposed to ensure the link between human advancement and scientific progress, suffered the same fate as Kant's legislation. The course of scientific development exceeded the limits set by those who wished to add the power of its testimony to the ideological structures on which society is founded. Auguste Comte's prejudice against excessive abstraction was laughable in the light of the development of logic (the work of Bolzano and Boole), algebra (Abel, Galois), arithmetic (Gauss), non–Euclidean geometry, the axiomatic method.[52] Astronomers studied the stars and thus broke the bounds that enclosed the positivist system. Even the separation between the various disciplines, a central element in the positivist guarantee, collapsed in the face of advances in astrophysics. Determinism, "the fundamental dogma of positivism,"[53] was seriously shaken. However, this dogma was precisely what enabled a subject capable of regarding an object "subjectively" to discover in it the objective element which would make others accept the evidence of what had been perceived. This is what Auguste Comte stated explicitly: "Thus positivism associates with its subjective principle, the preponderance of feeling, an objective basis, the immutable external necessity which alone makes it possible to subordinate the whole of our existence to sociability."[54] The "so–called calculation of chances" could only be a "radical aberration," even if it were characteristic of "virtually every present-day mathematician."[55] It is, however, precisely chance that provided laws of the two most significant fields of 19th century scientific development: biology, with the laws of Mendel and Darwin's theory; and thermodynamics with the theories of Boltzmann. To make man the guarantor of knowledge without his becoming "the measure of all things" was the challenge that Kant and Comte had tried to take up, both in the same fashion, by rejecting psychological man, the self, which is the image and product of pragmatism.

After the transcendental subject of critical philosophy, it was the turn of the positivist collective subject to yield. Psychology and pragmatism appeared simultaneously in Germany and the United States. But (and this showed that an aging Europe was less comfortable with this exercise than a youthful America) two Europeans were needed for this task for which a single American sufficed. William James could easily produce both a psychology and a philosophy, since his pragmatic philosophy was in perfect harmony with the pragmatic character of psychology. In Europe, on the contrary, while Brentano produced a psychology founded on the notion of intentionality, what he did enabled another thinker, Husserl, to build a philosophy of intentionality that rejected all psychologism and, therefore, limited the pragmatism involved in its foundation. And to do this, Husserl invoked Descartes to refute against the Sophists: ". . . the skepticism of Antiquity, inaugurated by Protagoras and Gorgias, challenges the episteme, that is, the scientific knowledge of the being–in–itself, and denies it. . . . This skepticism, which negated the practical-ethical (political) orientation, lacked already in ancient times what it lacked in subsequent epochs, namely the original Cartesian motive. This original motive was the passage through hell through which, by an almost skeptical *epoche* that nothing could now surpass, it was possible to force an entry into the celestial sphere of an absolutely rational philosophy and even to construct it in all systematicity."[56] A new hell has had to be faced by those who have had to found an objective system of knowledge since the end of the 19th century for, paradoxically, the very achievements of science have abolished its foundation. Even in physics, the subject of knowledge is no longer separated from its object. With the theory of relativity, the categories of time and space become dependent on the observer's position and speed. In quantum physics, the observer affects the object observed in a such way that the fiction of the isolated system loses all its utility. The science that triumphs is a pragmatic one, a science that enables pragmatic philosophy to triumph with it. The other sciences must face Husserl's hell, which is none other than the hell of the data directly supplied by the consciousness (the type of data Bergson cherished). This hell has few exits: philosophy, which distinguishes the subject of knowledge and, in so doing, distinguishes it from the self of psychology; logic, a formal structure which seems to contain a hard core of evidence on which a cosmos can be built; the social consensus which, in the manner of the positivists, makes it possible to recognize the existence of knowledge.

Hell for Husserl is the *epoche*, the discarding of all knowledge, the radical doubt from which a rejuvenated Cartesian *cogito* may emerge. In logic, hell is Frege's devoting all his efforts to tracing the steps by which man can count with no mistakes up to one. But logic also has its purgatories: for example, Cambridge, where Russell, Moore and Whitehead became the architects of formal systems while intermittently submitting to Wittgenstein's radical critique.[57] Logic even had its paradise when logicians, philosophers and physicists came together in the famous Vienna Circle to lay down the canons of knowledge in the way that Auguste Comte had done all alone a century earlier.

But if paradise thus came within their reach—a paradise in which "positivism and the older empiricism (of Comte and Mach), the study of the foundations, purposes and methods of the empirical sciences, the axiomatic sciences and finally hedonism and positivist sociology"[58] could coexist in harmony—this was very probably because Wittgenstein (who inspired the Vienna Circle without actually belonging to it) had kept all of hell for himself. After Kant's legislation, founded on the source of knowledge (understanding, reason), after the method of Comte's school, founded on the purpose of knowledge (order and progress), there came the age of scientific methodology founded, as its name indicates, on the method of knowledge. The positivist method forbade any questioning of the immediate data of consciousness: logic, language and signs, on the one hand, psychology and observation, on the other. Neo-positivism, on the contrary, sought to deduce from a critical analysis of the role played by these mediators of knowledge the criteria for a legitimate way of conducting scientific action.

But to found a new othodoxy, it was necessary to raise barriers. Thus, a logic shielded from the disquiet caused by questions (deemed metaphysical) on language and psychology tempted people to build metalanguages, which would be standards of rigour applicable to all sciences. In a similar manner, the observation of phenomena, shielded from questions of logic, language and psychology, which made their objectivity a relative thing, enabled Karl Popper to propose an empirical criterion for science, "the fact of exposing oneself to being falsified by rigorously prepared experiments"[59] (that is, the criterion of falsifiability).

By separating the objective (logic and observation) from that which was loaded with subjective meanings (language and psychology), neo-positivism proposed to replace the separation of nature from culture by a separation between what is science and what is not science. The knowledge thus produced could not violate Kant's injunction againt paying excessive attention to the immediate data of the consciousness without incurring the consequences. If logic is science, it meets the fate of all sciences: as it grows, it destroys the postulates on which it is built: for Gödel's Incompleteness Theorem states that in any sufficiently complex language, there are well–formed sentences of which it cannot be said that they are true or false. Logic itself is acquainted with uncertainty. If it was not, the question of matching logic with observation would remain. Kant made it the object of an a priori certitude; the neo–positivists were to make it the object of an *a posteriori* probability: theory would be deemed to be true because its propositions had been verified with a high degree of probability, or, on the contrary, as a sequel to Popper's criterion, it would be deemed to be true because it had been exposed to the risk of being "falsified" with a high degree of probability. Whether it opted for the probable or the improbable, what was certain was that theory henceforth eluded certainty. If there was no *a priori* agreement reached between logic and observation, and if psychology and linguistics, which would introduce the ambiguities of subjectivity into science, were to be kept at a distance, then it became necessary to stipulate the law of their *a posteriori* agreement: for some philosophies (realism), scientific categories reflect reality, for others (nominalism) they result from convention or the consensus of scientists. Here again is the opposition that divided the Sophists into the defenders of the *nomos* and those of the *physis*.

The advance of science had managed to overwhelm Kant and Comte: it was to leave their successors no respite. History implants doubt in the heart of the most eternal categories. It became necessary to seek protection. Kantian legislation having failed, Comte had imagined that the mediation of the specialists of generalities would produce a method in the manner of jurisprudence. It was this separation that the neo–positivist tried to preserve by distinguishing the study of the justification of science (or methodology as such) from the study of the discovery of science, "which tries to explain the illogical factors at work in the invention of theories" by appealing to psychology, sociology and history.[60] Karl Popper's the *Logic of Scientific Discovery* thus proposes to do away with the "irrational element" or creative intuition in the sense that Bergson gave it, whose existence he recognized at the center of every theory.[61]

Paradoxically, while this attitude is coherent with the pragmatic needs of the scientific community, it is incompatible with a truly pragmatic approach by scientific practice. This practice requires that "independently of the reasons for accepting a theory, there should be reasons for producing it."[62] Now this theory can only mix psychology and logic, science and meaning. Epistemology becomes the study of beliefs. Reduced thus to no more than a collection of believing selves, the scientific community could be the object of a sociology, and this sociology claimed to be the equivalent of an epistemology.

For Thomas S. Kuhn, the consensual methodology of the neo-positivists has been replaced by rival paradigms, each of which is defended by a group of scientists.[63] Since the unique reference to the truth no longer works, opinion becomes the criterion of the success of a scientific theory. Science is no longer the doing of the scientist (who does not constitute an opinion by himself) but that of research centers or of the university department fighting for prestige and funds. Pressure to conform becomes the essential means of setting up competing scientific ideologies. The legitimacy of a scientific bureaucracy of this kind is no doubt contestable. But how can it be contested without resorting to a special paradigm, and hence without actually placing oneself in the very structure one criticises? The scientific establishment's lack of legitimacy and the absence of a legitimate discourse of science leaves the dissenter with no solution other than that of anarchy. This is the viewpoint defended by Feyerabend. And even then, in doing so he has to explicitly use the Sophists' own approach. One of the processes proposed consists in developing "counter–inductive" theories, that is, elaborating "hypotheses that do not tally with well-established theories and/or well-established facts."[64] That there is really an echo here of the Sophists' dissoï logoï is confirmed by the author's caveat: "Always bear in mind that the demonstrations and rhetoric which I use express no deep conviction on my part. They only show how easy it is to lead people by the nose in a rational way. An anarchist is like a secret agent who plays the game of Reason to undermine the authority of Reason (truth, honesty, justice and so on)."[65]

Thus science also entered the realm of belief, consensus and Sophistry; attempts to separate the logic and observation of psychology from those of science failed. When its back was to the wall, science looked to psychology and even to language for reasons to believe in Reason. It was in Europe that these two preoccupations were pursued: in Switzerland with the genetic epistemology of Piaget and at Oxford with the analytical philosophy of language and its developments. Piaget's school was concerned with getting multidisciplinary groups of scientific logicians and psychologists to participate in the study of "the relation between epistemology and the development, or even the psychological formation, of notions and operations."[66]

The linguistic philosophers at Oxford, led by Austin, dedicated themselves to "highly intensive and painstaking studies on ordinary language,"[67] studies which could be considered as the propaedeutics of any scientific work. The pragmatism of this approach was expressed in the distinction made between constative propositions (which record) and performative ones (which constitute an action by themselves), for example: "I name this ship "Liberty.")[68] Thus language is action: it is speech-act. The proof of the pudding is in the eating and the meaning of the sentence in the saying. The truth of the sentence is measured by its effect: here the Sophist recognizes the tools of his craft.

The division between subject and object breaks down. Pragmatism dominates science. To clothe this fragmented epistemology in coherence, the principle must be found by which to knit the most contradictory pieces together. Having become a servant to two masters, nature and culture, science must don the motley garb known as the science of systems. In 1924, Harvard University gave the Cambridge logician, Alfred N. Whitehead, the opportunity to cross the Atlantic, build his own system and thus complete the geographical and mental voyage of modernity that Wittgenstein had embarked upon when he moved from Vienna to Cambridge. Whitehead's work is an organic philosophy or a philosophy of the organism, that is, "it refuses to chart arbitrary bifurcations in nature . . . , the dualism of body and soul, of the knowing subject and the known object, of thought and sensations, of man and his environment."[69] In this philosophy of the concrete, only "events" or "drops of experience" exist: they are the elements of a perpetual becoming, whose combination forms "concrescences." The subject is none other than the event: the identification of that which perceives and of that which is perceived. Appearance is not distinguished from reality, it is the concrete: Our perceptions of the apparent world are nature itself.[70] The subject is thus also the object. Whitehead calls these new entities *superjects*. They are the locus of sufficient cause and final cause. The organization of these two types of normally incompatible causality is made possible by the systemic or organic approach. Concrete realities, says Whitehead, are always organisms, so that the overall plan of the totality influences the particular characteristics of the various subordinate organisms that compose it. Mental states enter into the system of the total organism and thereby modify the systems of successive, subordinate organisms unto the smallest electrons. Thus an electron inside a living body differs from an electron outside it because of the existence of the total system.[71]

It remains to be seen how such a system could find legitimacy from the very fact that it implies creativity and liberty. Legislation goes on at two levels: that of eternal objects and that of God. For there exist, in this world of process, "eternal objects"; these are "eternal forms" which "determine how apprehensions take place, how the subject prehends its data."[72] Thus, in Whitehead's philosophy, we rediscover the principle of the legitimation of action by the methods according to which it is determined. In particular, complexity and hierarchy, which as we know constitute fundamental elements of the architecture of systems, require the existence of corresponding eternal objects: "Every finite or infinite hierarchy of abstraction is based on some group of simple eternal objects."[73] However, such a system of legitimacy does not escape the crisis induced by the question of how it happens that there is this order rather than any other.[74] This is why philosophy needs God: "The fact of the religious vision as well as the history of its continuous development is the basis of our optimism."[75] In other words, if the system wants to do without God, it must produce optimism by other means.

As a philosopher of the confusion between nature and culture, between subject and object, Whitehead is quite close to becoming a Sophist, a philosopher of appearances: "Our perceptions of the apparent world are nature itself." As for eternal objects, they recall the dogmatic core that all types of Sophism need, whether it be the existence of the self or the rules of rhetoric. From Greece to America, the self has ceased to resemble a man and has become an entity; the rules of rhetoric have ceased to be those of dialogue between equal parties and have become those of the hierarchical organization of systems ("mental systems enter the system of the total organism and thereby modify systems of successive subordinate organisms unto the smallest electrons").[76] To legitimate such a hierarchy, so contrary to principles of equality and liberty that characterize free–market democracy, Whitehead had to crown it by placing God at its summit. By accepting the optimism of Whitehead's God, cybernetic ideology would exclude itself from the system of legal rational legitimacy fom which it has sprung.[77] But it could avoid this. To do so, it only had to draw upon its well-known talent for simulation. What it had to imitate this time was the intellectual foundation of free–market democracy.

But before describing the way cybernetic ideology is able to perform such an imitation we should stop for a moment to consider the manifold and fruitful activities which are designated by a new catch word: Artificial Intelligence (A.I.).

The development of modern computing machines has been accompanied from its beginning by the emergence of a popular myth: the myth of the thinking machine. This myth has given rise to a vast field of research which orients its efforts in two directions. First, the development of information processing systems which emulate the work produced by man's mental activity. One exemple is expert systems use for diagnosing be it illness in a man or a breakdown in a machine. Second the development of research which aims to understand the mechanism of human understanding. In that sense A.I. is nothing other than a branch of the fast-growing field of the cognitive sciences.

The development of A.I. has transformed the popular myth of the thinking machine into a heated intellectual debate between specialists. Hubert L. Dreyfus and many others like him insist that there is a gap between man and machines.[78] They argue among other things that confusion is often raised by the mere fact of using words ambiguously: "intelligence" in artificial intelligence could be as remote from actual human intelligence as a computer's memory is from human memory. Confronting those who insist on the difference between human and machine intelligence are those who believe that "all that is relevant to intelligent behavior can be formalized in a structured description."[79]

The debate is itself quite complex. However it is possible to outline why this very debate can be understood as the extreme expression of the epistemological crisis we have been describing. If we had to characterize this crisis in a few words we would say that it occurs when sophism replaces philosophy, when the subject of knowledge is confused with the object knowledge and when nature is confused with culture. The reign of Sophism is the time when things are no longer what they are but what they appear to be. In that sense the Sophistic attitude would consist in taking the notion of artificial intelligence at face value that is including all the ambiguity contained in the words that comprise it. Taken at face value, artificial intelligence expresses the most extreme form of confusion between the subject and the object of knowledge. Not only does the subject of science consider itself as an object of science but moreover the subject of science considers the possibility of transforming his own object of science—an artefact—into a substitute for himself in his quest for knowledge: that is a substitute for intelligence.

The notion of artefact we just used reminds us that artificial intelligence contains the word "artificial" which represents a complete confusion between nature and culture. From that point of view we may note that if our times are characterised by complete confusion between nature and culture then everything in artificial. The question of artificial intelligence in that context no longer consist in knowing wether an artefact can be intelligent but how anything can be characterized as being natural and for that matter intelligence.

Notes

1. Norbert Wiener, *The Human Use of Human Beings: Cybernetics and Society,* Discus Books, 1967. Ludwig Von Bertalanffy, *General System Theory Essays on Its Foundations and Development,* Braziller, 1969.

2. *Pragmatisme et Sociologie*, Vrin, 1955, p. 28–29.
3. *Ibid.*, p. 28.
4. See Chapter II: "Laissez-faire and the Crisis of Legitimacy."
5. H. A. Simon, *La Science des systémes*, Paris, EPI, 1974.
6. Ilya Prigogine and Isabelle Stengers, *La Nouvelle Alliance*, Paris, Gallimard, 1979.
7. The beginning of this chapter owes a great deal to the work of Louis Dumont *Homo equalis*, Paris, Gallimard, 1976.
8. Cf. Louis Dumont, *op. cit.*, pp. 50–67.
9. *Ibid.*, p. 51.
10. *Ibid.*, p. 76.
11. *Ibid.*, p. 98.
12. Leon Walras, an economist of the late nineteenth century, to whom we owe a completely finalized mathematical representation of market equilibrium.
13. Quesnay and Malthus. Malthus was to develop a concept of the economy centered on the limitation of natural, agricultural resources. On Malthus, See J.-F. Soulet, *De Malthus a Marx, l'histoire aux mains des logiciens*, Gauthier-Villars, 1970.
14. J.-F. Soulet, *op. cit.*, p. 36.
15. Kenneth Boulding, *A Reconstruction for Economics*, John Wiley and Sons, 1950, p. 5.
16. Immanuel Kant, *The Critique of Pure Reason*, trans. G. M. D. Meiklejohn, Dent, London and Melbourne, 1984, p. 210.
17. Immanuel Kant, *Anthropologie*, Vrin, 1979, Introduction by M. Foucault, p. 12.
18. Immanuel Kant, *The Critique of Pure Reason*, London, Oxford University Press, 1958, p. 351.
19. *Ibid.*, p. 232.
20. *Ibid.*, p. 244 ff.
21. A. Koyre, *Etude Newtoniennes*, Gallimard, 1968, p. 60.
22. *Ibid.*, pp. 42–43.
23. *Auguste Comte*, presented by Paul Arbousse–Bastide, PUF, 1968, pp. 80–81.
24. Quoted by Henri Gouhier, *La Jeunesse d'Auguste Comte*, Vrin, 1970, Vol.III, p. 244 ("taken from a letter to Valat, dated 24th September 1819").
25. Quoted in Arbousse–Bastide, *op. cit.*, p. 84.
26. *Auguste Comte*, presented by Pierre Arnaud, Bordas, 1968, p. 16.
27. Arbousse–Bastide, *op. cit.*, p. 84.
28. *Ibid.*, p. 86.
29. *Ibid.*, p. 79.
30. *Ibid.*, p. 71; Auguste Comte, *Cours de Philosophie Positive*, p. 31–32.
31. Gertrud Lenzer, ed., *Auguste Comte and Positivisme: The Essential Writings*, New York, Harper Torchbooks, 1975, pp. 78–79.
32. M. Serres, *La Traduction*, Paris, Edition de Minuit, 1974. p. 165.
33. P. Arnaud, *Textes choisis*, Paris, Bordas, p. 65; Comte, *Cours de Philosophie Positive*, Chapter 45.
34. *August Comte*, presented by Pierre Arnaud, *op. cit.*, p. 69.
35. Immanuel Kant, *The Critique of Pure Reason*, *op. cit.*, II, p. 203, *The Antimonies of Pure Reason.*
36. M. Serres, *op. cit.*, p. 165.
37. *Auguste Comte*, presented by Rene Hubert, Louis Michaud, ed., p. 134.

38. *Ibid.*, p. 134.
39. In "The Essential Writings," *op. cit.*, p. 101.
40. Henri Gouhier, *op. cit.*, p. 244.
41. Ilya Prigogine and Isabelle Stengers, *La Nouvelle Alliance, op. cit.*, p. 50.
42. *Ibid.*, p. 49.
43. *Ibid.*, p. 119.
44. Lesson 40 of *Cours de la Philosophie Positive*, quoted by G. Canguilhem, *Connaissance de la Vie*, Paris, Vrin, 1969, p. 25,
45. *Ibid.*
46. *Ibid.*, p. 65.
47. Canguilhem, *op. cit.*
48. Pascal, A. J. Krailsheimer trans., *Pensées*, Harmondsworth, Penguin, 1966, p. 95.
49. *Ibid.*, p. 80.
50. Quoted by Canguilhem, *op. cit.,* p. 133.
51. Cf. Canguilhem.
52. M. Serres, *op. cit.,* p. 166.
53. Auguste Comte, "Discours sur l'Ensemble du Positivisme," I, 24, in R. Hubert, *op. cit.*, p. 88.
54. *Ibid.*
55. *Ibid.*, p. 87.
56. E. Husserl, *La Crise des Sciences Europeennes et la Phenomenologie Transcendantale,* Paris, Gallimard, 1976, p. 89.
57. Purgatory was also experienced by the American, Charles S. Pierce when he made Cartesian doubt not a certainty, but a problem of belief, seeking in the *Critique of Pure Reason* (to which he devoted two hours a day for three years) not "God, freedom or Immortality," but "cosmology and psychology," which led him to a pragmatic logic of the sign, which, to judge by his own criterion, (that of its practical effect) was more logical than pragmatic in the meaning of William James since James said of Pierce that "he was the strangest example of an unsuccessful talent." By an irony of fate, this pragmatic logician was to be the keeper of the weights and measures for several years in the United States. Cf. C. Wright Mills, *Sociology and Pragmatism*, Paine Whitman publishers, 1964, pp. 130–134.
58. P. Jacob, *L'Empirisme Logique*, Paris, 1980.
59. *Ibid.*, p. 125.
60. *Ibid.*, pp. 229–230.
61. K. R. Popper, *The Logic of Scientific Discovery*, New York, Torchbooks, 1965, pp. 3–5.
62. P. Jacob, *op. cit.*, p. 230.
63. The succession of paradigms brings to mind the succession of scientific questions presented by Bachelard. Bachelard succeeded in establishing an epistemology in harmony with "the land of brooks and rivers" (Cf. Paul Ginestier, *Bachelard*, Bordas, 1968, pp. 3–5). In the realm of meanings, starting from the barn, the fire in the hearth and the water in the river, the imaginary cosmology needed for intuition was free to flourish. In the realm of knowledge, the gaudy tumult of the history of sciences could be ordered by means of clearly defined epistemological divisions by which every word could look on the one that preceded it as an inferior version of itself. Thus, in a dream, science escaped from the bounds of pragmatism.

64. P. Feyerabend, *Contre la Méthode*, Paris, Seuil, 1979, p. 26.
65. *Ibid.*, p. 30.
66. J. Piaget, *Psychologie et Epistémologie*, Paris, Gauthier — Meditation, 1970, p. 11.
67. J. O. Urmson, "L'Histoire de l'Analyse," in *La Philosophie Analytique* Colloquium at Royaumont, Paris, Edition de Minuit, p. 20.
68. J. L. Austin, ("Performatif, Constatif"), *ibid.*, p. 27.
69. F. Casselin, *La Philosophie Organique de Whitehead*, Paris, PUF, 1950, p. 5.
70. A. N. Whitehead, *Principles of Relativity*, pp. 61–62.
71. Whitehead, *Science and the Modern World*, 1926, p. 79.
72. Cf. Casselin, *op. cit.*
73. *Ibid.*, p. 49.
74. *Ibid.*, p. 82.
75. *Ibid.*, p. 86.
76. Cf. *supra.*
77. "God is the ultimate limit and his existence is the ultimate irrationality," Whitehead, *Science and the Modern World, op. cit.*
78. Hubert L. Dreyfus, *What Computers Can't Do,* Harper and Row, New York, 1972.
79. Hubert L. Dreyfus, "From Micro World to Knowledge Representation" in *Mind Design: Philosphy, Psychology, Artificial Intelligence,* John Hangeland, editor, MIT Press, Cambridge, Mass., 1985.

Chapter 9

The Workings of Cybernetic Ideology

Thus one can no longer say that things are what they are but rather that they appear to be what they seem.

Free-market ideology recognized the separation between nature and culture; cybernetic ideology recognizes the pseudo-separation between information and energy. The former founded the objectivity of its knowledge (especially the knowledge of the separation between nature and culture) on the separation of subject from object, the latter founds the objectivity of its depiction of the world on the pseudo-objectivity of *chance* and *necessity*.

Thus cybernetic ideology legitimates its world, peopled with entities (systems and sub–systems) and with categories (flows and stocks), by setting itself up in the image of liberalism, for to cybernetic ideology *evidence* is nothing but resemblance.

Information and Energy

Thermodynamics and genetics are the true sciences of cybernetic ideology, as physics had been the science of free-market ideology. Just as market mechanisms hid the reality of the factory, so Newton's celestial mechanics concealed the steam engine. Kant, completing his system, had remained indifferent to the jiggling lid of the kettle which so fascinated Denis Papin. James Watt was perfecting the steam engine at the very time Adam Smith, writing his work on the causes of the wealth of nations, "could not imagine any use for coal other than to provide heating for workers."[1] For there where the machine replaces human work, nature and culture recognize a common measure between them: energy.

Newtonian physics had chosen the point of view of God, the eternal being, contemplating his work; thermodynamics, on the other hand, confined itself to the modest viewpoint of man looking to the machine for some practical result. What he saw was not the perpetual motion of stars but that machines always wear out. And it is from this iron law that ma-chines wear out that thermodynamics derives one of its principles: two bodies of different temperatures placed in a closed system move irreversi-bly towards some common mean value. If the total energy is conserved by virtue of a fundamental principle of physics, its quality and its usefulness deteriorate. Carnot's principle shows that the motion of a heat engine is derived from the difference of temperatures. Clausius defined this function, which tends inexorably towards a defined maximum and thus cancels out differences and destroys the power of engines, and he called it S or entropy.

August Comte had interpreted Fourier's law as an example and an image of the world's progress towards equilibrium. Later on, others, in spite of Comte's prohibitions, tried to give this macroscopic phenomenon a micro-scopic interpretation based on the movement of molecules contained in a closed system. This resulted in a scientifically similar vision (reversibility was still the law of motion), but, at the same time, an ideologically converse one (the system evolved towards maximum disorder). The approach pro-posed by Boltzmann considered the probabilistic behaviour of all particles contained in a closed system.[2] It was shown that such a system would spontaneously move towards its most probable state, one corresponding both to maximum entropy and to maximum disorder.

To define useful energy, the science of energy resorts to a notion of order. Maxwell imagined a demon who, without expending energy, moved an ideal hatch by which he prevented certain molecules from moving from one chamber to another.[3] If the high-energy molecules were brought to-gether in one compartment and the low-energy molecules in the other, order would be increased, entropy diminished and the result would be that free energy would also be increased. Alas, the energy needed by the demon to recognize the various particles would consume an amount of energy equivalent to that which he would thus release. Information and energy are therefore at the heart of thermodynamics. Biology, in its search for the elementary mechanisms of life, was to encounter chemistry and physics, and seek to express itself in the laws of thermodynamics. The proliferation of living beings, of bacteria, to take Monod's example, seems to realize Maxwell's demon paradox, giving birth to highly ordered systems in a way that apparently contradicts the principle of thermodynamics, which pre-dicts a constant degradation of order. In fact a precise energy balance sheet would show that the thermodynamic debt corresponding to the operation has been duly settled.[4]

What thermodynamics produced for cybernetic ideology through the science of heat engines and the science of life are two key words in the vocabulary of the confusion between nature and culture: information and energy. Information is what is closest to nature in culture. Carrying meaning without itself being meaning, identified with the material medium to which it is reduced, yet breaking away from it as its existence supposes the presence of a subjectivity, it is the inert witness to the living. Energy is what is closest to culture in nature, it is matter causing motion, it is rocks that are substituted for manpower by being burned in the bowels of machines. Energy even manages to make sense of the nonsense of its most extreme manifestations: a storm is seen as the manifestation of divine wrath, a thermonuclear explosion as the deserved punishment of those who steal the secret of fire.

Information and energy are the two central terms of the cybernetic cosmology.[5] The theme of the communication society gives birth to new developments in social accounting, where the output of the information sector is assessed, and where marketing, data processing, etc. are all lumped together. The theme of energy, of its economy and of its new sources also dominates the world scene. However, while information and energy make it possible to describe the world in a pragmatic way, they have not brought about a radical separation into two absolutely heterogeneous realms as occurs with the pairs of opposites: sacred, profane, nature, culture. As products of the ambiguity of the living and of the inert, these notions are capable, at the heart of science, of changing into each other: thus, in thermodynamics, the free energy of a system, the energy that can be used to make an engine work, is related to the entropy of this system, which itself is interpreted in terms of order or information. Thus it is also possible to calculate the energy needed to cause a given support, a computer memory for example, to reproduce and maintain a given piece of information. The prevailing confusion over the notion of information is all the greater as its use by thermodynamics (in the notion of entropy), by biochemistry (in the study of genetic codes), by the science of telecommunications (in Shannon's definitions for example), by the theory of automatons and by data processing, legitimates its status as a precise, quantifiable and universally meaningful notion. Cybernetic ideology is hardly affected by differences in definition, or even by challenges from those very disciplines that make the most rigorous use of this notion.[6] Cybernetic ideology prefers to believe that it is possible to define *information* (a term which it will replace by *order* or *complexity* if necessary) in an unequivocal way, which it will apply as easily to physics and to biology as to sociology, economics, history, linguistics, or even daily conversation, using the universal, all–purpose, Sophism–producing machine: analogy.

Philosophy of this scientific attitude has been perfectly described by Henry Greniewski, a planner: "All scientific research is a game, the researcher, the scientist are team mates; the object of the research is the adversary. And there is always the public. If that is true, the researcher or the scientist is a professional player and when one is a professional player, one occasionally has an urge to cheat. Often even a professional player becomes a cheat. Here is a rather well-known way to cheat: instead of playing the game with the object of the research, another player, another adversary is put in its place, that is, a very simple model; the game becomes easy, one wins, one adopts a triumphant air, but what has one done in fact? The same as if a boxer were to announce a fight with the world champion and then come up with some poor idiot he would easily defeat. This method of cheating is all the easier as there is no stable boundary between models that are simple and models that are too simple."[7]

To compensate for the ambiguities of the distinction between information and energy, as compared with the sharpness of the distinction between nature and culture, cybernetic ideology has at least two sciences (biochemistry and thermodynamics) instead of one (Newtonian physics). On the whole, the illusion is an effective one and the composition is successful, except perhaps that the actor goes too far, and in doing so suggests that the guarantees of the new science are not as good as those of the old: the essential is missing, namely the objectivity which guarantees that the subject of knowledge is separated from its object.

Chance and Necessity

The cybernetic sciences are needed to construct a cosmology on the model of that which lies at the foundation of the free–market ideology, but which do not suffice to give it legitimacy. All this fine work would have served only to create a rather fragile ideological veneer if it were not possible to use the emergency repair kit for broken–down legitimacy systems, chance and necessity.

Instructions for Use

Here is how to use this kit, which must be brought out only when legitimacy breaks down: if it becomes impossible to state the law, it is necessary above all to keep talking, which can be done by naming the various forms of silence that might be encountered.

Example number one: something unwarranted happens: this is the perfect opportunity to evoke the notion of chance. Example number two: something has happened: experienced people recognize that here is an instance where the word necessity will fit marvelously well.

Let us consider the following exercise: something has happened by chance. What should it be called? It should be called a necessity. The absence of law can thus completely be expressed in terms of chance, that which does not yet exist or, more subtly, what might not have occurred: ("This has happened to you by chance") and of necessity (which, as everyone knows, is a law unto itself). The use in justice of acts of God and happenstance, the way in which the accidental absolves guilt, if not responsibility, illustrates the fact that the legitimate discourse and the discourse of the illegitimate complement each other. Chance is that which obeys no law. Modern times add the stamp of their own genius by formulating, along with the laws of chance, the laws of the absence of law, the laws of the absence of legitimacy. And it is therefore not by chance that chance and necessity have been put forward as the key terms of an ideology founded on biology by the Nobel Prize winner Jacques Monod.[8]

The Last Breakdown

The characteristic feature of the logic of chance and necessity is that it is always handy. We should therefore not be surprised to see builders of legitimacy systems defend their handiwork against the return in strength of the pragmatism that this logic represents. It is not by chance that Kant and Comte, going against the Scientific development of their times, banished chance from the science that they needed in order to found a well-constructed system of legitimacy. And yet chance was neither a new idea nor a new science. To understand this paradox, one has to be willing to make a long detour: one which will enable us to see chance and necessity at work during the last great breakdown of legitimacy, which preceded the establishment of the democratic State and which went from the end of Scholasticsm to the philosophers' triumphant entry into the University in the eighteenth century. This long backward look is necessary to see how alive the philosophy of chance and necessity was when Kant set it aside to establish the reign of reason that classical pure free-market ideology needed. The crisis of the free-market ideology does not correspond to the emergence of the ideology of chance and necessity but to its return. Let us state at the very outset of this visit to Descartes, Pascal, Spinoza, Leibnitz and Kant that we shall have occasion to observe the appearance and disappearance of a constellation of systematically related notions (chance, necessity, the infinite, the self and rhetoric), which constantly appear and disappear together in their work.

Chance and Necessity According to Descartes

Between the schoolmen and Kant, the foundation of the legitimacy of political power shifted from faith to reason. This transformation could only have occurred by stages. These stages lead from Descartes, who constructed reason leaving faith and politics aside, to Kant, who managed to fit politics and religion within the bounds of reason, taking in, on the way, the meditation of Pascal on the relation between faith and reason and that of Spinoza on the relation between reason and politics. From the challenge to the role of faith in the School to the triumph of reason in the University, the philosophers of our story are Descartes, who took refuge in Holland for 20 years; Pascal, close to the recluses (who were soon to become the outcasts) of Port–Royal; and Spinoza, keeping his manuscripts secret and hiding behind the lenses that he polished. In the seventeenth century, the search for the certitudes of reason presumed the full acceptance of life's uncertainties. "That century, as we now know, was rather more a battlefield than the absolute realm of a rational order; the blinding sun of Louis XIV dazzles us and hides those tremendous struggles in which everything said on the finite and infinite, the relative and the absolute, reason and faith, man and God was greeted with contradiction and retort."[9]

In such troubled times, breakdowns in legitimacy must have been numerous and frequent recourse was probably had to chance and necessity. The philosophy of the order of reasons (ie. Cartesian philosophy) might have been expected to leave nothing to chance. In fact it gave unto Caesar what was Caesar's and to God what was God's, and for the rest it established the rule of the clear and distinct ideas of reason. However, it would be an exaggeration to say that doubt was unknown; this would mean overlooking, in the name of the victory of the *cogito*, the extent of disorder that could be contained in methodical doubt. Descartes himself did not hide the fact that: ". . . before commencing to rebuild the house in which we live . . . it is necessary that we be furnished with some other house in which we may live commodiously during the operations; so that I might not remain irresolute in my actions, while my Reason compelled me to suspend my judgment, and that I might not be prevented from living thenceforward in the greatest possible felicity, I formed a provisory code of Morals. . . ."[10]

Thus there is a pragmatic parenthesis in Cartesian dogmatism, formed by the crisis that separated the challenge to ancient beliefs from the establishment of new ones. And this parenthesis is occupied by nothing other than chance and necessity. Thus the second maxim of the provisory code of morals prescribes continuity in action, ". . . although it might be chance alone which first determined the selection; for in this way, if they do not exactly reach the point that they desire, they will come at least in the end to some place that will probably be preferable to the middle of a forest. In the same way, since in action it frequently happens that no delay is permissible, it is very certain that when it is not in our power to determine what is true, we ought to act according to what is most probable. . . ."[11]

The third maxim brings our desires up against necessity: "My third maxim was to endeavour always to conquer myself rather than fortune, and change my desires rather than the order of the world, and in general, accustom myself to the persuasion that, except our own thoughts, there is nothing absolutely in our power; so that when we have done our best in respect of things external to us, all wherein we fail of success is to be held, as regards us, absolutely impossible: and this single principle seemed to me sufficient to prevent me from desiring for the future anything which I could not obtain, and thus render me contented; for since our will naturally seeks those objects alone which the understanding represents as in some way possible of attainment, it is plain that, if we consider all external goods as equally beyond our power, we shall no more regret the absence of such goods as seem due to our birth, when deprived of them without any fault of ours, than our not possessing the kingdoms of China or Mexico; and thus making, so to speak, a virtue of necessity, we shall no more desire health in disease, or freedom in imprisonment.[12]

What Descartes put between protective parentheses was the self; what he sought to bring out of them was truth. Between these two, there is doubt: the radical questioning of all opinions capable of being contradicted, those that are acquired "by example and by custom."[13] "I took into account also the very different character which a person brought up from infancy in France or Germany exhibits, from that which, with the same mind originally, this individual would have possessed had he lived always among the Chinese or with savages, and the circumstance that in dress itself the fashion which pleased us ten years ago, and which may again, perhaps, be received into favor before ten years have gone, appears to us at this moment extravagant and ridiculous. I was thus led to infer that the ground of our opinions is far more custom and example than any certain knowledge. And, finally, although such be the ground of our opinions, I remarked that a plurality of suffrages is no guarantee of truth where it is at all of difficult discovery, as in such cases it is much more likely that it will be found by one than by many. I could, however, select from the crowd no one whose opinions seemed worthy of preference, and thus I found myself constrained, as it were, to use my own Reason in the conduct of my life."[14] The first maxim, which caps the other two, defines the parentheses. Their form is that of obedience to laws and customs, respect for teachings and moderation in opinions. Their function is to guarantee the right to self–contradiction.

Abandoning (within the parentheses) the guarantees of faith and those of tradition, the mind confronts itself as it would Gorgias, the object of the contradiction eternally possible between all opinions, so much so that for his provisory (pragmatic) code of morals, Descartes finds nothing better to propose than faith and tradition. The rejection of the doubtful is the quest, starting from the pragmatic self (subjected to absolute relativism), for a proposition that appears (an appearance which would be called *evidence* and qualified as being clear and distinct by way of precaution) to be impossible to contradict. With Descartes, philosophy became the result of the effort of persuasion exerted by the self upon the self: a Sophist to himself (insofar as one can be a Sophist to oneself),[15] the philosopher finally falls prey to his own seduction the day he convinces himself that he has found an idea which cannot be contradicted by any other idea that he might later come across in the voyages of the mind. In order not to attribute to mere lassitude the end of the search through the infinity of words and places, the first clear idea found (by chance) must be the very idea that there exists a prime idea from which other ideas flow, and flow according to an order, namely the order instituted by reason when it manages to emerge from its chaos: the self abandoned by kings and gods.

Now that the principle of reason is established, Descartes may come out of the parentheses in which he was confronted with doubt and exposed to the persuasive power of contradictory arguments. His first act is then to refute the power of rhetoric compared with the clarity and the intelligibility of thoughts. It is at the very beginning of the Discours de la Methode that he declares that those whose reasoning is the most powerful, and who can best direct their thoughts to make them clear and intelligible are always those best capable of winning approval for what they propose, even if haven't been to school and have never learned rhetoric.[16]

By finding the prime idea, Descartes had vanquished chance. There remained the question of whether he had not vanquished chance by chance,[17] whether in confronting the infinity of possibilities he might not have remained "in the middle of the forest."[18] Conscious of this, "Descartes always reminds us of the limits of our understanding."[19] He was to make this limit central to the idea of the infinite by stipulating that, although it is possible to have a philosophy of the infinite (and although it is even necessary to ask God to guarantee the correspondence between what there is in a thought and what is found in extension), it is impossible to think it. To claim otherwise would be to set oneself up as a rival with the power (of thought) of God, whom man needs as a guarantor, or to run the risk of falling back on a philosophy of chance.

To found Reason on science, Descartes had to confront pragmatism and its dangers. To bring Reason up against the pillars of the old order, religion and politics, Pascal and Spinoza also had to confront the risks of Sophism. And, if they managed to escape the pure logic of chance and necessity, it was only because Spinoza chose necessity over chance and Pascal chose chance over necessity.

Pascal and Chance

Reason as founded by Descartes seemed capable of doing without God. "I cannot forgive Descartes: in his whole philosophy he would like to do without God; but he could not help having him nudge the world into motion; after that he had no more use for God."[20] Pascal's voyage to the sources of the true faith led him into the worldly, life where libertines raised on the human sciences (hence disciples as much of the Sophists as of Montaigne) affected a disdain for religion in the name of reason.[21] He realized the force of their pragmatism and, being a pious and moral man, he yielded, for the purpose of his research, to the temptations of "diversion," a provisory code of amorality, by which he wished to bring out the obviousness of the preoccupation with salvation.

What Pascal was to encounter in his voyage towards the true faith (for it was essential for him that this faith, discovered by man, should not be discovered by chance), was the condition of man lost between the infinitely large and the infinitely small. With the return of the philosophy of the infinite, it was chance which came back itself as the sole and meagre justification of what happens. "Chance giveth thoughts and chance taketh away. There was no art whatever to preserving or acquiring them. My thought has fled, I wanted to note it, I note instead that it has fled."[22]

Pascal was to encounter chance in quite a real way in the problems of gambling posed by the Chevalier de Mere, to which he found the mathematical solution by his famous use of the arithmetical triangle. With Pascal, chance, far from being systematically cast aside, was made central to the human condition. A human condition without a center, hence a restless one which could find rest only by setting for itself the goal of salvation. For, to judge, man needs such a fixed point: "Those who lead disorderly lives tell those who are normal that it is they who deviate from nature and think they are following nature themselves; just as those who are on board ship think that the people on shore are moving away. Language is the same everywhere: we need a fixed point to judge it. The harbor is the judge of those aboard ship, but where are we going to find a harbor in morals?"[23] As a way out of the absolute relativism of the sophistical libertines, Pascal proposed the certainty of Salvation, compared with which all is vanity. And to incite the libertines to take the leap, he was to speak their language, the language of chance, by tempting them with a promising wager.

Just as Descartes pulled certainty out of an ultimate doubt, so Pascal expected the reign of certainty to come from a final roll of the dice. Confronted with infinity of thoughts and with the hazards of circumstances, the Pascalian man encountered the pragmatic self: "The nature of self–love and of this human self is to love only self and consider only self. But what is it to do? It cannot prevent the object of its love from being full of faults and wretchedness; it wants to be great and sees that it is small; it wants to be happy and sees that it is wretched; it wants to be perfect and sees that it is full of imperfections; it wants to be the object of men's love and esteem and sees that its faults deserve only their dislike and contempt. The predicament in which it thus finds itself arouses in it the most unjust and criminal passion that could possibly be imagined, for it conceives a deadly hatred for the truth which rebukes it and convinces it of its faults. It would like to do away with this truth, and not being able to destroy it as such, it destroys it as best it can, in its own consciousness and that of others."[24]

It was to this pragmatic self, this "man full of needs"[25] bounded to "false powers" namely "senses and memory," "imagination," "custom," "self-love," "pride and the spirit of vanity,"[26] that the convincing discourse of rhetoric was addressed. For, in certain subjects, there "are well–established things on known truths, yet things which are at the same time contrary to the pleasures that most affect us." The danger grows then that the "mind most determined" to "act only by reason" will "by a shameful choice" follow "that which a corrupt will desires."[27]

Then it is necessary to know "the spirit and the heart, the principles that they agree with, the things that they love; and then to observe the relations of the thing in question with the principles avowed or with objects that are delectable by the charms that are attributed to it. So that the art of persuasion is as much that of pleasing as it is of convincing, so much do men govern themselves by whim rather than by reason."[28]

In all these movements, Pascal was a faithful Jansenist, even to his friendship with the libertines, for "after the Fronde, Port–Royal welcomed, sometimes as disciples and sometimes, friends and protectors, many members of the Fronde (translator's note: this term covers a series of outbreaks in France from 1648 to 1653, caused by rivalry between the *Parlement* of Paris and the royal authority as well as the discontent of the great nobles), more humiliated than repentant, people like Mme de Longueville, Mme de Sablé, La Rochefoucauld etc."[29] For them it was "at once a haven of salvation where they could expiate the dazzling libertinage of their past lives and the only place where they could still oppose the State honourably and discreetly."[30] A circumstance which owed no more to chance than did the *Logique de Port–Royal*, the first line of which, nevertheless, proclaims: "The birth of this little work is due entirely to chance and to a species of *diversion* rather than to a serious design."[31] This was because *diversion* was precisely the space where chance reigned. By including social life and royalty in the category of diversion, Port–Royal illustrated the fact that the Pascal's meditation on reason and religion, far from sparing political power by being ignorant of it, condemned it by reducing it to the status of a diversion without legitimacy. Even the King's condition was not spared by Pascal's implacable rhetoric: "Kings are surrounded by people who are incredibly careful to see that the king should never be alone and able to think about himself, because they know that, king though he is, he will be miserable if he does think about it."[32] "Is not the dignity of kingship sufficiently great in itself to make the possessor happy by simply seeing what he is? Does he need to be diverted from such thoughts by ordinary people? . . . Put it to the test; leave a king entirely alone, with nothing to satisfy his senses, no care to occupy his mind, with no one to keep him company and no diversion, with complete leisure to think about himself, and you will see that a king without diversion is a wretched man indeed. I am not speaking here of Christian kings as Christians, only as kings."[33]

The confrontation of reason with faith had produced the expected result. Reason could no longer account for everything, in particular it could no longer give answers to questions about the difference in laws and customs on either side of the Pyrenees, or about the gulf of infinity and the omnipresence of chance. But infinite space could, without difficulty, contain reason—the results of which Pascal developed in the sphere of science, especially by founding the theory of probabilities—, as long as one could refer to a religion as the sole "fixed point," a necessary element for the salvation of souls, for the legitimacy of their fate through the intercession of grace and its choices.[34] Pascal's argument against the casuistical probabilism of the Jesuits showed that the religion whose legitimacy he had just established, in accordance with reason but not subject to reason, could not accept the presence of chance in its decrees. Casuistry suggested the uncertainties of a pragmatic approach where the certitudes of salvation alone should have emerged. "Take away probability and you can no longer please anyone, bring in probability and you cannot displease them."[35] (PASCAL) If there had to be casuistry, Pascal wanted it to be "as it had been among the first Fathers of the Church, as it had been among the Stoics themselves, an invitation not to let ourselves be trapped by the Sophistry of passions, a reminder of the purity of the rule."[36]

Spinoza and Necessity

Pascal had dealt with reason and faith by setting aside politics and in so doing he maltreated politics to some extent. Spinoza dealt with the relationships between reason and politics, putting aside religion, which thereby considered itself ill-used enough to excommunicate him. It is to the most radical political pragmatism that Spinoza makes reference in the *Treatise on Politics*: "What means an omnipotent prince, whose sole motive is lust of mastery, should use to establish and maintain his dominion, the most ingenious Machiavelli has set forth at large."[37] Political pragmatism is faced with a population of empirical selves hardly different from those described by Pascal: "Inasmuch as men are led, as we have said, more by passion than reason, it follows, that a multitude comes together, and wishes to be guided, as it were by one mind, not at the suggestion of reason, but of some common passion—that is common hope, or fear, or the desire of avenging some common hurt."[38] The path taken by Spinoza, like that of Pascal, like that of Descartes, leads through the acceptance of Pragmatism as a necessary way to the truth." Therefore applying my mind to politics, I have resolved to demonstrate by a certain and undoubted course of argument or to deduce from the very condition of human nature, not what is new and unheard of, but only such things as agree best with practice. And that I might investigate the subject matter of this science with the same freedom of spirit as we generally use in mathematics, I have labored carefully, not to mock, lament, or execrate, but to understand human actions; and to this end I have looked upon passions, such as love, hatred, anger, envy, ambition, pity, and the other perturbations of the mind, not in the light of vices of human nature, but as properties just as pertinent to it as are heat, cold, storm, thunder, and the like to the nature of the atmosphere, which phenomena, though inconvenient, are yet necessary, and have fixed causes, by means of which we endeavour to understand their nature, and the mind has just as much pleasure in viewing them aright, as in knowing such things as flatter the senses.[39]

Spinoza dealt with the facts of culture as facts of nature. In this he went against the separation set up by Descartes between thought and extension. But it is true that he contradicted this position even in his metaphysics, where thought and extent, far from being (as with Descartes) two separate substances whose harmony was ensured by a good spirit, became two attributes of one and the same substance, nature, two attributes whose parallelism was ensured by the fact that all thought was thought about something[40] and that the first thought was the thought of the body.[41]

This confusion between nature and culture, which, as we have seen, characterises the crisis of legitimacy of the rational–legal system, can already be found in the philosophy of Pascal, who, while he accepted the separation between the human mind and the automaton, could not accept their total dissociation when he came to thinking about the mechanisms of persuasion that come into play in conversation: "For being both body and soul at the same time . . . we are automatons as much as we are mind and this is why the instrument of persuasion is not demonstration alone. How few are the things that are demonstrated! Proofs only convince the mind. Custom makes for our strongest and barest proofs; they subdue the automaton which drags the mind without its thinking of it. . . . We must therefore put our faith in sentiment."[42] And to come out of the pragmatism from which he had agreed to start and in which mind and automaton were identified, Pascal ended his demonstration by "the trichotomy of the three orders of bodies, spirits and grace."[43]

Spinoza, too, had to make reference to an additional category to get out of the total pragmatism where right is nothing else than the right of the mightiest, where the big fish is destined to eat the smaller fish. This category is none other than the type of knowledge to which the individual has access. If he remains at the level of the first type of knowledge, he is subject to passions in a way so immediate that he becomes a totally passive object of history. At the second level of knowledge, where he has access to causes and effects, he may become conscious of the chances on which his fate depends and, to a limited extent, he may use strategems to struggle with events. But only the one who reaches the third level of knowledge understands that his position in the world (however fragile and unflattering this might be) is a necessary one, for his mind then rises to apprehend his position in infinite nature and in the participation of what he calls the intellectual love of God. God who, is nothing other than nature.

At this level, it is because man becomes free that politics can emerge from the pure tautologies of force and its motto ("things are what they are"). Now the freedom of man is a power, the power to be his own master, and therefore this power necessarily expresses itself in law. In particular, this living man, guided by reason,[44] will be able to formulate the best rules of government and, if the whole of society is made up of free men, their government can be the best government. Thus when men are dominated by affection (passions and feelings), the basis of the polity will be *the fear and respect* that it inspires in its subjects. "Hence to remain master of itself the polity must maintain the causes of fear without which it is no longer a polity."[45] Whether rhetoric and arms can serve the ends of the Prince is for the reader to judge. However, when the men of the polity are free, the result will be the better government by virtue of the fact that the best is the product of a being (man or polity) which is most completely its own master.[46] The purpose of the State then will be *the peace and security of those who live in it.*

Descartes, Pascal and Spinoza wrought havoc with the legitimacy of the traditional, feudal order. Descartes gave man access to his own Reason as opposed to Tradition. Pascal gave man access to his Salvation as opposed to the Church, and Spinoza gave man access to his Liberty against the State. The common danger that these three attitudes represented to the dominant order was that they made the individual the source of legitimacy, a danger that was concretized with Kant, who defined a Politics and a Religion within the bounds of Reason. For it was really political power that was at stake, and the main result of the revolution begun by Descartes was to make (individual) Reason and not (the Church's) Religion the source of the legitimacy of political power. History was to show that reason tended to make each person, equally and without hierarchy, the source of power. To combat a philosophy that had become too powerful to be ignored, the feudal hierarchies of the day had to set up another philosophy. This philosophy had to meet the dual condition of not contradicting science, a far too effective source of faith in reason, and of re–establishing the primacy of the divine, which alone could, by crowning a hierarchy, give it the support of the legitimacy that it needed. No less than the versatile genius of Liebnitz was needed to attempt such a contradictory program with any chance of success.

Leibnitz and the Probable

In order to admit a thesis and overturn it at the same time, it suffices to turn it inside out like a glove. Thus all its structures are accepted while its meaning is reversed.

Descartes had discovered reason, sheltered by a God who was kept away from polemics, Leibnitz was to welcome the reason thus produced and attribute it directly to God himself. He thus identified reason with divinity. Turning the arguments of Descartes against him, he cast doubt on a method that still left far too much to chance.[47] For, in the infinity of possible imaginations, "success in solving a problem was but a mixture of luck and chance with art and method."[48] Cartesian intuition, which claimed to discover that which escaped chance and its doubts, was thus left to chance. To get out of this difficulty, it was necessary to accept the existence of a direct relationship between God and thought, and hence the possibility of a thought of the infinite. Leibnitz knew how to use science as a rhetorical argument. He discovered infinitesimal calculus: at the heart of reason, Cartesian reason was shown to be lacking." Between Descartes and Leibnitz there was a reversal of perspectives: in the first perspective, that of Descartes, one starts with the *cogito,* and the clarity of the order of reasons coincides with certainty itself; in the latter, that of Leibnitz, one starts from being, the same words describe the mechanisms of divine understanding, which expresses itself in the order of the world, and the logical mechanism of our understanding, which imitates that of God and expresses that of the world, so that the clarity of order or rigour do not always coincide with truth or certainty."[49]

Thereby, "Leibnitz argued against the methodological solipsism (the source of pride in individual reason which was such a danger to the traditional order) implied by the practice of doubt. Doubt is so linked to passion that it is more of a rhetorical procedure than a precept of method. . . ."[50] For doubt, Leibnitz suggested another fate: the constitution of *a logic of the probable* and (there was a final paradox here) the temporary discarding of what remained of doubt, even if it was doubt about the value of axioms and postulates, so that at least "what was demonstrable" could be demonstrated.[51] Thus the consideration of the infinite led, as it ought to have done, to the acceptance of chance. Leibnitz was to turn the argument inside out, and here this took the astonishingly real form of the adjunction, to Pascal's arithmetical triangle, of the harmonic triangle, constituted by replacing each term of the former by its converse in the latter. Thus we move from probabilities to the continuity of the infinite, and what appears to us to be chance is in fact necessarily included in the infinite power of possibles.

The combinative system that gives us the rules of the probable is the very structure of God, who includes all possibilities. And by this combinative science, man, far from being solely the unknowing toy of some fate as of God alone, participates in divine knowledge: "While Arnauld made a sharp distinction between the ideas that man found in himself and the mystery of divine thought, while for him notions themselves were those that we find in ourselves, Leibnitz wrote 'As for me I had thought that notions are represented in divine understanding as they are in themselves.'"[52] If confrontation with the infinite led to chance in Leibnitz's thought, it was not referring to the absurd but to the meaning borne by some fragment of the divine combinative system. Far from it being necessary to emerge from the "forest" of Cartesian doubt to see the light of clear and distinct ideas, there is no confused idea, imagination or dream which does not participate in the parade of divine possibilities. "Leibnitz does not take into account this existential judgment of unreality. It is as a logician that he describes and analyzes the difference between sensation and image: thus he finds between them only a difference of degree in the criteria invoked and consequently a simple difference of probability between sleep and wake."[53]

This probability, relating sensation as much to knowledge (through the combinative logic) as to God (the source of all combinative systems and identical to them), enables man to participate in the one without sacrificing anything of infinity and to participate in the other without sacrificing anything of Reason. The pragmatic self of dreams and illusions, the self of diversion, can enter without discontinuity into the order of the world which rises, in one and the same movement, towards God and Reason. This self is none other than this ". . . intelligent soul which, because it knows itself and is capable of saying this self . . . does not merely survive as do the souls of beasts and subsist metaphysically much more than others more than the souls of beasts but furthermore remains the same morally, and acts as the same character. For it is this recollection of the knowledge of this self which renders it capable of chastisement or recompense. . . . But in order to judge, by natural reasons, that God shall always preserve not only our substance but also our person, that is, the memory and the knowledge of what we are (although distinct knowledge of this may be sometimes suspended by sleep or lapses) morals must be joined to metaphysics, that is, God should be considered not only as the principle and the cause of every substance and every being but also as the chief of all persons or intelligent substances and as the absolute monarch of the most perfect city or re-public, as is the city of the universe composed of all minds together. . . ."[54] And since the best of all possible worlds, which would seem to anticipate contemporary society, is just beginning to emerge here, let us note that, far from stopping at the notion of the self as a constituent element of the world, Leibnitz moves directly to a more abstract notion that would fill our cyberneticists with satisfaction, so similar is it to the entities from which they build their systems. He names these entities *monads*: they are the building blocks that constitute the world (somewhat in the manner of Whitehead's *superjects*). Monads have a three–tiered hierarchy: the sim-plest monads are endowed with perception and appetition, they pursue a goal to which they are guided by signals that they receive from the world; endowed with memory, these monads become souls capable of good, evil and responsibility (it might be said that souls are monads endowed with feedback); finally if monads accede to the "necessary and eternal truths, as are those of logic, numbers, and geometry," they are definitely differenti-ated from "beasts" and become "reasonable animals" or "spirits," for these souls are capable of "performing reflective acts and of considering what can be called the self, substance, soul, mind."[55]

The method used was always the same: turning the adversary's argu-ments inside out like a glove. Leibnitz is a past master at replacing the duel of philosophies by the victory of dual thinking. Spinoza knew only one substance, Leibnitz knew an infinity of them: the monads. Communicat-ing with one another while remaining autonomous (with neither "doors" nor "windows") monads reflect one another and all express divine logic. Divine logic gives birth to an infinity of possible worlds, the machine for generating possibles being the combinative art of which God provided the pattern as well as he attributed to each monad an autonomous capacity to act, thus reintroducing (through appetition) final cause into the world of modern philosophical thought. The product of these logical machines, of which all representations are probables that engender some possible, is the *compossible*. Reality is neither chance nor pure contingency—nor necessity; it is the result of the confluence of all possible series, it is that which corresponds to the greatest accumulation of compossibilities.

But once again, just as with Whitehead, human reason that led to such a description did not suffice to produce the optimism needed for legitimizing a system that had abandoned the necessity that authenticated it. To found the legitimacy of what is, it became indispensable then, for Leibnitz as for Whitehead, to appeal to God: "Until now, we have spoken as mere physicists, now we must raise ourselves to the level of metaphysics by using the great PRINCIPLE according to which NOTHING IS DONE WITHOUT SUFFICIENT REASON, that is to say that nothing happens without its being possible for he who knows things sufficiently to render a Reason which suffices to determine why it is so and not otherwise. This principle being posed, the first question that one is entitled to ask will be WHY IS THERE SOMETHING RATHER THAN NOTHING. . . . Moreover, assuming that things must exist, a reason must be given FOR WHY THEY MUST EXIST THUS AND NOT OTHERWISE. Now this sufficient Reason for the existence of the universe cannot be found without a substance . . . which is its cause and which is a necessary being carrying the Reason for its existence with itself. . . . And this last Reason of things is called God."[56] Leibnitz thereby inverted Spinoza's "God, i.e. nature," a god who had only to account for the necessity of his own existence, since it was enough for him to found the necessity of things and not their possibility, or their compossibility.

All this effort of inversion made it possible to vanquish feudalism's adversary: Spinoza's free man appropriated the right to make the distinction between a political system founded on *fear and respect* and another, better system, founded on *peace and security;* the spirit of Leibnitz's system recognized the world chosen by God as the best of all possible worlds. Spinoza's necessary world had become Leibnitz's best of all possible worlds. The hierarchical society, the reality of that time, was for Spinoza a necessity (like everything that occurred) which the free man could compare to the best of all governments, the one that would be constituted by a society of free men. The hierarchical society was, for Leibnitz, a possibility, the best possible one, the society in which each individual occupied a place suited to his gifts. Just as Leibnitz based his faith in God on Reason by putting Reason in the place of God, so he based his political optimism on the place that politics was capable of giving to the person who possessed the most reason: "The goal of monarchy is to bring about the reign of a hero of eminent wisdom and reason such as our present king. The goal of aristocracy is to give the reins of government to the wisest and most expert men. The goal of democracy or politics is to make peoples themselves agree on what is their good. And if there were, all at once, a great hero, very wise senators and reasonable citizens, that would make for a mixture of all three forms."[57]

Leibnitz's best of all possible worlds was already that of the Bureaucrat Prince's reign: "Good princes, however, whatever their power, always remember that, in the eyes of God, they are never the proprietors or even the usufructuaries of their countries but mere administrators of a good that belongs to God. . . ."[58]

To the Duke of Hanover and Peter the Great, Leibnitz suggested the importance of statistics and archives, the institution of retirement benefit funds and life insurance, State pawn shops; offices for various kinds of advertising, the monopoly of road transport, a general workshop for workers in search of employment.[59] If Leibnitz had no need to constitute a rhetoric, it was because all was rhetoric and communication in the best of all worlds, since communication was nothing but the convergence of languages that issued from the divine art of combining symbols. Completing the series of inversions, science, far from destroying rhetoric, itself became rhetoric. In this too, Leibnitz reminds us of the cybernetic universe. Evidence brought the Cartesian out of the shadow of doubt, henceforth doubt recognizes in itself the light of the probable which, when projected on the possible, gives it the appearance of the best.[60]

Descartes, Pascal and Spinoza had tried to ground metaphysical certainty in the individual alone, Leibnitz re–established the power of opinion. Thus the Cartesian proof invoked a metaphysical certitude "which concluded with necessity the existence of some body." The Leibnitzian proof asks only for a moral certitude.[61] "For Leibnitz, the problem was to account for the variety of our thoughts. To speak of an external world is to speak of a world which gives the appearances of extension but which in itself is composed only of souls"[62] and this is why "rather than rejecting opinion, a science of opinion must be made."[63]

To get to the foundations of a legitimacy at the heart of the individual, Descartes, Pascal and Spinoza had to go through the hell of pragmatism: the trials were named doubt, *diversion,* the law of the strongest. There they discovered the finite self confronted with the infinite universe, confronting chance and necessity, subjected to the artifices of rhetoric. Faced wih the strength of reason, the old order had only one way out: to negotiate. The agreement between the two competing systems of legitimacy could be none other than the reconciliation of God and reason as proposed by Leibnitz. And since opinions no longer seemed to converge as a natural result of tradition, they had to do so as a result of the activity of schoolmasters: "The Masters of the various levels of teaching have a precise role to play in the State for it is always necessary to provide for the union of wisdom and power, to work for the collaboration of those who think with those who act.

Teachers would be the delegates of the State in the provinces, and, in the towns, university professors would be the counsellors of the court and they would be assisted by abbeys and other ecclesiastical benefices."[64] And so it was. At least enough so for the thought of Leibnitz to reach Kant through Wolf, the man who was to be called "the school master of Germany."

To hypnotize a person, it is necessary to prevent him from seeing anything other than what is shown to him. The formalism and the final cause of Wolf's dogmatism had the capacity to put a mind of Kant's power to sleep, at least until Hume lifted the veil of verisimilitude and probability which covered the radical incertitude of empiricism. Kant had found his hell and his trial: empiricism. It was for Kant to submit to reason the God who had appropriated reason.

Kant, Comte and Cybernetics: The Rejection and the Return of Chance

In Kant's philosophy, the empirical self, relegated to "anthropology from a pragmatic viewpoint" is carefully isolated fom the subject of knowledge.[65] The power of the infinite, when the transcendental subject has no access through the *a priori* categories of knowledge, is abandoned to the unknowable, the thing–in–itself: chance is banished, necessity is the necessity of physical law; as for rhetoric, its power is such that it will perhaps be necessary to resort to it as a weapon against itself: "But where the mass entertains the notion that the aim of certain subtle speculators is nothing less than to shake the very foundations of public welfare and morality—it seems not only prudent, but even praiseworthy to maintain the good cause by specific arguments."[66] It was therefore not a matter of chance that Kant and Comte rejected both the self and chance, and insisted on keeping the infinite within reasonable limits. It was therefore not surprising that the self, chance and the infinite reappeared at the same time, thereby signalling the advent of pragmatism and the replacement of law by games.

Newtonian science did not know about games, it "feigned no hypotheses," it discovered the eternal laws of the world. The economic subject of liberalism, at grips with the vagaries of the market, knew that all misery, all frustration was but the expression of a discourse lacking dignity before the certainty of long–term equilibrium. Social legitimacy was established beyond all pragmatism. Justice was rendered by nature itself. The science of Auguste Comte replaced the laws of nature by the rule of the game of knowledge: method. Henceforth complaints and woes could no longer be ignored in the name of the eternity of economic laws. They were in part prohibited in the name of the principles of *love, order* and *harmony,* which guaranteed to each a suitable place in the social organism, and partly fated to disappear as and when progress achieved its task of putting things in order. Thus the vagaries of individual fates were subject to the certainties of collective destiny.

With cybernetics, methodology became a matter of probability, and science a game of chance. Complaints and woes could no longer be referred to a law or to a rule of a legitimate game. In the absence of law, making a virtue of necessity amounted to making a necessity of chance. W. C. Fields sees a sucker in a saloon and suggests a game of cards; "Is it a game of chance?" asks the victim. "Not the way I play it," replies the hero of *My Little Chickadee.* If W. C. Fields won every trick, it was because he knew the cards. Even so, the partner still has to accept the rules of the game. For that matter, however paradoxical it may seem, rules seem safer if they exclude chance.

A system of legitimacy can accept the existence of contingency only within the categories of eternity. God, the eternal being, accounts for the hazards of chance by the ministrations of his providence. For tradition, submitting to the vagaries of life is a custom whose origins go back to the dawn of time and for reason it is the laws of eternal nature that take over the burden of a God who has lost his place for having hidden himself too long. With the risk that, worn out by the rigours of the Eternal, one asked for meaning from history, thus rediscovering the consolations of providence by another route.

Legitimacy is as closely related to time as illegitimacy is to contingency. The divinity is replaced by the scientist, who derives the necessity of a scientific and objective law from the succession of chances: needing time to stage the series of its caprices, chance manages, through the law of large numbers, to become the law of time itself.

The Time of Chance

Darwin's and Wallace's evolutionism was the first to achieve this transformation at the heart of the conception of the world by which the contingent, having broken the legitimate ordering of species, went on to proclaim itself the law of this ordering. "What radically separates the evolutionism of Darwin and Wallace from all previous thinking is the notion of contingency applied to living beings. Until the nineteenth century, the great chain of beings participated in the harmony of the universe. There was the same necessity in the world of beings as in the stars."[67]

It was the world of Auguste Comte or the world that was dominated by Lamarck's transformism that collapsed at the same time. "So long as the living world was arranged as a continuous chain, the succession of transformations could be imagined as nothing other than a series of gradations, in the manner of Lamarck, progressing in a linear course from the simplest to the most complex. Once the continuity of the horizontal relationship among living bodies was broken (for zoological geography had shown the independence of the development of life on the various continents), once beings were redistributed into "branchings," the vertical relationship could no longer be seen in terms of a unique sequence. And these groups of beings isolated from one another no longer presented any character of necessity. The variation of beings is not necessarily linked to the idea of utility, of need, of progression, it can be gratuitous."[68]

Darwin, the scientist, worked this contingency out immediately in terms of the law of large numbers. "With Darwin, the mishaps and misadventures which can befall such and such an individual are of no interest . . . the object of the transformation is not the organism but the totality of similar organisms that live in the course of time. . . . The whole theory of evolution rests on the laws of large numbers. Not that Darwin resorted to complex mathematical processing in order to study variations in populations; he was satisfied with intuition and common sense; to study transformations, he considered solely those fluctuations that always occur in large populations. . . . His attitude was that of statistical analysis which would change the small advantage granted to a few into a rigid mechanism with unavoidable consequences, through a small increase in the chances of survival and reproduction. Hence, necessity did not entirely disappear from the world. It only changed its nature."[69] When necessity does not succumb to the determinism of a law that etches it in time or eternity, it is time that seems to result from necessity and chance: "Time has no importance, says Darwin, and in this respect its importance is great only in that it offers more opportunites for the appearance of advantageous variations. . . ."[70] Chance becomes the measure of time. If what had been impossible with Kant and Comte was to become the law, there had to be a new Copernican revolution. The first had lost the earth its central place in the universe, the second lost life its central position in relation to the inert. "Not only could the living world have been entirely different from what it is today, but it could have equally well never existed."[71] The identification of subject with object became a matter of confusion for the subject. But since the separation between the subject and the object tended to disappear, what affected one could not but affect the other.

And indeed Francois Jacob [72] saw this transformation as "the effect of the change in the very way of considering objects, the result of a completely new attitude which emerged in the mid–nineteenth century"; and he adds: "That this transformation was not a mere accident is proved by the fact that it appeared independently and more or less simultaneously in quite separate fields: in the analysis of matter with Boltzmann and Gibbs, in that of living beings with Darwin and Wallis, and then Mendel."[73] This change marks the passage "between two ways of considering a collection of objects that belong to one and the same class, like the molecules of a gas or the organisms of a same species. They can be seen firstly as a set of identical bodies. All the members of the group are exact copies the same model. . . . What must be discovered is not the objects themselves, but the type to which they relate. Only the type has a reality. . . . Quite on the contrary, we can find a population of individuals, in the same collection of objects, who are never exactly identical. Every member of the group then assumes a unique character. There is no longer a model . . . but an identikit picture which only summarizes the average properties of each individual."[74]

And what is true of the manner of considering the object of science (statistical biology and statistical thermodynamics) is also true of the way in which the subject of science is considered. Thus for Auguste Comte, "If the idea of society still seems to be an abstraction, it is above all by virtue of the old philosophical order, for, in fact, such a tract belongs to the idea of the individual, at least in our species."[75] With the triumph of pragmatism, the psychological self became the measure of all things. And if additional evidence were needed to illustrate the point that the emergence of chance as law was not fortuitous, it would be enough to recall that it was a sociologist who inspired Maxwell's and Boltsman's way of treating gases: this sociologist was none other than Quetelet, the inventor of the average man, who closely resembled the identikit evoked by François Jacob. For, with the average man, society was represented by an abstraction composed out of a diversity of features taken from a population of "selves." Just as man abandoned by God saw that he had created God in his own image, so the subject of knowledge, abandoned by the objectivity of science, perceived once again that it was in his image that he had created the object of his faith.

From Philosopher Scientists to the Philosophy of Scientists

In order to realize that he had been deceiving himself, the subject of knowledge would still have to retain a sufficiently good recollection of his past image if he was not, like Narcissus, to be contented with recognizing himself, rapturously, in the object that he had produced. And the temptation of his present image would be all the greater as the recollection that he put away was that of the painful work of separating the object of knowledge from the subject of knowledge. Perhaps Descartes' greatest merit was to have staged the birthing, by reason, of a single man at grips with the immediate data of consciousness: "Among the branches of Philosophy, I had, at an earlier period, given some attention to Logic, and among those of the Mathematics to Geometrical Analysis and Algebra,—three Arts or

Sciences which ought, as I conceived, to contribute something to my design
. . . and although this Science contains indeed a number of correct and very
excellent precepts, there are, nevertheless, so many others, and these either
injurious or superfluous, mingled with the former, that it is almost quite as
difficult to effect a severance of the true from the false as it is to extract a
Diana or a Minerva from a rough block of marble."[76] This painful gestation
lasted nine years. Nine years went by, Descartes said, before he took any
sides in the difficulties that are customarily disputed among the learned or
before he began to seek the foundations of any philosophy more certain
than the vulgar.[77]

To be born, Reason had need of that heroism which makes the subject of
knowledge and its object spring forth at the same time from the same body.
To live, it needed to be protected from the return of confusion and for this,
it needed to separate the philosopher from the scientist. When Descartes'
heir awoke from his dogmatic slumber, he had become a university philosopher, borrowing the model of a science from a scientist in order to
establish the laws of Reason.

The separation of the philosopher, witness and guarantor of science's
potential, from the scientist, the producer of science, could be perpetuated
for as long as the object of knowledge remained separate de jure from the
subject of knowledge. Cyberneticized science was to end this distribution
of tasks.

With logical neo–positivism, scientists set themselves up as the tribunal
of their own output; if they needed a philosophy, they asked for it from a
scientist: Whitehead. But, having become a philospher, Whitehead took it
into his head that he needed God. Cybernetic science cannot mimic the
science of laissez–faire ideology if, acting like Leibnitz's science, it demands
to be crowned by the divinity. To complete the simulation, it is science[78]
itself that must be put in the place of this untimely God.[79] And since even a
scientist devoting himself full–time to philosophy runs the risk of discovering something beyond science, it is from practicing scientists that a philosophy will be sought.

Henceforth, far from philosophy being the foundation of knowledge, it
is the results of science that found the philosophical representations that
cybernetic ideology requires. If they respect this cybernetic character of
their own knowledge, scientists like Monod and Prigogine will produce an
ideology of chance and necessity.

Chance and Necessity According to Monod

The proof that Jacques Monod's *Chance and Necessity* is "a break-
through," in the words of Michel Serres,[80] can be seen in Louis Althusser's

"admiring and rigorous" commentary,[81] as well as in the way Ilya Prigogine and Isabelle Stengers replied to him when they proposed the hopes of *La Nouvelle Alliance* (the New Covenant) in place of his uncertainties.[82]

Jacques Monod's work can be read like a drama. Desirous of discovering the difference between the natural and the artificial, "which appears immediate and unambiguous to each one of us," Monod knows that all he has available to him are the possibilities of cybernetics. "To make sure of the complete objectivity of the criteria chosen, it would doubtless be best to ask oneself if, by putting them to use, a program could be drawn up that enables a computer to distinguish an artifact from a natural object."[83] Drawing closer to the separation between nature and culture, Monod discovers the artificial and tries to produce the difference that separates it from the natural. As he goes along, he discovers the living: "Living creatures are strange objects. At all times in the past, men must have been more or less confusedly aware of this. The development of the natural sciences beginning in the seventeenth century, their flowering in the nineteenth, instead of effacing this impression rather rendered it more acute."[84] And this continues until the desperately sought reference is found in molecular biology: "the secret of life could then have seemed to be inaccessible in its very principle. Today it is, to a great extent, unveiled."[85]

But for this to be an unveiling, and not a simple description, there has to be a theory of science which can distinguish appearance from objectivity. And it is at this point that the play reaches its climax, for Monod has inserted the requirement of a knowing subject into his computer program: "The cornerstone of the scientific method is the postulate that nature is objective. In other words, the systematic denial that 'true' knowledge can be got at by interpreting phenomena in terms of final causes—that is to say, of 'purpose.' An exact date may be given for the discovery of this canon. The formulation by Galileo and Descartes of the principle of inertia laid the groundwork not only for mechanics but for the epistemology of modern science, by abolishing Aristotelian physics and cosmology."[86]

In his search for the reference, the secret of life, Monod goes equipped with a reference, the tradition, which, from Descartes to Kant, tried to abolish the domination of scholasticism over science, and which to this end defined the conditions of the objectivity of knowledge. At the very moment when these conditions were abolished in science (that of computer programming), they had to be reintroduced as an ethical value. For Monod, true knowledge knows no values, but to give it a basis, there must be a judgment or, rather, an axiom of value. It is evident that to pose the postulate of objectivity as a condition of true knowledge *constitutes an ethical choice and not a judgment of knowledge*, since, according to the postulate itself, there can be no true knowledge prior to this arbitral choice.[87]

Monod's problem therefore is that of the search for the reference by someone who knows that he has lost it. But someone who knows that he has lost the reference has not completely lost it, since it exists in his memory. It has become his tradition: The *Method,* says Monod, proposes a normative method, but it should be read also and, above all, as a moral meditation, as an ascesis of the mind.[88] The miracle for Monod is that, between the two principal criteria that he can define for his computer program in the search for "the secret of life," teleonomy and invariance, it is possible to choose invariance over teleonomy, that is, the eternity of material nature over the project of the animated nature which characterizes the "old covenant." Once the invariant is defined, it can be shown that its reproduction is necessary. What remains is the question of the origin of the constant and the question of its mutations. What Monod's objectivity reveals through the description of microscopic cybernetics is that life is the product of chance and necessity.

This discourse, which legitimates the absence of law, cannot silence the finalist discourse, and at the very outset of his work Monod notes: "Objectivity nevertheless obliges us to recognize the teleonomic character of living organisms, to admit that in their structure and performance they act projectively–realize and pursue a purpose. Therein lies, at least in appearance, a profound epistemological contradiction. In fact, the central problem of biology lies with this very contradiction, which, if it is only apparent, must be resolved; or else proven to be utterly insoluble, if that should turn out indeed to be the case."[89] This insoluble contradiction brings Monod back to the accents of Pascalian philosophy: "If he accepts this message—accepts all it contains—then man must at last wake out of his millenary dream; and in doing so, wake to his total solitude, his fundamental isolation. Now does he at last realize that, like a gypsy, he lives on the boundary of an alien world. A world that is deaf to his music, just as indifferent to his hopes as it is to his suffering or his crimes."[90] It is the crisis of legitimacy that is thus revealed: "But then who defines crime? Who will say what is good and what is evil?"[91] Monod describes modern man given over to himself and turning "against science"[92] in the way that Pascal showed man turning against God. The solution is the same: it is necessary to bet on reason (the tradition of the rejection of finalism) as Pascal proposed to bet on heavenly eternity.

Chance and Necessity According to Prigogine and Stengers

With the work of Ilya Prigogine and Isabelle Stengers, we take final leave of the realm of tragedy. The mirror of cybernetic science and its simulations no longer reflect the nostalgic image of Newtonian eternity. We now enter firmly into the age of chance. What one gains in hope one loses somewhat in rigour.

Prigogine and Stengers know that if Monod's tone is dramatic, it is because it carries the nostalgia of Newtonian eternity. "It is not possible to be unaware of the persistent, cultural, theoretical weight of the concepts that underlie the science that we call classic. Monod's conclusions provide us with an eloquent example here: no sooner has he situated the discovery of certain determinant mechanisms of cellular functioning in the context of a classical view of the world, than he is led to the idea of man's solitude in a strange world."[93] The rejection of pragmatism makes Monod incapable of fully enjoying his achievements: "His story is that of a dazzling success which ends on a tragic note."[94] This tragedy reveals the crisis of legitimacy that the ideology of chance and necessity was to mask. "Classical science is therefore characterized by an unstable cultural insertion: it simultaneously provokes enthusiasm, the heroic assertion of the painful implications of rationality, as well as rejections and irrational reactions. . . ."[95]

Newtonian science had for a time produced the illusion "that the attraction which the law of gravity puts into formulas makes it possible to attribute an intrinsic and generalized animation to nature, which would explain the genesis of increasingly effective forms of activity up to the interactions that make up human society;"[96] all it managed to produce was "a disenchanted world."[97] Positivism had replaced the "proposal of understanding" by "the mere proposal of manipulating and foreseeing; all it managed to do was to add the dangers of the myth of the domination of the world to those of its explanation." "Man, a stranger to the world, poses as the master of the world."[98] If the new subject of knowledge is to look at himself with indulgence in the mirror of science, he must (unlike Monod) choose teleonomy over the constant.

While Monod, the biologist, could marvel at the presence of an invariant at the heart of the living, Prigogine, the physicist, could only be pleased to discover that matter had purpose. It is the processes of statistical thermodynamics that produce the probable in an irreversible way. Even more, these purposes are macroscopic, engendered by a multitude of particles acting haphazardly and producing the improbable. "A striking example is that of the first stage in the construction of an termite hill . . . the construction of the pillars can be engendered by a host of disordered behavior patterns by the termites who are thought to carry and abandon balls of earth in a haphazard manner. . . . The information communicated by a hormone with which these balls of earth are impregnated is enough to explain the initial fluctuation capable of generating, in a purely probabilistic way, pillars whose spacing will depend on the distance the hormone can travel from the balls of earth."[99]

Thus the statistical aggregation of locally oriented behaviour makes it possible to produce the improbable with certainty. In such a system, the random activity of an individual may be "either doomed to insignificance," or (if it is placed in a strategic location of the process) determine the appearance of an order or provoke bifurcation toward "another order of functioning."[100] What is thus proposed is a new way of building a model of the political sphere, and in the process, a legitimation that it can use: "If the models of order by fluctuation can teach us something, it is that every norm is the product of a choice and contains an element of chance, but not of arbitrariness."[101] "Far from being opposed to natural legality as Monod saw it, chance produces law. The fact remains of course, and Leibnitz noted this, that it had to be possible to reply to the twofold question: Why is there something rather than nothing? and why is there this thing rather than another thing? The reply given by Prigogine and Stengers is a simple one: to pose, as Monod does, the problem of the necessity of man's existence, is to make room for the arbitrary. But if one has the wisdom to be concerned with phenomena of self–organization (in their growing complexity) then one may be reassured for, if the improbable exists, it is because it was necessary: man in his singularity was certainly neither called for nor expected by the world. However, if we liken life to a phenomenon of the self–organization of matter, evolving towards increasingly complex states, then, in well–determined circumstances *(which do not appear to be exceptionally rare)* life can be expected in the universe, it constitutes a phenomenon in the universe as natural as the falling of heavy bodies.[102] Chance become law finally fulfills its pseudo–legitimating role. Even better, the concomitantly individual and collective character of the processes engendered by its law make it possible "for the first time" to "thematize" that which "escapes manipulation *or cannot be subjected to it except by tricks and with losses."* To thematize manipulation is no doubt to exorcise it, it is not to destroy it. Confined to wiles, morally condemned by the idea of loss, it will soon reappear crowned with the glory of poets. "In the midst of a rich and diverse population of cognitive practices, our science occupies the singular position of a poetical listening to nature, in the etymological sense of the word where the poet is a maker, it is an exploring science, active manipulating, calculating but henceforth capable of respecting nature to which it has given speech. This singular feature will probably continue to provoke the hostility of those to whom all calculation, all manipulation is suspect, but no longer the hostility that certain summary judgments of classical science quite legitimalely provoked."[103] Since science thus loses some of its legitimacy, and since a new coherent system cannot be established, every resource available to legitimacies must be used: charisma, tradition, reason. The charisma is that of the poet who produces the "re–enchantment of the world" promised by way of conclusion. Tradition and reason (which by now has also become tradition) will be dealt with by means of respect: "We should also learn to respect other intellectual approaches, whether they are the traditional approaches of sailors, of peasants, or the approaches created by the other sciences."[104]

But since three leaky boats do not a watertight vessel make, disquiet remains: "This world which seems to renounce the safety of stable and permanent standards is certainly a dangerous and uncertain world. It cannot inspire any blind confidence on our part, only perhaps the mitigated sentiment of hope that certain Talmudic texts are supposed to have attributed to the God of Genesis."[105] Even mitigated, the hope of a new covenant requires the evocation of a God. To found the optimism of a science of systems, Whitehead (following Leibnitz on this point) had to call upon God; to found their mitigated hope, Prigogine and Stengers call upon Whitehead. "In order to recognize the convergence between physical theory and philosophical doctrine on the connection between being and becoming, we propose to call this third representation the Whiteheadian representation."[106] This representation is called to become the universal characteristic for decoding the natural and social world: "We feel, following Leibnitz, that making partitions is as vain as separating the waters of the oceans, even if this gesture is not without intellectual and institutional consequences. Let us, however, pay special attention to certain considerations on the communication between physical chemistry and the sciences of living populations and societies."[107]

The Limits of Chance

Perhaps this is the time to recall that the philosophy of chance and necessity also creates partitions in at least two ways. For probabilistic processes to be irreversible (whether they go towards the probable or the improbable), it is necessary to keep time within its pragmatic limits and to cut it off from its potential infinitude. The probable, even the most probable, is a notion whose meaning is profoundly different when seen from the viewpoint of God and that of man. Even if God accepts the game of chance proposed to him by Boltzman, He can play an infinite number of gambits available to Him, and this is logically quite sufficient to make the phenomenon reversible. The gambler at the casino does not play with the same luck as the house, and, if the devil takes a hand, the house wins every time. As long as it is human, subjectivity is dependent on time: what occurs by chance will end by conforming to the law of large numbers, which is the clock that shapes their history. History itself most often seems like a conjunction of chance events and necessity. Here a second partitioning comes in: to tell a story of chance, its occurrences must be divided up. If chance and information are related, it is because there is no more chance without the encoding of facts than there is information without a frame of reference. "There is still a problem, that of the code: how is the correspondence between the signified object and the signifying symbol established? How to ascertain that the relationship is a correct one? This problem can be solved by drawing upon a criterion of efficiency of the total chain, efficiency in attaining certain goals that the organism sets itself."[108] This amounts to saying that the correspondence between the representation of the world and the world henceforth depends completely on the "subjectivity" of organisms. Since these organisms themselves belong to the representation of the world, they must above all, for their criterion to be considered, get themselves acknowledged, and acknowledge themselves as organisms. Only then will they be able to participate in the production of codes that will produce chance and necessity.[109]

The Production of Cybernetic Ideology: Entities and Categories

Where laissez–faire ideology had the theoretical sciences available to explain economic and social relationships and to legitimate their consequences, cybernetic ideology has cyberneticized science, models and simulations. The theory of markets is replaced by building models in terms of information and energy, and the theory of the social optimum, by the statistical rhetoric of chance and necessity. Hence, understanding the workings of society does not consist of listening to the narratives produced by models, but of analyzing the mode of composition of these narratives. Now everything that can be narrated in the science of systems can be recounted on the basis of two elementary constituents: entities and categories. Entities are the systems and sub–systems that the specification of the social model is willing to include in its representation. Categories are encodings of flows and stocks which are exchanged among entities, it being understood that they may sometimes be flows and stocks of entities. But an encoding can only be evaluated with respect to the "purposes of the organism" or of the entity, each entity will tend to produce its own representation of the world and, as it happens, its first preoccupation will be to ensure that it is itself represented in this representation. Laissez–faire society is characterized by the existence of an infinity of free individuals, whose interaction produces collective development. The invisible hand of the market guides society towards well–being. In turn, these free individuals have very precise characteristics: their size is equally small compared with the infinity of their numbers, and so is their power.

Since none of them is big enough to possess any autonomous power over social development, they can all freely use all the power that they hold according to whim, interest or desire. This situation is reflected in the principle of the *self–determination of the will* which governs the drafting of contracts (for these determine, in a way, the "flows" among the "entities" of the free–market system). From the standpoint of information, this situation is reflected in a strict separation between the internal information that constitutes the subject, with its memory, its opinions, its whims (what in moral terms is called the innermost conscience) and external information, the information that circulates freely in the market and which is restricted to the expression of bids on contracts. This can be perfectly illustrated by representing the individual as a "black box." All internal information is marked with the seal of secrecy. If the "black box" must undertake an engagement demurrable by third parties, it will ratify the contract with its signature, the family name being the necessary and sufficient representative of the black box. In the cybernetic society, the size of certain social actors grows to an extent sufficient to make the equality of power of parties to the contract a fiction. Most often these are deeds of consent wherein, by definition, the individual's choice is limited. Freedom of the will is breached even more profoundly by the fact that, in order to satisfy the individual, the big organization draws up plans which it bases on hypotheses about what can be found inside the black boxes. By accumulating information on the behavior and contents of black boxes (through psychology and social psychology for example), the big organization encroaches upon the innermost consciousness of the person, stopping in principle only at the private life, the secret garden where the individual is protected from any intrusion.

This trend is symbolized by the fact that the signature is becoming less and less necessary for transactions by computer. It can be replaced by a code number. Similarly, the use of computers has radically changed the value of the signature as proof in accounts. This change in the status of the individual can be found in the specific example of the medical profession. With the socialization of health expenditure and with data processing, the status of the doctor, founded on the personal relationship between himself and his patient, a status that guaranteed respect for the innermost conscience of each individual through the obligation of professional secrecy, has undergone a veritable revolution. Already, administrative control of medical prescriptions interposes, between the doctor and the patient, the statistical norm of the behavior of others.

With firms, the challenge to their identity as separate entities comes above all in the form of mergers and takeovers. Here again the name of the entity is the symbol of its essence. Proper nouns, Chevrolet, Buick, Cadillac, etc. disappear behind a generic name, General Motors Corporation;

and the game of mergers and takeovers causes even the meaning of the generic name to be lost in the conglomeration of activities. The organization constructs an acronym for itself keeping only the initials of its name, abandoning (along with the words that composed it) the remains of whatever related it to a referent other than itself. But, since in order to impose its model of the world, the organization must obtain the adhesion of the entities that constitute it, it must set itself up as a referent for the others. It will define its image, a coherent construction built from its modes of appearance. A construction, the most obvious model of which is undoubtedly the one where certain organizations rebuild a word from the letters that make up their acronym, or even fabricate a suitable name when their acronym does not "naturally" lend itself to a metamorphosis of this kind.

But an entity is not necessarily an individual or an enterprise. It may be anything that is assembled within a circumscribed identity: segments of a population (of diverse entities), professions or even functions. This point is perfectly illustrated by the mode of production of Ivan Illitch's pragmatic Utopias. The recipe is a simple one. Take a society and look at it from the standpoint of systems analysis. Choose any sub-system (education and health have already been dealt with, but the method can easily be generalized). It is enough then to know that, if this sub-system is removed, all the other sub-systems could (should) take over responsibility for all (almost all) its functions. A huge mass of statistics and efficiency assessments will be used to register the (proposed) decision for eliminating the entity within the ethical decision-making framework of cybernetic ideology: chance and necessity. In cybernetic society, when two entities meet, they talk about information and energy, or rather about information and power, power being the name given to energy when it is available to a particular entity. The commonplace in this chat between entities is the famous equivalence of information with power, an equivalence which gives all its spice to what is exchanged in this chat, from which each entity no doubt hopes to glean some information and thus icrease his power. It would be futile to want to show that this model of the world is false, since its purpose is nothing but resemblance and its criterion is verisimilitude. At least one might try to show that it can be a source of confusion whenever it is used to draw more from this equivalence than the tautology that it contains.

One of the most common ways by which the social sciences interpret the relationships between information and power is to say that whoever holds information, because he holds it, has power. Another version of this proposition attributes power to whoever controls uncertainty.[110] Since cybernetic information can be expressed in terms of probability, these formulations are equivalent ones. Now it would seem that it is also possible to maintain the contrary, mainly that it is the person who holds power who, by the very fact that he holds power, possesses information. This argument, since it cancels out the previous one, would have only the feeble value of bringing out the tautological character of an equivalence were it not an opportunity for illustrating the value of an approach based on entities.

The meaning of the equivalence between information and power lacks precision as long as the nature of the information involved is not qualified. Not all information is equally important in the game of power which determines the fate of a given system. Its importance will depend, first, on the reduction of uncertainty it is supposed to provide about what the system will become; second, on the acknowledgment of the value of that information which, in turn, depends on the status of the transmitter of information and on his capacity to broadcast the information. Hence the equivalent of power is not information in general but qualified information. If the notion of entity can be used to provide some clarity in this discussion, then the concept of power is characterized by the fact that it is necessarily the attribute of a subject, of an entity. From this viewpoint, it can be asserted that the primary power of an entity is to exist, that is to be incapable of being reduced to a set of data and therefore to remain a black box. The primary power of an entity is therefore that of being a black box, which assumes the power to disqualify a part of the information produced about it by other entities and the power to qualify information, namely to make others accept the data that it proposes.

To be a subject, an entity, there must be a boundary between the interior and the exterior, which assumes a division of exchanges of information into three flows: 1) internal information, which circulates easily, abundantly and in a way that is secret from the exterior; 2) external information; 3) the information that crosses the bounds of the entity in one direction or the other, the essential characteristic of which is to be, on the whole, controlled by a centre representing the entity. The development of computers tends to intensify the challenge to these boundaries from the level of the individual up to that of society. Like the individual, firms are the subject of centralized databanks which, by accumulating "qualified information" about them, tend to deny them the status of autonomous entities. In firms that are grouped into conglomerates, this phenomenon also affects the autonomy of each entity, which can be measured by the degree of secrecy that it is capable of maintaining. Even nations find their frontiers becoming more porous when, over and above the growth in the traffic of goods and persons, they experience the development of trans–border data flow.

From the standpoint of power, gathering information serves no purpose if one is not capable of producing "qualified information." The power of information is above all the power to qualify information without power.

Cassandra knows all that will come to pass and tells it to the population, to the chorus of the Greek tragedy, but she is not believed for she is a slave and a foreigner. More recently, and in a less mythical way, Lysenko's theories, although false, were able to dominate because those who possessed information about their falseness did not have the power to diffuse it. From this point of view, it is doubtless more important to be a recognized entity, that is a *black box,* than to possess information. Power is above all the power to appear in the depiction of the world provided by the cybernetic model. There, in the interlacing of circles and arrows, is a black box, and it has a secret. Even if the secret is that there is no secret. The *black boxes,* the entities, produce the categories by which they recognize themselves, define themselves to one another and describe the flows that they exchange with one another. The entities of systems analysis echo Whitehead's *superjects* which in turn evoke Leibnitz's monads. Their essential characteristic is to be the site of a final cause,[111] emergence point of an action aimed at a purpose.

The liberty of this action depends on the mystery of its origin. If its purposes, its strategies, the representations of the world that accompany it are known, it is reduced to the status of efficient cause, and thereby loses the dignity of a separate entity. However informed one may be, if there is a persisting doubt about the determination of the other, the outcome of the negotiation with him remains a mystery. The laissez–faire system of legitimacy is the result of the long effort which, from Descartes to Kant, made it possible to exclude final causes from the realm of science, leaving only efficient causes. The pragmatism of cybernetic ideology marks the return in strength of finalism to the models of the world. Through Whitehead it is Leibnitz, and through Leibnitz it is scholasticism that the systemic ideology rediscovers. A new scholasticism where neither entities nor categories entertain a relationship with eternity. They are only the product of their own representative activity.

Notes

1. Ilya Prigogine and Isabelle Stengers, *op. cit.,* p. 139.
2. Take a population of N particles in a box divided into two equal compartments (Cf. *La Nouvelle Alliance,* p. 139). We may consider the probability of finding $N1$ particles in one compartment and $N2-N-N1$ particles in the other. Combinatorial analysis can be used to show that where N is sufficiently large, the probability that $N1-N2$ is so great that "any other state of equidistribution may be described as being highly improbable." Hence, regardless of the initial division ($N1$, $N2$) of the system, this state becomes an attracting state towards which the system tends irreversibly. Boltzmann thought that he could measure the entropy of the system ($N1$, $N2$) by the number of combinations of particles compatible with this division.

3. J. Monod, *Chance and Necessity: An Essay on the Natural Philosophy*, pp. 80 and 83.
4. *Ibid.*, p. 19
5. See for example, J. Attali, *La Parole et L'Outil*, PUF.
6. See *Le Concept d'Information dans la Science Contemporaine*, Royaumont colloquium, Paris, Edition de Minuit, 1965, and especially, Mandelbrot, "La Théorie de l'Information est-elle encore utile?," pp. 78-98, and L. Lwoff, "Le Concept d'information dans la Biologie Moléculaire," pp. 173-202.
7. Henryk Greniewski, "Le Concept d'Information et de la Science Contemporaine," *ibid.*, pp. 231-251.
8. Jacques Monod (1910-1976) Biologist, won the Nobel Prize in Medicine in 1965 for his work on DNA.
9. M.Serres, *Le Systéme de Leibniz et ses modèles mathematiques*, Paris, PUF, Vol.II, p. 651.
10. Descartes, *The Method*, Washington and London, M. Walter Dunne, 1901. Part III, p. 164.
11. *Ibid.*, p. 165.–166.
12. *Ibid.*
13. *Ibid.*, p. 155.
14. *Ibid.*, p. 159.
15. On the theme of the philosopher as a Sophist toward himself, Rousseau states: "of all the Sophists, reason is undoubtedly the one that wrongs us the least," quoted in the *Robert dictionary*. Moreover in the case of Descartes the story of the philosopher seduced by himself can be told: in the second part of *The Method*, Descartes recalls the time when he stayed "shut in every day in a heated room where I had all the leisure to commune with my thoughts." It is Descartes' biographer, the reverend Baillet father, who describes the three dreams which visited Descartes on the night of 10th November 1619. In the first of these dreams, someone announced that a certain "Monsieur N had something to give him. M. Descartes imagined that it was a melon brought from some foreign country." (*La Vie de Monsieur Descartes*, P. de Baillet, 1693). After this dream Descartes woke up and felt "*a real pain* which made him believe that it was the work of some evil spirit who might have wished to seduce him (*ibid.*). Now it so happened that this night was precisely the first anniversary of the meeting between Descartes and a "Dutch scholar, by far his elder, with whom he had had struck up a very deep friendship" (*Descartes par lui–meme*, Samuel de Sacy, Seuil, 1973). To this friend he wrote : "In reality it is you alone who has woken me from my indolence, recalled me to a knowledge that had almost vanished from my memory, brought me to better, serious pursuits from which my mind had moved away" (in Baillet, *op. cit.*). Later, "Beeckman was to boast of that he alone had been entirely responsible for making Descartes, who proved to be extremely short in his replies" (Sacy, *op. cit.*). The point, as Samuel de Sacy notes, is that "although the first impulse did indeed come from Beeckman, Descartes could well have believed that he had left Beeckman far behind him, and the claims of the Dutchman amounted to a denial of both illumination and the nine years during which his thought had matured." For it took Descartes nine years to produce *The Method* out of his doubt and his long silence, nine years of slow and difficult distillation at the very centre of the sciene of his age: "and although this Science contains indeed a number of correct and very excellent precepts, there are, nevertheless, so

many others, and these are either injurious or superfluous, mingled with the former, that it is almost quite as difficult to effect a severance the true from the false as it is to extract a Diana or a Minerva from a rough block of marble" (*The Method, op. cit.,* p. 160). What remains is the mystery of how the project was conceived in the dreams of the 10th of November 1619. Samuel de Sacy reports that Descartes was so moved that he turned to God "and prayed Him to make His Will known" and "even tried to interest" the Blessed Virgin "in this matter which he deemed to be he most important of his life," and "vowed that he would make a pilgrimage to Loretto."

16. *The Method, op. cit.,* p. 153.
17. This is why it is important to attain the sometimes "jealously guarded" secret of such fecundity in order "to be able to discover by method what was usually dscovered by chance," Belaval, *Critique de Descartes,* p. 94.
18. *The Method, op. cit..*
19. Belaval, *op. cit.,* pp. 42–43. "To discover by chance is to discover without knowing the how and the why of it."
20. Pascal, *Pensées, op. cit.,* p. 355.
21. E. Baudin, *Pascal,* Edition de la Baconniere.
22. Pascal, *op. cit.,* 218.
23. Pascal, *Citations,* Pleiade, p. 274, quoted by M. Serres, *La Systeme de Leibniz...,* *op. cit.,* p. 659.
24. Pascal, *op. cit.,* p. 347.
25. *Ibid.,* 77.
26. *Ibid.,* 143.
27. *Ibid.,* Chapter II.
28. Pascal, *L'Art de Persuader,* Pedagogie Moderne, 1979.
29. E. Baudin, *op. cit.,* Vol. II, p. 82.
30. *Ibid.*
31. Arnauld and Nicole, *La Logique de Port–Royal,* Flammarion, Coll. Champs.
32. Pascal. *Pensées, op. cit.,* p. 72.
33. *Ibid.,* p. 71.
34. M. Serres, *Le Systeme de Leidniz, ... op. cit.,* Vol.II, p. 702, "Le Paradigme Pascalien."
35. Pascal, *op. cit.,* 351.
36. M. Brunschvicg, "Pascal et Port–Royal," in *La Genie de Pascal,* Hachette, 1926, quoted by E. Baudin, *op. cit.,* p. 79.
37. Spinoza, *Political Treatise and Theologico–Political Treatise,* New York, Dover Publications, 1951, p. 315.
38. *Ibid.,* p. 316.
39. *Ibid.,* p. 288.
40. Spinoza, *Ethics.*
41. *Ibid.*
42. Quoted by E. Baudin, *op. cit.,* Vol.I, p. 60.
43. *Ibid.,* p. 69.
44. Spinoza, *Political Treatise, op. cit.,* p. 37.
45. *Ibid.,* p. 311.
46. *Ibid.*
47. Belaval, *Leibni, Critique de Descartes, op. cit.,* p. 33.
48. Leibnitz, quoted by Belaval, *ibid.,* p. 34.
49. Belaval, *ibid.*

50. Belaval, *ibid.*, p. 60.
51. Belaval, *ibid.*, p. 62.
52. F. Brunner, *Etude sur la Signification Historique de la Philosophie de Leibniz*, Paris, Vrin, 1951.
53. Belaval, *op. cit.*, p. 82.
54. *Leibniz et les deux Labyrinthes: Textes Choisis* PUF, 1973, p. 150-151. From this point of view, the animals also have souls: "You argue that there is no basis for giving souls to animals, and you believe that were there a soul, it would be a mind, that is to say, a substance that thinks because none of us knows anything other than bodies and minds and we have no idea of any other substance. Now to say that a trout thinks, or that a worm thinks is difficult to believe. This objection is also relevant to those who are not Cartesians. But ... I believe that I have shown that every substance is indivisible and that, consequently, every indivisible substance must have a soul or at least a form which has some analogy with the soul, for otherwise bodies would be nothing else but phenomena." Note also the distinction between "perception, which is the inner state of the monad representing external things and APERCEPTION which is the CONSCIOUSNESS or the reflective knowledge of this inner state, which is not given to all souls nor even at all times to the same soul. And it is for lack of this distinction that the Cartesians have been wanting, by taking little account of perceptions that are not perceived, just as the people take no account of unfeeling bodies." (Leibnitz, Les Principes de la Nature et de la Grace, Paris, PUF, 1978, pp. 36–37. Thus, once again, we see that the realization of the unconscious always accompanies the acceptance of the central value of the pragmatic self; thus, it is to the Sophist Antiphon that we owe the idea of healing by speech, and Kant, in *The Anthropology of the Pragmatic Viewpoint*, gives unconscious thoughts their due.
55. Leibnitz, *The Principles of Nature and Grace, op. cit.*, p. 41.
56. *Ibid.*
57. Letter from Leibnitz to Barnet and Kemvey quoted by E. Naert, *La Pensee Politique de Leibniz* , Paris, PUF, 1964, p. 21.
58. Leibnitz, "Letter to Landgrave," 1688, *ibid.*
59. Naert, *op. cit.*, p. 43.
60. A parallel should be drawn between the work of Leibnitz and that of Berkeley. To the former, we owe the anticipation of the cybernetic world and, to the latter, that of the world as pure depiction, from which Husserl and Bergson later claimed to have derived inspiration. Just as Leibnitz, Berkeley took part in the political life of his day and held high office. The immaterialism of Berkeley and the formalism of Leibnitz are philosophies of a world without referent, at least when the reference to God vanishes.
61. Belaval, *op. cit.*, p. 81.
62. Belaval, *ibid.*, p. 82.
63. Belaval, *ibid.*, p. 104.
64. E. Naert, *op. cit.*, p. 37.
65. "Empirical psychology should be entirely banished from metaphysics, and it is already entirely excluded by the idea of this science," Kant, "The Critique of Pure Reason," *op. cit.,* III, 547.
66. *Ibid.*, III, 489.
67. F. Jacob, La Logique du Vivant, Paris, Gallimard, 1970, p. 170.
68. *Ibid.*, p. 171.

69. *Ibid.*, p. 184.
70. Charles Darwin, *The Origin of the Species*, in F. Jacob, *op. cit.*, p. 188.
71. *Ibid.*, p. 180.
72. Francois Jacob: born in 1920. Biologist genetician, so on the Nobel Prize in Medicine in 1965 for his work on DNA.
73. *Ibid.*, p. 191.
74. *Ibid.*
75. *Note on the relationship between chance and the history of the bourgeoisie: Pascal drew up the laws of probability in order to resolve the problems of the game of the Chevalier de Mere.* The story of chance was subsequently related to the "economics of life annuities and the sociology of *bills of mortality*" (Michel Serres, *La Traduction, op. cit.*, p. 64). Finally, with the average man, Quetelet produced the model that thermodynamics was to use. Throughout this story, the object of science reflected changes in the social subject. The aristocrat drew his essence from the patronymic name which was assigned to him with certitude through direct–line consanguinity. The essence of the bourgeois was connected with the happenstance of adventure, above all the Great Adventure of spice–laden boats trading beyond the seas, and then the more modest adventure of the games of chance that occupied the *Chevalier de Mere*. Finally, it was the adventure consisting in the sinister calculation of life annuities. The (symbolic) worth of the bourgeois is the worth of his inheritance. For this product of chance to become the characteristic feature of an essence, it was necessary to await property–based suffrage which made the possession of a certain amount of property the hallmark of the adult citizen. The abolition of property–based suffrage marked the rise of the petty bourgeoisie, the bourgeoisie without inheritance, which, henceforth, availed itself to measurement by the sociologist (Quetelet). The citizen is as free as the air that makes up thermodynamic systems. In order to escape the common destiny, some will seek a new way of defining the essence of individual legitimacy through the hazardous heredity of the genetic code.
76. Descartes, *The Method, op. cit.*, p. 160.
77. *Ibid.*, p. 58.
78. On this subject, see Louis Althusser, *Philosophie et Philosophie Spontanée des Savants*, (1967), Maspero, 1974.
79. Unless the professional philosophers were to help them to formulate and propagate their doctrine: for example, Raymond Ruyer for the scholars of Princeton and Isabelle Stengers for the theses of Ilya Prigogin.
80. Michel Serres, *La Traduction, op. cit.*
81. In fact this comment relates to Jacques Monod's inaugural lecture at the College de France; Cf. Althusser, *op. cit.*, p. 119.
82. Ilya Prigogine and Isabelle Stengers, *La Nouvelle Alliance, op. cit.*
83. J. Monod, *Chance and Necessity, op. cit.*, pp. 20-24.
84. *Ibid.*, p. 17.
85. *Ibid.*, p. 34.
86. *Ibid.*, pp. 37 and 21.
87. *Ibid.*
88. *Ibid.*, p. 22.
89. *Ibid.*, p. 21.
90. *Ibid.*
91. *Ibid.*

92. *Ibid.*
93. Ilya Prigogine and Isabelle Stengers, *La Nouvelle Alliance, op. cit.*, p. 16.
94. *Ibid.*, p. 10.
95. *Ibid.*, p. 61.
96. *Ibid.*, p. 36.
97. *Ibid.*, p. 38.
98. *Ibid.*
99. *Ibid.*, pp. 175–176.
100. *Ibid.*, p. 190.
101. *Ibid.*, p. 191.
102. *Ibid.*, p. 193.
103. *Ibid.*, p. 288.
104. *Ibid.*, p. 265.
105. *Ibid.*, p. 295.
106. *Ibid.*, p. 283
107. *Ibid.*, p. 188.
108. See "L'Information est–elle Objectivable?" in *Le Concept d'Information dans la Science Contemporaine, op. cit.*, p. 316.
109. *Note on theses that tend to subject chance to necessity or to finality*, the limits of the ideology of chance and necessity lie in its incapacity to produce more than a mitigated hope for the time being. More resolutely optimistic versions are certainly possible, although these versions must remain mitigated if they refuse to assign responsibility for what is left of chance to the God of Whitehead or of Leibnitz. There is a strong temptation to produce systems that have the completeness and harmony of Leibnitz's system. Among the numerous signs of such a trend, note the attempt made in the *Gnosis of Princeton* presented by Raymond Ruyer and Rene Thom's theory of catastrophes. About Thom, the commentator of the *Encylopedia Universalis* says that "his project, which reactivates the dream of the Leibnitzian universal characteristic, is obviously still in its initial stages. "For those who might be impatient, the *Gnosis of Princeton* provides a whole which is apparently in working condition. This work also falls under the patronage of Leibnitz "there are fathers of the Gnostic Church, patron saints rather than fathers, far before its recent founders. Leibnitz, first of all, as a Rosicrucian as much as a scholar or philosopher and also as an intelligent politician, a social conservative looking at the same time to the future." For Rene Thom, chance is "that which defies all description"; his definition is, therefore, an "entirely negative, empty concept, hence one without scientific interest. Determinism, on the contrary, is a subject of fascinating richness to whoever knows how to scrutinize it." (in *Le Debat*, no. 3, July–August 1980, p. 130). "As a philosopher, the scholar may leave the question open, but as a scholar, it is an obligation of principle for him (under pain of internal contradiction) that he must adopt an optimistic position and postulate that nothing is unknowable *a priori*" (*ibid.*, p. 120). Statistical laws are therefore the measure of our ignorance, our ignorance of hidden variables which would make it possible to state everything about (to describe) nature. Thus Rene Thom brings optimism to the champions of the *physis*. For Raymond Ruyer, although "chance indeed plays a major role in the conscious invention of forms and information" (Gnosis of Princeton), it is nonetheless true that "in the beginning was order, or the Great Ordinator or Anti–Chance or Consciousness or Cosmic Subjectivity"; chance would not become

organized without the presence of "choosers" and in fact, the world is made up of entities, endowed with consciousness and subjectivity, whose inter–subjectivity produces a sort of world consciousness (*ibid.*, p. 13). Thus, the Gnosis of Princeton brings optimism to the champions of the *nomos*. Whether the world is absolute natural determinism (capable of being completely described) or absolute consciousness (capable of being interpreted universally in terms of finality and meaning), these two paths lead to the certainty revealed by science. Faced with the merit of both of these paths, some may hesitate. To choose, there is always the possibility of tossing a coin.

110. See Michel Crozier, "The bureaucratic phenomenon," Seuil, Paris, 1965.
111. The final cause is "the purpose for which everything has been made," the efficient cause is "that which produces an effect," Robert Dictionary.

Chapter 10

Social Classes and Statistical Destiny

Once—out of twice—there was a lucky man.

The Bureaucratic Genesis of Fates

Identity Crisis

The approaching legitimacy crisis was visible in the depletion of traditional and natural referents and the destabilization of the symbolic order of the world.[1] The same is true of the traditional tasks of the family, increasingly taken over by bureaucracy (from teaching dental hygiene to inculcating respect for the old). Family relationships, traditionally founded on parental authority, are challenged by a huge body of legislation (especially in countries ruled by social-democratic parties), which reorganizes them on the contractual model of labor relationships:[2] for instance, in Sweden, where the commission for children's rights in society describes family relationships in terms of "participation" or "co-determination" or intends to give children the legal right to freedom of speech.[3]

The vanishing middle class. People no longer present themselves as they used to. IBM's employees identify themselves with the firm rather than with a social group. Social movements widely tend to give themselves a brand name or the name of a place or the name of a specific action. Identity is portioned out; it fluctuates according to action, moment and place. The same crisis of identity can be found, *a contrario* in the success of those categories which are too large not to be all–inclusive like the famous middle class. Many people have run into trouble with this concept, finding that it covers little else than a traditional amalgam of categories comprising a small part of the population to be identified, and a large formless group, monopolized to a great extent by "executives or management" who are themselves so difficult to pin down.[4]

The middle class is unaffected by the traditional analysis of class conflict,

233

which seeks to dissolve it without great success; it also resists analysis in the statistical terms which it suggests: according to a recent study, only 17% of the French population combines the average characteristics of the whole population. These characteristics, as it happens, comply so little with the national image of Mr. Dupont as a "petty bourgeois" and with all the stereotypes of the average Frenchman that, before the group they constitute can be described, it is rechristened "the new middle–class."[5] Thus, the elusive middle-class marks the dual incapacity of tradition (of classes) and science (of statistics) to give meaning to this no–man's land in which, nonetheless, a large majority of the population (more than 90% in the United States, it seems) recognizes itself. A residual category, therefore, but a monstrous residue in its dimensions, a category that in the end can be apprehended only by the place it occupies in various administrative codes for income, educational qualification, social stratum, etc.

The end of grand principles. Even the most "natural" phenomena of existence are susceptible to this syndrome. The hiatus between the two terms in pairs of strictly incompatible conditions like life and death, sickness and health, madness and reason, guilt and innocence, all these ancestral certainties inscribed in the nature of things, are "threatened." So long as nature decided between life and death, science or tradition between reason and madness, law between guilt and innocence, the primordial rules of our life in society could consist of a few simple and immutable principles, the Ten Commandments for example: thou shalt not kill, honor thy father and thy mother, etc. And the road to happiness was all charted out: the goal was to push back the boundaries of death by technological development, to help madmen return to reason, to chastise the guilty.

These eternal categories, when left to the impious hands of the bureaucracy, were thoroughly refashioned. The immutable frontiers of the natural, divine or traditional order, were now replaced by indistinct, variable limits, namely the "thresholds" of the bureaucracy's cultural order. The irreducible principle that made sense of the distinctions between life and death, reason and madness was replaced by the purposes of bureaucratic action. The threshold is pragmatically defined at a level beyond which it would be desirable to consider a man as dead rather than alive, guilty rather than irresponsible. The grim reaper's scythe has lost some of its edge; the scales of justice have lost some of their precision. The cleavages are no longer sacred. The old adages are threatened: life henceforth has a price, and its price is the one accorded it by a bureaucracy. Gone is the sacred duty to assist persons in danger. The doctor now has the duty to enquire into the costs graph of his patient as much as into his temperature chart in order to select, on the basis of thresholds defined by the available budget allocation (in the interests of balanced management), the moment when it will become necessary to unplug the machine, (unless, for some reason, it seems necessary to retain the dying man at the threshold of death). "The doctor is caught between the (moral) obligation to use the most up-to-date means and the (managerial) need to make strict economies: the conflict of duties he is bound to face one day is not merely a choice of society but a choice of civilization: what price do we wish to pay or are we able to pay for human life?"[6]

The Designating Bureaucracy: Segmented Man

The name used to be the emblem of the subject's identity. Even this is now challenged by the growth of bureaucratic practices; the growing use of the national I.D. number or the social security number instead of the proper noun contrives to break the individual down into as many attributes as are needed for administrative action. Thus, with the "medical identity card," the user will carry, in his pocket, his magnetized medical mini-file, encoded and accessible to doctors alone, part of his portrait as a fragmented man. The process could easily be extended so that the same card carries police and work records.

The individual entity has lost the irreducible character, the inviolable, innermost consciousness which characterized him in the philosophy of the Enlightenment. The bureaucracy constructs man by statistical recomposition—based on the splitting up of all the symbolic elements that characterized the individual as a subject. The man of the marketing society is a segmented man. The principle of his segmentation or segmentations is provided by the universe of goals and resources of big bureaucratic organizations. Thus the individual entity is described by its position in a set of lists (sex, income, age, blood type, blood pressure, parents' profession, etc.) The administration dissolves the subject by breaking it down.[7]

Managing the bureaucratic language. The consciousness of identity is suggested by the relationship with the other. Because the "other" is increasingly some big organization, the perception of self tends to be organized around the terms that various bureaucracies lay down. Bureaucracy has taken the place of tradition: it names. Because bureaucracy takes possession and charge of everything, no action will be effective if it is not performed in bureaucratically relevant categories. And these categories are in the process of becoming the universally necessary mediators of relationships among individual or collective entities and bureaucracies and among entities themselves. Categories tend to universality by their extent but not by their duration. Administration is another term for the management of the things of this world, and this world is itself a changing one. It is the nature of administrative language to fluctuate like the meaning of the world that it voices. This is a grave defect in a language and only an excess of administrative activity can maintain the dignity of such a language as a universal medium of communication: to survive as a means of intelligibility, administrative categories assume that communication between the organization and individual or collective entities can be managed. For its categories to be efficient, a bureaucracy must continuously learn from these entities what they are and it must continuously teach them where they are supposed to be. Thus a game of mirrors grow up between entities and bureaucracy. It might be called the consensus game. The legitimacy of this game can be managed by organizing its popularity. The game lends to become serious as governments increasingly use the feedback from their audiences provided by constant polling to adapt their policies.

Statistical Destiny

The man segmented by bureaucracies is defined by his location on various lists.[8] In France, for instance, in the early 80's,[9] a woman is entitled to unemployment benefits if she:

- has at least one dependant child (list: number of dependant children)
- or is widowed, divorced or legally (separated for less than 3 years marital status list)
- and has had specific basic training (specific training list)
- or possesses an officially approved certificate of preliminary or vocational training and has been looking for work for at least six months, except for those who have undergone training (job list).

In this bureaucratic portrait, each term refers to rules defining its exact meaning from the viewpoint of the bureaucracy.

During the same period, the "high cardiac risk population" is defined as:[10]

- having a systolic blood pressure of more than 160 and a diostolic blood pressure of more than 95,
- and having a blood cholesterol level of more than 2.80 g,
- and having a blood sugar level of more than 1.5,
- and having a blood urea level of more than 70 mg.,
- and being diabetic (declared or latent),
- and smoking more than 20 cigarettes a day,
- and being overweight,
- and have a family history of cardiovascular and cerebrovasculor disease
- and belonging to a so-called "type A" psychological group (consisting of

ambitious, competitive, overworked, tense persons who are always in a hurry).

Through these operations the bureaucracy becomes the statistical master of destinies. It gives existence to each individual by describing all the attributes that expose him to a certain type of treatment warranted by a certain probable type of future (treatment such as sanctions against offenders, preventive action directed at high–risk categories, etc.). It is because the *a posteriori* probability that young first–job seekers will not find jobs is excessive by bureaucratic standards that they are given unemployment benefits. It is because of the high probability that persons whose systolic blood pressure exceeds 160 will have a heart attack that preventive campaigns are aimed at them.

Man in the marketing society is segmented by the probable cost that he will entail for the bureaucratic organization that deals with him. The thresholds of tolerance are defined by the corresponding costs. It is because the social costs of the ills named "unemployment" and "heart attack" exceed the level defined by the bureaucratic organization as being tolerable that it creates categories said to be "at risk." The general nature of treatment by organizations thus induces the propagation of the notion of risk, accident risk for road safety authorities, good and bad risk for bankers, big and small risk for national health, risk of delinquency for justice, school failure, risk for education, cardiovascular risk for doctors. We are all on the brink of the probable, overlooking an abyss opened up by the numerous lists that break us down according to the age of our vehicle, the level of our blood pressure, our psychological type, our social and professional origins, our family antecedents and our school reports and records.

In certain cases the whole population is potentially in danger: thus as soon as it gets into a car, every French family runs the risk of having an accident; the category of car drivers or passengers is therefore likely to receive certain instructions according to the cost assessment of its specific risks, as well as the resources to reduce them, the effects of which are assessed statistically. In other cases, the possession of certain attributes puts the individual into a high–risk population, but this predisposition can be decreased by the possession of other attributes which act in a way as antidotes: thus the predisposition to heart attack, as a result of a high level of cholesterol, will be decreased by membership in the category of non–smokers, just as a predisposition to failure at school, arising out of certain conditions of income and housing, will be decreased in the only child.

Each individual therefore can calculate his conditional probability of (physically and morally) succumbing to risk. Bureaucracies assume responsibility for this. They methodically compose the types or profiles that correspond to different risk thresholds on the basis of the most varied attributes, on condition that these are statistically discriminating. Through their objectivation they produce a new characterology which reminds of one of Borges's lists.[11]

Games of Fate

Beset by bureaucratic categories, the entities are led to perceive their individual and collective fates in the terms that these categories impose on them.

They are led to do so first of all in their very philosophy of existence: the hallmark of identity is henceforth the statistical category to which one belongs, by which the *a priori* probability of fate is defined. Thus each individual is led to assess his chances of salvation statistically. Henceforth each individual knows that he runs a multitude of risks. He can even know the probability of his being affected. All that is missing are the names of the victims. Here perhaps is one of the sources of the increasingly widespread *feeling* of insecurity.

Seen from this viewpoint, life is a game with the probable. It consists of drawing up strategies to appropriate the best attributes and maximize the advantages that may be drawn from them on the basis of one's knowledge of the environment, all the while minimizing the disadvantages of harmful attributes which cannot be eliminated.

This game can be played individually or collectively. In the latter case, it will be possible to create the conditions for the game by making alliances in groups organized according to the pragmatic criteria of segmentation used by bureaucracies. It follows that communication between bureaucracy and individual and collective entities is ensured by mutual recognition that the segmentation criteria used are valid. When this is achieved, it will be called "consensus." But it is never achieved without work. The work of obtaining knowledge about the public by polling and market studies, the work of educating the public into bureaucratic categories, by which each individual internalizes his standard destiny based on his attributes, is met by resistance from the categories struggling for classification,[12] that is for a more advantageous position than the one granted them by the bureaucracy. This is how it is in struggle for the definition of classifications in industrial relations,[13] this again is how it is in struggle for the bureaucratic recognition of new categories, for example, women, unemployed, white collar workers, etc.

To sum up, if we look at all existing organizations, the public appears as the intersecting point of various lines on a grid. The fate of each individual entity, each segmented man, is determined by the specific way in which he is held in the meshes of descriptions of the world proffered by organizations. He is led to recognize himself as the product of these descriptions. It is on the basis of this image of himself that he must enjoy the advantages related to it or try to elude the fate that it predicts.

The New Categorical Imperative: Statistical Morality

Risk, Security, Profile: Chance and the Majority

The new social norm is defined statistically on the basis of bureaucratic categories. It forbids individuals and groups to cross thresholds that it defines as limits, from the viewpoint of the pragmatic criterion of its action.

Files and regulations. Thus, we see an increase in the number of files by which various bureaucracies can simultaneously define the thresholds of the acceptable and the profiles of categories whose behavior is intolerable: individual medical files,[14] nationwide school guidance files for students, and school performance files,[15] statistical files on the medical profession,[16] bank files,[17] road accident files, etc. The file serves first of all to analyze risk in order to define the rules most likely to reduce it. The existence of an excessive cost for social management is generally what determines the investigation of the nature of risk. Risk acquires a bureaucratic existence when it concerns a substantial portion of the public.

A car accident, for example, is analyzed by the characteristics of the vehicle (the condition of the tires, maintenance, etc.), the passengers (alcohol consumption, eye–sight, etc.), the road system (danger points). The rules concerning these different characteristics depend on their discriminating value on effects, measured by statistical analysis: the life of the tires, the obligation to wear a safety–belt, the obligation to dim headlights in town, the breathanalyzer test, etc.

More and more frequently, the rules thus seek legitimacy by measuring risk according to an experimental procedure. It is by the same type of procedure that the rules come to be contested. Thus when government officials [18] declares that the rule on dimming headlights in town has been decided upon after scientific (hence irrefutable) investigation, some body of concerned citizens will challenge him in the name of inquiries apparently as dependable as the previous one.[19] But motoring risks are not restricted to accidents: there are also the risks of traffic jams, which cause individual discomfort, as well as excess consumption of fuel and an increase in accident risks. Hence the campaigns to spread out people's vacation times.[20] Traffic efficiency *versus* War on Waste:[21] it is all a question of statistics in the service of minimizing costs through marketing directed at the public.

Henceforth the new categorical imperative of the state is to stimulate a reduction in costs in line with a goal of comprehensive regulation.

Profiles, standards and normality. Rules, stimulation, but also prevention. Files serve to define high–risk categories so as to organize prevention. Deviation from the mean behavior or performance, established as a norm is used to define the high-risk segment; this is the reign of the majority in its most restrictive sense, in its statistical meaning. Thus we see the growth of the notion of the statistical profile: the profile of the perfect soldier,[22] the perfect pupil,[23] the medical profile or again the profile of the criminal or the madman, the profile of the insolvent bank client, etc.

In her report of March 1979 to the Council of Europe on the financial deficit of the French national health insurance, Madame Veil (then Health Minister) blamed the system of private medicine, exposing the pressures that it created in offering treatment. To affect supply, it is necessary to achieve full control over its components so that each agent in the medical profession is aware of his share in it. Madame Veil therefore pleaded in favor of control and self–discipline of doctors (which could be matched with sanctions or economic and financial stimulants).[24] In fact, she suggested the use of "statistical tables of activity" and "medical profiles" by which every doctor could see the number of the acts that he performs and compare himself with the average activity of other doctors. In the event of abuse, which would be detected by a medical commission, a doctor could be excluded from the agreement that linked doctors to the national health system.

The same purpose governed the preparation of school files,[25] designed to follow the pupil from the kindergarten through the *lycée*, by systemizing information from various earlier files, in order to prepare a document by which the causes of failure at school might be understood. The same reasoning again governs the use of tests: intelligence tests, tests of various kinds of aptitude. For example, the French Army project for a conscripts' test:[26] the test was set up in two stages. In the first stage, a long questionnaire was to be administered to two groups of soldiers, chosen on the basis of criteria of normality (one group being known as a high military-consensus group and the other as a low military-consensus group). The aptness of the questions was assessed by their capacity to differentiate the first group from the second in an optimal way. In the second stage, the optimal questionnaire was to be created, and it would automatically discriminate between conscripts according to their adaptability to normal military life. Similarly, intelligence tests are created in two stages. In the first stage, a questionnaire is administered to a representative sample of the population which will be the subsequent object of the test. Then, questions corresponding to variables whose distribution is not statistically normal are eliminated.[27] Finally the population can be tested.

These profiles, constructed on the basis of an *epidemiological* knowledge of the population, share a common feature, regardless of the field in which they are used (schools, banks, the army or medicine): they are designed as aids to decision–making. They subordinate every action to a knowledge of the statistical mean as a mark of normality and the divergence of the case being treated from this mean. What statistics treat as *variance* becomes, in normative bureaucratic terms, *deviance* or *marginality*.

Consequently, the decision taken is always arrived at in the same way, but varies according to the nature of the context: thus the banker aims at differentiating good risks from bad risks, that is at identifying the categories for which he might take the "good" risk of making a loan. In the same way, the knowledge of the customer's profile enables the insurance company to protect itself against the risk of costs that the customer might entail for it. This is the object of the bonus/malus system.[28] In schools, the knowledge of profiles is used for defining pupils' orientation; it may also be used to ratify these with scientific arguments: thus, Professor Debray–Ritzen has no hesitation in recommending "the scientific organization of school (stages, tracks, levels) by doctors specialized in neuro–psychological curricular guidance."[29] It is natural, he says, that in a social class where the average I.Q. is below 100, the number of children who come up to university requirements will be relatively small.[30] Hence, as it has been aptly said, the school would become a "machine for manufacturing a destiny for every child":[31] Starting from the quantified knowledge of the categories of educational bureaucracy, it would transform a probable but indeterminate individual fate into a certain destiny, the nature of which would be defined by the deviation of an individual's group's position from the mean of all pupils and by the threshold of tolerance defined at a given moment by the educational bureaucracy.

Similarly, for health insurance,[32] the knowledge of profiles can serve to discriminate between small risks and big ones. Social insurance could, as life insurance already does ask, define high–risk categories to make malus payments. Until now, this knowledge has only been used for setting up systems of reimbursement differentiated according to the nature of the risk.

The definition of profiles, moreoever, makes it possible to define sanctions for deviations from the norm. Here again it is enough to set the threshold beyond which the deviation will be considered intolerable. Bureaucracy takes care of this. In certain cases, when the choice is between only two alternatives (for example, to wear or not to wear one's safety–belt) the definition of the threshold raises no problem. In other cases (for example, the permissible level of alcohol for a driver, the number of prescriptions beyond which a doctor's work will be deemed to be abnormal), the difficulty is far greater. Thus doctors will be deemed to have behaved unusually[33] when the number of their prescriptions is 50% above the threshold set by a special commission. They will be punished by being struck from the rolls of their health-insurance organization. One must obviously ask, then: are "unusual" doctors "normal"? As it happens, this is the question that seems to be suggested by the way profiles are interpreted in the profession, where this deviation is often attributed to the anxiety and perfectionism of the "guilty" doctor.[34] In so doing, one accepts to see oneself in the system of categories given by the bureaucracy. The traditional policing of the profession by its order tends to be replaced by bureaucratic control by method. In turn, the system of evaluation tends to impose a normative vision of good medical practice which goes against the way in which doctor traditionally saw themselves as members of a profession, exercising an art, that is a technique that has no automatic procedures.

Finally, although it has not yet received its statistical credentials, the concept of psychic normality proceeds by the same mode of reasoning. Deviation from the norm is assessed before civil courts in order to determine the responsibility of the criminal, that is to decide the relevance of his treatment by the judiciary.[35] Some go so far as to assert that the law has evolved as a result of the development of criminology and has henceforth entered its "psychiatric phase."[36] Others complain that the life of the accused is scrutinized without his having a word to say about it.[37] It is the segmentation of the subject according to criminological categories (such as dangerousness and accessibility to punishment) and psychiatry (madness and reason) that determines the mode in which cases put up for judgment are understood and the nature of the treatment prescribed. Before the innocence or guilt of the accused is judged, his responsibility or irresponsibility must be assessed with the help of specialists.

Segmented man on probation. The marketing society produced segmented man out of a universe that postulated individual freedom. All that is now left for him is to hope that he will receive favourable treatment or to try and escape. But this is not easy as can be seen from the true story (in the form of a fable) of the Overamstel model prison in Amsterdam. The purpose of this prison, according to the authorities, was to make the prisoners happier. Various material and psychological devices were used. "Escape is not easy, but it is possible. Overamstel's public relations officer told the Justice Minister that this should be so because if a prisoner puts all his creativity into his escape plans, we cannot sabotage them without making him go mad." The newspaper that reported his words adds: "Everything has been provided for: even the right to dream."[38] But when the dream is provided by the institution as one of the normal categories in its repertory, will it still be a 'true' means of escape? One solution remains for segmented man: to seek the "right category." And, first and foremost, to know which category he belongs to in order to draw up the best strategy. Unless of course he belongs to one of those categories that are deprived of imagination.

On the Importance of Categories

Administrative categories have always provided food for conversation on bureaucracy and guided the action of the governed in relation to it. We might recall, for example, the old custom of self-mutilation to evade military obligations.[39] We also know the nasty tricks that administration can play with individual fates: how old and perfectly sane people end their days in psychiatric hospitals simply because, unlike in old-age homes, in these hospitals full responsibility is taken for their care,[40] how the "soldier on leave should stay healthy,"[41] because he cannot be reimbursed for medical expenses if he is unwise enough to be stricken by acute appendicitis in a place where there is no military hospital; we also know how individual fate can depend on the right classification of the individual on a form, and of the form in a clerk's papers.[42] In short, we know about what one ombudsman called "the martyrdom of the administered,"[43] who may at any time fall victim to ignorance of their rights or to the grain of sand that stops the cogs of the administrative machine. The time has come when the omnipresence of bureaucratic categories means that the risks and advantages of belonging to them are everywhere.

Grids and tracks. Who am I? What shall I do? Where am I going? These anguished and age-old questions were until now put to priests, family and the specialist press of astrologers and palm-readers. Today the specialist press has expanded: magazines and newspapers propose articles on "The price of managers,"[44] "A guide to salaries,"[45] "The cost of marriage,"[46] etc. Opinion pollsters provide typologies, portraits of the average Frenchmen, etc., for the asking. Not to mention tests: "Are you well matched with your partner?"[47] and also: "Are you moving up as you should in your career?,"[48] thanks to which each individual can identify himself in a universe whose complexity everyone makes it a point to stress. Thus one French newspaper gave managers the opportunity to assess themselves by the criteria of big organizations and in relation to their colleagues: "The purpose of this survey is above all to enable each person to assemble the data for a personal diagnosis. . . . Where are you in your career? (We would like to . . .) enable every manager to find out how far he is ahead or behind in his career within

the sector that he has chosen. . . . Have you really maintained your purchasing power? . . . The table enables the reader to situate his own progress
compared with that of managers with the same profile and in relation to
prices. . . . The section entitled "Those who earn half as much as the
others" gives the branches of specialization and types of education of managers whose earnings are far greater than the average for their category. . . .
The graph "Are you one of those hit by the crisis?" shows that during the
last five years, certain positions in firms have been favored while others
have been particularly hit by the recession . . .", etc.

Another newspaper gives its readers statistical tables on schools: "Have
you chosen the *right lycée*?"[49] Yet another asks: "What is the use of a degree
from a *Grande Ecole*?"[50] (one of a group of elite university–level schools in
France, specializing in professional training). Not to mention the annual
ratings of schools published in *Le Monde de l'Education*.[51] It is because
each person seeks the information that he considers necessary for the
preparation of intelligent strategies that these publications sell. To situate
yourself is to be able to situate the others: from the viewpoint of categories,
knowledge is the means to determine what is owed to you, where you are
heading, to act on your destiny or to try to do so, by getting into the best
possible position or by optimizing your chances of reaching a better position. This approach calls for shrewdness and sometimes guile. You have to
know that, in order not to find yourself at a dead–end at the age of 45, you
must change your sector in the firm at 35:[52] you have to know that, even if
you do not like calculus, it is preferable to graduate from high school with a
major in mathematics, since it opens many doors. Which no doubt explains the calculations made by a French daily to show for example that "it
is possible to graduate in science with a low grade in maths."[53] And even
then, once this has been achieved, there are still the traps laid by selectors
in the path of candidates for higher education: you should know for example that one university looks favorably on graduate in mathematics, but
only one with a good grade in the main subject. *Le Monde* also published
an article on "the cost of marriage" according to which "anyone who
would like to make an exhaustive study should have a mathematical model
and a computer in order to plot the optimum curve of the life of a couple:
Get married when your incomes are in such and such a configuration but
not before; get divorced before buying your country home or playing the
stock market; have one, two or three children at such and such a time;
remarry then get divorced and so on."[54]

Even drinkers are not forgotten: when the breathanalyzer test became
compulsory, every restaurant used to offer its customers a small sheet
edited by the *Compagnon Gourmets*, which specified for each category of

height and weight, the quantity of alcohol of different kinds that could be absorbed within the limits permitted by the law.

Manuals, Games and Scenarios

In short, to be in a category and to remain there takes a lot of work. There are many manuals and other guides on this subject.[55] They make it possible to situate oneself in the universe of bureaucratic categories: "Who is a student?" asks one of them for example, "When do you have the right to unemployment benefits?", etc.

While legal *codes* are supposed to rule every aspect of the citizen's public life, guides bring together various definitions for use by the target groups of the bureaucracy in all phases of existence. Henceforth it is at school itself that the student is explicitly taught to maximize his chances in the jungle of categories. Witness business schools, which teach their students the basic strategy to be followed by a manager offering his services: how to prepare his curriculum, analyze his situation, in a word how to master his future.

Even the military art is called to the rescue in these war games for the conquest of the future.[56] Games of strategy, which are becoming such a popular pastime, are also used as a means of learning and as techniques of innovation: role–playing in the firm, where real or credible situations are simulated; role–playing to learn a trade;[57] scenario–building (the future in kit form, build your own future) at all levels, from the firm in search of new ideas[58] to planning commissions in search of a presentable future. According to the journalist, J. Grapin, the instructions given to the Eighth Plan International Forecasting Group were essentially the following: "Describe as precisely as possible the events that France will have to take into account in the coming years, state the priority goals and conclude on the available room for manoeuvre."[59]

When the Categories Take to the Streets

The management of one's own future is an individual task, but it is also a collective one involving the defense of group interests. Simultaneously with the growth of systems for category identification, we are witnessing the development of collective categorial expressions.

Let us with the expansion of categorial groups themselves. Traditionally marginal social groups such as "artists" now have a recognized social status in Europe.[60] Groups change their system of reference by receiving a new name: artisans and workers collectively become manual workers.[61] The professions, the oldest of which were already organized into orders, are

Probable level of alcohol in blood
(Subjects without counter-indications).

	On empty stomach						After a meal					
	Vol.	Weight (in Kgs)					Vol.	Weight (in kgs)				
		50	60	70	80	90		50	60	70	80	90
Table wine 11%	7 cl	0.19	0.14	0.12	0.11	0.10	37 cl	0.72	0.53	0.43	0.39	0.33
Table wine 11%	—	—	—	—	—	—	50 cl	0.96	0.70	0.57	0.53	0.44
Fine wine	7 cl	0.22	0.16	0.13	0.12	0.11	37 cl	0.79	0.57	0.47	0.43	0.36
Kir or Cardinal	7 cl	0.21	0.15	0.12	0.11	0.10	12 cl	0.25	0.18	0.15	0.14	0.11
Sangria 13.5%	7 cl	0.25	0.18	0.15	0.13	0.12	12 cl⁻	0.28	0.20	0.17	0.15	0.13
Wine-based aperitif 16.5%	6 cl	0.26	0.19	0.16	0.14	0.13	6 cl	0.17	0.13	0.10	0.09	0.08
Aniseed-based aperitif 45% (5 parts water)	2 cl	0.23	0.17	0.14	0.13	0.11	2 cl	0.16	0.11	0.09	0.08	0.07
Cognac												
Armagnac 40%	4 cl	0.50	0.38	0.33	0.31	0.28	4 cl	0.333	0.25	0.21	0.20	0.18
Whisky, rum 40%	4 cl	0.56	0.43	0.38	0.33	0.30	4 cl	0.37	0.29	0.25	0.24	0.21
Apple brandy, Mirabelle												
Plum liquer 48%	4 cl	0.61	0.47	0.41	0.38	0.35	4 cl	0.40	0.31	0.27	0.25	0.22

now grouped together in a *Union Nationale des Associations des Professions Liberales* (UNAPL–National Union of Professional Associations, 1977), with a view to an offensive strategy towards the public authorities.[62]

In addition to professionally based groups, concerned citizens associations come together for self–defense against administration, with the purpose of acting as pressure groups for the defense of the environment, quality of products or accessibility of educational resources, etc. The list is a long one: the Association for the Development of Progress Associations has 2000 members, and it is estimated that France had around 3000 such associations in 1978.

The establishment of associations is correlative with the crisis of expression in trade unionism and the transformation of social movements to which the sociologist Alain Touraine drew attention: "All social movements today are directed to contesting, in some sphere of social life or other, the needs that the machines define for us and the mode of satisfaction that they prescribe for us . . . whether these are consumer movements, anti-nuclear protestors, women, ecologists, high–school students, or Breton, Corsican, or Occitanian nationalists. These movements are not the instruments of parties or theories which look to a future society. They seek to assert their existence here and now. . . . History no longer has any meaning that the movement can or wishes to claim for itself. It is therefore its own sole guarantor of the rightness of its purposes and of the legitimacy of its ends. This is why its means must confirm its ends."[63] Touraine's analyzes are partly endorsed by certain views expressed in the trade union movement which stress the breakdown of the traditional concept of the "working class."

As Touraine clearly points out, by the very fact that they are constituted in the forms necessitated by communication with the bureaucracy, all these categories have a pragmatic viewpoint. In order to act, that is in order to defend or win their rights and privileges, they use all the traditional or new resources that are offered to them as means of expression. Thus the associations, unlike the old committees, are no longer limited to exerting indirect pressure on the political system or to holding discussions with the administration in the rarified atmosphere of offices or, again, to publishing confidential documents.

Being good tacticians, all is grist to their mill: they develop an offensive press which opposes its investigations to those of the administration and of big firms. They do not hesitate to put up candidates for the presidency despite the indignation of politicians who invoke the grand principles of traditional political democracy to protest that politics concern the citizen and the General Interest, and not the user, professional categories or private interest. It is in the name of managers,[64] Protestants,[65] couples or even "misfits, derelicts, drug–addicts"[66] that people run for president.

The categories and associations have taken the idea of strikes and boycotts from trade union action: when European ministers are forced to ask veal consumers to be reasonable and responsible towards producers, the world seems turned upside down. Finally, categories have abandoned the legendary reticence of the silent majority and have no hesitation in taking to the streets. The reason the categories defend their privileges so tenaciously, while each individual seeks to build or maintain his position in a good category is that henceforth, without categories there is no power. To escape statistical fate, there is only one solution: flight. Flight towards pure chance as a rediscovered law of fate, this is borne out by the great success of lotteries of all types. Flight towards new charismas, from astrology to mystical sects via alternative medicine which restore symbolic order of the world. Flight towards the irrational and by the same token towards the unknown for this man whose reference points were established by the rationalistic revolution of the eighteenth century.

Notes

1. J. Habermas, *Legitimations probleme in Spätkapitalismus, op. cit.*
2. Characteristically, it is in those countries that have followed the path of social democracy for the longest time that such legislation is the most developed.
3. *Le Monde*, 16th November 1979.
4. C. Baudelot, R. Establet, *La Petite Bourgeoisie en France*, Paris, Maspero, 1974.
5. Cofremca survey, *Le Monde—Dimanche*, 25th May 1980.
6. Professor J. Cottin, *Le Monde*, 28th/29th January, 1979.
7. Like the great analyst of W. Gombrowitz, *Ferdydurke*, New York, Grove Press, Inc., 1968: "He operated analytically and his speciality was to split up of the individual into parts by calculation and, more particularly, by means of flicks of the finger. With a flick of the finger he could invite a limb to an independent existence and make it move spontaneously from one side to the other, causing wild agitation in its owner," p. 88.
8. Whence the dangers of the incongruence of the various fates defined for one and the same person when different bureaucracies taking care of him do not use the same lists or categories. This situation is known to the French as the guêpier *administratif* (the administrative hornets' nest).
9. *Travail—Information*, notes of the Labour Ministry, Press Information Service, no.25, October 1979.
10. *Le Monde,* "Entretiens de Bichat: pour une bonne gestion du patrimoine—santé," 3rd October 1979;
11. It is difficult at this point not to think of Borgès's list which Michel Foucault named as the source of the thinking which inspired *Les Mots et les Choses*. According to "a certain Chinese encyclopedia, says Borgès, animals are divided into the following categories: (a) those that belong to the Emperor (b) em-

balmed animals (c) tame animals (d) suckling pigs (e) sirens (f) fabled animals (g) dogs at liberty (h) animals included in the present classification (i) animals that are agitated like mad beings (j) innumerable animals (k) animals drawn with a very fine camel's hair brush (l) etc. (m) animals that have just broken the pitcher (n) animals that follow flies from far off." Thus, for example, there is the list of qualities registered in the various school reports that are filled in, as the case may be, by teachers, parents or social workers (Cf. *Le Monde*, 16th November, 1978) where children are classified higgledy–piggledy, according to the assessement of the respondents as: bold/fearful/active/cool; disciplined or capable of self–discipline/disciplined through fear of punishment/through passiveness/undisciplined and disorderly; works at a quick/normal/slow rate; rarely/frequently absent; wearing clean/dirty/inadequate clothes; maladjusted/adjusted/flirty; apathetic/shy/inhibited/passive/quiet/sleepy/given to telling stories; plays alone/in small groups/in gangs; has a normal/affectionate/dependent/antagonistic relationship with his teacher; hot–tempered/cheerful/sad/calm/excited/quick–spirited/slow–spirited; has had the measles/chicken–pox; has his own room/must be approached in a certain way.

12. P. Bourdieu's expression.
13. M. Cézard, "Les qualifications ouvrières en question," *Economie et Statistique*, April 1979.
14. *Le Monde*, 27 March 1979.
15. *Le Monde*, 27 June 1979.
16. *Le Monde*, 28 March 1979.
17. *Le Monde*, 3 November 1978.
18. See, for example, an interview with J. Le Theule, *Le Matin*, 19 December, 1979.
19. This is the mode in which all the controversies grew over the breathanalyzer tests (*Le Monde*, 3 November 1978), the dipping of headlights in town (*France-soir*, 22 February 1980; *Le Matin*, 13 November 1979), the use of safety belts ("Is the safety belt effective?" *Le Monde*, 28 March 1978; see also *Le Monde* dated 16 November, 1978).
20. *Le Matin*, 9 June 1979 and 2 July 1980.
21. It is worth noting how this action of the bureaucracy "resocializes" time which the free–market society had "desocialized." For the concrete time of tradition, organized by the rhythms of cosmic and collective life, the free–market society had substituted abstract, mechanical time made up of quite similar elementary units which could be combined at will. The marketing society tends to reorganize the timetables of each of its members in accordance with its imperative need to minimize the costs that it assumes. How long will it be before every Parisian whose telephone number ends with a "2" will have to leave for his annual vacation between midday and 2 p.m. on the 1st of August?
22. Université de Vincennes, *Le Nouvel Ordre Intérieur*, Alain Moreau, 1978.
23. GAMIN project, *ibid.*
24. *Le Monde*, 28 March 1979.
25. The project for school performance files, established by an order dated 8th August 1977, was cancelled, after vigorous protest by parents and teachers, by an order dated 5th July 1980. But since the forms were already distributed and had cost a great deal of money, it was decided that they would continue to be used, each respondent replying to the questions that he or she thought were permissible. Cf. *Le Monde*, 27 June 1980.

26. *Le Nouvel Ordre Intérieur, op. cit.*

27. The implicit hypothesis being that intelligence, a psychological or physiological attribute and not a sociological one, is distributed by chance in the reference population, namely that no characteristic of the subjects (other than age, whose effect is neutralized by the construction of specific tests for each age) affects the quality of their replies, apart from their intelligence itself.

28. In the game of insurance against chance, the strangest example is surely the one reported by the French satirical magazine, *Le Canard Enchaîné* holders of the French Electricity Board's (1947) premium bonds, which were given out in compensation for nationalization and carried the right to a share in 1% of the company's profits, took out insurance against the risk of receiving full compensation, since such compensation put an end to an increasingly exhorbitant privilege inasmuch as each time lots were drawn, the number of share-holders grew smaller while the amount to be shared out grew larger.

29. G. Debray–Ritzen; *Lettre ouverte aux parents des petits écoliers*, Paris, Albin Michel, 1978.

30. *Le Monde*, 1st December 1978.

31. "Manifeste des philosophes de l'Ecole Normale," in *Le Monde*, 8 Mai, 1979.

32. Here again, we can see how the definition of health risk imposes a bureaucratic definition of *health*. Now it appears that nothing is less clear than the idea of "health": "it is not a scientific concept, but a felicitous agreement between the person who feels well and those around him. Does this have anything to do with the right to health granted to us by the WHO or by the State health system which is being set up? "(Study theme at the congress of private psychiatrists at Evian, quoted in *Le Matin*, 11th October 1979); or again: "is it possible to define a medecine for the healthy man? Does the healthy man exist? Is health the absence of illness? The absence of suffering? A statistical datum?" *Le Monde* report on the XXVIth seminar on preventive and social medecine); or yet again: "Health is not non-illness. It is adaptation to the environment." (A. Battle and J. F. Blondeau, "Les insécurités sociales" in *Le Monde*, 12th October 1980.

33. Within the framework of the Evreux pilot experiment: Cf. *Le Monde*, 15th August 1979.

34. Work on the definition of the medical profile is itself aimed at gaining deeper knowledge of the factors that determine the variation of doctors' prescription rates. Cf. A Letourney, *Rapport sur l'Etude de la pratique médicale du généraliste en médecine liberale de cabinet, formulation d'un modèle de comportement du médecin généraliste de ville,* CORDES 1977.

35. Since, in effect, article 64 of the penal code states that "there is no crime or offense when the accused is in a state of dementia at the time of the action or when he has been obliged to it by a force which he was unable to resist."

36. Mr. Dorwling–Carter, deputy public prosecutor at the Paris court of appeals, during a seminar on psychiatry at Lille, 14th November 1979, quoted in Le Monde, 19th November, 1979.

37. Mr. L. Csiznadia, advocate at the Lyons court of appeals, *ibid.*

38. *Le Matin*, 20th April 1979.

39. Cf. J.-P. Aron, E. Le Roy Ladurie, *Le Conscrit Français*, Paris, Mouton, 1972.

40. *Le Matin*, 28 February, 1979.

41. *Le Matin*, 6 March, 1979.

42. *Ibid.*

43. *Ibid.*
44. Annual survey since 1975.
45. Survey in 1978.
46. *Le Monde*, 5 February 1980.
47. The magazine *Elle*, for example.
48. "Le prix des cadres 1980," *Expansion*, 20th June–3rd July 1980.
49. *Le Matin*, 23rd September 1980.
50. *Le Monde*, 20th June 1980.
51. Since 1976: "The palmarès des universités," *Le Monde de l'Education*
52. "Le prix des cadres," *op. cit.*
53. *Le Matin*, 23rd September 1980.
54. J.-J. Philippe, "Le coût du mariage," *Le Monde de l'Economie*, 25th November 1980.
55. The market for these text books of a new type has expanded at a dizzy pace in recent years: *Manuel de la Vie Pauvre*, Paris, Stock, Coll. Vivre, 1974; *Guide de l'Etudiant*, les dossiers de l'étudiant, 1978; *Répertoire Québecois des Outils Planétaires*, Flammarion, Coll. Mainmise; *Guide des Jeunes CFDT*, Paris, Montolon–Service, 1980; etc.
56. See articles on the subject in *Le Monde–Dimanche*.
57. The New York Times dated 2nd October 1979 has a report on the use of this method to train future doctors by bringing them into contact with patients.
58. *Le Monde,* 20th April 1980.
59. *Le Monde*, 2nd February 1980.
60. *Le Monde*, 25th October 1975.
61. *Le Travail Manuel, Horizon 85*, documents from the Secretariat for Manual Work, 1979.
62. Whose competition they condemn, and to which they refuse to pay high health insurance contributions. Cf. *Le Monde* dated 1st and 25th November 1980.
63. Interview with Alain Touraine, *Le Nouvel Observateur*, 8th January 1979.
64. *Le Monde*, 8th November 1980.
65. *Le Monde*, 7-8th December 1980.
66. Coluche, the late satirical showman: "Profession of faith," *Le Monde*, 18th November 1980.

Chapter 11

Managing the Impossible

*09/82/95 complains that he is being treated like a
number.
If you have no choice, offer it.*

The categorical imperative of the Bureaucrat Prince is pragmatism. Counting, rhetoric and cybernetics enable him to take on the Necessity of confronting Chance. Pragmatism did not, of course, wait for the legitimacy crisis in order to exist. It may be argued that, without pragmatism, free-market system in its purest form could not have lasted a single day. However pragmatism then remained implicit, or at least subordinated, to a symbolic system founded on law and science. It is this symbolic system that endowed acts, however pragmatic they might be, with their dignity as legitimate acts. The efforts of the entrepreneur in the face of chance in the market constituted the sacrifice that believers offered up to providential nature. The initiatives of administrators were the expression of obedience to the law which bound them to the governors. As for the legislative nature of the governors' pragmatism, it proceeded from the will of each individual as expressed by the vote. In other words, pragmatism was necessarily a subordinate, hidden discourse, clandestine as it were.

Something like the mysteries of the inner life which the principle of free will grants to whoever deigns express himself in the forms of law. However, once the market brought public virtue into agreement with private vice, the pragmatic discourse of the management of firms and management itself was able to develop freely since its absence of reference to any criterion other than success was the very sign of its obedience to divine providence. For this, of course, it was necessary that the entrepreneur should no longer be the solitary hero speaking to himself about his projects, joys and sorrows and commanding the factors of production in a sovereign manner.

This is why managerial language emerged only at the end of the nineteenth century, when it became necessary to divide the intellectual work of the management of the firm among a relatively large number of persons.

Although it was first developed in enterprises, management has a more universal meaning. As the application of a rational approach (ie. legitimation of a rational legal system) to the functioning of an organization, it is the form in which bureaucratic pragmatism is expressed. Complex reality is described by means of circles (entities) and arrows (flows); these arrows are defined and counted in the categories that suit the different actors. Cybernetics, counting and rhetoric are the essential components of this language, which henceforth will be learned in the business schools that came into existence at the end of the last century in the United States. The pragmatic character of this teaching expends to the very methods used: students learn to confront the hazards of a situation by defining strategies in the same way Machievelli's Prince learned to display virtue in the face of the manifestations of fortune. Military art, Political art and the art of management come together in the evocation of the great decisions of the past (the Battle of Austerlitz, Alexandre Borgia's last meal, the launching of a new product) and training based on games of strategy—the case method—simulation, large–scale miltary manoeuvres, etc.

We may note an essential characteristic in these situations compared to those examined in the last chapter: each situation, each decision is considered in its singularity. When masses of entities are randomly confronted with one another, the laws of chance make it possible to give these phenomena, which follow no law, the form of a law, the law of the absence of law. When, On the contrary, the Bureaucrat Prince considers a singular situation, he can no longer resort to the laws of chance. To give meaning to his destiny, he must face uncertainty head on. In a crisis of legitimacy, the use of managerial language spreads to all bureaucratic entities, regardless of their nature. This is what the development of political marketing and public management shows. And if this language were to meet with an obstacle, it should able to take part in the working of systems whose function is to be symbolic, namely law and science. We can distinguish three situations with respect to the relationships between bureaucratic pragmatism (management) and legitimacy systems.

1. An entity assured of the legitimacy of its action (for example: a firm in a competitive situation) seeks a goal for itself (e.g. profit). From the standpoint of legitimacy, it acts in a deterministic universe; from the standpoint of its purpose, it acts in an uncertain universe (hence a pragmatic one).

2. An entity which is not assured of the legitimacy of its action (for example: an enterprise in a dominant position) seeks a goal for itself (e.g. profit). Henceforth from the standpoint of legitimacy as well as that of

its own goal, it acts in an uncertain (hence pragmatic) universe. It may be said that henceforth legitimacy becomes a goal for this entity.[1]

3. An entity is entrusted with preserving the symbolic value of a system of legitimacy in crisis (for example, law, science). It finds itself faced with an impossible task. The ultimate degree of pragmatism is therefore, more than the management of the uncertain, it is the management of the impossible, which can only be symbolic.

The examples of the management of the impossible (management of the symbolic), that we shall invoke belong either to the sphere of the management of the law or to the management of science (the management of the Apocalypse).

Managing the Law

The laissez–faire crisis of legitimacy is above all the crisis the law; and thereby it is the crisis of the boundary between the public sector and the private.

The Law Itself

In an exaggerated fashion, it may be said that from being presumed to be known, stable, universal and prescriptive, the law becomes unknown, flexible, specialized and stimulative.

The unknowable law. A joke going around in the States has it that the Tables of the Law were contained in ten lines, the Declaration of Independence in one page, the Gettysburg address in three pages, and the West Coast Lettuce Growers' Charter in two hundred and fifty pages. With the proliferation of specialized texts, it is becoming impossible to know the law, even for those whose role it is to enforce it. Hence the principle according to which ignorance of the law is no excuse is tending to become virtually ineffective and it is becoming increasingly necessary to assume that knowledge of the law is no obligation. This means replacing a judicial structure as such by pragmatic structures which provide for satisfactory communication among various entities: this could imply the use of mass communications, setting up structures for information, contact and even negotiation. Henceforth it is necessary to "sell" the law, to make it known and to tailor its application to the concrete conditions of its achievement. Replacing one principle by the other implies a complete change in the character of law itself. From a categorical imperative laying down the universally binding prohibitive force evoked by the Tables of the Law, the law becomes a prescription to be published, understood and eventually accepted.

Law as a flexible institution. Increasingly the law is not only sold according to the principles of management, but is pragmatically designed to follow the behavior of entities: henceforth, law increasingly follows fact. In the highly symbolic realm of family law, sociology is now asked to set the standard. To formulate a law on divorce, we no longer start from a symbolically coherent view of the family but from the sociological analysis of behavior patterns. And if perchance some deep–rooted conviction, coming from the legacy of tradition, is offended, the opinion poll is resorted to in order to find out at what moment such a principle might be considered to be outmoded.

Law as a stimulator. While the law may be henceforth derived explicitly from behavior, it also happens that behavior is in turn affected by the law. Six months after the promulgation of a new divorce law in France, newspapers were reporting the effect that the law seemed to have on behavior and were asking questions about the future of marriage.

With increasing frequency, the law is used as an auxiliary to State action programs. Any private action can be singled out by the State in terms of its economic and social consequences, and in return can be made the subject of a policy addressing these very forms of behavior, whether it is smoking, brushing one's teeth or drinking and driving, or even wearing safety belts and dimming headlights in town, etc. In these cases, the law has value only if it is actually known and accepted.

To see that the law remains the law when it has lost all the characteristics of law: such is the impossible task whose symbolic management is increasingly entrusted to market research and communication techniques.

Public Sector and Private Sector

The impossible task is that of continuing to act as if it were possible to make a clear distinction between public and private sectors, when the boundary increasingly runs down the center of each acting entity, or even down the center of each act.

To state, following Max Weber, that the free–market system comes under the system of rational–legal legitimacy, means that, because the acts of the various entities that make up society are rational, they can be justifed by a legal language. Thus, the firm and the consumer need no other guarantee for their actions than compliance with the forms of private contract which guarantee the freedom of will and, by the same token, the social optimum. Thus, because it acts within the strict framework of the spheres of traditional sovereignty (the boundary of the public sector) and within the strict framework of the delegation of power, attributed impersonally to each agent of the State, the administration can enjoy prerogatives that it gains by being subordinate only to the political power which draws its legitimacy from the vote.

The real functioning of a legitimating language leads to a distinction between what, in this language, is self-evident (complies with the nature of things) from what, in this language, is not self-evident (is liable not to be respected). Thus, every well–formed legitimating language must contain in itself the possibility of its own breakdown and the possibility of its repair. The breakdown of the legitimating language is what happens when a given power refuses to recognize the boundaries set up by the law. Repairing the legitimating language can only mean the intervention by another power, equal at least to the former one, whose sole function is to know the legitimating language and to make it respected. Hence, to be legitimate, every power needs to be confronted with a double, a legitimating institution, in the way that the agents of the laissez–faire system may be brought before legal institutions. The crisis of a legitimacy system therefore is the crisis of the dialogue between power and its double; the crisis of free–market ideology therefore is the crisis of the dialogue between power and legal institutions.

The practicing jurist generally recoils from the idea that a legal system might undergo a crisis. Since the law can be defined as that which the judge states, it will be respected for as long as there is a judge to go on stating something.

This holds true for the principle of the independence of the judiciary which may be interpreted as meaning either that to be a judge it is necessary to be independent of power or that by the very fact of being a judge one is independent of power. Of course, this principle assumes the existence of certain ways of dramatizing the possible opposition between power and its double: the normal functioning of institutions, where conflicts are resolved by dialogue (conducted in legal language) between power and its double, contrasts with the crisis of the system where power and its double confront each other like two characters on a stage. These characters are, for example, on one side the administrator, the State, possessing a power that it tends to abuse, especially in the sense that it encroaches on the domain of the invisible hand, and on the other hand, a wise and independent constituted body ready to resist pressures. Its legitimating power is entirely contained in its capacity for resistance, a capacity which requires that the legitimating institution does not itself draw its own power from the power that it has to legitimate. This means that the legitimacy of the legitimating institution should have its own autonomous sources.

In the legal–rational liberal system, the legal institution draws its power from two sources: the rationality of the language that it uses, the rationality of the persons who use this language. To the legitimacy of the rule therefore, which is based essentially on the fact that it can be understood by all, is added the legitimacy of the judge, which derives first of all from his capacity to speak the language (competence), and second from his determination to speak it in all circumstances, including those that correspond to the crisis of the system of legitimacy (courage, reponsibility, integrity, autonomy). And since, following Max Weber, there are only three forms of legitimacy (charismatic, traditional and rational–legal), the legitimacy of the judiciary may be said to be partly of rational–legal origin (when it concerns the legitimacy of the rule), and partly of charismatic origin (when it concerns the personal legitimacy of judges), and, for the remainder, of traditional origin (insofar as it is agreed that habit is a second nature). Democratic's crisis of legitimacy occurs when the judge can resort less and less to the legitimacy of the rules and must increasingly resort to his personal legitimacy. This process can be followed by considering how the jurisprudence of the French *Conseil d'Etat* has tried to resolve the problem of the control of the State's discretionary power. The initial formulation of laissez–faire ideology corresponds to the delimitation of State action on the basis of a purely legal criterion: every agent of the public authority necessarily comes under public jurisdiction. In its pure form, the rational–legal system asks the jurisdictional control only to guarantee the legality of the status of the agent and of the legality of its intervention in a given domain. But this agent does not have to account to anyone (legally) for the rationality of his decisions. Thus the control of legality cannot be confused with the aptness of the decisions taken, and, for this reason, the discretionary actions of the administration (known as "acts of higher administration") can or even should be beyond the control of the public judge.

The passage from the criterion of public power to the criterion of public service marks the first stage in administration's crisis of legitimacy. Henceforth the extension of the public sector is defined on the basis of functional criteria. The question that comes up then is how to limit the administration in such a manner without directly raising the question of the rationality of the actions taken. It was impossible to find a solution which did not entail a detailed analysis of the decisions themselves. Thus the idea arose of making a distinction, in the decision, between, on the one hand, the explicit purpose of the act, the exactness of the facts invoked by the administration to justify its decision, which could be the subject of legal supervision, and, on the other hand, appreciation and the qualification of the facts, which remained unsupervised. This distinction between the (legal) analyst of the decision and the (administrative) decision–maker recalls the distinction, cherished by Auguste Comte, between spiritual and temporal powers.

With the crisis of the criterion of administrative law, it becomes impossible to state a clear rule by which each individual may know in advance and in all circumstances whether an action falls within the public or the private sector. Concomitantly, the discretionary power of the administration has grown with the intervention of the State in all aspects of economic and social life.

It is becoming increasingly difficult to identify clearly the goals pursued by the administration. Legal control henceforth has no choice but verify the expediency of actions or abandon the whole idea of supervision. To verify expediency is to dive resolutely into the pragmatism that characterizes State action. At the very moment when the judge seeks to make a direct assessment of the rationality of public action, he abandons the *grounds* of the legal rule which guaranteed his power beyond his own authority. As Judge Kahn (a presiding judge in a division of the *Conseil d'Etat*) said, legal control is not possible if "the judge is not capable of advancing or suggesting the rule on which his decision is based."[2] Otherwise, "his control is exercised at random, without principle, that is in a form which is not that of the control of legality." We would then be led to formulate the hypothesis that in this situation, the *Conseil d'Etat* has no other solution than to resort to management both in its internal functioning (the development of jurisprudence) and in its external functioning (public relations). From the standpoint of its internal functioning, if it must formulate the principles of its decisions, it must resort to pragmatism itself. This is the case with major creations of jurisprudence in recent years: the "theory of the balance sheet" and the "theory of patent error." The former directly evokes the balance of advantages and disadvantages that firms use to assess their own situation. The Conseil d'Etat can now use this pragmatic means to see to it that none of the concerned parties is excessively damaged by public decision. In the theory of patent error, the judge retains the possibility of issuing a warning when administrative act appears to be "excessive," "immoderate," "unreasonable."[3]

Thus the judge does not confine himself to encoding facts, he assesses them directly. The worth of his judgment is no longer derived from the rule that he applies but from the legitimacy of whoever states the judgment. The legitimacy of the judge becomes the essential tool of judgment and the essential source of the legitimacy that this judgment can provide to the State. In order to provide legitimacy, the judge must see to it that he gets legitimacy in an autonomous way. This legitimacy, which he now cedes in the form of pragmatic judgements, must be procured in a pragmatic way.

Marketing techniques therefore ought to find a new field of application here. The recent emergence of a public relations department in the Conseil d'Etat, the numerous surveys made on the image of justice and even the use of advertising to recruit public prosecutors for the Ministry of Justice[4] are all so many signs that this is already the case.[5]

This trend towards pragmatic legislation seems to be opposed by the promulgation of a new law on the motivation of administrative acts. It does seem as if this law, according to which actions should be motivated, extends the field of what can be controlled from the strict standpoint of legal regulation. This regulation would formally resolve the crisis of legitimacy of the administration by achieving a Copernican revolution in its own functioning which, until then, could simply invoke the general interest that it was established to protect. However, the practical import of this law will probably be far more restricted. It is precisely when decisions are based on an increasing number of increasingly specific motives and when they come from an increasing number of increasingly disparate decision–making centres that the administration is asked to state publicly the ins and outs of its decisions. From a purely logical point of view, this is an impossible task. Unless the purpose of this law is to prop up the myth of the existence of rational decisions at a time when this myth has lost a substantial part of its reality. From the standpoint of our hypothesis, it may be thought that the practical application of the law consists of drawing up decisions that can be understood and accepted by those whom they concern. However, the essence of such a law resides in its effect on the quality of the relationship between the administration and the public. If a law is necessary, it is because unlimited power is illegitimate power: when the law restrains such a power it allows it, by the same process, to accomplish all that such a constraint tolerates. The legitimating force of such a law is added to the direct management of the legitimacy of the legitimating institution. We have already seen how the permitting power of the prohibiting law works during the first stage of the crisis of legitimacy of the private firm. By prohibiting firms from becoming too big and by dividing up those which contravene this new categorical imperative, the anti–trust law ensured, in the process, that all other firms were sufficiently small. In France, the new stage of the legitimacy crisis of private firms is also marked by a law: the law that requires firms to demonstrate the legitimacy of their motives by publishing a social balance–sheet.

However, these laws alone cannot ensure that the Laissez–faire system will remain the basis of the legitimacy of firms. In the sphere of competition (which the anti–trust law was supposed to resolve), it has been necessary to develop legitimating institutions of a less legal and more pragmatic style inspired by the example of the United States. It is the administration itself that goes to war against price fixing [6] or organizes a "Commission de la Concurrence" (or fair competition authority). Such commissions, which are pragmatic, legitimating institutions (by definition), are entrusted with managing the symbolism of the market by making pronouncements—sometimes on the concentration of companies (four times between 1977 and 1980)—and by applying sanctions. Their impossible task is to re-establish the normal working of the laws of the market. If they apply sanctions too frequently, they run the risk of replacing the laws of the market by administrative control; if they do so too rarely, these markets risk coming under the control of coalitions of big firms. Another symbolic solution to the problem of competition consists in promoting the creation of small firms which, by their glorious or tragic fates, demonstrate that the market is still real enough to stimulate new entrepreneurial vocations. But today, in France, the entrepreneur's calling itself requires administrative procedures, financial assistance and even administrative advertising campaigns.

Managing the Apocalypse

Knowledge is a tree, and the fruit of this tree, a prohibition, a temptation and the beginning of the history of men on the face of the earth. Similarly in Greece, knowledge was Prometheus saving the men he had created by giving them the secret of fire stolen from the gods. Thus were linked the themes of procreation (childbirth, the creation of man, the arts and techniques of the potter's fire), of knowledge (the secret of fire, knowledge, science) and of transgression. It is also the theme of the punishment of human pride, of Hubris. Disquiet in the face of the computer, the atom, and genetic engineering, is quite simply the resurgence of the curse of whoever cannot resist the temptation to know what no man has known before.

For a long time, knowledge was a matter of secrecy and sects: the Pythagoreans and their science of numbers, the alchemists and the science of the fire that transformed stone. It was fire that threatened those (like Bruno and Galileo) who revealed a knowledge unknown to revelation, and it was an alchemist, Newton, who opened the way to a new political order in which religion was replaced by reason.

In the face of so much pride, what is surprising is that we have had to wait so long for divine wrath to manifest itself and for the specialists and the leaders of the world to ponder anxiously the consequences of the Faustian choices[7] that society now makes daily. For this, was needed a break in the alliance between science and society. From science, laissez-faire society asked first of all for a representation of the laws of nature to which it could submit. Technology and practice belonged to the power of men. Since men obeyed the laws of nature, technology and practice were by the same token bound by these laws. The fire of the factories was supposed to disappear behind the cold law of markets. The productive passion of industrialists could not stand this silence.

With Auguste Comte, what society asked of science was no longer only the revelation of nature but its transformation. With this pragmatism, the danger of the Promethean temptation reappeared. Thus, in order to preserve his optimistic faith in progress, Auguste Comte had to mark the boundaries of knowledge by eliminating the infinitely great and the infinitely small from the horizons of science: he defined a practical limit to knowledge. Science is the preoccupation and the technique of closed systems. The dramas that are born in these systems also die there. Practice and technology have a limit. Prometheus promises to remain bound. As for the power that he might have conquered within these limits, its legitimacy is found in the ordering of the theory of public service. When this order collapses, the sciences, which have once again become pragmatic, become irresistible and boundless temptations. What the computerization of society reveals is nothing else than the cybernetic character of society, that is the collapse of the symbolic systems that legitimate it. What this pragmatic society asks of science henceforth is to be a series technologies. The atom—the technique of fire and of the transmutation of matter, this public alchemy—causes anxiety because it makes it impossible to confine experimental apparatus strictly within limits of time and space. Because it can be split or fused, the atom, whose very name was synonymous with indivisibility, now symbolically consecrates the fragility of the individual. Even the self, according to Kant, the object of the only dogmatic assertion of the Sophists, has been challenged the new entities that man, the new Prometheus, wants to create by the processes of genetic engineering.

The Logic of the Necessary and the Impossible

With laissez-faire ideology, science stolen from the gods, unlike divine law which confined it to secrecy, establishes human law by its own lights alone. Henceforth it is no longer with God that science comes into conflict, but with society, whose laws it constantly tends to transgress. The crisis of the relations between science and society is the crisis of languages which legitimate the use that society makes of science. This crisis is first of all the legitimacy crisis of society itself (see Chapter 7, The formation of the Cybernetic Ideology). It is also the crisis in the relationship between science and society. This relationship must in turn be considered at two levels: the symbolic and the pragmatic. From the symbolic standpoint, science and society exchange legitimacy with each other: either science is used by society (in the form of laissez–faire theory or in the name of the authority of scientists) or science uses the legitimacy of society (for example Lysenko, the condemnation of Galileo, etc. . . .).

From the pragmatic standpoint, society asks science to build and maintain machines, or to participate in solving social problems. In doing so, it tends to make concomitant use of the languages of various sciences for some specific purpose. Since these languages have validity in their own sphere, society, by using them, tends to ask more of them than can be said in scientific language. What no science can state will be asked of multi-disciplinary studies, which can be understood as the art of making many sets of language (or laws) speak on one and the same fact. This crisis of language, this breakdown of legitimacy can only lead to radical fragmentation. Even then, it is necessary that this pragmaticism should preserve what is needed of the symbolical structure so that the risk of transgression is not unlimited. For that purpose, it will make use of the discourse of chance and necessity.

When the action of society threatens the very order that founds it, it may claim necessity, but it cannot admit that it has abandoned itself to chance without causing anxiety.

To avoid this pitfall, it is enough to speak of the action of society according to the logic of the necessary and the impossible; that is to say, the art of managing technology becomes the art of managing what is simultaneously necessary and impossible.

The general problem is as follows:

—Since the danger implied by new technologies cannot be assessed (it is *impossible* to know the social impact of "fire"), these technologies should be developed only to the extent that they are or have become *necessary*.

—Since a danger results from this, safety measures should be taken to render this danger impossible. These measures would be safety norms for technical questions or social laws for the social consequences of a given temptation if any.

—Since it is *impossible* to show that danger is *impossible* (science, whether social or natural, says so), there will be a tendency to make it very *improbable*. With time, the proliferation of opportunities and the persistence of human temptations, the improbable becomes *necessary*.[8]

At first sight, it would seem that the logic of the necessary and the impossible is no more capable of soothing anxiety than the logic of chance and necessity. It even seems to aggravate the situation, which avoids chance only to fall into fatality. However since this fatality is only the logical consequence of the logic of chance, it is a good idea to take this logic of chance as a starting point to consider what is needed to make this necessity bearable. In order to manage the apocalypse, it is necessary to produce a language with which we can continue to speak. But before giving examples of the symbolic procedures by which society can fulfill the impossible missions implied by the use of technology, we must first describe these impossible missions.

Missions Impossible

Mission Impossible NO. 1: Making nuclear power safe. The risk of nuclear explosion seems to be ruled out for ordinary nuclear plants because the quantity of fissile materials is not sufficient in any case to set off a chain reaction. A breeder reactor has enough plutonium to manufacture a bomb, but the conditions required for the explosion of this bomb are unusual enough (they have to be set up very carefully for military purposes) to make the explosion in fact impossible. However, in either case, there could be a "nuclear leak," with the possibility that radioactive products might escape into the atmosphere. The transportation of radioactive materials entails the risk that they might be leaked either by accident or through the malicious intent of groups or individuals. And radioactive wastes have to be stored in such a way that they can be kept safe for the centuries that are needed for them to become harmless. Precautions are taken to make all these risks improbable but, with the proliferation of nuclear plants, these risks tend to increase regularly.

Mission Impossible NO. 2: Using computers without curbing freedoms. We have already looked at the way data processing challenges the secrets of the black box which is the very essence of the notion of the subject's liberty in the laissez–faire system (see Chapter 8, The Workings of Cybernetic Ideology).

Even beyond the direct attack on the innermost conscience, the use of computers challenges the very constituents of free will: memory and language. Human memory, which is soon going to be dethroned by gigantic electronic memories, may one day be used for nothing more than nostalgia. As for language, the machine may attain it in three ways: through the propagation of the language of access to the machine, the automated production of texts and, above all, the structuring of data banks. In the last case, the very language of the different fields of specialized knowledge is centrally organized, with each individual having to submit to this form of organization in order to obtain access to "his" ("its") memory. A situation is described in the terms of the machine, the machine replies; there remains the interpretation, the personal language by which what the machine says can be related to what has been said to the machine. However, with artificial intelligence, even the domain of human autonomy is increasingly invaded by the language of the machine.

Mission Impossible NO. 3: Developing genetics without affecting the natural reproductive processes. Genetic manipulations on bacteria might create some surprises. Genetic manipulations on man might cause some anxiety. The eighteenth-century ideology assumed a natural man discovering nature and the advantage that he might derive from obeying nature. Henceforth even the reproduction of the species comes within the ambit of his artifices: the field of temptation is open.

Symbolic Management of the Impossible

The only way to manage the impossible, were this to prove necessary, would be to manage it symbolically. Here is the catalogue of tools for the symbolic management of the impossible.

The law that authorizes. We have already encountered an example of this type of procedure with the anti–trust laws, which prohibit firms from being too big and which undertake to make them small enough to guarantee pure and perfect competition.

These laws are necessary when a technology (genetics, computer science, nuclear science) threatens society's system of legitimacy. These laws place a limit on the use of these technologies. This limit is supposed to ensure that the old system of legitimacy will not be modified. In practice, these laws that make it possible to take certain offenders to court cannot stop others from evading prosecution. They cannot make absolutely sure that every person who has decided to exceed the limits they have set will be stopped in his endeavour. The temptation will be great enough that such persons will exist. If need be, the argument of international competition ("we cannot help doing what everybody else is doing") or that of national defense is used to justify such attempts. In matters of defense, the seal of secrecy may remove these attempts from the controls of the law.

It follows that the practical consequence of such laws is essentially to facilitate the task of the very persons who develop these technologies and are tempted to exceed the prescribed bounds. Before the law, anything can be transgression. With the law everything that is done in laboratories and worksites which come under the law becomes legitimate on principle.

Consequently, it will be worthwhile for anyone who wishes to develop new technologies to have laws that restrict his activity and which, by that very fact, authorize it. The so-called "Information Privacy laws" (the

French version of which is called the "Informatique et Liberté" law) are an example of such laws.

Sometimes attenuated forms of this procedure are proposed. This involves a code of professional ethics, a sort of private law given to those who are most exposed to temptation. Ulysses had himself tied to the mast of his ship to resist the sirens' song. Similarly research scientists in genetics, at the Asilona conference in 1975, laid down the bounds within which experimentation was possible. This followed a seven–month moratorium on all experiments provoked by the disquiet that such experiments had caused. But since this code of professional ethics did not allow sufficient scope for research (coming after an excess of fear, it displayed an excess of caution), the safety measures were made less stringent by the U.S. National Institute of Health (NIH) in 1978.[9] However such laws can stop abuses and errors only in principle, as is shown by examples of experiments applying genetic manipulation techniques to human beings[10] or again by Doctor Kennedy's mistake: He thought he was making Sindbis vaccine proteins when, in fact, he was handling Semiliki, a closely related species but one that is potentally deadly to man.[11] In this field as in many others, it can be seen that Snark–hunting is a fruitful art, on condition that your Snark does not turn out to to be a Boojum.[12]

Mr. or Mrs. Technological Danger. A second procedure consists in entrusting a person well known for his knowledge and wisdom with the task of closely supervising the danger. Thus we can sleep better knowing that Mr. or Mrs. Technological Danger is watching over us.

The committee of sages. If one person does not seem to suffice in an age where, as we all know, scientists work in teams, this work of supervision may be entrusted to a committee of sages. Thus in 1974, a committee of this kind was set up in France to monitor genetic manipulation. "The sages (under the leadership of Professor Jean Bernard) include Professor Jacob, Professor Gros and Professor Monod, whose professional ethics are inseparable from a profound knowledge of the subject."[13]

Commissions. Further institutionalization may lead to setting up commissions. These bodies, like the *Informatique et Libert* (information privacy) commission in France, may have a quasi–jurisdictional role. The situation of the wiseman (alone or in a commission) before the Prince has already been evoked by Thomas More in Utopia: either the wiseman agrees with the Prince (but if he does so all the time then he is no longer wise), or he disagrees and shows his disagreement, and the Prince then may no longer follow his advice. Thus it is in the nature of these commissions that the sages sometimes resign and sometimes are removed.

Safety standards. The essential role of safety standards is to make danger "improbable" since it is "impossible" to make danger "impossible." These safety standards are sometimes produced by committees of sages or by safety commissions.

Five points may be noted:

1. Since no catastrophic accidents have as yet taken place, the calculated probabilities are based not on real experience but on imaginary experiments that anticipate the consequences of causes some of which are as yet unknown.[14]

2. From this point of view, the long–term consequences are those that remain hypothetical for the longest period of time.

3. Since there are no means of calculating probabilities on the basis of experiments, "*a priori*" "subjective" probabilities will be formulated. To say that an event will occur with a subjective probability of one half is to say that one is going to act as if long experience had shown that this event occurs once every two times. To use *a priori* probabilities is to create a tradition (a history) in a domain where by definition there is none.

4. Often what are published are accident probabilities and not "mathematical expectations." If the danger is infinite, an infinitesimal probability may lead to an expectation of infinite risk.[15]

5. Every standard implies a cost in time or in money. A trade–off must therefore be considered between *"impossible"* security and *"necessary"* economic activity. This choice is related not to science and technology alone but also to the social sciences. To define safety standards is to define a language (a technical and social one) in which it is possible to state that the risk is "sufficiently small."

Information. If the above procedures were sufficient, the job of informing would be confined to making known the law, sages, committees, commissions and standards. Sages and scientists would also be seen from time to time explaining aspects of the doctrine that guides their judgment to those who wish to share in the workings of human prudence and appreciate its extent. But the legitimacy crisis of society, of science and of society's use of science does not allow such a Comtean scheme to function. If it is suspected that the subject who is supposed to know in fact does not know, if the subject who is supposed not to know realizes that no one can be held to account for anything, then anxiety is aroused. And if there is one remedy for this anxiety, it is still the word, speech or, as we now call it, information.

Yet those who were entrusted with attempting the impossible initially resorted to secrecy. With nuclear power, for example, everything was supposed to stay secret, including even the French civilian safety and emergency plan, the efficiency of which, however, clearly depended on the active participation of all those who risked becoming the passive victims of an accident or of the ensuing panic. It took the Three Mile Island accident in early April 1979 to show that the possibility of the improbable was not just the daydream of a few unhealthy minds gazing at the tail–ends of statistical distribution curves.

After this accident, the public had to be informed. It was informed first of all that the prefects were preparing "plans of action" for each nuclear plant (Le Monde, 24th April 1979). However these plans were to remain secret "even as far as their civilian aspect was concerned." The then Industry Minister, Alain Giraud, explained: "if weak points were revealed they could be used by saboteurs." However, a Cabinet meeting on November 7th, 1979, decided to "make an effort to facilitate access by citizens to information in the field of nuclear power."[16] In particular, it was decided to publish the emergency plans for all the nuclear plants in operation.

A Council for Information on Nuclear Power has been in existence since 1978. This body has, on occasion, exposed instances when authorities failed to inform the public[17] and has expressed a desire "for more systematic and regular publication of technical reports by the various organizations that deal with public safety in atomic energy."[18]

As for the control of technology, the accident at Three Mile Island shows that it was possible to neglect defects known for more than a year[19] perhaps because the economic costs of safety measures seemed to be excessive when compared with the risks entailed. This accident showed also that the control systems were of no use. A hundred warning signals were set off simultaneously during the first stages of the accident without its being possible to turn off those that were not important while keeping those that were important.[20] It must be known that human error continues to be a factor of incalculable risk,[21] that "belief in adequate safety of nuclear plants has become a conviction. This attitude ought to be modified. It must be known that nuclear power is potentially dangerous by its very nature and that we should continually ask ourselves if the safeguards already in place are enough to prevent serious accidents."[22]

Finally, it must be known that lack of information provokes panic: thus Alain Giraud observed that the major problem seemed to him to be the "absence or insufficiency of information and of education of public opinion" in the face of this "mysterious problem which the phenomenon of radiation still represents for many people."[23] On this point, the politicians agree that it is important not so much "to produce cubic metres of additional reports"[24] as to seek a language suited to facilitating communication with the concerned populations in the event of accidents and to familiarize opinion with nuclear problems.[25] Mr. Giraud's point of view was echoed by Helmut Schmidt, in Germany, who urged the experts to "develop a language for dialogue with public opinion and not to be content with some sort of popularization of the problem."[26]

Henceforth dialogue with the public has become the ultimate recourse. Three symbolic procedures correspond to this preoccupation: the opinion poll, the referendum and the construction of a new language.

Opinion polls. The opinion polls which point to public fears about nuclear power and public confidence in its safety are too numerous to be cited: thus according to Le Matin (20th August 1979) 85% of the population fear nuclear power and 65% feel that its development is necessary.

Referendums. In a reversal which is not without its share of irony, governments are sometimes led to submit this business of specialists, scientists and sages to universal suffrage. Sweden and Austria have done so. A variant of the appeal to public opinion consists in having the citizen participate in the decision. This technique, as yet little used in France by State authorities, is already widespread among Parisian taxi drivers. They know that they have to go from one place to another and they know that it is impossible to avoid traffic jams. So they have taken to asking passengers which route they would prefer. They realise that when one has no choice the only thing left is to offer it to others.

The creation of a new language. The principal law rediscovered by politicians, which is referred to above, is that one should never be at a loss for words to state things. When what is involved is a threat to the symbolic structure itself, it is not enough to abandon oneself to chance and necessity: necessity has to be recognized, and chance has to be controlled in a way which ensures that chance is not allowed more than its fair share. Recognition of necessity may take the shape of expert advice, the sentiment of public opinion or a judge's decision. Thus the *Conseil d'Etat* decided that "the imbalance between energy needs and available resources on French territory calls for the development of electrical power production by processes different from those used at present; that severe regulations should be laid down for builders and users of nuclear installations and that precautions should be taken to ensure that installations are safe; finally, that the construction of the plant should not lead to any grave threat to the environment."[27] But, regardless of the jurisdiction of a given institution in the creation of the legitimating language, this language henceforth cannot elude the laws of multidisciplinary creation. All the more so as it is not just a question of formulating judicial decisions but of resolving discrepancies in the logic of the necessary and of the impossible in such a way that one is no longer led to self–contradiction, first of all, it is not dangerous, and, then, we have taken every precaution, and, moreover, there are far worse things, and, in any case, everybody else is doing the same thing. We may quote a proposition of this kind about genetic engineering: "What we fear is not that a laboratory might invent some manipulation which transforms the personality and creates a Brave New World. Besides there are already enough drugs and enough psychic techniques for this.[28]

To define a language that links the logic of the necessary and of the impossible with the languages of science, technology and society, nothing less is needed than the vast effort made to create this new discipline, STS (Science, Technology and Society), whose purpose is to produce the language that the crisis of science and society have made necessary. Thus we discover an ultimate symbolic procedure by which it is possible to manage the impossible: the creation of a new field of research whose name (STS), from the outset, already veils what may not be contemplated without a veil of words.

Notes

1. This is the situation when a new form of management develops: public management. See Romain Laufer et Alain Burlaud, Management Public Gestion et Légitimité, Dalloz, 1980.
2. "Le Pouvoir Discretionaire de l'Etat," *Cahier de l'IFSA*, Cujas, 1978, No. 16, p. 11.
3. Cf. Guy Braibant, *ibid.*, p. 60.
4. *Le Monde*, December 1980.
5. A striking example of the crisis in the relationship between the State and its double is provided by the creation of the "Conseil Constitutionnelle"; see the article by Réné de la Charriere, *in Pouvoir*, no. 13, 1980, pp. 133–150.
6. Cf. *Le Matin* dated 11th and 27th November 1980, *Le Nouvel Economiste* dated 5th February 1979, p. 30.
7. Herman Kahn, "Choix Faustien," *Futurible*.
8. R. Laufer, "Science, Technology and Society: A Conceptual Framework," *Information Privacy* No 4, November 1981.
9. Cf. I. Andrieu, "La Déontologie des Manipulations Génétiques," in *Science et Vie*, December 1980. See also *Le Monde*, dated 1st November 1978: "The U.S. moves towards the relaxation of safety regulations on genetic manipulation."
10. Cf. *Le Monde* dated 1st December 1980.
11. *Science et Vie*: article quoted above; see also *Le Matin* dated 11th August 1980.
12. Lewis Carroll, *The Hunting of the Snark*, in *The Works Of Lewis Carrol, Spring Books, Hamlyn, Feltham, Middlesex, 1965*, "If your Snark be a Snark, that is right: Fetch it home by all means—you may serve it with greens And it's handy for striking a light.'" But oh, beamish nephew, beware of the day, If your Snark be a Boojum.' For then you will softly and suddenly vanish away, And never be met with again.
13. *Science et Vie* article quoted above.
14. The material behavior of technical objects can be known only through experi-

ence. Thus, it is experience that tells us to reinforce the joint between the wheel and the axle in a particular way. It is experience that indicates the long-term effect of stresses on a complex system.

15. Cf. Daniel Saint–James, *Le Monde*, 5th April 1979.
16. *Le Matin,* 8th November 1979.
17. *Le Monde*, early October 1979.
18. *Le Matin*, 8th November 1979.
19. *Le Matin*, 16th November 1979.
20. *Le Monde*, 1st November 1979.
21. "Human Error," *Le Monde*, 4th April 1979.
22. *Le Monde*, 14th November, 1979.
23. *Le Matin*, January 1979.
24. *Ibid.*
25. *Le Matin*, 25th April 1979.
26. *Le Matin*, 8th May 1979.
27. *Le Matin*, 7th May 1979: "The Nuclear Industry: the Super–Phenix project gets the go–ahead."
28. *Science et Vie*, article quoted above.

Chapter 12

1989: Two Centuries Later.

Dissidence is good sense inasmuch as it differs from common sense.

1989, two centuries after 1789: the three estates—the clergy, nobles and commons—have become four, as is fitting. The fourth estate, which was small to begin with, has grown. Its name is the bureaucracy. The bureaucracy has such a poor reputation that its name has become pejorative in itself. To pronounce it is to denounce it. So much so that anyone who wishes to characterize the society in which we live will speak of the society of abundance, the post–industrial society, the state–monopoly capitalistic society but never of the bureaucratic society. Indeed, we have to keep reminding ourselves that Max Weber, at the beginning of this century, thought that the concept of bureaucracy designated the most rational form of human cooperation, the form that provided for the use of the bodies of scientific knowledge while, at the same time, protecting the people from the (arbitrary) power of the Prince.

Today the Bureaucrat Prince reigns and his first act of government is to search public opinion for the name he will give his own power. How can we name such a society of changing names if not by the act on which it is founded and by which it finds its name? We shall call it the "marketing society."

However, such an appellation cannot be justified completely, if it is not confronted with the store of rival denominations which have already had their day and which cry out to be used again. Now, these denominations have come to us from the history of ideology, and it is this history that we must chart from 1789 to recent times in order to try and show that the marketing society is its necessary result. But since the word 'necessity' evokes truth, we shall ask the reader who has an open mind on the diversity of opinions about truth to assume that, in the rest of this chapter, we shall act as if such a necessity and such a truth existed. Since ideology is nothing but the self–consciousness of the social subject (whoever he might be), its

273

history ought to lend itself to description according to Hegel's method, which described the world as the history of self–consciousness. Nearer to our times, Alexandre Kojève, gave a masterful description of the method in a famous seminar attended by minds as diverse as those of Georges Bataille, Jacques Lacan and Raymond Queneau. We have adopted Kojeve's approach in describing the succession and the multitude of social ideologies as developments of the dialectic between an individualistic thesis and a holistic anthithesis, as Louis Dumont put it.[1]

Adam Smith and Rousseau

Briefly, the process may be described as follows: 1789 symbolized the abolition of the three estates, which represented the (by then quite illegitimate) residue of an order that went back to the Middle Ages.[2] By this act, what was abolished was tradition as the founder of a social organization characterized by the symbolic division of tasks (prayer, defense and production) and by the hierarchy which resulted from it. This traditional order expressed its own legitimacy in the categories of the sacred and the profane, for the hierarchy ranged from the clergy (which took its origin from the sacraments and devoted itself to their perpetuation, and was thereby twice sacred) through the nobility (the King was the anointed one of the Lord: his power was also of sacramental origin but his function was of the profane order) to the third estate which belonged entirely to the profane order.

To reverse tradition was to challenge the relativity of what then appeared as merely culture. How then could a legitimate order be founded if not on nature?

But nature does not seem to require any system of legitimacy. Animals are satisfied with instinct, for this is what men, sometimes admiringly and sometimes contemptuously, name the absence of mediation which, according to them, characterizes the relationship of the animal to his action. Man himself depends on the mediation of language. To describe his relationship with what is not language, his relationship with nature, he has to find a name or more precisely two names for, since this relationship is not immediate, it cannot be designated adequately by a single word like instinct: these names are *desire* and *knowledge.*

To legitimate a culture in the name of nature is to create, on the basis of the terms *desire* and *knowledge*, a mediation by which the culture can found itself wholly on nature. This is the program achieved by the individualistic thesis which is at the origin of the story we are narrating.

To symbolize this position we shall use the name of Adam Smith because the constitution of modern political economy is the foundation on which this thesis is built.

Following this thesis, individual desire should be conceived in the categories of physics: it is equivalent to the concept of force, its accomplished form will be the concept of utility from which every trace of social psychology, sociology or history has been erased and which consequently is completely subject to nature. But this *desire*, having thus become *utility*, is not instinct, for instinct has no need to recognize itself as such, whereas man can become conscious of the fact that desire is utility only through the mediation of knowledge. In this instance, it is knowledge of political economy which shows him that, since the force of desire is exerted freely, that is in the market, the best result flows naturally from it.

This individualistic thesis is the opposite of the collective or holistic antithesis, in its complete form which we owe to Jean–Jacques Rousseau. We have left aside his point of view until now, because we were concerned above all by the development of current modes of legitimation in the western development countries which, to varying degrees, claim their authority from laissez–faire principles. Rousseau's viewpoint is an antithesis also in the sense that it is a thesis of political opposition to the dominant forces of his time. And this can be seen in his famous *Discourse on the Sciences and the Arts*, where he challenges everything that symbolized the Enlightenment. For him, the sciences and arts are the instruments of decadence and depravity. To understand this paradox, we can turn to the *Discourse on Inequality* which reveals the foundations of the project described in the *Social Contract*.

To tell a story of decadence, Rousseau must begin with man the savage. This man is quite close to the animal "given up by nature to instinct alone." At least, as far as ends are concerned, he is the equal of the animal, for in means of action he is both inferior and superior: his instinct is "perhaps" insufficient but it is supplemented by a faculty that characterizes him, perfectibility. Knowledge thus results from passions (desires) and "passions in their turn draw their origin from our needs and their progress from our knowledge." Thus there already exist the elements of a dialectic of desire and knowledge, but in the good savage it is limited by the horizon of the animal: like the animal, he does not know death at the outset of his history, or in that pre–history which constitutes the savage man, for the knowledge of death and its terrors is one of the first things that man acquires when he moves away from the animal condition. This pre–history remains outside of time: "His soul, which nothing disturbs, dwells only in the sensation of its present existence, without any idea of the future, however close that might be, and his projects, as limited as his horizons, hardly extend to the end of the day." Perfectibility may lead certain men to develop a special way of doing things, but these skills will not be transmitted and they will die with their inventor, leaving savage man in his natural state. What changes this situation is nothing less than the birth of language. It is difficult to know "which was the most necessary: society already linked to the institution of language or languages already invented at the beginning of society."

With language, society, man leaves the state of nature to enter culture, that is a state where man is confronted for the first time with his need for another man. Now this encounter is badly prepared by nature: "Whatever these origins may be, we see at least from the small pains which nature has taken to unite man through mutual needs or to facilitate the use of speech how little she has prepared their sociability."

So long as man only relates to things to satisfy his true needs, inequality remains limited, for natural needs are more or less equally distributed. At any event, equality is achieved in principle by the absence of a common measure and comparison. But once society is set up, man sees his desires perverted when another looks on them: "The savage lives within himself; social man lives always outside himself; he knows how to live only in the opinion of others." The perfectibility of his capabilities, his knowledge, technology, the development of wealth only increase the possibility of expressing this desire for recognition which forms the basis of inequality. This basis is symbolized by Rousseau in this brief myth: "The first man who, having enclosed a piece of land, thought of saying 'This is mine' and found people simple enough to believe him was the true founder of civil society."

Thus language, the right to property, the confrontation with the desires of the other and the discovery of death come together at the beginning of civil society, whose history will be the history of a fall. Desire and knowledge cannot be separated from the culture that perverted them: freedom and property, much vaunted by the individualists, far from leading to natural law and its benefits, lead to a cultural law whose goal is inequality. The reference to nature is henceforth impossible.

Only a new cultural act, initiated by the mythical figure of the legislator, can bring this story to completion: each individual will alienate itself from the general will, which will immediately be restored in what constitutes the essence of its original freedom, namely equality. By this gesture, the holistic, collective nature of society is established: "The public good or evil is not only the sum of specific goods or ills as in a simple aggregation, but lies in the links that unite them. It is greater than this sum and far from it being the case that public fidelity is established on the well being of individuals, it is its source."[3]

Individual desires and knowledge, perverted by culture, cannot by themselves provide access to legitimate order: "The people by itself always wills the good, but by itself it does not always see it. The general will is always right, but the judgment that guides it is not always enlightened. It must be made to see things as they are, sometimes as they ought to appear; it must be shown the good road it is seeking, safeguarded against seduction by particular wills."[4] Direct mediation by individual desire and knowledge cannot resolve the political question: the solution here can be found only at the collective level.

Since the essential subject of political life is henceforth society, it is on this level that it is necessary to define what could be the equivalent of a desire and a knowledge on which social relationships could be based. Such was the role that Rousseau gave the concepts of *public force* and *general will*.

The coupling of public force with the general will replaces the pairing of desire with knowledge: "As in man's constitution, the action of the soul on the body is philosophy's unfathomable gulf, so the action of the general will on public force is the abyss of politics in the constitution of the State." This abyss will be filled by the intervention of the *deus ex machina* the legislator, who comes to save the people that "wants the good it cannot see."[5]

But what source of legitimacy could be invoked by Rousseau, who does not come to point out evidence as a manifestation of nature in the manner of laissez–faire reasoning but to unveil a hidden truth, one contrary to the common sense, which he will draw forth from the relative universe of the cultural?

An additional mediation is needed to make this hidden truth fully manifest: "Since therefore the legislator cannot employ either force or argument, he must necessarily have recourse to another species of authority, one which can enroll without violence and persuade without convincing. This is why the founding fathers of nations have always had to resort to divine intervention and honour the Gods for their own wisdom, so that the people, submissive to the laws of the state as to the laws of nature, and recognizing the same power at work in the formation of the city as in the creation of man, might obey freely, and wear with docility the yoke of public felicity."

It might be noted that, if the system is completed by appealing to a divine guarantee, the God in question is one who restores the unity of nature and culture, and thus founds social order on eternal nature. The abstract nature of the explanation of these two doctrines should not give cause for surprise: a well–constructed system of legitimation is a form of logic. This logic is founded on a division of the world into two elements, namely a source of legitimacy (the sacred, nature) which is separated from what it governs (the profane, culture). 1789 overturned tradition; behind the dichotomy between the sacred and the profane, the Enlightenment revealed the presence of another dichotomy between nature and culture. Now, it is possible to found an indisputable system of legitimacy on eternal nature alone: culture is arbitrariness. But human beings are such that submission to nature would not be a sufficient argument if there were not the additional idea that such a submission is worth their while.

Therefore those who overturn tradition can do so only by the notion of a benevolent nature. For Adam Smith and his followers, it was a harmonious nature which composed individual liberties into collective providence. For Rousseau, this so–called nature was only an illusion, a product of culture. The truly good state of nature lies hidden in the human past. Man cannot rediscover this past unless culture is transformed from within so as to revert to the virtues and simplicity of this lost paradise. But behind these various representations of benevolent nature, from which the social con-tract proceeds or towards which this contract enables us to move once again, there looms the possibility that nature might be bad and that the social contract only puts the seal on the submission of frightened peoples to the tyrant.

Hobbes, who maintained this disturbing point of view, was attacked by both individualists and holists. If nature were malevolent, it would be only derisory to deprive the Leviathan of his garment of tradition. A well–constructed system of legitimacy (thesis or antithesis) is a notion so ab-stract that, as soon as the concrete workings of society are considered, one has to introduce the destructive seed of the opposite thesis: for each of these theses sees its opposite as none other than the Leviathan. Let us look at what brings thesis and antithesis together, namely what they both reject: tradition. What tradition provides for is the legitimation of constraint by inequality: hierarchy. Thus individualism and holism were to have the same motto: liberty and equality, with individualism making liberty the condition of equality and holism making equality the condition of liberty.

But how then can one legitimate the authority of a government which is compelled to be hierarchical? This difficulty exists both in individualism and in holism.

To individualism, government represents the contradictory concern of a general interest which strongly resembles the general will invoked by Rous-seau. To those who ask for submission to the general will, choosing gover-nors runs the risk of having the special interests of governors dominate the general will of which they ought to be merely the interpreters (cf. *The Social Contract*). Thus the State will be reduced to the minimum. In indi-vidualism, this restriction of the role of the general will was to be ensured by restricting the spheres of its action (justice, the police, foreign affairs, defence) and by the separation of powers (the legislative, executive and judicial powers). In non–traditional, post–revolutionary holism, the ideal solution was the participation of everyone in government (and therefore, in a sense, the dissolving of government as a separate body). Even the most realistic solutions proposed by Rousseau uphold the guarantee implied by the total absence of any representative system; the legislative function belongs to the entire people. But as soon as thought is given to the judicial and executive functions, the general will tends to be opposed by special interests (of each of the members of the government on the one hand and of these persons as a social body on the other hand): thus Rousseau speaks of "the abuse of government and its tendency to degenerate" and further on, "of the death of the public body" which, "just like the human body, begins to die as soon as it is born and bears in itself the causes of its destruction."

These two theses are no doubt basically even more abstract than has been stated until now. To found a system of legitimacy, facts must be set aside. The disappearance of the sacred, the collapse of tradition leave "natural" man at grips with his desire and with his knowledge. Legitimation systems must deny him direct mediation of his desire by his knowledge. The pragmatism implied by such a course cannot be a source of legitimation without mediation, and this mediation is precisely the business of legitimation systems. In the individualist position, pragmatism is dissolved by abstraction, which opens the way for theoretical knowledge to found the existing order as the best possible one. Thus the market will tend to hide the factory, as trees hide the forest. In Rousseau's position, the social contract is truly the realization of a pragmatic project: "What man loses through the social contract is his natural liberty and an unlimited right to all that tempts him and which he might expect; what he gains is civil liberty and the ownership of all that he possesses. To make no mistake about these compensations, we must distinguish natural liberty, which is limited only by the force of the individual from civil liberty, which is limited by the general will; and possession, which is but the effect of the force or right of the first occupant, from property which can be founded only on a positive claim." For good measure, Rousseau immediately adds the possibility of participating in a new version of Pascal's wager: "To the preceding, we might add moral liberty which alone makes man a true master of himself; for the impulse of appetite alone is slavery and obedience to the law that one has prescribed for oneself is liberty. But I have already dwelt far too much on this matter, and the philosophical meaning of the word 'liberty' is not my subject here." But if he is thus led to adding arguments whose nature is more hypothetical, it is because of his own will, the man who enters into the contract abandons his concrete condition and submits to the sovereign, who "is by nature only a legal entity with a purely abstract and collective existence." And in fact, when a material problem is put to an individual, "the matter becomes contentious and cannot be resolved by the general will, which is only one of the parties, hence subject to error. The people then no longer acts as a sovereign but as a magistrate."

While Rousseau's ideas on the different forms of government reveal an interest in the interaction of real forces, these forces can exist only around the margins of the legitimacy system, and lend to remain separate. They are destined to fade away just as, in the liberal thesis, market imbalances can only be passing phenomena which will necessarily be resolved with time.

Ideological History

Thus, following Alexander Kojève, we have stated that the starting point of this ideological history of the last two centuries was the product of a thesis and an antithesis which we have developed and which can be summarized thus: to the thesis according to which the legitimate will is the free will of the individual is opposed the antithesis according to which the legitimate will is the general will.

Henceforth, following Kojève, one could only repeat what had been said by these two pure systems of logic, until a synthesis resolved their contradiction, by bringing them together and dissolving them in a thesis which would finally be a truly new one.

There is a particular aspect about the history of the restatements of the thesis and the antithesis: unless one sticks to repeating them exactly, one is led to mix more or less skillfully (but from a logical point of view, always incoherently) bits of each discourse with the other. Furthermore, it is the beginning of this history that we saw just breaking through at the end of our development on holism and individualism. Kojève calls these mixtures *paratheses*. But there is an order to the the art of mixing two substances: one might, put more of one, more of the other, or equal amounts of both. According to Kojève one would then obtain thetic paratheses (if one has put in a lot of individualism and a little holism), antithetical paratheses (if one has put in a lot of holism and a little individualism) or again synthetic paratheses (if one has put in appreciably equal parts of holistic and individualistic propositions). The history thus narrated could be schematized as follows:

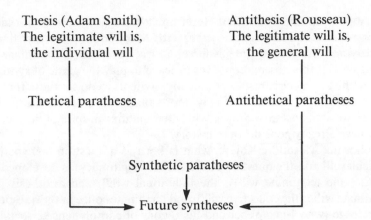

Thesis (Adam Smith)
The legitimate will is,
the individual will

Antithesis (Rousseau)
The legitimate will is,
the general will

Thetical paratheses

Antithetical paratheses

Synthetic paratheses

Future syntheses

In narrating the history of an ideology one must take the standpoint of the synthesis, whose discovery alone makes it possible to organize the "parathetical" small talk. If the synthesis is truly the Bureaucrat Prince, it must associate the theme of legitimacy with that of bureaucracy: it was Max Weber who achieved this for the first time, and without him this history would have been inconceivable.

If we must find this history an origin in modern times, let it be Machiavelli describing "this adventure of changing from a private man to a Prince."[6]

Curiously enough, individualism was to accomplish this Machiavellianism by matching private vice with public virtue, while holism was to condemn it by considering the legislator as sacred. The fact is that having eliminated history, the new individualism had nothing more to fear from its wiles.

This very history was narrated by Max Weber although he did not conceptualize it. This is because he founded a science of the social in the way that Kant founded a science of nature. On the side of the object of knowledge, he separated the phenomenon (modes of representation structured in systems of legitimacy) from the noumenon (history, power, the nature of things); on the side of the subject of knowledge he separated *understanding* from reason which provides values (axiology) to guide the research of the scientist. Thus he substitutes a "comprehensive" sociology for both the political economy of the individualist thesis and the theory of the history of the holistic antithesis.

To think history, even in the manner of a fairy tale,[7] is therefore to situate oneself in relation to Weber just as Hegel situated himself in relation to Kant, from the standpoint of the accomplished synthesis. This would be utter impertinence if Hegel himself did not come to our aid by stating that all history repeats itself, with Marx adding: the first time as tragedy and the second time as farce, a farce based on the mimicry of a tragic past. If this observation gives us leave to play the game of synthesis, certain historical circumstances actually invite us to do so: those that lead us to seek an explanation of why, more than half a century after Max Weber, we are constantly drawn to his formulations in spite of the fact that they have already gone down in history.

Following Alexandre Kojève, what is born as a question or hypothesis (Machiavelli and the question of the Prince's legitimacy) is developed as a thesis ("the legitimate will is the individual will") and antithesis ("the legitimate will is the collective will") and terminates once in the question of knowledge (with Max Weber and his theory of comprehensive sociology: "legitimacy is that which can be known") and a second time in "discursive wisdom."

This discursive wisdom draws the lesson of the story which has just been narrated: the will is legitimacy. This is a formula that includes the thesis and the antithesis and their development through history, and it therefore constitutes their synthesis. Hence the pattern of the history thus narrated is the following:

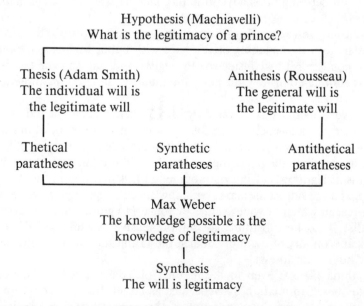

Hypothesis (Machiavelli)
What is the legitimacy of a prince?

Thesis (Adam Smith)
The individual will is
the legitimate will

Anithesis (Rousseau)
The general will is
the legitimate will

Thetical
paratheses

Synthetic
paratheses

Antithetical
paratheses

Max Weber
The knowledge possible is the
knowledge of legitimacy

Synthesis
The will is legitimacy

Narrating the history of ideology thus amounts to bringing the various paratheses into dialogue.

Thetical and antithetical paratheses meet on two points which are common to the thesis and antithesis: the rejection of all hierarchy and the abstract (non–pragmatic) character of the knowledge that founds them. On the side of individualism, this knowledge is a science of nature, economics, by which each individual, against the evidence of common sense, can recognize harmony where there appears to be nothing but strife and chance. On the side of holism, this knowledge is a science born of the dialectics of nature and culture, a science that expresses the way in which nature demoted to culture cannot return to a condition close to that of nature except by an act of culture performed by the legislator: it is therefore history and its meaning which enable individuals to escape the temptation of common sense, which would lead them to consider present constraints as (eternal) necessities.

The legitimacy of individualism eludes common sense by economic theory, which gives the political sphere its meaning, role and boundaries. The legitimacy of holism eludes common sense through the intervention of the legislator, the hero of the tale who, in acknowledging history, alters its course.

The absence of hierarchy assumes equality and liberty. Through economic theory, individualsm tends to make liberty the condition of equality (albeit equality of opportunity). For holism, the only worthwhile liberty is the liberty to alienate oneself from the representative of history (the general will) which restores the equality peculiar to the State of nature. Parathetical paratheses suffer the fate of all that seeks to reconcile contraries before it is possible to transcend them. The contradiction between thesis and antithesis leads parathetical parathesis to seek the means for reconciling them in what preceded them. Theses and antitheses rejected hierarchy in a contradictory manner, parathetical paratheses bring up the question of *hierarchy* in an attempt to reconcile them. This could lead either to the *organicism* of Saint–Simon and Auguste Comte, if the hierarchy is acknowledged to be necessary, or to the *anarchism* of Proudhon and Fourier, if the hierarchy is recognized as a danger.

Wishing to reconcile a science of nature with a science of history, parathetical paratheses will go on to develop a *concrete pragmatic knowledge* of which sociology is the model. The way by which the legitimacy of synthetic paratheses eludes common sense is to assert the possibility of producing a science of common sense itself. It is the confusion between nature and culture that explains why the pragmatic sciences and especially sociology usually have recourse to the notion of complexity to describe the world.

The essential function of parathetical small talk, like all forms of small talk, is to pass the time. It is people who have the gift of conversation that make the biggest impression here. Their role is to contribute new ways of arranging arguments. If they wish to be heard, they must take everything that has been said into account; making mixtures of mixtures, they produce new mixtures in which the proportions (of holism and indivdualism) gradually approach each other and, finally, reach the level of equal distribution which suggests that the synthesis is at hand. The numerous paths which bring Adam Smith and Rousseau to our times, through the masters, major and minor, of ideological construction, may be narrated in the manner of a story told in dialogue form.

The New Feudal Lords

To place the dialogue in its proper setting, it might be a good idea to give a quick description of the scenery and the position of the characters at the beginning of the action. "What is being played is the tragedy of a people who are unable to complete their revolution, and who keep bungling their restorations: the Directory, the Consulate, the Empire, the Constitutional Monarchy of 1814, the liberal Bonapartism of the Hundred Days. The French Revolution had been far too deeply felt as a spiritual fact for it not to impose a spiritual problem of Restoration."[8] The spiritual problem is that of establishing a well–formed system of legitimacy. There has been no lack of claimants to this role, from the successors of Adam Smith to those of Jean–Jacques Rousseau, to whom we might add the representatives of the dethroned tradition. Their thoughts are expressed in the collection of the nine Constitutions that France had from 1789 to 1816, forming a veritable logbook of the ship (of State) crisis. The antithetical character of Rousseau's thought, which opposes and protests against a previous form of thought, is illustrated by the fact that it appears explicitly only once in 1793 and then in the course of the maelstrom, a moment when values were overturned, something that was possible for a time only and only through the Reign of Terror. Henceforth the pen was to be wielded by individualists who, faced with the "indiscribable bewildering frenzy that has been called the Reign of Terror" were filled with a "deep aversion for revolutionary tyrants."[9] But the thesis does not manage to close all discussion by a constitutional writ which finally puts an end to the overthrown tradition and establishes a new order. The new feudal lords, to use Henri Gouhier's expression, challenged the emphasis laid on the letter of the law. For the Comte de Laborde, the constitutions were overthrown not because they were bad but "in spite of all of them being good"; for what is of import in a constitution, is the "unwritten but acting, active part of institutions" and the mistake lies in clinging "more to the text of the laws than to the movement that ought to guide them in their actions."[10] For the Comte de Maistre, "precisely the most fundamental and most constitutional (part) of a nation's laws cannot be written down," "What is written down is nothing."[11] What is new with the new feudal lords is that for them, too, tradition henceforth is questionable; "Whether they analyze the structure of France" like Montlosier, whether, like Bonald, they try to discover ideas drawn from the nature of society, natural ideas or whether, like Joseph de Maistre, they look for laws of 'the moral order'. . ., all agree that institutional reform is subordinate to precise knowledge of the living society for which these institutions are intended. But life extends the past into the present; order will be deciphered within a history where disorder and progress are clearly distinguished."[12]

Saint-Simon

In spite of the appeals made to "history" and "natural ideas," the new feudal lords, because they are feudal, are not directly a part of the parathetical small talk which alone is of interest to us here. Its beginning required that a Count gave up his title, make a fortune from national property, be curious about every science, in a word that he preserve all that was new in the new feudal lords and give up all that was feudal. If we add that he possessed the gift of conversation to the highest degree, we have the portrait of Claude Henri de Rouvroy, Comte de Saint–Simon who was also "Citizen Bonhomme" in 1790.

The first attempt at a synthesis was to be as chaotic as the life of his author in which he experienced the storms of history and took a passionate interest in every new thing produced by science and philosophy. Moreover, those among our contemporaries who wish to defend him admit that "Saint-Simon's thought shows very serious and even obvious weaknesses."[13] More at ease with speech than with writing, "he needed the help of secretaries (Augustin Thierry), sons (Auguste Comte) or Saint–Simonians"[14] to write his work. So much so that Henri Gouhier wrote: "Saint–Simon enters the history of ideas not by his ideas but by his magnetism; he traversed the life of Comte like a magnificent passer–by whose words touched the heart and then flew away."[15] While his work did not yield a perfectly coherent philosophy, it was the first display, and a "magnificent" one of synthetic, parathetical small conversation, and while he was unable to link and articulate its arguments completely, he discovered most of its key words: the industrial society, social sciences, sociology, industry, organization, the separation of spiritual and temporal powers, the opposition between the critical period of the revolution devoted to the task of destruction, led by the "jurists" (metaphysicians), and the constructive period devoted to the building of a new world, the importance of science and scientists, the role of scientists and philosophers in spiritual power, the role of the proletariat, etc.

Discovering the industrial society did not just mean demonstrating a genius for coining new expressions, it also meant designating a new reality: "France's industrial strength was established between 1780 and 1815."[16] This reality made it possible for Saint–Simon to oppose the individualists, the disciples of holism and the new feudal lords all at once. In contrast to the individualists, for whom civil society, governed by economic laws, had to be strictly separated from State power, Saint–Simon spoke of the transformation that industry had brought to the art of "managing public business": "the old doctrine had entrusted governors chiefly with the task of commanding, the new doctrine gave them the functions of administrating well." This administration can extend to planning. As opposed to the disciples of holism, for whom the civil society is identical with the State and merges into the unique category of the General Will, Saint–Simon maintained that reality is not found in the State, which is an abstraction, but in "the organization of the social sphere," as a system can think itself out only through "the inventions and the actions of men and social classes."[17] Finally he could differentiate himself from the new feudals lords, from whom he drew the idea of the "utility of systematic unity"[18] by substituting industry for God as the principle of unity. Scientists, the new spiritual power, rely on observation to draw up a social science capable of guiding actions.

Perhaps Saint–Simon's lack of rigour enabled him to become the source of philosophies as diverse as those of Marx, Proudhon, Comte and the famous Saint–Simonians, builders of railways and canals. However, we must turn towards Auguste Comte to grasp the synthetic parathesis in its coherence.

Auguste Comte

With Auguste Comte, the first synthetic mixture is achieved with all the purity of which such an operation is capable. The purity of the synthetic movement is first of all the consciousness of being the result of a historical evolution, then it is the substitution of sociology for history and economics, finally it is the place reserved for public opinion. Positivist history leads us from the theological to the metaphysical, and then to the scientific age, not in a gradual and peaceful sequence but through a tumultuous and ineluctable dialectic.

The theological age, the Middle Ages, possessed the formula capable of founding a legitimate hierarchy: the separation of spiritual power from temporal power. "Submission, by taking on with the character of voluntary assent, ceased to be servile; while remonstrance was no longer hostile, at least within certain limits, since it rested on a moral power legitimately constituted." It seemed that nothing could affect the fruitful understanding between these two powers if the "Western revolution" had not put the seeds of decay within each: "By bringing on the Western revolution, the entire Middle Ages left a legacy of inseparable problems: How to incorporate the spontaneously risen proletariat into modern society, to substitute demonstrable force for theologism, which was irrevocably exhausted."[19] With science questioning the legitimacy of faith precisely when the proletariat was troubling the very heart of ancestral social classifications, the way was thrown open to challenges of the established order: "During the entire course of this period (16th, 17th and 18th centuries), which may be justly described as revolutionary, all sorts of anti-social ideas were put forward and reduced to dogmas as agencies for the demolition of the Catholic and the Feudal system. . . . For example, the dogma of unlimited Liberty of Conscience was first constructed to destroy the theological power, then that of the sovereignty of the People to overthrow the temporal power, and lastly, that of Equality, to dissolve the ancient social classification."[20]

This struggle between liberty and equality heralded the coming of the metaphysical age, an intermediate age marked by a twofold ambiguity: to combat the old order, the metaphysical age had to draw its doctrine from the same order; to establish the new order, all this age had was a fighting doctrine adapted to social warfare: "Such is the primitive negative doctrine, drawn originally from theology as a means of warfare against the ancient system and which was subsequently seen as an organic idea."[21] This doctrine was none other than what we have recognized as the thesis and the antithesis in the history that we are narrating. Auguste Comte accomplished the duty of anyone attempting a synthesis: he recognized and condemned them: "The dogmas of the revolutionary camp have never stopped wavering between two contrary aberrations, individualism and communism . . . [22] the one proclaims a disorder of altruism whilst the other consecrates the preponderance of selfishness."[23] Fully recognizing thesis and antithesis implies recognizing them even in the utility of their weakness: "By an irresistible fate, the various dogmas which compose the critical doctrine were able to acquire the degree of energy essential for the complete fulfillment of their natural destination only, by assuming an absolute character; but this renders them necessarily hostile not only to the system they attacked, but to any social system."[24] For every social system assumes the existence of a hierarchy. In denying hierarchy by principle, and in letting it flow, in practice, from the play "of wealth and force," the critical doctrine proves to be incapable of constructing a legitimate order. Thus, the historical necessity of the positivist synthesis becomes obvious: "A scientific polity must therefore arise, some theory being indispensable, or we should otherwise be driven to assume the reconstitution of a theological polity since the metaphysical polity is not, correctly speaking, a true theory but a negative doctrine suitable for a transition."[25]

If positivism made it possible to prevent "theological politics" from being reconstituted, it was only by drawing from them its principle of legitimate hierarchy: "The retrograde are, at the bottom, the only persons whose theories adequately assert the dignity of human nature, since they make moral superiority the corrective and regulator of force or wealth.[26] What remained to be found was the principle on which this moral superiority could be based. The theological age was over, the feudal lords had failed. The process of thesis and antithesis had led to the triumph of reason: "All classes in the Occident, even the retrograde ones, adhere more or less to the fundamental principle of revolutionary doctrine: the supremacy of individual reason with regard to any question."[27]

The principle of this individual reason remained profoundly anarchical, since it allowed each individual to claim equal competence with the rulers: "Opponents of the absurd pretension of rulers to exclusive political wisdom have fostered among subjects the prejudice, less dangerous but equally absurd, that everyone is competent to form, by mere instinct, just views in politics, thus encouraging each citizen to set himself up as a legislator.[28] The positivist synthesis, a synthesis of two abstract theses, could only be concrete; what made it possible to found a legitimate order was that, over and above knowledge, there were scholars and scientists who could play a concrete role in social organization, not only because they knew but also because their authority was acknowledged by the public: "The intellects really competent to construct the true organic doctrine destined to end the existing crisis would therefore labor in vain unless, from their previous position, their authority was in fact recognized. . . . Thus, apart from their being the only ones competent to form the new organic doctrine, they are exclusively invested with the moral force essential to secure its recognition."[29]

Spiritual power could thus pass from the clergy to the scientific community while temporal power would pass from the feudal lords to the "leaders of industrial enterprises." This history is complete when, in putting an end to a "deplorable antagonism," positivism manages to surmount "backwardness and anarchy, which can only die simultaneously."[30] However the retrograde forces may be supposed not to have been completely eliminated; to found the legitimacy of the hierarchy, Auguste Comte could not stop with knowledge or even with the scientific community, he had to make them into a Church: this was the "religion of mankind" which irrevocably established the "fundamental separation" between "counsel and command."[31]

The metaphysical character of individualism and collectivism is thus reflected in the twofold abstraction that marks them: the abstraction of the sciences that found them and the abstraction of their view of government. Compared with the richness of sociological analysis, political economy accounts for only a minute proportion of social phenomena: "In the positive order of society, organization, whether considered as a whole or in detail, is nothing but the regulation of the division of labor, this expression being understood not in the very narrow sense given to it by economists but in the most extended sense, that is to say, as embracing all the various kinds of coexisting labors, theoretical or practical, which work together to the same end, including distinct national as well as individual functions.[32] This vision of the division of labor became compatible with history, for Auguste Comte made of its development the measure of social progress.

While the role of history was by this very fact recognized in sociology, it remained strictly limited: "Thus, whatever may be the indispensable function to be fulfilled by history in sociology in order to sustain and direct its chief speculations, we see that its use must remain essentially abstract." It is only when the birth of sociology has been completed that "the truly rational history of various individual and collective existing beings" can begin, its role being to put down "a rational sequence of markers" to indicate the stages of social progress[33] a history of progress which is opposed as much to the "individualists," who assert the primacy of the present over both the future and the past, as to the collectivists, who will thus learn that solidarity should be subordinated to continuity.[34]

In their pure expression, the thesis and the antithesis identify civil society with government. According to individualism, economic and social development devolves, in principle, entirely upon the laws of the market even if, in France especially, industrialization "was the result of the action of government, royal, revolutionary or imperial."[35] For holism, the only way to preserve the purity of the general character of the political will is to make all people participate in decisions as in actions for, as Rousseau noted, as soon as certain people are designated to fulfill the functions of a magistrature, there is the risk that their special interests will prevail over the collective interest.

For individualism as for holism, the conception of a government which supposes a hierarchy can only pose a problem. This problem is quite simply that of practice, and sociological pragmatism appropriates it in order to turn it into the essential structure of reality: "Although it may be useful and, in certain cases, even necessary to consider the idea of society, abstracted from that of government, it is universally recognized that these ideas are in fact inseparable. In other words, the lasting existence of every real association necessarily supposes a constant influence, at times directive, at times repressive, exercised, within certain limits, by the whole on the parts, in order to make them converge towards the general order from which they always naturally tend to deviate, more or less, and from which they would deviate indefinitely could they be entirely left to their own impulses.[36] This pragmatically necessary government has two modes of pragmatic action available to it: it can act on actions by "force or by wealth, which amounts to the same thing," it may act on opinions by "that moral authority which, in the last resort, belongs to intellectual superiority and knowledge."[37]

The miracle of the thesis and antithesis is to make individual desire and knowledge the source of all legitimacy while at the same time avoiding the reign of opinion. For individualism, opinion finds redemption through the market. For holism, opinion sacrifices itself in order to take rebirth purified in the general will. In each case, desire is mediated by knowledge: knowledge of the laws of the market, knowledge of the alienation of individual desires. Every man is the source of legitimacy without being the measure of all things: politics is free of Sophism. The reason for the miracle is theory. For it is only by dint of theory that the established order can be attacked: "Guided by the traditions of the fallen regime, the retrograde have, properly speaking, no need whatever of any formulated doctrine nor of any spiritual leaders. On the contrary, revolutionaries cannot move towards social progress without a theory capable of portraying the future to them and legists competent to develop it."[38]

The doctrine prepared by the metaphysicians was spread by the jurists who specialized in eloquence. Thus, with a sort of irony, Auguste Comte shows that even the critical party knew something of the dissociation between spiritual power (of the metaphysicians) and the temporal power (of the jurists). The victory of the synthetic parathesis gives the practical viewpoint primacy over the viewpoint of the absolute. However, it could not give itself up wholly to the influence of opinion: "It is doubtless absurd to claim to manage the reorganization of society by looking at it as a purely practical matter and without carrying out any necessary theoretical work beforehand."[39] Having broken with tradition (since the social structure had gradually become more plastic), the positivist power needed a doctrine: "The necessity for such a doctrine is the greater in this respect because the classification of individuals being, under this system, far more variable than in the old one, each person is thus naturally less prepared for the special function which he must fulfill."[40]

Thus the synthetic parathesis was faced with a contradiction: as a pragmatic approach to government, it must take opinion into account; as a new and moving system, it had to provide and guarantee the "government of opinion, that is the establishment and maintenance of principles which ought to preside over the various social relations."[41]

To prevent knowledge and desire from acting without mediation, since the mediation of individualism and holism had been rejected, Auguste Comte proposed to institute a dissociation between theory and practice. The practitioners of government (the command) are far too involved in practice to produce the theory (the counsel) that will guide their action. As for the people, it is good to distinguish its desires from its opinions: "It is reasonable, natural and necesary that every citizen should have political aspirations, since all have an interest in the conduct of social affairs. . . . But a political opinion expresses more than desires. It includes a judgment, for the most part decided and absolute, that these can only be satisified by particular measures and not by others." Now, it is ridiculous and unreasonable to pronounce on this count without special study."[42] Moreover when desires are considered and opinions set aside, it is perceived that a broad agreement is more easily achieved: "Regarding unenlightened men as confounding in their political estimates the end and the means, it will be seen that a greater uniformity exists than is commonly imagined in the political aspirations of a nation."[43] If we add to this point the fact that the authority of theoreticians relies above all on the credit that they have with the masses, we find that we are not far removed from what was to become, a century and a half later, the marketing society. The essential difference lies in the existence of a guild, the scientists, whose authority is laid down in the manner of a new traditional power, and in the "religion of mankind" which bears witness, after the man whom Comte called "the great Leibnitz," to the fact that, for the legitimacy of an organic and pragmatic society, God is not yet a useless hypothesis. However the positivist regime did not deny itself the use of extensive means of indoctrination, through education and the proper use of jurists, the masters of eloquence: "They will not be useless . . . owing to their means of persuasion, which they possess even more than any other class . . . they must play a powerful role in the adoption of the organic doctrine."[44]

This rigorous indoctrination makes it possible to grant freedom of opinion: "Nothing justifies the restriction by the temporal power of the freedom of discussion, since the dangers that such freedom creates in times of mental and moral anarchy can be sufficiently overcome by the spiritual power based on a complete and decisive doctrine."[45] The thesis and antithesis bring about the mediation of desire by knowledge, and thus give each individual access to reason, even if this should only lead the individual to deliberately alienate his individual freedom. The synthetic parathesis achieves the mediation of desire by a social organization of knowledge capable of accounting for desire without submitting to opinions and capable of shaping desires until they can express themselves freely.

Fourier and Proudhon

With Saint-Simon and Auguste Comte, the synthetic parathesis posed, as it must, the problem of hierarchy at the same time as it tried to look at the organization of society in a more pragmatic way. Although hierarchy can be seen to result from a pragmatic combination of the requirements of equality and liberty, it does not overcome their contradiction Saint–Simon and Comte made it possible to think the factory which the students of pure economics had forgotten, but in order to completely legitimate the hierarchy, they had to find its principle among the "retrograde thinkers." Thus to these synthetic paratheses we must add those which, while recognizing the problem of hierarchy, treat it as an evil which has to be rooted out. It was the utopian, anarchistic or community philosophy of Fourier and Proudhon that fulfilled this role.

There is something that Saint–Simon, Auguste Comte, Fourier and Proudhon have in common: this is the recognition of the social role of organization. It is in this that they all belong to the synthetic parathesis since organization is the pragmatic mediator between the individual and the collective, liberty and equality. It is a mediator because it can be used to measure what remains of each of these contradictory categories when they are associated. It is pragmatic because it assumes that in reality beings and things are arranged in a limited space instead of conceiving of itself in the unlimited space of the ideal where liberty and equality are more at ease. If there is something in common between the pairs formed by Saint–Simon and August Comte on the one hand and by Fourier and Proudhon on the other, it is that both pairs are composed of socially and morally opposite characters. Saint Simon was a nobleman, August Comte a commoner; Fourier was the son of a merchant, Proudhon the son of a worker. Saint–Simon renounced his nobility, Auguste Comte claimed his commonness; Fourier detested commerce, Proudhon worshipped labour. Saint–Simon and Fourier were as self–indulgent with their desires as Auguste Comte and Proudhon were preachers of an austere moralism.

For two beings as unlike as Fourier and Proudhon to share something, it had to be the hatred of what Saint–Simon and Auguste Comte represented. This feeling was so common to them that for once they used the same words to condemn the objects of their hatred. Saint–Simon and Auguste Comte were the representatives of "industrial feudalism" according to the term invented by Fourier and repeated by Proudhon.[46]

To struggle against hierarchy, Fourier and Proudhon both renounced the theoreticism and dogmatism of the thesis and the antithesis. Recognized as a concrete question, hierarchy was to receive a concrete and pragmatic response that accounted for all the complexity that reality revealed when the strict distinction between nature and culture was abandoned. In this complexity, Proudhon was to see the expression of a dialectic on which he had long meditated, enthusing about the antinomies of reason to be found in the *Critique of Pure Reason*. However, to remain parathetical this dialectic had to reject synthesis: "Antinomical terms do not destroy each other any more than the opposite poles of an electric cell destroy each other. The problem is finding not their fusion, which would mean their death, but their ever unstable equilibrium. . . . Their equilibrium comes not from a third thesis but from their reciprocal action." Pragmatic thinking had to accept the presence of antinomies and reject the synthesis which led to the "preponderance of the State"[47] and to the "re–establishment of authority."[48] Proudhon struggled against the shadow of Hegelianism by countering it with a dialectic that had no third term; Fourier for his part, was contented with considering complexity as the manifestation of the ambiguous.

It was from Cartesian doubt rather than from Hegelian certitudes that Fourier was to derive the principle of the subversion of all categories: "Descartes made a partial and erroneous use of doubt." He challenged emotional and palpable existence of which there is no doubt, instead of seeking the conditions of its full manifestation. The "absolute doubt and absolute divergence," on which Fourier prided himself, rejected the inhuman world built in the course of centuries, "but they consist in doubting doubt itself, in the name of the existence and the hope which reside in it."[49] Now that Descartes' provisory code of morality had become permanent, the long series of ambiguities could now spill forth without shame, "the amphibians, the orangutans, flying fish, bats, eels and many others of which the most remarkable is quicklime, the link between fire and water."[50] To the pain of Proudhon's handicapped dialectic, Fourier preferred the gentle bonds of ambiguity: nothing would be linked without the ambiguous. What Fourier and Proudhon shared here was the "synthetic" conviction of the confusion between nature and culture, of the knowing subject and the object of its knowledge. For Proudhon, "the author of economic reason is man; the architect of the economic system is still man. . . . The idea emerges from action and returns to action."[51] For Fourier, everything "is related to the convenience of man" since he accedes to the world by his existence, he locates it at the heart of movement. He founded knowledge on "a naive and comprehensive understanding, of which calculation must specify the connections. . . . The task of science is not to determine simple, linear causalities but reactions, in such a way that all is simultaneously cause and effect, and the calculations themselves enter into universal reciprocity: they transform and bring into harmony the passionate attractions which underlie them and set them moving endlessly."[52] Proudhon and Fourier are at one in rejecting hierarchy and accepting the complexity of the world. In all else, they are at odds. The reference to Descartes and Hegel indicates the opposition between the individual and the collective at the very heart of the synthetic parathesis. The side of the individual is illustrated by Fourier, who chooses desire, if not over knowledge at least over reason.

And he was to reveal the "arrangements" of reason, demonstrating them by "ridiculing the uncertain sciences,"[53] starting with metaphysics, which taught "that human reason can, by itself and without the aid of divine revelation, invent a social order which will bring happiness to human beings. . . . While the three sciences, economics, politics and morality, share God's remains, the direction of the social movement, we see reigning everywhere the three degeneracies, physical, political and moral, which attest to the degradation of humankind and to the idiocy of the sciences that it has chosen for guides. Metaphysicians, when you see this unfortunate civilization which moves from revolution to revolution, from torture to torture, what are you waiting for to make a massed attack on the three sciences which so badly fulfill God's functions which they have appropriated?"[54]

If the reason of the moralists ends in such degeneration, it is because it "campaigns against our instincts, our spontaneous desires, our passions" while it is God himself who created them. To restore Universal Harmony, it is enough to give oneself up to the here and now of this creation instead of revolting against it by trying to combat it: "It is now that we make the choice to be free."[55] Universal harmony, the paramountcy of the present, the reference to Descartes (for "absolute doubt") and to Newton (for the "law of universal attraction"), the freedom and preeminence of individual desire, all these themes would be close to the individualistic thesis were the science that founded it not totally subverted, and did the descriptions of the phalanstery not demonstrate the central place given to organization.

Far from denying hierarchy,[56] Charles Fourier transfigured it, inventing the "spherical hierarchy."[57] And if he put God at its center, it was to put the stamp of legitimacy on the science of unreason that he proposed. Certain people see in this science a foreshadowing of psychoanalysis: when the synthetic parathesis chooses to centre itself on the individal, it discovers its pragmatics: psychology, social psychology, psychoanalysis. As much as Fourier gave himself up to desire, Proudhon tried to re–establish the rights of knowledge": My mind no longer submits to anything other than what is proved to it, not by syllogisms, analogies or metaphors as in the phalanstery, but by a method of generalization which excludes error."[58] This requirement is similar to Auguste Comte's: moreover, it is from Auguste Comte that Proudhon borrowed the notion of "sociability," distinguishing among "spontaneous sociability," which is emotional, sociability as justice, and finally sociability as the "equality of conditions which has never yet been achieved."[59]

For sociability to exist, the smallest division of the social realm must already contain it. If it is not to constitute a legitimation of the hierarchy, this smallest division of the social realm must be unaware of such a hierarchy; Auguste Comte, following Bonald and Maistre on this point, had made the family the "organic molecule of society." Proudhon was to replace the family by the workshop: "If I may say so, the family is not the organic molecule of society. . . . The family is the type and the cradle of monarchy and patriarchy; in it resides and is preserved the idea of authority and sovereignty which increasingly disappears in the State . . . the constituent unit of society is the workshop."[60]

For a form of sociology to destroy hierarchy, knowledge itself should be incapable of being a factor of legitimate differentiation between individuals and groups. It is necessary to banish the positivist sociologist, who, with his knowledge, constitutes the legitimacy of his own distinctive place in society. Far from being distinctions which differentiate social groups, theory and practice are two aspects of the functioning of every social being: "The organ of collective reason is the same as that of collective force; it is the group of workers, instructors; the industrial, scientifc and artistic company; the academies, the schools, the municipalities; it is the national assembly, the club, the jury."[61]

Finally, for these organs themselves to avoid the temptation of hierarchy, it will be enough to establish the principle that the mode of organization of the future society will be based on "positive anarchy," "industrial democracy" and "workers' self–management."[62] Such a construction remains to be legitimated. Like Auguste Comte, Proudhon had recourse to progress. "Progress is the justification of humanity by itself under the incitement of the ideal."[63] Unlike Auguste Comte, he condemns all recourse to divinity; "the egalitarian morality" necessarily rejects "the scandalous thesis of the existence of a transcendant Lord, of a Master of the World."[64] Equality must reign from the cosmos to the elementary social molecule. Alone among the defenders of the synthetic parathesis, Proudhon claimed to do without God where other philosophers of industry had found it worthwhile to make him descend in the form of a *deus ex machina* in order to provide pragmatic functioning with an added symbolic guarantee. It could not, however, escape the inevitable fate by which, being unable to found the legitimacy of his system on a system of pure knowledge where nature and culture, subject and object, were properly separated, he had to resort to the existence of a common representation: "Since the reality of the State's collective force is beyond dispute, what must be considered is the spirit that animates it, its philosophy, its soul, its idea. It is by their idea that governments live or die. Let the idea come true and the State, however reprehensible may be its origins, however faulty its organization may appear . . . will be sheltered from all blows from without and from all corruption from within."[65] Hence, to show that the present State is not "true," it is necessary to produce, if not a theory, if not a God, at least a hypostasis capable of seeing the world and of judging it; this hypostasis is "collective reason" or "collective consciousness"[66] which reveals egalitarian morality to man: "Collective reason reveals that society, that pre–eminent moral being, differs essentially from living beings (individuals), in whom the subordination of organs is the very law of existence. This is why society revolts against any idea of hierarchy, as can be understood in the expression: all men are equal in dignity by nature and should become equivalent from the viewpoint of their condition and their dignity."[67] Proudhon carried the separation between hierarchical nature and egalitarian society out to the very cosmos. Far from founding morality on science as Auguste Comte did, Proudhon was to try to found the science "of society" on morality: "Get rid of property while preserving possessions; and by this single modification in principle you will change everything in laws, government, economy, institutions: you will banish evil from the earth."[68]

For those who might be shocked by the idea of encountering utopians only in a description of synthetic paratheses, since the pragmatism of the latter is opposed in principle to the idealism of the former, it must be asked whether thetical and antithetical paratheses have not also produced their own utopias. In the thesis, Utopia is excluded by the sole fact that a system of legitimacy in action is utopian in itself, it is nothing other than the ideal representation of that which is.[69] On the side of the antithesis, Utopia does exist; it consists, quite simply, in dreaming of taking the place of the thesis, that is, of dreaming of collectivist revolution of which Gracchus Babeuf was undoubtedly one of the first and most eminent representatives.

Marx

If utopians dreamed, it was because the enlightenment of reason no longer managed to keep them awake: "We have seen how the French philosophers of the eighteenth century, the forerunners of the Revolution, appealed to reason as the sole judge of all that is. A Rational Government, Rational Society were to be founded. . . . The State based upon Reason completely collapsed, Rousseau's *Contrat Social* had found its realisation in the Reign of Terror. . . . The society based on Reason had fared no better. The antagonism between rich and poor, instead of dissolving into general well–being, had become intensified by the elimination of the guild and other privileges, which had to some extent mitigated it, and by the removal of the charitable institutions of the church, which had softened it."[70] "In a word, compared with the splendid promises of the philosophers, the social and political institutions born of the 'triumph of reason' were bitterly disappointing caricatures. All that was wanting was the men to formulate this disappointment, and they came with the turn of the century. In 1802, Saint-Simon's *Geneva letters* appeared; in 1808 appeared Fourier's first work, although the groundwork of his theory dated from 1799; on January 1, 1800, Robert Owen undertook the direction of New Lanark."[71] What characterized the age of reason was arrival at a certain maturity: the individual no longer confined himself to being the object of desire and the subject of knowledge; he managed to mediate desire by knowledge, in that either it indicated to him (as did individualism) that the free play of desire necessarily established "the society of reason," or that it convinced him (as did holism) that the abandonment of individual desire to the benefit of the general will realized "the state of reason" which universally restored a desire unalienated by rivalry with the other. What the synthetic parathesis had recognized was the discrepancy between these ideals and reality. In Saint–Simon, on the one hand, this was reflected in adventures of the imagination which, noting the discrepancy between government and civil society, tried to produce the conditions of their reconciliation, while with Auguste Comte, on the other hand, it took the form of a mediation between knowledge and desire achieved through the constitution of a theory. However, this theory could not be part of the synthetic parathesis were it not a sociology which founded the legitimacy of scientists on the legitimacy of knowledge as much as it founded the legitimacy of knowledge on the legitimacy of scientists. The strict separation of desire from knowledge culminated in the sacrosanct principle of the separation of command from counsel.

With Fourier and Proudon, immaturity made its entry into ideology: the divergence between the known reality and the desired idea was pragmatically felt as a contradiction, it was denounced as an evil. Knowledge no longer managed to resolve antinomies, to dissolve ambiguities; it barely managed, by the seesaw motion of the former and the fascination of the latter, to cradle those who suffered until they could at last dream dreams: "To the crude conditions of capitalistic production and the crude class conditions corresponded crude theories. The solution to the social problems, which as yet lay hidden in undeveloped economic conditions, was supposed to spring spontenaously from the brain. Society presented nothing but anomalies; to eliminate these was the task of reason. It was necessary, then, to discover a new and more perfect system of social order, and to impose this system on society from without by propaganda and, wherever it was possible, by the example of model experiments. These new social systems were doomed to remain Utopian. . . ."[72]

The role attributed to propaganda, to opinion was already characteristic of the utopian standpoint. Individualistic and holistic theories having been criticized, the suppression of all hierarchies left each individual at grips with his own desire and his own knowledge: "With all this, absolute truth, reason and justice differ with the founder of each new school. And as each one's special kind of absolute truth, reason and justice is again conditioned by his subjective understanding, his conditions of existence, the measure of his knowledge and his intellectual training, there is no other ending possible in this conflict of absolute truths than that they shall be mutually exclusive one of the other. Hence, from this nothing could come but a kind of eclectic, average Socialism which, as a matter of fact, has up to the present time dominated the minds of most of the Socialist workers in France and England. Hence a mixture allowing of the most varied shades of opinion; a mixture of critical statements, economic theories, pictures of future society by the founders of different sects such as excite a minimum of opposition; a mixture which is the more easily brewed the more the sharp edges of the individual constituents are rubbed down in the stream of debate, like pebbles rounded in a brook."[73] Auguste Comte had been capable of assessing the political power of rigour in theory at its true value: "The various dogmas which compose the critical doctrine were only able to acquire the degree of energy essential for the complete fulfillment of their natural destination, by assuming an absolute character."[74]

Now the diversity of theories was not only the consequence of the existence of many sects, it was also the theoretical position of at least one of them, namely Proudhonism. Proudhon pointed to a distinction between the "individual, absolutist reason, proceeding by genesis and syllogisms, constantly tending, by the subordination of persons, functions and characteristics, to synthesize society" and the "collective reason . . . invariably proceeding by equations and energetically denying, as regards the society that it represents, any system."[75] And if there had to be a superior institution, a "collective reason" or a "collective consciousness," none should be able to state its law unless it existed and unless it revealed itself pragmatically in action. The reason Proudhon does not appear in the list of utopians cited by Engels is undoubtedly because of the very special relationship by which he was both tied to Marx and separated from him.

What tied them was Marx's enthusiasm for the French socialist movement and his interest in Proudhon's thesis on property and religion. It was also Proudhon's interest in Hegelian dialectics which Marx tried to inculcate in him. What separated them was in particular their fundamental, mutual opposition on the status of theory. In a letter announcing the coming publication of the *Philosophy of Poverty, a System of Economic Contradictions*, Proudhon defined his position thus: "Let us search together, if you will, for the laws of society, the mode in which these laws are fulfilled, the progress by which we are able to discover them but, for God's sake, after demolishing all *a priori* dogmatisms, let us not think in turn of indoctrinating the people . . . let us not create new tasks for humankind through new mistakes. . . . Because we are at the head of a new movement, let us not become the chiefs of a new intolerance. . . . Let us welcome and encourage all protest. . . . Let us never consider any issue as being a dead one, and when we have used our last argument, let us start again, if necessary, with eloquence or irony. On this condition, I will join your association with pleasure. If not, no."[76]

What Marx's reply, *The Poverty of Philosophy*, established was not just a difference of opinion but rather a difference in the status granted to opinion. Marx described this opposition in the way in which Proudhon dealt with both economic and philosophic categories. On the economic side: "To make the antithesis even more clear-cut, he (Proudhon) substitutes a new term, putting '*estimation value*' for '*exchange value.*' The battle has now shifted its ground and we have on one side *utility* (use value, supply), on the other, *estimation* (exchange value, demand)." Is there a point of comparison between these two contradictory forces? . . . 'Certainly,' cries, M. Proudhon, there is one: free will. In my capacity as a free buyer, I am judge of my needs, judge of the suitability of an object, judge of the price I am willing to pay for it. On the other hand, in your capacity as a free producer, you are master of the means of execution, and in consequence you have the power to reduce your expenses. . . . How can this opposition be removed so long as free will exists?"[77] This reign of opinion does not stop with economic categories, it invades philosophy by transforming it into a place of insoluble contradictions, which once again recalls the Sophists.

"Let us now see to what modifications M. Proudhon subjects Hegel's dialectics when he applies it to political economy. For him, M. Proudhon, every economic category has two sides—one good, the other bad. . . . The good side and the bad side, the advantages and the drawbacks, taken together form for M. Proudhon the contradiction in every economic category. The problem to be solved: to keep the good side while eliminating the bad."[78] Proudhon's pragmatism, through opinion and contradictions without solutions culminates in the notion of "the problem."

"Hegel has no problem to formulate, he has only dialectics."[79] Whether he dealt with economics or philosophy, as it happened a philosophy of history, Proudhon, as a good synthetic parathetician, reduced them to the pragmatic categories of sociology. This sociology is capable of expressing its desire by bringing together opinions, by appealing to common sense, namely a better, egalitarian, free and unalienated world. It is capable of denouncing what it knows of the reality of the world: opinion and common sense converge in the statement that this world is inegalitarian, unjust and alienated. For the rest, it imagines solutions. Its discourse feeds on the distinction between "expressed desire" and "perceived reality," this dual empiricism reducing the theoretical force of its arguments to virtually nothing.

For idealism and Utopia to be left behind, for the better society to exist on earth and not in the starry sky of the mind, one would have to rely on the determinisms of history themselves and not on the dreams of generous souls.

This theory of history is opposed not only to those who dissolve it in the sociology that it produces in passing; it is opposed also to those who, like Robespierre and others, took themselves for the legislators invoked by Rousseau, and tried to set up a State on the faith of the "Social Contract." In other words, Utopia lies also in seeking to bring about the end of a period come before its time: "The have–not masses of Paris, during the Reign of Terror, were able for a moment to gain the mastery, and thus lead the bourgeois revolution to victory in spite of the bourgeoisie themselves. But in doing so, they only proved how impossible it was for their domination to last under the conditions then obtaining."[80] This theory of history is quite analogous to the one sketched out by Rousseau in his *Discourse on the Origin and Foundation of Inequality among Men* which Engels called a "masterpiece of dialectics."[81]

For in the duality of theory and practice, we can see a metamorphosis of the pair formed by the general will and collective force. But while this pair concerns the entire people, theory and practice concern only each class. These two pairs therefore are similar only when society is constituted of a single class. While for Marx and Rousseau a time comes when classes (special desires inasmuch as they oppose one another) are abolished, this moment is not the product of the legislator's will alone but the result of the necessities of history.

To give a non–utopian form to the antithetical parathesis, history had to be made a science, a theory. This theory drew its logic (the dialectic) from Hegel and its categories and its reality from the economists. Hegelian dialectic could become scientific because, far from being the unfolding of the spirit over a period of time, it was the very logic by which it was possible to grasp in their development the true categories of the relationship of man to nature: the economic categories.[82] By making political economy a his-

torical science, Marx deflected the thetical argument to establish the inev-
itability of its subversion by history. This is the history of class struggle, the
struggle of classes which express economic relations which in their turn are
revealed in the political relations between civil society and government, the
latter appearing as the expression of the domination of one class by another.

Theory, as distinguished from practice, made it possible to escape the
direct mediation of desire and knowledge, and allowed practice to escape
pure pragmatism. Contrary to the viewpoint of August Comte, theory and
practice were not the prerogatives of two specialized groups. Contrary to
Proudhon's viewpoint, theory and practice were not what resulted from the
theoretical and practical activities of all. Marxism's first theoretical thesis
relates to the existence of classes, and it makes it possible to attribute this
unequivocal theory to the revolutionary class. Henceforth the antithesis
had an absolute theory capable of political effectiveness.

Far from rejecting the theses of individualism, it gives them a place in
the history of economic categories, it explains their evolution, economic
crisis, the concentration of enterprise, etc. With regard to pragmatism, it
can analyze the hierarchy existing between government and civil society as
an expression of the existence of the hierarchy among classes. Similarly, it
replaces thinking about organization and industry by a thinking about
modes of production, technical development, and the type of production
unit that is dominant at a given moment. From the standpoint of the
antithesis, it can formulate the thesis which expresses the necessary evolution of the capitalist world towards socialism and thus help in formulating
revolutionary strategies.

Theory is what enables certain people to open their eyes to the future
while others act, still blinded by the evidence of the synthetic parathetical
universe or the impatience of antithetical utopias. Henceforth the eyes that
are closed are no longer those of a dreamer but those of the mole which, as
we all know, is a stubborn burrower. In replacing the pair desire/knowledge
by theory/practice, Marxism set aside pragmatism, and with it sociology, to
constitute a science of history, the central element of which is economics.
Freed from the weight of opinion, the movement could take flight, even if
certain people, for whom the truths of class (class in itself) remained hidden, would need time and action to discover their true condition (class for
itself).

Contrary to synthetic parathesis, Marxism takes no pleasure in complexity and the concrete, it tries to bring out a (simple, abstract) knowledge that
is rigorous, in the way that political economy (which it sometimes takes as
a model) proceeds. Contrary to thetical paratheses, Marxism does not
confine itself to abstractions produced by "bourgeois political economy"; it

recombines these abstractions until it reaches the concrete, which it then takes as the starting point of its inquiry. This point is reached not in order to repeat it (as the pure empirical perception of the real), but in order to produce it as thought–out concrete reality, the result of an elaboration which allows the concrete to avoid the naiveties of pragmatism and empiricism. The "concret-pens" (thought–out concrete) of theory diverges from "concret peréu" (the perceived concrete) of common sense."[83] This "concret-pens" (thought–out concrete) belongs to the realm of thought and not that of the concrete that is produced by thought. To be an antithetical parathesis, one must reject the concrete as such (the sociological). However, before the coming of the legislator or of his time, the concrete may be interpreted on the basis of the simple categories of science which may eventually be combined so as to reconstitute the complexity of the concrete for thought. By this means, the concrete, the evident, common sense become not unrestrictedly acceptable but at least open to interpretation.

"Since the sun has shown in the firmament and the planets circled around it, no one has yet seen man standing on his head—i.e. on the Idea—and building reality on the idea."[84] The French revolution seen by Hegel was "the time when . . . the world was stood on its head."[85] Tradition gives Marx the credit for having brought the world out of this uncomfortable position by being content to put Hegel back on his feet.[86] But describing Marx as a moment in a Hegelian dialectic, even if it were a hypothetical one, might pass for a way of standing Marx on his head. Hence we must try to justify the threefold qualification given to his work: parathetical, antithetical, non–utopian.

To start with the most formidable task, it will be said that Marxism is a parathesis, namely that it is a mixture of thesis and antithesis and, thereby, it is "incoherent from the purely logical point of view."[87] Now, while one cannot raise any eyebrows by speaking of Saint-Simon's logical incoherence—there are many who consider him to be inconsistent in the very fecundity of his ideas—while the philosophy of positivism can live with and even take pride in having escaped the absolutism of logic as it preaches the triumph of the relative—and while the utopians (Fourier and Proudhon) can very well do without a rigor to which they lay no claim, the same cannot be said of Marx, who retained from Hegelianism that which will not be altered by being set back on its feet: precisely the idea of a logic.[88] If parathesis means mixture, then there is truly parathesis here since Marxism, by its own admission, results from the confluence of French socialism, British political economy and German philosophy. If paranthesis means incoherence, this incoherence could well be no more than the expression of our own incapacity to understand the dialectic, and the way in which it makes it possible to transcend contradictions. We must therefore specify what we mean here by coherence, and to do this we must recall that coherence refers to the essential characteristic of thesis and antithesis: in other words to speak of incoherence in regard to Marx amounts to confronting his philosophy with that of Jean–Jacques Rousseau.

This confrontation should turn to Marx's advantage if we consider the succession of countradictory propositions, "disadjustments" in the expression of Louis Althusser, which constitute the "Social Contract."[89] First of all there is this strange contract between two parties, the individual and the people, one of whom (the people) does not exist before the signing of the contract.[90] Then there is the strange exchange stipulated by this strange contract, by Rousseau's own admission: "What is singular in this alienation is that, far from despoiling individuals of their goods in accepting them, the community only ensures their legitimate possession of it . . . they have, so to speak, acquired all that they have given."[91] And although the individual preserves those of his goods which do not interest the community, he does so only after he has placed them at the disposal of the community. "It is agreed that all that is alienated by each person of his power, goods and liberty through the social pact is only that part which is of importance to the community, but it should also be agreed that the sovereign is the sole judge of this importance."[92] The difficulties of Rousseau's text do not stop here. The contract, which links the individual will to the general will, has nothing to fear from either. "If the citizens had no communication among one another when the people, being sufficiently informed, deliberated, the general will would always result from the large number of small differences, and the deliberation would be always good."[93] The sole enemy of the contract is the group, the "intrigues," the "partial associations," and, Althusser adds, the classes. The true special interest which can harm the general interest is "the special interest of social groups."[94] The reason the *Social Contract* is obscure is because it clearly states these "contradictions," these "disadjustments," and denies them at the same time. However, when we follow this discourse carefully, we discover a logic in it. "The disadjustment is not what Rousseau says it about it . . . but the constituting act of Rousseau's philosophy, its theoretical object and its logic."[95] However in order for a series of "theoretical difficulties" (to use Althusser's expression) to form a complete logic, there must be an ultimate proposition to resolve them.

Following Althusser, "the task of solving existing theoretical difficulties" is entrusted to practice. The solution involves removing from reality that which can no longer be avoided, namely social groups and their effects."[96]

The question raised then is whether, starting from the moment when reality is no longer avoided, that is starting from Book III of the Social Contract, which deals with government, Rousseau completes his thesis by resolving it in practice or whether, on the contrary, he embarks on the parathetical road of a thesis which is entirely contained in Books I and II.

If we choose the former interpretation, we turn the Social Contract into the incoherent discourse of a possible reality. If we choose the latter, we make the Social Contract the coherent discourse of an impossible reality. Althusser chooses the first solution: entrusting "practice" with the task of resolving the antimonies in the Social Contract, he comes upon a double dead–end: "The flight forward into ideology,"[97] by which Rousseau appeals to education and finally to religion for the control of opinion in order to "unceasingly defend and restore the 'purity' of the individual consciousness . . . in a society where it is dogged by the pernicious effects of special groups," and the "regression into (economic) reality"; and the "proposal for economic reforms which aim "at proscribing the effects of the established economic inequality"[98] so that "none may be so wealthy as to purchase another and none may be so poor as to be forced to sell himself."[99] Rousseau himself acknowledges that these proposals are only a dream, a pious wish. How can "this impossible regressive reform" be achieved if not by "moral preaching, that is by idealogical action"? Thus, for Althusser, the Social Contract ends in reality, for whose transformation it offers only "two practices, both of which are impossible": "Since we are in reality, we can do nothing but go round in circles (ideology—economy—ideology, etc.), and there is no longer any flight possible in reality itself. End of disadjustment."[100] The latter reading of the work supports the idea that the three contradictions that Althusser noted in the Social Contract (the first three "disadjustments") are resolved, not in practice as it is studied from Book III which deals with government, but in a fundamental theoretical thesis that appears in Book II, which Althusser's analysis avoids somewhat and which deals with the role of the legislator. The legislator is an eminently dialectical character since he embodies the possibility for a cultural being to become independent enough of culture to guide men towards the state of nature, or rather, since the state of nature is definitively lost, towards what most resembles it in the midst of culture, that is the state created by the social contract inasmuch as it institutes a people: "To discover the rules of society best suited to nations would require a superior intelligence which saw all the passions of men and experienced none; which had nothing in common with our nature, and knew it thoroughly; whose happiness was independent of us, and which nevertheless was willing to concern itself with ours; and finally, one which, looking to distant glory in the course of time, would be able to work in one century and reap its reward in another. It would take gods to give men laws"[101] The use of the conditional here is a telling reminder of the fact that Rousseau does not claim that such a reality exists: he merely says that it is necessary[102]

Jean–Jacques Rousseau's coherence lies entirely in the fact that, once the state of nature is left behind, there is no reality, not even an economic one, which can be seen in any way other than through culture: "How can a blind multitude, which often does not know what it wants, since it rarely knows what is good for it, by itself execute so great and difficult a project as a system of legislation?"[103] Only the legislator with his paradoxical (dialectical) characteristics can give the social body the guidance that it should desire and, if this guidance is regressive, this is because, for Jean–Jacques Rousseau, history is, until the arrival of the legislator, a process of decadence which the latter can stop only by turning towards the past. Thus, in this sense, there is no flight forward towards ideology but a return to the past with the help of ideology. Hence there is no regression in reality but progress towards the past. For Rousseau, the development of economics, like that of the arts and sciences, cannot be a progress because it produces inequality just as the arts and sciences produce the corruption of morals. What characterizes the antithesis in its pure form is its refusal to identify, mix, or even articulate the natural with the cultural. Man is in culture and has access only to culture. Although the state of nature is the historical reference, it is a hypothetical state of nature and, in a way, a prehistoric one: "It has not even entered the heads of most of our philosophers to doubt that the state of nature once existed, yet it is evident from reading the Scriptures that the first man, having received the light of reason and precepts at once from God, was not himself in the state of nature; and giving the writings of Moses the credence which every Christian philosopher owes them, one must deny that even before the Flood men were in the pure state of nature. . . ."[104] Hence, far from basing himself on the concrete, following the method proposed by Marx, Rousseau begins by "setting aside all the facts,"[105] thus displaying the love of abstraction shared by the thesis and the antithesis when they attempt to be coherent discourses. Preoccupied with making a rigorous separation between what belongs to nature and what belongs to culture (to history) in "man's present nature," Rousseau turns towards a "state of nature" which "no longer exists, which has never existed, which probably will never exist, and yet, about which it is necessary to have correct notions in order to properly judge our present state."[106]

To support the primacy of the concrete over thought, Marxism cannot confine itself to founding its theory on a hypothesis: when the anthropologist Lewis Henry Morgan furnished the description of a primitive form of communism, Marx and Engels recognized it as the material basis that their (materialistic) theory of history needed.

Marshall Sahlins, in his work "Culture and Practical Reason," shows that anthropology displays two logics: a practical logic and a signifying one. Sahlins makes the hero of the former logic none other than Lewis Henry Morgan; the latter is entrusted to Franz Boas.[107] For the former, culture is the result of an adaptation ("biological in the first stage, technological in the later") of man to his environment, a process of a natural character since "the beaver's mental qualities are essentially the same as those displayed by the human mind."[108] The latter on the contrary was to complete his meditation on society by discovering that "the seeing eye is the organ of tradition,"[109] a sentence which echos Marx's: "The development of the five senses is the work of all world history until today."[110] Here is a twofold relationship of Marxism with a "natural" anthropology and a "cultural" anthropology, which illustrates the parathetical character of his work: "Finally, in the context of the concrete analysis, Marx's notion of meaning would be positivized and functionalized. The categories as well as relations of production embody the instrumental logic of a given state of the productive forces, a logic that also has a secondary reincarnation as the functional ideology maintaining a given type of class domination. This combined play of continuity and discontinuity helps account for what I have called 'cultural and natural moments' in Marx's theory and, more important, for the evident contradiction between the social constitution of the material logic, which follows from Marx's permanent conception of a humanized nature, and his material constitution of social logic (which became the dominant notion of 'historical materialism').[111] In making a detailed analysis of the role of nature and culture in Marx's work, Marshall Sahlins is led to question the way in which economics and history are connected, and goes so far as to suggest that Marxism is a historical and utilitarian materialism in which it is possible to discover the "almost ghostly" presence of *homo economicus* and of the "bourgeois rationality" that he represents.[112]

If Marxism is really parathetical, that is a mixture of thesis and antithesis, the question that might be asked is whether it is still antithetical. The way to dose the mixture is as follows: measure the proportion of thesis by the place of political economy, the proportion of antithesis by the place of history and the proportion of synthesis by the place of sociology. To say that Marxism is an antithesis is tantamount to saying that, although economics has a bigger and more positive place in it than in the work of Jean–Jacques Rousseau (economic progress does not produce decadence but the very conditions for transcending the inequalities that decadence produces), its essential point continues to be a theory of history which reveals the cultural character of what the individualistic thesis proclaims to be natural: the laws of political economy. History is also the possibility for culture to become self-conscious, to return to its past and to free itself: the advent of the lawmaker with Rousseau, the advent of communism with Marx: "Communism is distinguished from all movements that preceded it until now by the fact that it overturns the basis of all previous relations of production and exchange and that, for the first time, it consciously treats all prior natural conditions as the creations of men who have preceded us until now, strips them of their natural character and submits them to the power of individuals." Marx substituted the proletariat for the lawmaker; he thus eliminated metaphysical intervention by a purely cultural agent "who had no relationship with our nature and who knew it to the bottom. . . ."[113] The notion of social class mixes the natural with the cultural in the same way as it links economics to history. Social classes result from the development of productive forces. Social classes produce history as the history of their struggles.

The ambiguous (natural and cultural) nature of the subject of Marxist history gives rise quite naturally to contradictory interpretations: if the emphasis is placed on nature then the result is economism, a thesis that passively gives itself over to the necessary development of the relations of production; if the emphasis is placed on culture, the result is what might be called activism, a thesis that ascribes autonomous efficiency to the development of class consciousness. These contradictory interpretations of theory were to acquire their full significance when they were confronted with practice throughout the history of the concrete application of Marxism, and this history was made necessary by the non-utopian character of Marx's work. For it was above all against the utopians that Marxism developed: the utopian discourse fed the opposition between expressed desires (for a better, egalitarian, unalienated world) and a perceived reality criticized in terms of value ("property is theft"). By this dual empiricism, the utopian remained enslaved to a consciousness alienated by history. To be freed of it, it was necessay to bar the way to the direct mediation of desire by knowledge. For want of a law given directly by the legislator, Marxism was to have the theory by which the laws of historical development could be discovered, a theory that revealed the role of the proletariat in the establishment of a classless world, that is, in the disappearance of social classes and of the division of labor: the dissolution of social mediations which until then were needed to link economics with history. Sociology faded out between the history of economics which accounted for it and the history of communism which dissolved it.

With the reintroduction of sociology into Marxism, the question may be raised of how the theory such a sociology requires differs from that of August Comte or Prudhon. In Auguste Comte, we find a theory which indicates that knowledge is a function of social position which determines practice, that is the mode of mediation of desire by knowledge. The only possible reconciliation here results from stating that certain categories (scientists) are inherently capable, by their position, of knowing, and that the others are good only for recognizing scientists and their knowledge. This recognition is essential if the knowledge of scientists is to legitimate the social order, since as it happens, the essence of their knowledge, from the standpoint of legitimacy, can be reduced to the definition of this order which designates them as knowers. Wishing to overthrow the industrial hierarchy, the thinker of the self-managed and federated workshop must give each individual equal participation in the formulation and revelation of theory. This soon leads every opinion to being as good as any other. Theory would then be reduced to the conflict of individual opinions were it not for the fact that a hypostasis, the collective consciousness, endows the anarchy of ideas with a legitimate outcome.

What Marx must produce is a mediation between desire and knowledge which eludes the miraculous character of the general will and collective force revealed by the lawmaker without falling into the relativism of the sociological view of the relationship between theory and practice. To do this it suffices for Marx to put the proletariat in the place of the lawmaker and to make theory into the theory of the existence of a class whose destiny is to recognize this theory which corresponds to its practice in order to accomplish, by its practice, the destiny that it designates. Thus constituted, theory has no accounts to render except to "the truth" from which it derives its force.[114]

Wishing to be non–utopian, Marxism exposed itself to confrontation not only with the criterion of theory but also with that of practice. The development of the antithetical parathesis is therefore the development of Marxism throughout the history of its embodiment in Russia. However, this history began only at the start of this century. We must now turn to the way in which the thetical, synthetical and antithetical discourses encounter the powerful arguments of the antithetical parathesis stated by Marx.

Pareto, Durkheim and Sorel

By this point in the game of the history of ideologies, the reader is undoubtedly familiar with its rules. He expects three authors to spring up, for example Pareto, Durkheim and Sorel. He expects to see the hero of the thetical parathesis (Pareto) entertain that privileged relationship with political economy which the hero of the synthetic parathesis (Durkheim) entertained with sociology and which the hero of the antithetical parathesis (Sorel) entertained with history. He probably also expects the proportions of these three mixtures, which are henceforth mixtures of mixtures, to approach equidistribution and hence, he expects all three of them to converge in one form or another of sociology. So much so that the economists (Pareto) and the historian (Sorel[115]) ought to be sociologists almost as much as the pre-eminent sociologist (Durkheim, founder of the first chair of social sciences in France). In this, we see already that the change from Jean–Baptist Say,[116] Auguste Comte and Marx to Pareto, Durkheim and Sorel is qualitative far more than it is merely quantitative. This is because the first three were speaking after the fall of the *Ancien Regime* and the triumph of science while the latter three were speaking after Marx, the development of socialism and the crisis of science. Pareto replied to Marx in a work devoted to socialist systems, Sorel replied to the Marxists in *Reflections on Violence*. "There is no doubt that it was a real disaster for Marx to have been transformed by young enthusiasts into the leader of a sect: he could have produced many useful things had he not been the slave of the Marxists." Finally although Durkheim kept Marx out of his major works, although he omitted Marx from his description of sociology in nineteenth-century France, he could not avoid dealing with "the definition of socialism," with the relationship between "socialism and social science" and finally with "the materialistic conception of history":[117] he even had to state emphatically that his similarities with Marx owed nothing to Marx: "As for us, we came to this point before knowing Marx, from whom we have undergone no influence whatsoever."[118] Living after Marx, whether they liked it or not, Pareto, Durkheim and Sorel came together to reject Marxism's claims to scientificness. For Durkheim, "fine, fruitful intuitions should not be mistaken for laws that are defined and methodically demonstrated . . . of all the criticisms made by M. Richard of Marx, the sharpest seemed to us to be the one that highlighted the gap between the fundamental proposition of the system and the observations on which it rested."[119] Similarly, Pareto noted that until the end of the nineteenth century, "sociology has almost always been presented dogmatically. Let us not be deceived by Comte's attaching the label *Positive* to his philosophy. His sociology is fully as dogmatic as Bossuet's in the *Discours sur l'histoire universelle*. They are different religions, but religions they are still."[120] For Pareto, science was characterized by recourse to scientific method, logical and empirical method as it happens. Sorel, for his part, found joy in separating Marx from that perspective of science, "petty science," which believes that "when it has attained clarity of exposition, it has attained truth,"[121] "useless pseudo–science,"[122] ". . . a would-be science . . . truly chatter."[123]

Curiously, Pareto, Durkheim and Sorel were also somewhat agreed in their assessment of Marxism's positive content as being mainly a myth or a religion, a myth or religion made necessary by the suffering of certain social categories: "Such discontent as existed in the Middle Ages expressed its need for reform through religious considerations and drew its arguments from the Gospel; if it existed now, it would express the same need by socialist theories and draw its arguments from Marx."[124] ". . . Socialism is above all the way in which certain strata of the population, particularly tried by collective suffering, represent themselves . . . regardless of the scientific value of the way in which its formulae are expressed. These are no more than symbols."[125] These positions are similar to those of Sorel for whom the "myth of the general strike" was the continuation of Marx's work. "Socialists must be convinced that the work to which they are devoting themselves is a serious, formidable and sublime work; . . . even if the only result of the idea of the general strike was to make the socialist conception more heroic, it should on that account alone be looked upon as having an incalculable value."[126]

Defending science against religion, Pareto and Durkheim seemed to meet on a common point of evidence, and yet, at the same time they had to acknowledge with Sorel and all their learned contemporaries that science was going through a crisis while pragmatism was triumphant. "We have nowadays abandoned all hope of discovering a complete science of nature; the spectacle of a modern scientific revolution is not encouraging for scientists and has no doubt led many people, naturally enough, to proclaim the bankruptcy of science, and yet we should be mad if we handed the management of industry to sorcerers, mediums and wonder–workers. The philosopher who does not seek a practical application of his theories may take up the point of view of the future historian of science, and then dispute the absolute character of present–day scientific theses; but he is as ignorant as the present-day physicist when he is asked how to correct the explanations given by the latter; must he therefore take refuge in skepticism? Nowadays, no philosophers worthy of consideration accept a skeptical position; their great aim, on the contrary, is to prove the legitimacy of a science, which, nevertheless, makes no claim to know the nature of things, and which confines itself to discovering relations which can be utilized for practical ends."[127] This very triumph of pragmatism led Durkheim in 1913 to devote his lectures to the relation between pragmatism and sociology: "What led me to choose the subject of these lectures? Why did I call them Pragmatism and Sociology? First because pragmatism is almost the only current theory of truth it.[128] And if we recall that, for William James, pragmatism and psychology were two complementary creations of a piece with one another, the beginning of chapter 2 of Pareto's manual of political economy, "Introduction to Social Science," underlines the absolute victory of this doctrine of the relative: "Clearly, psychology is the basis of political economy and, in general, of all the social sciences."

Whereas in Auguste Comte's time, belief in science was absolute enough for it to withstand the addition of a certain dose of pragmatism or even having its system capped by religion, by the time of Durkheim, Pareto, and Sorel pragmatism was dominant, and belief in science as the source of truth (beyond its achievements) had to be forcefully separated from the absolute reign of the useful. It is this effort not to be purely pragmatic that we shall now trace in the work of Durkheim, Pareto and Sorel. The triumph of pragmatism was contemporary with the beginnings of sociology in the university, the science of common sense became official at the same time as common sense triumphed. This simultaneity of facts provides clues to an objective complicity. Durkheim himself had to admit this: " . . . there is a sense of life and action in pragmatism which it has in common with sociology: both trends are the daughters of one and the same era."[129] Thus the task of separating them was an arduous one and "the whole duration of a year's course would not be too long. For there is a lot at stake. I do part totally, however, with the conclusions of pragmatism. It is therefore, useful to indicate the respective positions of the two doctrines. The problem raised by pragmatism is indeed of a very serious nature. We are currently witnessing an attack on reason which is truly militant and determined. . . . Pragmatism is in a better position than any doctrine to make us see the need for a reform of the traditional rationalism, for it shows us what is lacking in it."[130] The idea of "traditional" rationalism might cause amusement were it not for the fact that it was in the name of this tradition that Durkheim called on the French nation to react: "Our whole French culture is basically an essentially rationalistic one. The eighteenth century is a prolongation of Cartesianism. A total negation of rationalism would thus constitute a danger, for it would overthrow our whole national culture. If we had to accept the form of irrationalism represented by pragmatism, the whole French mind would have to be radically changed."[131] Thus it was to save tradition that Durkheim sought to defend reason, even though to achieve this he had to attack whatever was traditional in reason.

Now reason begins when tradition reveals its cultural relativity; hence it cannot be saved by remaining within a single (relative) culture. "It is not only our culture, with one exception, it is the totality of the philosophical tradition whose tendency is rationalistic, hence if pragmatism were valid we would have to proceed to overthrow the whole of this tradition." However, it would undoubtedly be too much to ask from reason, which teaches the relativity of tradition, that it should find its basis in a tradition be it a philosophical one. And this is all the more true as in the midst of this tradition there is "an exception," a real worm in the apple, an exception which is none other than sophistry: ". . . pragmatism comes close to the single exception already referred to, Sophism, which also denied all truth. This resemblance is not arbitrary and is admitted by the pragmatists themselves."[132] If we add that, following Durkheim, pragmatism finds its source in "the Anglo–Saxon environment,"[133] if we grant the equivalence between Sophistry and pragmatism on the one hand and Sophistry and marketing on the other, we might see the pragmatism combated by Durkheim as the juvenile form of what was to become the marketing society.

The advent of the marketing society marks the failure of a contradictory attempt: that of sociology, whose relativism, the enemy of tradition, seeks to rescue some absolute in the name of this very tradition that it has helped to destroy. To escape this contradiction, Durkheim (who is a champion of the synthesis) had to leave a bigger place for history and thus approach the antithesis: "It is here that we can establish a parallel between pragmatism and sociology." The "truth has to be softened" by "applying this historical point of view to the order of things human. Man is a product of history and hence of becoming. ... History begins nowhere and ends nowhere. ... Consequently, if truth is human, it too is a human product. All that constitutes reason, its principles, its categories, has been made in the course of history."[134] But to prevent the presence of history from leading too far towards the antithesis, he distinguished history as looking to the past from pragmatic history, which opens the way to the future. This retrospective history is the one which reveals tradition in its various successive forms, namely myth and science. This history knows how to stop at the threshold of the present and leave to sociology the task of dealing with individual and group projects: "There is also a science which, with the help of history, is called to play the most important part in this area. That science is sociology." How are sociology and pragmatism opposed? Pragmatism appears as the complete form of the synthetic parathesis. From the thesis (individualism), it draws its first principle of relativity: "Truth cannot be one because this oneness would be incompatible with the diversity of minds."[135] From the (holistic–historical) antithesis, it draws its second principle of relativity: " ... truth cannot be immutable because reality itself is not immutable. Hence truth changes in time."[136]

Durkheim's essential objection to this absolute relativism was that it could not account for two characteristics of truth: it is laid down as a "moral obligation," it has "a de facto necessitating power." "The true idea is binding on us. It is this characteristic that was expressed in the old theory of evidence."[137] These two traits are achieved in the "impersonal" character, that is, for Durkheim, the collective character of this representation. The usefulness of this "community of views, judgements, ideas," "was not entirely unappreciated by the pragmatists."[138] Their answer, as is proper for the heirs of the Sophists and the predecessors of the marketing men, was "the consensus of opinion" or the "stage of common sense."[139] Durkheim was to devote all his efforts to combating this proposition of pragmatism according to which " . . . the 'common truth' was the product of gradual convergence of individual judgments."[140] And he tried to do this by replacing "the will to believe" proposed by William James, the will which makes belief the result of human action by belief itself: "Myths have no essentially practical character. In primitive civilizations they are accepted for themselves, and are objects of belief. . . . They are groupings of representations aimed at explaining the world, systems of ideas whose function is essentially speculative. For a long time, myths were the means of expression of the intellectual life of human societies. If men found a speculative interest in them, it is because this need corresponded to a reality." The reference to need would contradict the concern with removing the useful if the need implied were not one of speculation for speculation's sake or again one of collective representation whose usefulness, if it exists, is mediate and not immediate.

For Durkheim, only collective history could account for the existence of "truth, reason, morality," and sociology was definitely differentiated from pragmatism by recalling that: " . . . what is social always possesses a higher dignity than what is individual. . . . The sociological point of view has the advantage of enabling us to analyze even that august thing, truth."[141] And if truth can be described as majestic, it is because its essence is in no way different from that of myth or religion: "The mythological beliefs encountered in primitive societies are cosmologies, and are directed not towards the future but towards the past and the present. What lies at the roots of myths is not a practical need: it is the intellectual need to understand. Basically, therefore, a rational mind is present there, perhaps in an unsophisticated form. . . ."[142] As for science, "speculation and practice" were "of course intermingled in the very early stages. . . . But as history progresses, scientific research loses the mixed character that it originally possessed. Science has increasingly less to do with purely technical concerns."[143]

And if scientific truths are opposed to mythological truths, it is only in the way in which organic solidarity is opposed to mechanical solidarity, in the way that contemporary society is opposed to primitive societies. Although scientific truths can be reached independently by each individual, they are nonetheless "collective representations,"[144] as are "mythological truths." And if one must find a philosopher in order to achieve the miracle "where individuals find communion in an object which is the same for all, with each retaining his personality,"[145] then it is enough to refer to Leibnitz and his monads.[146] But Leibnitz himself was never able to legitimate the structure of beliefs without placing God at its summit. Durkheim managed to do so by borrowing the "collective conscience" produced by Proudhon in opposition to Auguste Comte, and by surreptitiously putting it in the place of the God whom Comte placed at the summit of his own system. For Proudhon, if the "collective consciousness" is the object of a science, if it is a necessary hypothesis (even though each individual faces it from the position of the monad and not that of God), it is because it is the product of an absolute: *justice*, which each can experience in a practical way within the institution of the family. Far from being a family which a father rules with his patriarchal authority as if he were a pope of his own religion, society is the product of a conjunction of workshops, which consist of beings desiring the justice that they have come to know within their family, which is an "eternal institution." It is in the name of morality that Proudhon attacks God. And he is so conscious of laying down an absolute law here, that he notes in the margin of a text of Feuerbach: "Who knows if God is anything else than the force of the collectivity of beings?"[147] When Durkheim borrows the concept of collective consciousness from Proudhon, he abandons morality for science, that is, Comtean science, a science that follows the medical model and considers divergence from the norm to be not evil (or the suffering caused by evil) but illness or *anomie*.

Thus the sociologist, in relating the collective (the collective consciousness, tradition) with the individual (anomie and the possibility of mesuring it by statistics), could claim to escape from pragmatism. Instead of capping his sociology with a religion as Auguste Comte did, it was enough for him to produce, through the sociology of religion, the concept of collective representation. Perhaps he would thus manage to produce sociology as a monotheistic religion as opposed to the polytheism of pragmatism.[148] At the beginning of his lectures, Durkheim evoked Hume awakening Kant from his dogmatic slumber. By this invocation, he was trying to muster his courage in the face of his formidable adversaries, the pragmatists. But the parallel can be drawn even further. We have seen how Kant brought about the triumph in the University of that reason which had undertaken to destroy the law of Scholasticism two centuries earlier. Durkheim's establishment of a chair of social sciences in the university could well be the beginning of the return of Scholasticism to the university, a return prepared by a century of sociology which had been produced outside it by Saint–Simon, Auguste Comte, Fourier and Proudhon.

This return to the question of God can again be seen in Pareto's polytheism, which corresponds to the individualism of the thetical parathesis. To be a good champion of the thesis one must be an economist. Pareto would have had to be born fifteen years before Durkheim and Sorel to be their contemporary. This is because an economist, even an exceptionally gifted one, needs time to acknowledge the non–scientific character of his own effort.

"We imagine that in applying mathematics to political economy, the demonstration of this science would be given rigor and evidence which they lacked and that, consequently, everybody would be obliged to accept them. August Walras walked squarely into this error, not only for pure economics but also for practical questions for which he thought he could impose solutions in the name of scientific rigor. We do no need to add that he was completely mistaken."[149] From 1900 onwards, Pareto devoted himself to sociology, which he (as a thetical thinker) approached as a science founded on psychology: "It is therefore mainly feelings and interest that can be addressed in order to make men act and to make them follow the desired path. As yet, we know little about the theoretical basis of these phenomena."[150] As for practice, Pareto, as a true predecessor of the new sophists, had to develop a theory of argumentation.[151] However, he too, like Durkheim, sought to dissociate himself from the pragmatists by showing that the true is not the useful. For there are false things (myths) which are more useful than true things (scientific results). But the uselessness of scientific results (an argument already referred to by Durkheim) does not by itself account for their existence. For Durkheim they were the product of the collective consciousness. For Pareto they could only be the product of the individual consciousness. This consciousness could be described as an assemblage of instincts, needs, tendencies called "residues" (such as the instinct for groupings, sociability, sexuality, etc.). Some of these residues were related to the "need for logical development,"[152] and science is their product. And while the product of the action of these logical needs could rightfully be called scientific, this in no way implied that the product was superior or inferior in usefulness to all the non-logical products of the human spirit. In other words, while Pareto denounced the mythical character of Marxism he did not for all that underestimate its practical value. All the more so as his own science showed him that every society is structured into two social layers, one of which despoils the other. But here the analogy with Marxism ends, for Pareto believed that the socialist system would only be another modality of plunder. It would therefore be necessarily structured into social layers.

In this sense, history has no direction: it oscillates. The social categories, for their part, should be considered on the basis of the individuals who compose them and who can "circulate" among them. This circulation is that of the elites, who provide momentary stability to the system. It must be studied on the basis of the individual, the social atom, the eternal essence, the fundamental myth of the thetical position which Pareto, on the brink of pragmatism, finally retained in order to preserve the possibility of producing a truth independent of utility.

To be the representative of the antithesis (Sorel) after half a century of Marxism was to confront the theory of Marx with the practice of the

Marxists. Practice confirmed the existence of class struggle: "For some considerable time the Republicans denied that there was any struggle between the classes in France . . . the revolution was supposed to have suppressed class distinctions, wrote Joseph Reinach sadly in the 'Matin' of April 1895: but they spring up at every step . . . it is necessary to point out these aggressive return of the past, but they must not be allowed to pass unchallenged; they must be resisted."[153] Recognizing the effectiveness of socialist theory, Durkheim and Pareto fought it by denying its scientific-ness. Politicians, for their part, fought it by creating social peace and thus destroying its practical effectiveness. Thus socialists and radical socialists entered the National Assembly: "In France said Clémenceau, "the socialists that I know are excellent Radicals who, thinking that social reforms do not advance quickly enough to please them, conceive that it would be good tactics to claim the greater in order to get the less. How many names and how many secret avowals I could quote to support what I say! But that would be useless for nothing could be less mysterious."[154] Social peace was well worth the price of a few additional sacrifices. "Experience shows that the bourgeoisie is easily plundered, provided that it is made to fear the revolution."[155] Social peace was got in the Assembly, it was also got in negotiations with the representatives of the trades unions: "A more general culture and the inter–mixing with people of another region rapidly destroy provincialism: would it not be possible to destroy the corporative feeling by frequently bringing the important men in the syndicates into connection with the employees, and by furnishing them with opportunities of taking part in discussions of a general order in mixed commissions? Experience has shown that this is feasible. . . . People who are called on to intervene in disputes in this way are misled by what they have seen of certain secretaries of syndicates, whom they find much less irreconcilable than they expected, and who seem to them to be ripe for a recognition of the idea of social peace."[156] Faced with the success of theory and the failure of practice, Sorel reconsidered theory and practice. For the person who seeks the goal that theory sets for itself, the theory should be a pragmatism, a pragmatism for which theory is a contrivance that creates the desired reality. Durkheim's definition of the "pragmatic" concept was therefore perfectly suited to his vision of science. "In order to play this role, William James says, concepts do not need to be copies of objects. The word which designates them is enough to set in motion the necessary process and thus to guide our action, since it has dynamic relationships or at least potential connections. This interpretation is reminiscent of Bergson's *schema dynamique*."[157] And indeed Sorel called upon Bergson in expressing his own philosophy of science. And in Marx's theory he distinguished the tendency to form a model (a copy) of reality, what he called the share of "petty science," or utopia, which had excessively fascinated the Marxists; and the presence of the action–containing myth of the catastrophic and irremediable revolution from which there was no return, the myth of the withering away of the State. The role of passivity in the face of the necessities of history versus the role of activity, an element of economism versus an element of activism. To want to act thus was therefore to formulate this myth of the revolution or, rather, to reformulate it. It was the fate of pragmatic concepts to be replaced when they lost their efficiency. The revolution could be made impossible by the strategies of social peace, it could be made inefficient in the event that it did not destroy the State structures. If the revolution came about in a period of growth, as in France in 1789, it could prove to be a monument of conservatism, as Tocqueville showed.[158] If it came in a period of crisis and economic regression (the abandonment of economism makes this hypothesis plausible even for socialist revolution) then the heirs of the *Ancien Regime* would be seen to perpetuate its turpitudes, as happened at the end of the Roman Empire in the aftermath of the revolution which led to its Christianization: for as long as a social organization capable of preserving ideology stands, the revolution is destined to become the prey of the new State. This is why the myth of the general strike must succeed the myth of the revolution. "For a long time these myths were founded on the legend of the Revolution, and they preserved all their values as long as these legends remained unshaken. Today, the confidence of the Socialists is greater than ever since the myth of the general strike dominates all the truly working–class movement."[159]

Because it was recognized as a myth, the general strike was all–powerful: "No failure proves anything against socialism since the latter has become a work of preparation (for revolution); if they are checked, it merely proves that the apprenticeship has been insufficient; they must get to work again with more courage, persistence and confidence than before."[160] Sorel's pragmatism made division into classes the product of practice and not the result of theory. Right ideas came from practice. Just as Proudhon found the idea of justice in the practice of the family, so Sorel found the idea of class struggle in the practice of the strike within workshops. The strike equals violence, whose function is to preserve class antagonism: "To repay with black ingratitude, the benevolence of those who would protect the workers, to meet with insults the homilies of the defenders of human fraternity, and to reply by blows to the advances of the propagators of social peace, all that is assuredly not in conformity with the rules of the fashionable Socialism of M. and Mme Georges Renard, but it is a very practical way of indicating to the middle class that they must mind their own business and only that."[161] However, like Durkheim and Pareto, Sorel had to evade the radicality of the pragmatism that he proclaimed if he wished to avoid finding himself [162]in the marketing society where concepts form "an artificial world,"[163] the product of the confusion between nature and culture. To get out of pragmatism, Sorel did not invoke the non–utility of science but, on the contrary, the far greater utility of the myth, namely of the collective representation: "These artificial worlds generally disappear from our minds without leaving any trace in our memory; but when the masses are deeply moved it then becomes possible to trace the outlines of the kind of representation which constitutes a social myth." And since pragmatism and psychology go hand in hand, Sorel had recourse for his theory to a psychologist. However, it was a psychologist of crowds, a psychologist of socialism named Gustave Le Bon. The myth of the strike therefore had to be the myth of the *general* strike.

The antithetical, holistic character of the myth of a proletarian general strike becomes fully apparent when it is confronted with the political general strike: "In the first case, no detail ought to be considered by itself; in the second, everything depends on the art with which heterogeneous details are considered."[164] Hence Sorel's pragmatism owes nothing to that of politicians and sociologists: "To estimate then the significance of the idea of the general strike, all the methods of discussion which are current among politicians, sociologists or people with pretensions to political science must be abandoned."[165] To find a correct definition of the general stike, he must "question men who take a very active part in the real revolutionary movement amidst the proletariat . . . their testimony is decisive, sovereign, irrefutable when it is a question of knowing what are the ideas . . . which most appeal to them as being identical with their socialist conceptions and thanks to which their reason, their hope and their way of looking at particular facts seems to make but one indivisible unity."[166]

On its way, the theory of the myth of the general strike encounters the problem of its pragmatic realization. The proletarian strike may henceforth do without politicians, but it cannot do without myth. Is there not a danger here that the myth–making professionals will set about their task? "We cannot be suspected of seeking to carry on a kind of intellectual industry, and we protest every time people profess to confuse us with the intellectuals, who do, as a matter of fact, make exploitation of thought their profession."[167] To avert this danger, the intellectual must confine himself to listening to the workers' vanguard described above: "We have limited ourselves to recognizing the notion of the general strike."[168]

Between Durkheim, Pareto and Sorel, as transmitted to us by a brief tradition, and the authors whom we discover through "textual" reading, there is a distance that verges on paradox. A paradox which these authors themselves must have felt: "Professor Durkheim said recently, at the Société Francaise de Philosophie (February 11, 1906) that it would be impossible to suppress the religious element in ethics, and that what characterized this element was its incommensurability with other human values. . . . I do not want to discuss these propositions here. I simply cite them to show to what point the character of the sublime impresses itself on authors who, by the nature of their work, would seem the least inclined to accept it."[169] Religion, science and action used to entertain mutual relationships of demarcation, mutual exclusion or hierarchization. They have henceforth become mirrors which reflect one another. What we get then could be the useful religion of the useless, the useless religion of the useful, the science of religion, the religion of the useful, the non–scientific science of the useful, the scientific science of the useless, etc. In this game of exchanges and mirrors, distinctions which formerly founded certainty are dissolved and lost. Certainty no longer proceeds from such distinctions, it is these distinctions which henceforth proceed from belief.

Max Weber

Max Weber is the one who must be credited with having first formulated the synthesis of the thesis (the legitimate will is the individual will) and the antithesis (the legitimate will is the general will). The first synthesis is, according to Kojève, 'the question of knowledge.' Instead of asking what constitutes a legitimate will, it asks what can be known of a legitimate will. Weber replies in the manner of Kant: only the phenomenon can be known. This phenomenon is made up of the belief that certain *a priori* categories (principles of legitimacy) make it possible to understand what is meant by legitimacy. As for the unknowable, the thing–in–itself, it results from the plurality of beliefs which is such that no one can arrive at a complete picture of the world. History enables us to recognize the evolution of belief systems (legitimacy systems) which bind the believing individual to the collective representation of the world offered to his belief. This development reveals the advent of a "rational–legal" legitimacy borne by democracy. However, the extent to which these propositions on history can bind each individual depend solely on his "axiological" orientation, i.e. on his own system of values. As for the bureaucracy, we must not be surprised if Max Weber is the man who gave the world its first rigorous definition: it was the task of the synthesis to recognize bureaucracy as something which lies between the individual and the collective and which provides the model of a purely rational form of hierarchy. It is left to history to show the difficulties that the Bureaucrat Prince would encounter in getting himself acknowledged as Prince by virtue of the sole fact of being a Bureaucrat.

In the meantime, in Russia, the antithetical parathesis achieved its non–utopian nature.

Keynes and Gramsci

As long as the thesis and the antithesis remain abstract, they can exclude each other. For each of them, the other is but the Leviathan. The other is the State. The State which, for the individualist, makes the collective dominate the individual; the State which, for the holists, makes the individual dominate the collective. Thus the incarnation of the antithesis in Russia led thesis and antithesis to confront the non–utopian character of the other by placing the State at the center of their meditation. For the thesis to accept explicitly something of the antithesis without betraying itself, it had to be the work of an economist. This economist was John Maynard Keynes. For the antithesis to cope with the power of the thesis without abandoning the essence of its mission, it had to be the work of a historic political man: this man was to be Antonio Gramsci. "The analysis of the passage from the classic liberal State to the new forms of the State related to the New Deal or to fascism make Gramsci the contemporary of Keynes rather than of Weber."[170]

We have already seen how Keynes, in order to found the State as an actor of the free–market society, introduced the minimum necessary quantum of social psychology (of unemployment and of consumption) into political economy. A minimum social psychology which was enough for the State to change character and swap the repressive image of the garrison state for the more pleasing one of the welfare state. A social psychology that remained sufficiently discreet for consensus to be achieved in the name of economics. For the intervention of the State was confined to enabling the market to establish its equilibrium at the optimum level for society. While the thesis took it upon itself to achieve consensus by State action, thanks to Keynesianism, the antithesis was led to meditate on the dual nature of the State: the repressive State on the one hand and the State as ideological power on the other. For Antonio Gramsci, "the State is the whole set of theoretical and practical activities by which the ruling class not only justifies and maintains its domination but also manages to obtain the active consent of the governed."[171]

Our manner of tracing the lineage of the antithesis may cause eyebrows to be raised. To make Sorel the successor of Marx and the predecessor of Gramsci may cause some shock. How could a man who did not shy from associating with extreme right–wing groups before the First World War be the spiritual father of a man whom an extreme right–wing government imprisoned for fifteen years? How can we imagine that the anarchist whom Lenin called "a well–known muddlehead" could have contributed anything at all to a theoretician about whom a recent study says that "the Gramscian analysis of the State, because it is theoretical, constitutes a specific contribution to Marxism, to Leninism?"[172] The fact that he gave Marx as a reference is not a sufficient recommendation for Sorel, and while there is obviously a place for him in the history of anarcho–syndicalism, why should it be necessary to thereby make a place for anarcho–syndicalism in the procession of the antithesis? These are so many embarassing questions to which Gramsci himself provides an answer.

If we agree with Christine Buci–Glucksman, that "Machiavelli constitutes the phantasm through which Gramsci sees himself,"[173] then his *Notes on Machiavelli* constitute a form of self–portrait. It is therefore enough to read it: "The basic characteristic of about *The Prince* is that it is not a systematic treatment but a 'live' work in which political ideology and political science are fused in the dramatic form of a 'myth.' Before Machiavelli, political science had taken the form of either the Utopia or the scholarly treatise. Machiavelli, combining the two, gave imaginative and artistic form to his conception by embodying the doctrinal, rational element in the person of a *condottiere* who is a plastic and 'anthropomorphological' representation of the 'collective will.' . . . Machiavelli's *Prince* could be studied as an historical exemplification of the Sorelian myth—i.e., of a political ideology expressed neither in the form of a cold utopia nor as learned theorizing but rather by the creation of a concrete fantasy which acts on a dispersed and shattered people to arouse and organize its collective will."[174] There is an explicit reference to Sorel here which marks a three-fold agreement: agreement on the theory of myth, agreement on the criticism of utopia and agreement on the dual function of the State. With Gramsci as with Sorel, utopia is defined as the political theory that assumes a model to which reality must conform. If the model is taken as a guide for action, it appears in its claim to foresee and, thereby, to be science. Any presence of economism in Marxism thus appears to Gramsci, as it does to Sorel, as the presence of the germ of utopia: "Utopia consists in failing to see history as a free development, in seeing the future as an already outlined solid, in believing in pre–established plans."[175] "Political action is not directly determined by the economic structure but by the interpretation that is given of this structure and of the so–called laws that govern its development. These laws have nothing in common with natural laws; although the latter too are not established, objective facts but constructions of our thought, practical charts to be used for the convenience of study and teaching. Utopia is philistinism of the sort that Heine held up to ridicule. . . . Auguste Comte and Hippolyte Taine represent French philistinism. . . . The utopians are those who preach national, historic missions or believe in individual callings, they are those who mortgage the future and imagine that they can imprison it in their pre–established plans, those who do not conceive of divine liberty and groan constantly over the past on the pretext that events have taken a wrong turn."[176] The assertion of freedom and myth, the rejection of utopia, that encloses the vision of the future in representations of the present ideology, are made necessary by the recognition of the State's dual function of coercion and persuasion. To the forces of social peace led by the State and political society, Sorel could oppose only the violence of the civil society and the negation of the rule of the State. The sole task then became that of keeping the classes separate by maintaining confrontation in the midst of the civil society, and thereby keeping the political society separate from the civil society, politicians being denied the strike to the benefit of trade unions.

Although Gramsci accepted the questions raised by Sorel, he could not accept his answers. It is true that, soon, Sorel himself no longer knew to which State he should pledge his anarchism and, after putting his hope in the extreme right, he acclaimed Lenin's accession to power in Russia as the victory of the factory councils, the "Soviets," of which he could consider himself to be one of the first theoreticians. Coming later, Gramsci knew about the strange fate of anarchism; he knew, moreover, that, in addition to the danger of a political society which could succeed in seducing the civil society, there was the danger of political society which could establish itself against civil society when the latter was not sufficiently developed and organized and when it was incapable of producing a political party. In this constant concern with "the organization," Gramsci's arguments against Sorel sound strangely similar to those of Auguste Comte against the purely destructive philosophy of the metaphysicians: "A study may be made of how it came about that Sorel never advanced from his conception of ideology–as–myth to an understanding of the political party, but stopped short at the idea of the trade union. It is true that for Sorel the 'myth' found its fullest expression not in the trade union as organization of a collective will, but in its practical action—sign of a collective will already operative. The highest achievement of this practical action was to have been the general strike—i.e. a 'passive activity,' so to speak, of a negative and preliminary kind (it could only be given a positive character by the realisation of a common accord between the various wills involved), an activity which does not envisage an 'active and constructive' phase of its own. Hence in Sorel there was a conflict of two necessities; that of the myth and that of the critique of the myth—in that 'every pre–established plan is utopian and reactionary.' The outcome was left to the intervention of the irrational, to chance (in the Bergsonian sense of 'élan vital') or to 'spontaneity.' Can a myth however be 'non constructive'? How can an instrument conceivably be effective if, as in Sorel's vision of things, it leaves the collective will in the primitive and elementary phase of its mere formation, by differentiation, 'cleavage'—Will not that collective will, with so rudimentary a formation, at once cease to exist, scattering into an infinity of individual wills, which in the positive phase then follow separate and conflicting paths? Quite apart from the fact that destruction and negation cannot exist without an implicit construction and affirmation—this not in a 'metaphysical' sense but in practice, i.e. politically, as party program. In Sorel's case it is clear that behind the spontaneity there lies a purely mechanistic assumption, behind the liberty (free will—élan vital) a maximum of determinism, behind the idealism an absolute materialism."[177] The radical division between the classes assumed a radical split between civil society and political society which was itself related to a total split between culture (the myth) and nature (absolute materialism). It is from the dangers of metaphysics rediscovered that Gramsci was to save the antithesis by formulating a doctrine of the organic which, as we know, has to be a doctrine of the confusion between nature and culture. The antithesis, having begun with the figure of the legislator, a purely cultural being, continues with the "proletarian class" which, while it is at the same time cultural and natural, escapes from sociology and renders accounts to economics and history alone. Sorel tries to save Marxism from the dangers of economism by putting culture ahead of nature, in proposing "the myth" against "petty science." But the Sorelian myth is not sufficiently mythical to be unaware of nature. It is always "springing up" somewhere in the workshop. The myth of the general strike assumes the separation into classes which this very myth sets about creating. Dedicating itself to culture, it manages only to achieve the triumph of nature: behind the absolute culturalism of the myth lies concealed the most absolute economism.

Gramsci's work thus consists in rebuilding the links between nature and culture (through the new way in which he approaches the study of the relationship between the infrastructure and the superstructure), among social classes (by the way in which he defines the concept of hegemony, where the domination of the ruling class works by the production of an ideology capable of ensuring the consent of the population), finally between civil society and political society (by the way in which he deals with the role of the intellectuals, the point on which he is probably most opposed to Sorel). Far from being nothing but harmful exploiters of ideas, intellectuals can represent the interests of a class whose members are capable of expressing themselves only in the categories of "folklore" (tradition) and common sense by formulating the philosophy that corresponds to them. These intellectuals give civil society the means to exist in a condition other than that of submission to the state bureaucracy and to these other intellectuals who also constitute it. These intellectuals make it possible to formulate a hegemonic project whose victory will be the product neither of an immediate revolution nor of a permanent revolt but of a "war of positions," a war which will be joined by the political party, "the vanguard of every progressive historical movement ... an historical experimenter of philosophy ... a collective intellectual."[178]

Rousseau's conception of the legislator represented the superhuman effort man had to face to free himself for the very culture of which he was but a product.

The conception of theory in Marx is opposed as much to the caste of positivist scientists as to the Proudhonian notion of a theory resulting from a series of contradictory opinions. With Sorel we come closer to Proudhon's sociologism: it is in the workplace itself that the myth is created; to discover this myth, it is enough to listen to a workers' vanguard. With Gramsci we come closer to Auguste Comte's sociologism: not only can the myth be observed but it is possible to give a concrete definition of those who observe it, and it is possible to make them into the organic category of intellectuals. However, Gramsci's "Collective Prince" is not yet the "Bureaucrat Prince." His sociology is still strictly subordinated to politics. "The rise of sociology is related to the decline of the concept of political science and the art of politics which took place in the nineteenth century (to be more accurate, in the second half of that century), with the success of evolutionary and positivist theories. What is of real importance in sociology is nothing other than political science."[179] For political science to be something other than sociology, it should not be limited to the negotiation of social peace among political parties indulging in the game of alliances which Sorel condemned. Perhaps this antithetical requirement of a unity (the legislator, the class, the myth) leads Gramsci to formulate the theory of the historic bloc.[180] Thus is it guaranteed that politics "considers no detail separately" and is not confined to being "the art by which heterogeneous details are considered."[181]

Parsons, Lazarsfeld and the Sociology of Organizations

It seems that only the arrival of the synthesis can put an end to parathetical small talk. When the arguments are exhausted, the masters of conversation hold their peace, and the walls begin to speak. Throughout the world, in Germany, the United States, France, Mexico, Italy, Japan, Czechoslovakia, the year 1968 marked the beginning of the end of parathetical small talk.

On the side of the thesis, the concentration of firms, the development of State intervention, the interpenetration of the public and private sectors marked the legitimacy crisis we have examined throughout this book. On the side of the antithesis, de-Stalinization had been in progress for ten years, a sufficient time for the antithetical discourse to exhaust the joys of commenting on the works of the legislator incarnate. On the side of the synthesis, the place was free for the triumph of the marketing society, which Europe imported from the United States just as Greece once imported Sophism from Ionia. This was a reversal of the movement which had built the United States with the men and ideas of Europe. Moreover, until 1968, it was to Europe that the United States had recourse more than once in order to import some elements of the building blocks of the legitimacy system it required.

On the side of the thesis, it was Paul Lazarsfeld, a defector from the Vienna Circle, who made counting the triumphant criterion of scientificness. Who counts and what is counted do not count. What counts is the way of counting. This is the triumph of "abstract empiricism"[182] (as C. Wright Mills called it), in which the idea of science that evokes nature and from the idea of counting which, through multiplicity, evokes the idea of a possible plurality comprise the basic elements of the thesis.

On the side of the antithesis, it was Talcott Parsons who, from a visit to German universities, brought back one of the most systematic theories of American sociology. This theory diverged from the pure pragmatism of systems theory only to the extent that it assumed the existence of collective cultural values. While recognizing that "the determination of the extent of the consistency of pattern and deviation from (cultural models) in a given culture presents serious difficulties to the analyst"[183] and that "very close approximations to complete consistency in the patterns of culture are practically never to be found in large complex social systems," Talcott Parsons maintains the hypothesis that such a coherent system exists: for one of the most important functional imperatives in the maintenance of a social system is the fact that the orientations of the different actors in one and the same social system, in terms of values, should be integrated in a certain measure in a common system." It is these cultural values that education and socialization transmit from generation to generation, constituting the basis of the tradition which enables pragmatism to find its legitimacy. However, apart from cases where a symbolic structure is explicitly formulated (for example the law, systems of ideas), "explicit culture appears almost always to be fragmentary at first sight and its fragments appear to be disconnected." Furthermore, since it is not possible to remove the influence of the action of systems on the cultural system itself, we must recognize a dynamic of the theory of culture, the theory of innovation and of change which is concerned with: "The imperfections of the integration of cultural models and account for it in terms of interdependence of cultural orientations with the tensions and processes of the social system and of the personality." Since culture is thus the product of a laborious work of theory, we might wonder whether the theory put forward by Talcott Parsons (the "supreme theory" as C. Wright Mills put it) is not finally the essence of the culture it is supposed to discover. In fact, Parsons' theory, structural functionalism, is not resented as pure knowledge, it has itself "a function," hence it is itself a part of what it describes. This function is threefold: "First it should aid in the codification of our existing concrete knowledge. . . . Second (it should be) a guide to research. "By codifying, it enables us to locate and define more precisely the boundaries of our knowledge and our ignorance." Third, it should be "a point of departure for specialized work in the social sciences," a means for "the control of the biases of observation and interpretation which are at present fostered by the departmentalization of education and research in the social sciences."[184] This encoding and coordinating legislative institution, built on the model of positivism, can produce a legitimate system only if it finds a source of legitimacy for itself. While Parsons can say that "principles are the free creation of the human intellect," he immediately notes that it is to Henri Poincaré himself that we owe this definition of science.[185] And since even a "supreme theoretician" cannot claim that his imagination would have a validity in the social sciences identical to what it would have in mathematics, he is obliged to appeal to observation, measurement and the verification of hypotheses to support the relevance of his work. These principles "are useful in a practical sense . . . only insofar as they can be identified in some manner with sense data so that they can be used to predict occurrences which can be observed."[186] The foundation of the legitimacy of the "supreme theory" can therefore be found in the neo–positivism of Paul Lazarsfeld's "abstract empiricism." And, as a matter of fact, it is from Paul Lazarsfeld that the "methodology" of the only "empirical" chapter of this founding work is borrowed. For "Toward a general theory of action" could not have been concluded without some place, albeit symbolic, being devoted to empiricism: "I do not by any means maintain that the same kinds of theories which are used in physics must be used in the social sciences, but the spectacular successes of the theories in physics at least suggest that the procedure followed in these theories might be fruitful for the social sciences."[187]

Paul Lazarsfeld and Talcott Parsons are thus related directly to each other, Lazarsfeld using Parsons' codifications to legitimate his additions, Parsons welcoming Lazarsfeld in his own work to give his formulations an empirical expression. However, both seem to avoid considering the essential role of organizations in this dual work of counting and encoding. Organizations are not overlooked however by American sociology. From the side of the synthetic parathesis, the sociology of organizations has seen major developments: whether in terms of Etzioni's "complex organizations" or the cybernetic modelling of Simon, March and Cyert. 1968 marks the end of the holy alliance which defended the United States against the triumph of the marketing society. We ought to recount the end of the final elements in the "system of structured cultural symbols"[188] which gave the American consensus its legitimating significance. We shall confine ourselves to citing two examples: the end of the Gold Standard and the resignation of Lyndon B. Johnson, who acknowledged the defeat of American troops in Vietnam. The dollar is no longer "as good as gold." The United States is no longer invincible.

1968 marked a turning point in American sociology. The influence of Talcott Parsons and Paul Lazarsfeld began to yield ground to new currents in the theoretical field and from the point of view of method. For instance, in the theoretical field, a Marxist sociology developed in what was an eruption of the antithesis at the very heart of the thesis. From the perspective of method, ethnomethodology proposed to define the criterion of truth as the agreement between the knowledge produced and the common sense of the population studied. From there, the way was clear for the marketing society.

After 1968

France thinking before 1968 was the conjunction of an intellectual history, which pursued its autonomous course, with the gradual importation of productions from the United States. Michel Crozier imported the sociology of organizations Franois Bourricaud and Alain Touraine introduced Talcott Parsons's sociology of action, Raymond Boudon carried out the empirical analysis of social facts in collaboration with Paul Lazarsfeld, while the Durkheimian tradition was undergoing a revival through the work of Pierre Bourdieu.

The momentary interruption of parathetical small talk by the events of May 1968 ushered in the time of their final state: the confusion between nature and culture, the triumph of the artificial, the apotheosis of cybernetics, alone capable of describing the complexities of organizations. What marked the collapse of the thesis and the antithesis was the return of the question that they were supposed to avoid, that of the legitimacy of the hierarchy. Thus the last incarnation of the synthetic parathesis was as incapable of avoiding a two-faceted presentation as the first incarnation had been: the two facets were those of the acceptance of the hierarchy and of its rejection. In the acceptance of hierarchy, the marketing society was a distant echo of Saint-Simon and Auguste Comte. In the rejection of hierarchy it was self-management that took up the protest begun by Fourier and Proudhon. The last paradox of this long series of paradoxes is undoubtedly the fact that the Bureaucrat Prince can legitimate his hier-archical power only by declaring himself to be a partisan of self–management.

To end this history of ideology according to Kojeve's schema, there remains only to follow his argument on the synthesis, however abstract it may seem. The thesis states that the legitimate will is the individual will, the antithesis states that the legitimate will is the collective will, the first synthesis (the question of knowledge) states that legitimacy is that which can be known[189] and the second synthesis (discursive wisdom) that the will is legitimacy.

What do we mean when we say that the will is legitimacy? When we look at the past it is evident; when we look at the future, it remains an enigma.

Notes

1. Louis Dumont, *Homo Hierarchicus*, Gallimard. Holist means relative to the whole, is taken here as being synonymous with the primacy of the community as a whole, a meaning that is slightly different from the one given by Louis Dumont.
2. See G. Duby, *Les Trois Ordres et l'Imaginaire du Féodalisme*, Gallimard, 1980.
3. Rousseau, *Political Writings*, Edinburgh, Thomas Nelson and Sons, 1953.
4. *Ibid.*, p. 40.
5. *Ibid.*
6. Machiavelli, *The Prince*, Chap. VI, quoted by Pierre Manent, *Naissance de la Politique Moderne*, Payot.
7. Gerard Lebrun, *La Patience du Concept*, Gallimard, Bibl. de Philosophie.
8. Henri Gouhier, *La Jeunesse d'Auguste Comte*, Paris, Vrin, 1970.
9. Thierry Augustin, *Dix Ans d'Etudes Historique*, quoted by Henri Gouhier, *op. cit.*, Vol. III, p. 16.
10. Laborde, quoted by Henri Gouhier, *ibid.*, p. 13.
11. Maistre, quoted by Henri Gouhier, *ibid.*, p. 14.
12. Henri Gouhier, *ibid.*, pp. 14–15.
13. Ghita Ionescu, *Saint–Simon*, PUF, Bibl. Sociale, p. 89
14. *Ibid.*, p. 19.
15. Henri Gouhier, *op. cit.*, Vol. III, p. 407.
16. Henri Gouhier, *op. cit.*, Vol. II, p. 37.
17. G. Ionescu, *op. cit.*, p. 30.
18. Henri Gouhier *op. cit.*, Vol. II, p. 338
19. Auguste Comte, *The Crisis of Industrial Civilization: The Early Essays of Auguste Comte*, introd. R. Fletcher, London, Heineman Educational Books Ltd., 1974, p. 215.
20. *Op. cit.*, p. 277.
21. Gertrud Lenzer, ed., *Auguste Comte and Positivism, op. cit.*, p. 30.
22. Auguste Comte, "Appel aux conservateurs" in *Du Pouvoir Spirituel*, p. 465.
23. Ibid, p. 466.
24. Comte, *The Crisis . . ., op. cit.*, p. 217.

25. *Auguste Comte and Positivism*, 32.
26. *The Crisis . . .* , p. 225.
27. "Appel aux conservateurs," p. 454.
28. *Auguste Comte and Positivism, op. cit.*, p. 6.
29. *Auguste Comte and Positivism, op. cit.*, p. 26.
30. "Appel aux conservateurs," p. 451.
31. *Ibid.*, p. 453.
32. *The Crisis . . . op. cit.*, p. 231.
33. *Cours de la philosophie positive*, quoted by P. Arnaud, *Auguste Comte*, Bordas, 1968, p. 111.
34. "Appel aux conservateurs," *op. cit.*, p. 466.
35. Henri Gouhier, *op. cit.*, p. 37; Cf. Charles Ballot and Claude Govel, *L'Introduction du Machinisme dans l'Industrie Francaise*, Paris, Rieder, 1923
36. *The Crisis . . ., op. cit.*, p. 227.
37. *Ibid.*, p. 227.
38. "Appel aux conservateurs," p. 451.
39. "Plan des travaux scientifiques," *op. cit.*, p. 118.
40. *The Crisis . . ., op. cit.*, p. 242.
41. *The Crisis . . ., op. cit.*, p. 227.
42. *Auguste Comte and Positivism . . ., op. cit.*, p. 7
43. *Auguste Comte and Positivism . . ., op. cit.*, p.7.
44. "Plan des travaux scientifiques," *op. cit.*, p. 278.
45. "Du pouvoir spirituel," *op. cit.*, p. 327.
46. "The industrial feudalism that Fourier predicted nearly 50 years ago and whose praises were then sung by the Saint–Simonian school, now exists in effect," *Manuel d'un Speculateur a la Bourse*, 1857, quoted by Gurvitch, *Proudhon*, PUF, p. 51.
47. Proudhom, *What is Property?* quoted by Gurvitch, *op. cit.*, p. 21.
48. *Ibid.*
49. Simone Debout, *Charles Fourier*, Payot, 1978, p. 184.
50. *Ibid.*, p. 193.
51. *Ibid*, p. 200.
52. Cf. Gurvitch, *op. cit.*, p. 19.
53. Simone Debout, *op. cit.*, pp. 196–197.
54. Charles Fourier, *L'Ordre Subversif*, Aubier–Montaigne, p. 45.
55. *Ibid.*, p. 49.
56. *Ibid.*, pp. 36–37.
57. Perhaps, in order to persuade those who would regard such a definition as nothing more than an abstract concept, he draws up a table in which he has developed a hierarchy of cuckoldry wherein anyone concerned can place himself in one of 49 categories assembled in three groups of husbands: horned, slightly horned, hornified.
58. Quoted by Sainte–Beuve, *P.–J. Proudhon*, A. Costes, 1947, p. 108.
59. Gurvitch, *ibid.*, p. 32.
60. *Système des Contradictions Economiques*, p. 238, quoted by Gurvitch, *ibid.*, pp. 81–82.
61. Gurvitch, *op. cit.*, p. 40.
62. *Ibid.*, p. 46.
63. *Ibid.*, p. 30.
64. A. Vergez, *Fourier*, PUF, 1969, p. 32.

65. Gurvitch, *op. cit.*, p. 36.
66. This identification of the collective consciousness with collective reason astonishes Gurvitch, who sees it as a contradiction of the dialectical pragmatism of Proudhon; Cf. Gurvitch, *ibid.*, p. 39.
67. Quoted by Gurvitch, *ibid.*, pp. 39–40.
68. *What is Property?* quoted by Gurvitch, *op. cit.*, p. 77.
69. Pierre Rosanvalon, *Le Capitalisme Utopique,* Seuil, 1979.
70. Frederick Engels, *Utopian Socialism and Scientific Socialism*, Moscow, Progress Publishers.
71. *Ibid.*
72. *Ibid.*
73. *Ibid.*
74. *Spiritual Power, op. cit.*
75. Proudhon, quoted by Gurvitch, *op. cit.*, p. 40.
76. In Marx, *The Poverty of Philosophy*, Moscow, Progress Publishers.
77. Marx, *The Poverty of Philosophy*, Moscow, Progress Publishers.
78. *Ibid.*
79. *Ibid.*
80. Engels, *Utopian Socialism and Scientific Socialism, op. cit.*.
81. *Ibid.*
82. Hegelian dialectics becomes Marxist dialectics through a twofold process, namely the critique of Hegel by Feuerbach and the critique of Feuerbach by Marx; on this point, see *The German Ideology* and *Ludwig Feuerbach*.
83. Karl Marx, *Contribution to the Study of Political Economy*.
84. Hegel, *Philosophy of History*, quoted by Engels in *Utopian Socialism and Scientific Socialism, op. cit.*
85. F. Engels, *ibid.*
86. Tradition is represented especially by Engels, *Ludwig Feuerbach*, p. 31, and Althusser, *Pour Marx*, Maspero, 1965.
87. See the beginning of this chapter.
88. Turning Hegel on his head also meant turning Hegel's logic on its head. What remained was the notion that there was a logic of things historical: "Hegel provided his logic with a political body, he did not provide the logic of the political body."
89. On *The Social Contract*, see Louis Althusser, *"L'impensé de J.-J. Rousseau,"* in *Les Cahiers pour l'Analyse*, No. 8, Le Graphe.
90. Cf. Althusser, *ibid.*, pp. 18-19.
91. *The Social Contract,* Book I, Chap. IX, quoted by Althusser, *ibid.*, p. 26.
92. *Op. cit.*, Book II, Chap. IV, quoted by Althusser, *ibid.*
93. *Op. cit.*, Book II, Chap. III, quoted by Althusser, *ibid.*, p. 34.
94. Althusser, *op. cit.*, p. 35.
95. *Ibid.*, p. 22.
96. *Ibid.*, p. 38.
97. *Ibid.*, p. 39.
98. *Ibid.*, p. 41.
99. Rousseau quoted by Althusser, *ibid.*, p. 41.
100. Althusser, *ibid.*, p. 42
101. *The Social Contract*, Book II, Chap. VII.
102. *Ibid.*, end of Chap. VI, p. 6.
103. *Ibid.*, p. 46.

104. J. J. Rousseau, *A Discourse on Inequality*, trans. Maurice Cranston, Harmondsworth, Penguin, 1984.
105. *Ibid.*
106. Perhaps we should see the "metaphysical" (in the sense that Auguste Comte already understood this word) nature of Rousseau's thought as the reason why his work and his name appear so rarely in the work of Marx, when compared with the work and name of Adam Smith; cf. Marx, *The Jewish Question*, and Louis Dumont's commentary in *Homo Equalis*, Gallimard 1976, p. 151.
107. Cf. Marshall Sahlins, *Culture and Practical Reason*, Chicago, The University Press of Chicago, 1976.
108. L. H. Morgan, "The American Beaver and his World," quoted by Sahlins, *op. cit.*.
109. F. Boas, quoted by Sahlins, *ibid.*
110. Quoted by Sahlins, *ibid.*, p. 166.
111. Sahlins, *op. cit.*, pp. 175–176.
112. *Ibid.*
113. *The German Ideology.*
114. "Marx' theory is all–powerful because it is true" (Lenin).
115. "Socialism is a philosophy of the history of contemporary institutions, and Marx always reasoned as a philosopher of history when personal polemics did not draw him outside the laws of his system," and, further on, "history does not have to give out prizes for virtue. . . . Its role is to understand that which is less specific in events," in *Reflections on Violence*, pp. 61 and 63.
116. A liberal economist of the early nineteenth century.
117. Emile Durkheim, *La Science Sociale et l'Action*, Articles presented by Jean–Claude Filloux, PUF, 1970.
118. *Ibid.*, p. 250.
119. *Ibid.*, p. 241. ("Socialism and Social Science").
120. V. Pareto, *Sociological Writings*, New York, Praeger, 1966, p. 171.
121. Sorel, *op. cit.*, p. 208.
122. *Ibid.*, p. 206.
123. *Ibid.*, p. 209.
124. Pareto, *The Socialist System*, quoted by Julian Freund, *Pareto*, Seghers, p. 146.
125. Durkheim, *op. cit.*, p. 241.
126. Sorel, *op. cit.*, p. 202.
127. *Ibid.*, p. 220.
128. E. Durkheim, *Pragmatism and Sociology*, Cambridge University Press, 1983, p. 1.
129. *Ibid.*
130. *Ibid.*, p. 1.
131. *Ibid.*, p. 1.
132. *Ibid.*, p. 2.
133. *Ibid.*, p. 2.
134. *Ibid.*, p. 67.
135. *Ibid.*, p. 69.
136. *Ibid.*, p. 73.
137. *Ibid.*, p. 75.
138. *Ibid.*, p. 76.
139. *Ibid.*, p. 48.

140. *Ibid.*, p. 77.
141. *Ibid.*, p. 77–78.
142. *Ibid.*
143. *Ibid.*
144. *Ibid.*
145. *Ibid.*
146. *Ibid.*
147. In Pierre Haubtmann, *La Philosophie Sociale de P. J. Proudhon*, Presses Universitaires de Grenoble, 1980, p. 216.
148. Durkheim, *Sociology and Pragmatism, op. cit.*
149. Pareto, quoted by J. Freund, *op. cit.*, p. 32.
150. *Ibid.*, pp. 50–51.
151. *Ibid.*, p. 67.
152. Freund, *ibid.*, p. 86.
153. Georges Sorel, *Reflections on Violence*, New York, Peter Smith, 1941, p. 56–57.
154. *L'Aurore*, 14th August, 1905.
155. Sorel, *op. cit.*, p. 58.
156. *Ibid.*, pp. 59 and 60.
157. *Sociology and Pragmatism, op. cit.*, p.47.
158. Cf. Sorel, *Reflections on Violence, op. cit.*
159. *Ibid.*, p. 36.
160. *Ibid.*, p. 36.
161. *Ibid.*, p. 88–89.
162. *Ibid.*
163. *Ibid.*, p. 145.
164. *Ibid.*, p. 176.
165. *Ibid.*, p. 136.
166. *Ibid.*, p. 136–137.
167. *Ibid.*, p. 37.
168. *Ibid.*, p. 37.
169. *Ibid.*, p. 240.
170. Christine Buci–Glucksman, "Du Consentement comme Hegemonie," *Pouvoirs*, No. 5, 1978, p. 82.
171. Gramsci, quoted by Christine Buci–Glucksman, *Gramsci et L'Etat, Dialectiques*, Nos. 4–5, March 1974, p. 11.
172. Christine Buci–Glucksman, *ibid.*, p. 6.
173. *Ibid*, p. 7.
174. Antonio Gramsci, *Prison Notebooks, op. cit.*, p. 125-126.
175. *Ibid.*
176. *Ibid.*, p. 125.
177. *Ibid.*, p. 129.
178. Christine Buci–Glucksman, "Gramsci et l'Etat," ArtIcle quoted above, p. 17.
179. Gramsci, *op. cit.,* p. 243.
180. According to this theory, revolution results from the action of the organic grouping of intellectuals and of various fractions of classes: this grouping is called the historic bloc.
181. Sorel, *Reflections on Violence*, p. 176.
182. An expression coined by the American sociologist, C. Wright Mills, *The Sociological Imagination.*

183. Talcott Parsons, *Towards a General Theory of Action*, *op. cit.*, pp. 21–22.
184. *Ibid.*, p. 3.
185. *Ibid.*, p. 32.
186. *Ibid.*
187. *Ibid.*, p. 37. Our italics.
188. Talcott Parsons.
189. This means that our knowledge is restricted to the phenomenon. In the political and social spheres, the representations of power, the systems of legitimacy, are thus what it is given to us to know.

Conclusion

Marketing is the guiding concept we used to analyze the present state of modern society. The following four theses were explored in this respect.

1. Marketing is a fundamental social phenomenon and an expression of the present crisis in the exercise of power.

2. Marketing, which is usually associated with the dynamism of the private sector, characterizes the development of modern bureaucracies whether public or private.

3. Marketing is related in a very basic way to the intellectual foundations of our society. In defining it as the modern–bureaucratic form or Sophism, this book connects marketing directly to the history of reason in Western society insofar as this history can be considered as the continuation of the debate between Plato and the Sophists in 6th century Athens.

4. The above thesis derives from an analysis of society from the point of view of symbolic structures. This book attempts to show how such an analysis is methodologically possible using the notion of system of legitimacy.

From the point of view of understanding the world, acknowledging a crisis may be sufficient, as long as the crisis is coherently represented. However, from the point of view of our practical interests, the question of how to end the crisis cannot be avoided. Some will look to the past for an answer, as is the case of those hoping for a return to original laissez–faire capitalism, while others seek solutions in the fascinating economic prowess of Japan. As we cannot remain indifferent to their attempts, we will accompany them in their voyage through history and geography.

Between the United States and France, there is a privileged relationship which is associated with the names of Lafayette and de Tocqueville. Lafayette symbolizes what brings the countries closer together; two contemporary, interdependant revolutions with profound repercusions on world history. de Tocqueville symbolizes what separates the two countries; the distance required to know oneself.

In *The Old Regime and the Revolution,* De Tocqueville noted that the French Revolution was the most striking manifestation of a phenomenon concerning all of Europe and which was spreading like a religious movement. Today, we would undoubtedly call what spreads like a religious movement, a crisis of ideology, or even a crisis in the existing systems of legitimacy.

1789 marks the moment when rational/legal legitimacy, the basis of laissez–faire in the economy begins to conflict overtly with charisma and tradition which were characteristics of the Old Regimes. All the countries were hit by the crisis but its consequences differed in each of them. Thus, de Tocqueville noticed that England avoided a revolution such as the one that shook France: in France the aristocracy and the bourgeoisie clashed, whereas in England they formed an alliance.

In terms of ideological construct, France had to solve a particularly delicate problem, that is, found a system of legitimacy based entirely on reason. In England, given the interplay of alliances, tradition and even charisma continued to play a role in the legitimizing process. But de Tocqueville helps understand both what the revolution changed and what it did not change. What changed, and this was equally true for all the countries of Europe, was that reason was substituted for charisma and tradition as the new organizing principle. What did not change, and this affected each country in a different manner, was the extent to which tradition lasted into modern times.

By taking the influence of tradition into consideration, it is possible to understand why France and the United States interpreted the same principle—reason as the basis for the reign of natural laws—in two different ways. To provide a thorough account of this development, the following series of oppositions characterizing France and the United States respectively would have to be explored:

- longstanding unification versus recent federation,
- explicit class divisions with an aristocraty who avoided mixing with the lower orders and their activities versus a traditionally democratic society,
- absolute monarchy versus a democracy which had been liberated from English monarchy which itself was less absolutist than French monarchy,
- the dominance of Catholicism which was highly centralized and hierarchical versus that of Puritan sects which relied more heavily on individual autonomy or at least, small communities,

- Paris, an old, centralizing center of power versus numerous urban centers spread over the entire territory.

This group of well-known oppositions allows us to understand how tradition affects the form that rational/legal legitimacy takes in the two countries in terms of the conception of reason, the relative importance of the state and civil society, and the role of the private and public sectors respectively. Since the principle of reason may take different forms, the hypothesis can be made that tradition specifies the type of reason which lay at the heart of the newly constitued rational/legal legitimacy. Reason can be viewed in the Cartesian manner as in France where "I think, therefore I am" rings of "L'Etat c'est moi" or reason can be viewed empirically as Bacon, Hume and Locke viewed it in England.

Empirical reason is better suited to a country with a strong civil society where each individual contributes to building common knowledge through debate and consensus. Dogmatic reason is better suited to a strong state which finds in the unity of reason and the discourse of truth the best legitimation of its centralizing power with civil society subordinated to it. Rational/legal legitimacy assumes that the legal order is based on the separation of the private and public sector as is the case in the United States and in France; the specific form reason and civil society take in both cases explain why in France the public sector is the most legitimate and in the United States private sector is.

When a crisis of legimacy occurred as it did from 1880 to 1900, each country sought legitimacy in its most legitimate sector. France has made use of resources of legitimacy embedded in the public sector by developing the principles of the public service. These principles legitimized the development of an enormous administrative sector based on the ability of specialists to achieve objectives set by the political process on which the legitimacy of the state is based. Later in its history, France was to nationalize certain industries. The legitimization of the dominant enterprises occurred by their coming into the public sector where the ideology of public service was given the task of defining aims, principles and management.

In contrast, the United States has made use of the resources of legitimacy embedded in the private sector. This explains the existence of anti-trust laws and judges whose tasks it is to ensure that companies do not become too large. Management is given the task of applying scientific methods in implementing objectives defined in shareholders' meetings. Other aspects of this process include the development of various market-regulating bodies, the growth of non-profit organizations and foundations, and more generally, the permanent intervention of judges in all aspects of life in civil society.

Of course, management also exists in France and public spending also exists in the United States. However, these features in both countries do not have much legitimacy and do not give rise to elaborate ideological formulations. For example, in the early sixties France was obliged to import the teaching of management from the United States.

Two centuries after the French and American revolutions a crisis has begun to shake the world and seems to be spreading "like a religious phenomenon," as de Tocqueville said. 1968 marks the year in which a major symptom of this crisis developed under the form of a series of major ideological upheavals. The events of that year demonstrate that the crisis would henceforth be a world crisis and that it concerned France as well as the United States and the Eastern European countries as well as Japan.

In Western countries, the crisis is immediately recognized as a crisis of the welfare state, that is, a questioning of the systems of regulation of the private and public sectors that France and the United States established to correct what appeared in 1880 as unacceptable imperfections of the market. The attacks on public spending, regulations, and management are evidence of the concern and worry fostered by the loss of belief in continuous progress which until the sixties had bolstered systems of regulations based on positivist logic.

As in all crisis, the crisis of the welfare state has created great debate much of which focuses on the nature of the crisis and how to end it. The most commonly held attitudes spring directly from the history of the system of rational/legal legitimacy with the advocates of the welfare state on one side and the advocates of the market economy on the other. The welfare staters may have thought that the crisis was not very serious and that time as well as readjustments in the regulating, controlling and planning systems or even their strengthening would provide a solution. One illustration of this attitude can be seen in the ideas of the French Socialists when they came to power in 1981.

The upholders of the market economy tend to say that all the trouble comes from the very systems of regulation, control and planning which have been in place since the end of the 19th century. A return to an earlier phase—by privatization in France and deregulation in the United States—would be enough to re-invigorate the existing system and rekindle confidence in it. The prevalence of this attitude is apparently what brought to power Ronald Reagan in the United States and Margaret Thatcher in England.

The main argument developed in this book is that the present crisis goes much deeper than that. Therefore, no sufficient solution to it can be found either in the welfare state or in a simple return to laissez–faire capitalism. France, where the public sector has great legitimacy and where a party in favor of strengthening the welfare state came to power in 1981, offers an outstanding example of how serious the crisis of the welfare state really is.

During the period the Socialists were in power, it can be seen that the role of the two major state planning agencies in France, the Commissariat au Plan (Central Planning Commission) and the Delegation a l'Amenagement du Territoire (Urban and Country Development council) was greatly reduced rather than increased.

The nationalizing of companies went from a phase marked by the desire to develop a centralized, industrial policy to the gradual recognition of the need for autonomy of national firms and a growing confusion between public and private logic which had not been anticipated at the outset.

The idea of good management became a growing concern for nationalized companies, the unions and even public administrations. Hostile feelings towards advertising and marketing gave way to the increasing use of the logic of opinion polls and the media. This development was particularly salient in the way attitudes toward television changed moving from seeing television as the vehicle for implementing a deliberate, normative cultural policy using the existing state–run, non–profit channels to the setting up of two, new, purely commercial channels.

The socialists, coming to power on a platform which placed great emphasis on the welfare state, witnessed the advent of a veritable cult of private enterprise which began to invade the media. This period was marked by the discovery of the methods of regulation used in the United States, that is, management and regulation by competent and independent authorities. It is now France's turn to learn regulation by civil society rather than public administration.

Given the difference between France and the United States, it was normal that, in France, the welfare-state crisis, or to be more precise, the crisis of the positivist modes of regulation of economic and social processes should express itself in a different manner than in the United States. Thus, the question of nationalization or denationalization in France is the equivalent of question of deregulation or of the questioning of management in the United States. The symbol of deregulation is undoubtedly the putting into question anti-trust legislation which re-legitimized the natural laws of market, threatened by the excessive power of a few large companies. The symbol of the putting into question of management, is, beyond the ecology or consumer movements, the existence of a growing number of takeover bids and the resulting debate on the "raiders". The question here is whether the raiders are rendering justice by restoring power to shareholders which bureaucrats had confiscated or if they are "bad guys" who by ambush or

"Greenmail" are forcing managers to defend the independence of their firms in the short run thereby making them unable to take risky, long-term decisions in the face of Japanese competition.

Confronted with the crisis, France tried as a last resort to get the help of the upholders of the welfare state hoping that they would know how to implement a system that the supporters of the free market, then in power (Giscard d'Estaing's government), were only timidly managing. The result was growing awareness of the limits of the solutions available to the welfare state. Similarly, the United States has counted on the assistance of laissez–faire advocates hoping they would know how to impliment a system that the supporters of state intervention (the Carter administration) were managing reticently. The hypothesis of this book, related to the crisis of legitimacy of the rational/legal system, suggests that by doing this, the United States could very well be the perfect example of the limits of relying on laissez–faire logic.

Not being in a position to foretell the future, it is, however, possible to define some of the areas where the crisis of laissez-faire is present. We limit ourselves to citing the four below:

1. Public administration:

   The limits of the free-market system can be seen in the increase in public spending and the budget deficit.

2. Private administration:

   - Managerial efficiency suffers from the difficulty of forecasting and planning at a time when the investment in research and technology required to meet competition demand more and more money and time.
   - Also it is confronted with the dangers of bureaucratization. (We have already mentioned this as regards the activities of the "raiders." Other aspects include a large portion of managerial literature ranging from "management by walking around" to quality circles which attempt to give managers the marks of excellence which their traditional knowledge as "scientific managers" can no longer guarantee).

3. Deregulation: In deregulating markets the crisis results from numerous contradictory tensions between the desire to liberate certain markets and the need to control them. The tension between freedom and control is especially acute in issues such as the growing computerization of society, genetics, problems raised by ecological disasters such as Three

Mile Island and Bhopal and even the regulation of market processes themselves. The latter concerns the reform of anti–trust laws and stock–market regulation with respect to such practices as insider trading. Insider trading raises the question of defining precisely what is meant by inside information when a firm is so large that its limits are hard to define. The reform of the anti–trust law also poses the question of limits. Should competition be measured within a country, i.e., the United States or on a worldwide scale? In the first view, a judge dealing with an anti–trust case works within national legislation in order to measure and define the size of a firm in order to guarantee necessary competition. If firms become too large to be dealt with in this manner at the natural level one has to turn to a second view according to which the problem has to be considered at the level of world markets—this is not without consequences for the range of national sovereignty.

4. International relations: The foregoing leads us directly to the question of international relations, one of the areas where the crisis of laissez–faire should appear most blatantly. Here the universal nature of market mechanisms and the national characteristic of public sovereignty and its interests are in opposition. Thus protectionist measures, economic agreements on the organization of international markets and international agreements between huge corporations of all countries, as in the car and telecommunications industries, are in opposition to the ideal of free competition leading the world to optimum performance. One example of the crisis of laissez–faire capitalism can be found in the U.S./ Japan agreement on electronic components signed in 1986.

The analysis of the present crisis as a crisis of the rational/legal system of legitimacy explains why neither recourse to laissez–faire nor recourse to the welfare state, which are two expressions of legitimate rational/legal power, can solve the crisis we are undergoing.

When we dealt with laissez–faire and the welfare state, our analysis only covered Western democracies. It is undoubtedly logical to turn to the third form that the rational/legal system can take, that is, the holistic or collectivist conception of legitimacy.

Although most of the analyses in this book deal with Western democracies, the analysis of the history of ideology in the last chapter demonstrates the way the history of Marxism can be viewed as the antithesis of the history of the Western world. We have even shown how in the works of Marx, Sorel and Gramsci, this antithesis followed a course parallel to the history of liberal ideology and its amendments. The fate of holism in the countries which chose it as the founding doctrine of their constitutions has not been discussed due to the length to the subject.

If the history of the rational/legal system in Western countries can be

conceived as the result of a debate between the dominant thesis of individualism and the subordinate thesis of holism, it is valid to ask if the choice of
holism as the dominant thesis made in Eastern European countries may
preclude a crisis of reason in those same countries.

Precise answer to this question requires an in-depth study of the history
of the successive phases of the ideological debate in the Soviet Union. Such
a study would explore how a dominant thesis in which political action
played the dominant part was in opposition to an antithesis which placed
greater emphasis on economic determinism. This would involve examining the way the Bolcheviks were pitted against the Mencheviks during the
Russian Revolution and how war communism was in opposition to the
NEP which followed it. The notion of crisis of legitimacy, could be illustrated by the de-Stalinization process which was officially proclaimed in
Nikita Kroutchev's famous speech at the 20th Congress of the Soviet
Union's Communist Party.

Such a study is beyond the scope of this book. However, a certain
number of symptoms can be identified which reveal that Communist
countries are affected by an ideological crisis similar to the one in the West.
In Hungary, management is now being taught while Poland has joined the
IMF. In China there has been a bankruptcy—officially recognized as
such—followed by lay-offs, private ownership of capital stock has begun
and Chinese students are being sent to Western schools to study management. In the Soviet Union, small, privately owned companies have been
legalized. Gorbatchev's coming to power in the Soviet Union may also be
interpreted as a symptom of the crisis due as much to the stringent criticism he seems to be making of the evils of bureaucracy as to the "new
look" of his political behavior based on techniques such as seduction
through communication, the use of opinion polls and crowd-mingling.
The repercussions of the Chernobyl atomic power plant accident also seem
to point in this direction. At first, Soviet authorities were very reticent and
secretive about the affair and then began an intensive communication
campaign at home and abroad. This reversal of the way the Soviet Union
treats news events, along with the severe criticism of bureaucracy which
accompanied it, led to the much publicized firing of high-level bureaucrats.

It should be remarked that the changes in all the countries mentioned
have occurred concommitantly with considerable development of commercial advertising which apparently confirms the association we have
attempted to show between the crisis of rational/legal legitimacy and the
advent of marketing.

If charisma, tradition and reason are the three principles on which a
system of legitimacy can be founded, then the crisis of reason leads individ-

uals and organizations to turn increasingly to tradition and charisma to legitimize themselves.

The return to tradition can take two forms depending on whether it takes place within the history of rational/legal legitimacy or outside it, drawing directly on the traditions preceding it. Rational/legal legitimacy is based on the separation between nature and culture and on the subordination of culture to nature. The crisis of rational/legal legitimacy stems from the growing confusion which has arisen between nature and culture. One way to re–legitimize the system without going beyond the discourse of reason consists in a return to the sources of this system, i.e. the reign of the laws of nature. Neo–laissez-faire capitalism, recourse to the laws of the market, the rejection of public administration, the criticism of welfare, the re–legitimation of leaving the poor to fend for themselves as a mark of social virtue, deregulation, the exhaltation of individual effort and private enterprise can be interpreted as so many signs of the effort to legitimize modern times in terms of the past. Time passes and modern times become olden times. The situation is paradoxical, and, in its way, is an expression of what is known as post–modern society.

The return to the laws of nature does not guarantee the separation of nature and culture. To be convinced of this, one has only to see how the notions of culture, identity, and history have invaded managerial literature. Managers are not contented with obeying the laws of nature. They are managing a social system and their first role is to produce an acceptable representation of it for those who participate in it. But the most salient manifestation of this appeal to tradition is perhaps to be seen in the way managers are fascinated by their Japanese counterparts. Beyond quality circles and managerial theories, Japan offers an image of how traditional culture can provide force and cohesion for organizational activities. That's how it has been able to legitimize hierarchical power and to create strong ties of loyalty between the employer and his company as well as between the company and the nation as a whole. Based on the Japanese example, the West can gaze into the mirror of its own tradition.

With a sort of naturally regressive movement, the return to the sources of the modern world is associated with a nostalgia for what preceded it. Communist China provides a striking example of such an evolution as official historians discover a new way of looking at the role of modernist mandarins at the end of the XIXth century in their effort to open China to the western world.

One need not look so far to see efforts being made to entrench phenomena in tradition which seem to elude the reign of mere reason. The attempt to describe marketing as the modern form of Sophism could readily be seen as this kind of effort. To seek the model of contemporary social processes in Ancient Greece and to relate the history of reason and the history of social legitimacy is to remind those concerned with the issue that in the West the crisis of reason is part of a tradition which is largely a tradition of reason. The return to theory, philosophy and the study of intellectual structures which are the foundations of post–modern society is thus both the consequence of the present crisis and the means that our tradition provides us with so that we may experience it in accordance with age–old ideals.

Reason can be more readily associated with tradition than with charisma. The bewildering powers of magic are more radically opposed to reason than to tradition. Tradition can be grasped by reason using the category of repetition. The vocation of magic is to ruin the explanations and forecast of reason whether they concern the laws of nature or the features of social processes of which culture is comprised. The crisis of reason was to be associated with the development of the recourse to charisma. Examples of the latter are not in short supply: the current return to religious beliefs evidenced by the growth of religious sects (Moon, Hari Krishna, Scientology etc. . . .), and the rise of fundamentalist beliefs and even marketing itself. Marketing tells us how to make rational use of the widely held belief in the magical power of certain products, and political or economics leaders.

The reign of reason presupposed a world of individuals whose economic behavior was dictated by the laws of the market. The crisis of reason involves a world of organizations which are learning to live with the crisis by developing strategies of legitimation. With public opinion as witness, each organization justifies itself with social argumentation drawing on charisma, tradition and reason. The discourse of reason and science is thus replaced by a discourse of pure persuasion and rhetoric the justification of which derives entirely from its capacity to persuade. The concern and worry roused by the reign of this kind of rhetoric for which there is no guarantee, should not obfuscate the fact that through the practical and theoretical questions raised by the discourse of persuasion with regard to the status of opinion, marketing and Sophism loom over the centuries as two paradoxical images of liberty.

Index